THE BUILDINGS OF ENGLAND

BE 19

BUCKINGHAMSHIRE

NIKOLAUS PEVSNER

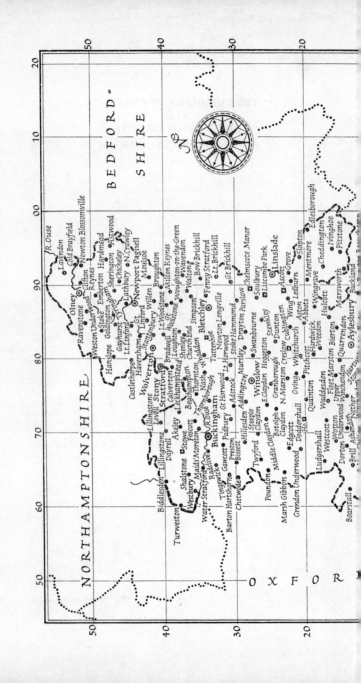

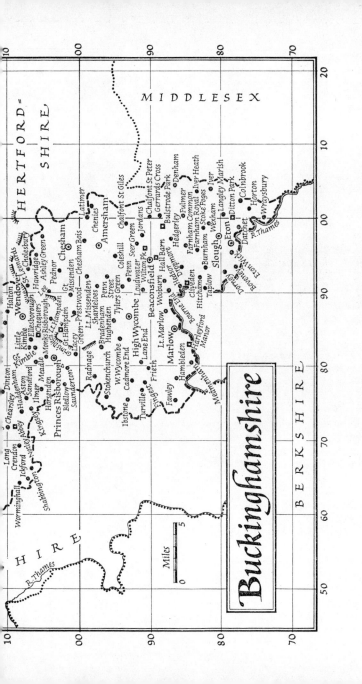

Buckinghamshire

THE BUILDINGS OF ENGLAND

Buckinghamshire

BY

NIKOLAUS PEVSNER

★

PENGUIN BOOKS

Penguin Books Ltd, Harmondsworth, Middlesex
U.S.A.: Penguin Books Inc., 3300 Clipper Mill Road, Baltimore 11, Md
AUSTRALIA: Penguin Books Pty Ltd, 762 Whitehorse Road,
Mitcham, Victoria

—

First published 1960
Copyright © Nikolaus Pevsner, 1960

TO LIS

OLDEST AND MOST FAITHFUL FRIEND

Made and printed in Great Britain
by William Clowes and Sons Ltd, London and Beccles
Collogravure plates by Harrison & Sons Ltd

CONTENTS

*

*

Map References

The numbers printed in italic type in the margin against the place names in the gazetteer of the book indicate the position of the place in question on the index map (pages 2–3), which is divided into sections by the 10–kilometre reference lines of the National Grid. With a few exceptions, the map contains all those places, whether towns, villages, or isolated buildings, which are the subject of separate entries in the text. Where a place is not named on the map, it is located by giving its distance from a neighbouring town, and to this town a map reference is given.

The first two figures of the reference number indicate the grid position of the place in question *East* of the Grid datum point near Land's End: the last two figures its grid position *North* of that point. Thus, for example, Emberton (reference 8040) will be found in the map square bounded by grid lines 80 and 90 *east* and 40 and 50 *north* of the south-west (bottom left hand) corner of the map; Oakley (reference 6010) in the square bounded by grid lines 60 and 70 *east* and 10 and 20 *north*.

FOREWORD

Buckinghamshire was prepared by Dr Mark Girouard during the one year he worked for The Buildings of England. *He made an excellent job of it, and if the printed text contains errors and omissions they are most probably due not to him (nor certainly to my then secretary Mrs Bailey, who kept all the material in impeccable order) but to me. Users of this book who may spot mistakes or gaps are invited to tell me or the publisher's office about them.*

The geological notes in the introduction were provided as usual by Mr Terence Miller, the notes on prehistory and Roman antiquities both in the introduction and the gazetteer by Mr J. V. S. Megaw. The Ministry of Housing and Local Government (here abbreviated MHLG) have a statutory duty to draw up lists of buildings of architectural or historic interest and have again very kindly put at my disposal the lists compiled by the Chief Investigator and his staff. I wish to thank them and also Mr Cecil Farthing and the staff of the National Buildings Record (abbreviated NBR) for their helpfulness. The sign GR means, as in previous volumes, that information comes from the Goodhart-Rendel list of Victorian churches, the sign TK refers to Sir Thomas Kendrick's lists of Victorian glass. I am most grateful to both the late H. S. Goodhart-Rendel and Sir Thomas Kendrick for allowing me the use of their lists. RCHM refers to the two volumes of Buckinghamshire inventories of the Royal Commission on Historical Monuments, VCH to the Victoria County History.

As regards individual places and problems, my thanks are due to the Provost of Eton, who took me round the premises in great detail, answered many questions, and in the end read my proofs. Exactly the same was done for me by Mr Michael Mounsey at Stowe, and I am equally indebted to him and also to Mr George Clarke at Stowe. Mr Mounsey in addition to all the other help provided me with a number of his photographs. Proofs were sent to nearly all rectors and vicars in the county, and some of them took much trouble over commenting on them. Many also answered letters enquiring about particular points. The same inconvenience was faced by the owners and occupiers of many houses. I have to thank them, and in addition to acknowledge their kindness in letting me examine their houses. Permission to see Chequers was obtained for me by Mr C. F. Penruddock, secretary to the Chequers Trust, and as this is a rarely granted privilege I want to place on record my gratitude to him. Mr T. A. Hume, Curator of the County Museum, helped me in various ways, including a good deal of tedious proof-reading, shared nobly by Mr E. Viney. Mr Philip James read and corrected my account of Waddesdon, Mr Leo Kelly my selected pedigree of the Rothschild family, Mr Christopher Hohler the paragraph on Long Crendon Manor. In connexion with prehistoric and Roman archaeology we have to thank the Director-General, Ordnance Survey, and the Inspectorate of Ancient Monuments, Ministry of Works, for information on otherwise unpublished sites, Mr A. L. F. Rivet for advice on Iron Age monuments, Mr B. R. Hartley and the Bucks Archaeological Society for information on the Roman villa at High Wycombe, prior to publication, and Mr J. F. Head and Mr A. D. Lacaille for reading the relevant sections in proof.

The principles on which my gazetteer is founded are the same as in the eighteen volumes of The Buildings of England which precede it. I have myself seen everything that I describe. Where this is not the case, the information obtained by other means is placed in brackets. Information ought to be as complete as the space of the volume permits for churches prior to c. 1830 and all town houses, manor houses, and country houses of more than purely local interest. Movable furnishings are not included in secular buildings, though they are in churches. Exceptions to the latter rule are bells, hatchments, chests, chairs, and altar tables. Brasses of post-Reformation date are only occasionally mentioned, church plate of 1715–1830 only rarely. As for churches and chapels of after 1830, I had to make a selection, and this is dictated by architectural value or by significance otherwise in the light of architectural history. The same applies to the buildings of the twentieth century.

INTRODUCTION

BUCKINGHAMSHIRE is not a large county. In size it stands thirty-first, in population twenty-seventh. Yet it contains a great deal of variety of nature-made as well as man-made landscape. Landscape depends on earth-scape, and GEOLOGY must come first. The geological structure of Buckinghamshire, when represented on a map, gives the impression of a piece of striped (and somewhat ragged) cloth. The stripes lie SW to NE, coming up out of Oxfordshire and running away into Northamptonshire, Bedfordshire, and Hertfordshire.

Between Buckingham and Olney, the valley of the Great Ouse (where it is not veneered by river and glacial deposits) is cut in Middle Jurassic sands, clays, and thin, shelly limestones, one of which was formerly cut and polished as 'Buckingham Marble'; this is the first strip. Southward of this first strip, and stratigraphically above it, since all the rock layers dip gently down to the SE, comes a group of three clay formations: first, the Oxford Clay, stretching out three miles on either side of the Winslow–Bletchley railway line; second, a very narrow and sinuous outcrop of Ampthill Clay from Oakley through Quainton to Stewkley; third, a wider, five-mile belt, of Kimmeridge Clay, from the SW county boundary on the Thame, up towards Wing. Although clay-based, this country is not all of a heavy soil, for sheets of sandy and limey glacial material scattered upon it have served to lighten and drain it. Carried as it were on the back of the Kimmeridge Clay of the Vale of Aylesbury lie isolated patches ('outliers') of the very topmost subdivisions of the Jurassic system, the Portland and Purbeck Limestones, in small hills between Long Crendon and Whitchurch, as at Ashendon, and the Winchendons.

Slanting down above the Jurassic rocks, but still gently inclined to the SE, come the various members of the Cretaceous system. The lowest of these, the Lower Greensand (which is invariably white or brown), occurs in Buckinghamshire only as odd outliers forming 'caps' to small hills like those of Brill and Muswell, and in a strip of country forming the l. bank of the Ouzel between Brickhill and Linslade. When well cemented, the Lower Greensand is an ironstone, and has been used in building, as for example round Brickhill. The Gault Clay, above the Greensand, continues

the triple clay-strip of central Buckinghamshire S and NE of Aylesbury in the low ground at the foot of the Chalk escarpment. This
steep scarp face and ridge, cut by the Princes Risborough and
1a Wendover gaps, stretches as the Chilterns right across the county,
and is the uppermost formation of the Cretaceous. Most of the
Chalk is a pure white soft limestone, formed almost entirely of the
skeletons of minute marine organisms. The lower beds are rather
clayey, and contain grains of the green mineral glauconite, so that
the rock as a whole has a greyish colour; higher up, one or two
harder beds ('rock-bands') occur, in colour almost pure white,
and nodular concretions of silica (flint) are scattered throughout.

The southerly lobe of the county, from the line Bourne End–
Chalfont St Peter down to Horton and the confluence of the rivers
Colne and Thames, is formed of Eocene sands and clays lying on
top of the Chalk. The main Chiltern plateau surface is partly
covered by a residual skin from these Eocene rocks, a deposit
known to geologists as 'clay-with-flints', which rests in hollows
in the Chalk and fills fissures and 'pipes' with a brown pebbly
clay or sand. From these sands large boulders of Eocene sandstone
and conglomerate ('sarsens' or 'greywethers') can be extracted.
Also in this part of the county, and N towards Wycombe and
Chesham, there are important spreads of a silty clay which has
been worked under the name of 'brick earth' as the raw material
for bricks and tiles. It is a product of the former extension of the
rivers and their alluvium.

It will be clear from this account of the geology that Buckinghamshire, particularly the northern part with its clay foundation,
is not rich in building stone. There are some quarries in the Jurassic limestones, particularly in the outliers of Upper Jurassic N and
W of Aylesbury, as at Hartwell, where fossil ammonites were
built into the park wall, and Long Crendon. But for the main
supply it was always possible to draw on the great freestone centres
of Oxfordshire and the Cotswolds to the W, and Northamptonshire (ironstone field) and Rutland and Lincolnshire (Barnack,
Ketton, and Weldon Stones) to the N, all within easy reach by the
water-lines of the Thames–Cherwell and Great Ouse. Thus at
Eton the stones of the College include Merstham Stone from the
Cretaceous Upper Greensand of Surrey, Jurassic Taynton Stone
from the Forest of Wychwood in Oxfordshire, and Caen Stone
from Normandy.

In South Buckinghamshire the flints extracted from the Chalk,
or gathered from the 'clay-with-flints', have been used in building
and facing, as in High Wycombe church; and the 'greywethers'

have been dug out of their sand matrix (after location by prodding with long steel rods) and trimmed for foundation-blocks, as in Chesham church, or for cornerstones, as at Hartwell. For the most part, however, the natural substrata of the county have been exploited for the making of bricks and tiles rather than for the getting of building-stone. This is particularly so in the s, on the Chiltern plateau and the slopes southward from it. Here, in the brick earth region, even church towers often contain brickwork, and in houses and cottages it is ubiquitous. The northern clay-belt was also extensively dug in former times, more of the production probably being of bricks than tiles, where material for thatching must have been abundant. Most of the older, smaller, claypits are now filled in, and since the coming of the railways a huge concentration of brickmaking has grown up in the NE.

Also since the coming of the railways the proximity to London has changed the appearance of Buckinghamshire greatly. Suburban trains run as far as Aylesbury, red buses as far as Wendover, green buses over most of the county. Londoners' houses have made of the Chalfonts and Gerrards Cross an Outer London, prosperous, snug, and devoid of visual coherence. Londoners' houses spread all along the Thames Valley and much into the Chilterns. It is a relief still to find large areas of the hills uninvaded by houses and favoured by ramblers. Round Turville especially, but also round Hampden, and N of Marlow and even N of Burnham, London is forgotten.

The architectural character of the county is determined by the absence of a big town of its own. The largest town of Buckinghamshire, Slough (with no more than 60,000 inhabitants), is a recent creation. Otherwise Buckinghamshire towns are small and frequent: Aylesbury, the county town, Buckingham, the medieval county town, High Wycombe, industrial but clean, Amersham, 3a Beaconsfield, Newport Pagnell, Wendover. Their chief attraction 3b is Georgian. At Amersham and Beaconsfield, the two towns nearest to London, the danger of loss of personality has been avoided by the development of 'new towns' away from the old. The finest villages, and there are very fine ones in the county, are a mixture of timber-framed and brick cottages and houses: West Wycombe with a straight street, Denham with a curved one, Bradenham with a spacious green, Hambleden with a little square. Near London, villages have lost their former attraction owing once again to London. The influence of London on Buckinghamshire can indeed not be overestimated. But it is, as has already been said, an influence confined to what the historian calls Modern

History, and before the Modern History of Buckinghamshire can be summarized, something must be said about its Ancient History and its Medieval History.

Concerning PREHISTORY of early structures, there is not much to be said. The countryside to the N is for the most part poorly drained low-lying ground and to the S the once heavily wooded chalk escarpment, intersected only at a few points by comparatively fertile valleys. Thus the Buckinghamshire of the past offered little to early man. Only these few fertile valleys and the wide Thames plain to the W of Taplow were naturally attractive, and here and along the great through-route of the Upper Icknield Way, running along the foot of the Chilterns chalk escarpment just above spring level and connecting Wessex with East Anglia, is concentrated the bulk of the evidence for the first patterns of settlement in the county. On the ill-drained ground below and at about a mile's distance is the straight line of the Lower Icknield Way – a route of much less antiquity or importance. To the Palaeolithic (Old Stone) Age belong large concentrations of flint implements found on the Pleistocene-deposited riverine terraces which rise above the Thames between Taplow and Slough. Included here is an important 'Acheulean' series from gravel diggings near Burnham on what is termed the Lower Boyn Hill or Furze Platt-Lent Rise Terrace. Other Palaeolithic series of mainly 'Levalloisian' type come from pits near Iver and Langley on the Iver and Taplow Terraces. The gravels of the Colne at Denham and of the Misbourne at Great and Little Missenden and Beaconsfield have also produced implements of the period. In the subsequent Mesolithic (Middle Stone) Age, with its more sophisticated, lighter stone industry, settlement seems again to have been concentrated on the riverine gravels; an important site is on Iver Heath in the valley of the Colne, while at Kimble Farm, Stonor, a group of these hunter-fisher people was established on a bench of the Chilterns. In the second half of the third millennium B.C. the innovations of a settled farming economy and the use of pottery arrived from the Continent, and the settlers of the Neolithic (New Stone) Age made use of two of the county's natural lines of communication, the Thames and the Upper Icknield ridgeway. Here the importance of the Saunderton – High Wycombe – Bourne End valley route is clear from this period on, as for example in the find of a typical leaf-shaped arrow-head near High Wycombe. For evidence we have, from Iver and the Cop, Bledlow, two polished flint axes traded in all likelihood from Cornwall, while from Whiteleaf comes a third axe whose origin is Westmorland. Also on Whiteleaf Hill, above the Icknield Way, is the site (excavated in 1934-9) of a kidney-shaped mound heaped over a central wooden revetted chamber – a variant perhaps, despite its single inhumation, of the stone-built collective tombs of the 'Severn-Cotswold' group. An apparently parallel site has been noticed at the end of Bledlow Ridge. Some of the pottery from the Whiteleaf Barrow is related to a group of Neolithic cultures evolving in part directly from the aboriginal Mesolithic communities. Such 'secondary' Neolithic finds occur at several places along the Thames – at Hedsor for example, at a gravel pit in Mansion Lane, Iver, and beneath the now destroyed Roman settlement on the Rye at High Wycombe. In this connexion two possible flint mines may be noted, one recorded in a railway cutting near High Wycombe, the other at Pitstone on the N edge of the Chilterns. At the Rye villa were also found fragments of the characteristic bell-shaped drinking cups of the 'Beaker Folk', the itinerant traders from the Continent who first introduced the use of metal into this country. Evidence for the N and W penetration into the county of this new group is to be found not only in the lower levels of settlement sites, as at Hitcham and Ellesborough, but in the round barrows beneath which they buried their dead. Some half-dozen of these are in the vicinity of the Icknield Way, the link with the area of the full 'Wessex' Bronze Age. The excavated mound of the Cop at Bledlow also contained evidence for reuse at a time when bronze had become common. Although once more there are no major monuments related to the period, single finds as well as dumps or hoards of tools and weapons – as at Lodge Hill, Waddesdon, New Bradwell, Wolverton on the Ouse, and the Slough Trading Estate – show the continued use of the twin lines of communication. Indeed it is not impossible that the dug-out canoes found at Marlow and Bourne End may belong to this time. Evidence of the new cultural influences of the later Bronze Age, apart from objects, exists only in the C 18 account of a cremation urnfield at Stokenchurch and similar sites at Stoke Poges and Hitcham.

We come now to the Iron Age, from which period date the first visible monuments of size and importance. An area of primary settlement in about the mid C 5 – perhaps more or less direct from northern France via the Lower Thames – was on the Icknield ridge. Here a group of undefended sites sprang up, particularly where the Risborough Gap and the Ellesborough Pass join the Upper Icknield Way. There are sites at Ellesborough itself, Lodge Hill, and Shimmel's Farm, Bledlow, as well as at Chinnor just across the border in Oxfordshire. The distribution of fortified camps supports the earlier pattern; few sites are known in the N of the county, and the largest, the hill-fort of Danesborough, Wavendon, is on the line of an ancient trackway leading S to the Icknield Way along the line of which is the major concentration. Other forts – those at Ashley Green, at West Wycombe, and at Medmenham on the Thames – are carefully sited in relation to other natural routes. Thus, although only two have been even partially excavated, it seems reasonable to regard the Buckinghamshire hill-forts as places of refuge and defence rather than of permanent residence. The largest hill-fort of all, the double-ramparted camp in Bulstrode Park, Gerrards Cross, contained evidence of occupation both in the Early Iron Age and by the Belgic peoples of the C I B.C. Here and at Cholesbury, between Wendover and Tring, which also had two phases of settlement, we have material proof of the occupation of the Catuvellauni. This was the Marnian tribe who, under Cunobelin, had control by the time of the Claudian conquest of an area bounded on the S by the Thames and the W by the Cherwell, and which extended E to Cambridgeshire and Essex and N into Northamptonshire. The tribal capital was at Wheathampstead in Hertfordshire until Caesar's sack of the town in 54 B.C., when it was moved to Verulamium. Evidence for the improved agricultural methods of the time, including the introduction of the heavy plough, may be seen in the cultivation terraces or lynchets visible on the fertile escarpment slopes. The best preserved of them are at Cheddington. The presence of the Catuvellauni in Buckinghamshire is supported by finds, made in 1826–7 on the slopes of Keep Hill, High Wycombe, of native coinage, including eleven gold staters of Tasciovanus, probably the son of Cassivelaunus. The early form of a hoard of 400 gold coins from Whaddon Chase in the N of the county proves them to belong to the Atrebates, inhabitants of an area to the S of the Thames. Occasional coins found throughout the county are inscribed with the name of Addedomarus of the Iceni, Boudicca's Norfolk and fen-dwelling tribe – evidence once more of the use of the Icknield route. Although strictly outside our scope, the 'pile dwellings' discovered at Hedsor in 1894 and attributed to the Iron Age may also be noted here. The position of the site and the numerous objects found in the Bucks reaches of the Thames – particularly a gold-studded spear-head at Taplow, a sword sheath at Amerden, and a bronze fibula inset with amber and blue glass – recall the not dissimilar sites at Codeham, Beds, and at Old England, Brentford, Middlesex.

Mention above of the native tribes brings us on to some consideration of ROMAN BUCKINGHAMSHIRE. The story is one of simple settlement, mainly near the military highways and in the favoured river valleys – particularly those of the Ouse, Wye, and Chess – where between the C1 and the C4 A.D. a simple farming life was continued. Unfortunately little remains above ground. The largest and richest villa was that on the Rye at High Wycombe, which boasted a fine tesselated pavement first discovered in 1722–4 and a bath house. It was fully excavated in 1954, following which it had to be destroyed to make way for a municipal swimming pool. The only major visible Roman monument now remaining is the section of C4 tesselated paving from Foscott now in the Queen's Temple, Stowe Park. However, the strategic needs of the Roman occupation can be seen in the ROADS which traverse the county and which must be summarized here. First is Watling Street, which makes its way NW from Verulamium (St Albans) to Lactodorum (Towcester) in Northamptonshire, where ends its first alignment. At the Watling Street crossing of the Ouzel stood the unwalled road station of Magiovinium (Dropshort), whose name is known from the C3 Antonine Itinerary. From here towards Buckingham stretches another road which for most of its course is as impressive as Watling Street; it seems to continue W out of the county towards Aynho. At Thornborough Mounds, one of which is certainly of Roman date, this last route is crossed by a road which, passing the site of the settlement at Foscott, offers a link between Akeman Street and Towcester. This road, though difficult to follow, seems to join the route between Venta Belgarum (Winchester), Alcester, Oxon, and Towcester. This turns abruptly N in Stowe Park, where its course is clear, and it is in this last stretch that it is joined by the road from Akeman Street. Akeman Street itself links Alcester with Verulamium, the cantonal capital. Its deviations from the present main road are particularly clear on the stretch between Aylesbury and Westcott, where at Fleet Marston the site of an intermediary station has recently been found. Finally a route from Dungee, Bedfordshire, on the Irchester road makes SW to the settlement at Olney. It is next to be picked up in Gayhurst Park, where it heads for Hill Farm, site of another extensive settlement. Crossing the Ouse W of the once extensive villa of Stanton Low, it intersects Watling Street just NE of Dovecote, site of yet another villa. Unlike the settlements, the three kilns which are the only evidence for industry in the period do not seem to be dependent on the fixed lines of communication. Indeed the sites – at Hedgerley

Green, Duke's Wood Fulmer, and Stone – which seem to have had a short life in the second half of the c2 – reflect much local Belgic tradition and may well have catered for purely local needs. As to sepulchral remains, we have already commented on the Thornborough barrows; the dedicatory silver plaques found at Stony Stratford point, as do similar finds at Barkway, Herts, to the presence of a near-by rural shrine. The burial high in the hills at Sprig's Alley, Radnage, 1 m. from the Icknield Way, was unusual not only in its position; a cremation contained in a fine bronze-mounted casket was encircled by nine 'terra sigillata' bowls, a plain earthenware pitcher, an amber glass jug, and a white and blue 'pillar-moulded' bowl also of glass and probably of c1 A.D. Alexandrine manufacture.

In the SAXON AGE, prior to the spread of Christianity, the generally uninviting nature of the county's topography seems once again to have protected the native inhabitants from the incursions of this newest of foreign elements. For our present purposes we need not go into the complex problems of the earliest date of Saxon settlement in the Chilterns; it is sufficient to say that, although the Anglo-Saxon Chronicle records Cuthwulf's capture of Aylesbury and three other towns from 'the Britons' following the battle of 'Bedconford' in 571, with the exception of the Bishopstone cemetery just outside Aylesbury itself, none of the Saxon sites placed along the line of the Icknield Way can be dated as early as the c6. However, this does not affect the balance of opinion which assigns a Saxon date to Grim's Ditch, the largest visible monument in the county, a monument possibly constructed as the E boundary to Cuthwulf's territory or later in the c8 when the demand for land had increased. Grim's Ditch is visible for considerable distances, from Park Wood N of Bradenham via the sharp E turn in Hillock Wood, Great Hampden, to Longcroft S of Tring, where the ditch crosses over into Hertfordshire. Its detailed course is to be found in the gazetteer. S of the ditch there are only two burial sites on the Wye, at High Wycombe and Loudwater, and two on the Thames, one at Hitcham, the other the famous barrow at Taplow of the town's eponym, Taeppa.

Now for CHRISTIAN REMAINS. As regards the Middle Ages, Buckinghamshire is not a county for the medievalist. It has hardly any castles or mansion houses, no cathedral, and not many churches of more than local interest.

For the ANGLO-SAXON centuries, apart from odd windows in naves, blocked when aisles were built and later revealed (Hardwick, Iver, Lavendon, Little Missenden), there is only one

building here to be commented on: Wing, probably of the late
c 10. Here the tall apse stands upright with a crypt underneath and 4a
the walls of the nave and an aisle. The piers between the two are
simply chunks of wall left standing, the arches are unmoulded,
and the imposts as simple as can be. The apse is polygonal inside
and outside, as is that of Deerhurst, and the crypt has an odd
hexagonal core surrounded by a kind of ambulatory – a variation
on the Italian theme of the ring crypt created in Rome before 600
(St Peter's) and adopted in a simple form at Hexham and Ripon
before 700. The exterior of the apse has the thin lesenes and round
and triangular arches familiar from Earls Barton and Barton-on-
Humber.

Scholars have spoken of a Saxo-Norman overlap, Norman
work with a Saxon flavour, and to this one may well assign the
NORMAN w tower of Bradenham with its Saxon-looking details,
and the far more impressive w tower of Fingest, which is so large 2
that Sir Alfred Clapham and others thought it must have served
as a nave, as Saxon towers sometimes did. What else needs sum-
marizing here of Norman remains requires no more than a few
lines: the churches of Stewkley and Upton, both very completely 9b
preserved, both with a nave, a central tower, and a straight-ended
chancel, and both with rib-vaults in their chancels. Stewkley is
uncommonly sumptuous in its decoration. Other lavish pieces of
Norman decoration are rare. The doorways of Horton, Dinton, 4b
and Twyford might be mentioned, and, for the uncommon interest of their sculpture, the doorways of Water Stratford. One of
them has a tympanum with Christ and two angels reminiscent of 5
the Prior's Door at Ely. The other has a Saxon-looking dragon.
Tympana or lintels with figure-work are rare otherwise (Dinton, 4b
Lathbury, Leckhampstead). One font has a scene with violent and
mysterious action: Stone. Among motifs of decoration beakheads 16
occur occasionally (Bletchley, Fawley), and occasionally they are
in a very interesting way reduced to an abstract shape no longer
reminiscent of beasts' heads or beaks (Hanslope, Radclive,
Twyford). In contrast to these somewhat barbaric performances
of the Norman carver is a series of Norman FONTS centred at
Aylesbury and decorated reticently with foliage in an upper band
and fluting below. The Aylesbury font has as its base what looks 15
like a reversed scalloped capital. The same type appears at
Bledlow, Great Kimble, and Weston Turville, and without the
base at Chearsley, Chenies, Haddenham, Linslade, Monks
Risborough, and Pitstone.* Another well-known type of Norman

* Base only at Great Missenden and Wing.

(and E.E.) font is to be found in a few places in Buckinghamshire: the table-top type made of Purbeck marble and as a rule
decorated with flat blank arches (Iver and Taplow C 12; Amersham and Denham C 13).

The TRANSITIONAL between Norman and E.E. is recognizable by such ornamental motifs as zigzag at r. angles to the wall,
or the scalloping of capitals turning into concave-sided trumpets
and also by the development from the Norman leaf to the E.E.
stiff-leaf. In arcades one has to watch for the unmoulded arch
becoming a single-step arch and later for arches developing
chamfered mouldings, and also for the round arch to become
pointed. The piers are round and have square abaci. The abaci
then turn octagonal and circular. All these nuances of transition
can be observed, but none in major examples. The chancel of
Wingrave may be mentioned with its blank arcading inside (and
also the odd, narrow tunnel-vaulted chamber to its N), and the
chancel of Shenley Church End with its intention of vaulting.
There are a number of good EARLY ENGLISH chancels in the
county (Aylesbury, Iver, Lillingstone Dayrell, Swanbourne). At
Little Missenden there is internal shafting so detached from the
wall that it forms a kind of fragmentary miniature wall-passage.
11a The same motif occurs at Great Missenden and Princes Ris-
10b borough. Chetwode is a special case. The nave and chancel of
the present church are no more than the chancel of a former
abbey church, founded in 1245.

On the whole MONASTIC REMAINS are uncommonly scanty in
Bucks. It is enough to refer to the chapter house, sacristy, fuel
house, and refectory walling of Burnham Abbey (Augustinian
Canonesses, founded 1266), the ornate refectory arcading and the
remarkably comfortable early C 16 abbot's house at Notley Abbey
(Augustinian, founded before 1164), the walls of the cloister and
the C 15 roof of the dormitory at Missenden Abbey (founded 1133),
the excavation of the Benedictine nunnery at Little Marlow
(founded in the second half of the C 12), the few fragments at
Abbey Farm of the Benedictine Abbey of Bradwell (founded c.
1155), the walling at Wraysbury of the Benedictine nunnery of
Ankerwyke (founded c. 1160), and at Tickford, Newport Pagnell,
of the Benedictine abbey (founded in 1100), and the one original
pier of Medmenham Abbey (Cistercian, founded early in the C 13).
Nothing survives of the Benedictines at Snelshall (originally Pre-
monstratensian) and Wing, the Augustinians at Ravenstone, the
Cluniacs at Newton Longville, the Cistercians at Biddlesden,
the Premonstratensians at Lavendon, the Franciscan Friars at

Aylesbury (the only Mendicant house in the county), the Templars at Bulstrode, and the Hospitallers at Hogshaw and Widmere.

A few E.E. postscripts to what has been mentioned: a good tower at Haddenham with blank arcading of the bell-stage, the crossing tower at Aylesbury,* the bellcote at Little Linford, a group of large capitals with lively stiff-leaf, located in the E and linked to Eaton Bray in Bedfordshire (Ivinghoe, Marsh Gibbon, 10a Pitstone, Wingrave), the rib-vaulted S porch of High Wycombe, and the very odd oaken arch with dog-tooth decoration in Upton church, probably not *in situ* and quite possibly a domestic piece (cf. Great Bricett in Suffolk).

Later medieval parish churches in England are characterized by very wide aisles. The change from narrow to wide aisles began in the C13, and Hanslope furnishes an example of this. Another change typical of the C13 concerns windows. Lancets were gradually given up and groups of them replaced by single windows of several lights with bar tracery. Bar tracery, introduced in England about 1245, seems to have entered Buckinghamshire some time after 1260 and to have been used in its simplest form: two lights and a foiled circle over, up to 1280 or 1290. A splendid example of the still Geometrical but freer forms of the end of the C13 occurs at Edlesborough, a church in a most impressive, 6a commanding position.

Such freer forms, spherical triangles and quadrangles instead of circles, intersected arches instead of arches kept separate, herald the FOURTEENTH CENTURY. But here also Bucks has little of more than local value to offer, such as the big E window at Emberton. There are two really fine spires, under immediate Northamptonshire influence, Olney and Hanslope, both built late 6b in the century (Hanslope rebuilt in the C19). Several Buckinghamshire towns are proud of their tall spires, but they are of the last sixty years: Marlow, Princes Risborough, and Slough, all three by *John Oldrid Scott*. Altogether, this may be the place to refer to the work of Victorian architects and restorers in the county. Especially near London it is hard to find a church which, owing to their zest, does not look wholly of their time. The attraction of these churches has retired into the interior.

A few aids to the dating of Gothic churches in the county may be appended. The most usual arch moulding from the C13 to the C15 is the double chamfer. In the early C14 it is often replaced by sunk quadrant mouldings. The most usual PIER SECTION, again

---

* There are over a dozen crossing towers in the county, the most impressive ones, such as Long Crendon, being Perp.

from the C13 to the C15, is octagonal. For dating here one must watch bases and capitals. Quatrefoil piers occur in the C13 at Long Crendon and Twyford, but are more characteristic of the C14 (Olney, Emberton). Again capitals must be used to distinguish. Variations on the quatrefoil section are the square with attached demi-shafts (Great Missenden), the quatrefoil with thin shafts in the diagonals (Clifton Reynes), or with a group of three thin 11b shafts in the diagonals (Bierton), or with the four 'foils' squashed into a flat surface and double curves along the sides (Hardwick). The most frequent Perp section is of four shafts with four hollows in the diagonals (Chenies, Denham, High Wycombe). This also exists in the C14, when the forms, especially of the hollow, are broader and bolder (Great Hampden). Perp piers are slender, Perp arches wide. On the whole, four-centred (depressed) arches are later than two-centred ones. But Buckinghamshire is not a county to visit in search of spectacular Perp parish churches. There is not a single church on the scale of those of East Anglia or the Cotswolds. Hillesden with its lavishly panelled chancel and chapel is the finest piece in the county, Maids' Moreton a good 7 & second.* This leaves out of consideration the chapel of Eton Col-12 lege begun in 1449 and completed c. 1475, one of the Royal Chapels which must all be counted among the foremost buildings of their date in England. The others are King's College Chapel, Cambridge; St George's Chapel, Windsor; and Henry VII's Chapel in Westminster Abbey.

No more important than medieval churches are medieval CHURCH FURNISHINGS in Buckinghamshire. There are a few curiosities interesting to the antiquarian: a Chrismatory at Gran-borough, the base of an Altar Cross of bronze at Stoke Poges, and a Vestment Press in the form of a wardrobe at Aylesbury. There are one or two pieces of early PLATE: a C14 paten at Bierton and a C15 one at Woughton-on-the-Green. There are two MONU-MENTS of oak at Clifton Reynes, both of c. 1300, there is at Taplow the earliest civilian brass in England (c. 1300), and there is a speci-ally good later brass at Thornton († 1472). There are Late Perp tomb recesses with elaborate detail at Beaconsfield, Hambleden, and Whaddon. There is an effigy of the late C14 at Chenies which was never completed and largely remains in the rough block. There is a PULPIT at Upper Winchendon, probably of the C14, 17a and a later one at Edlesborough; there are C14 SCREENS at Weston

---

* A footnote to record the vaulted porches of Amersham and Chesham (tierceron), Chilton (ribbed tunnel-vault), Great Linford and Newport Pagnell (sexpartite vaults), and Hillesden and Maids' Moreton (fan-vaults).

Turville and Saunderton; there are plenty of ROOFS of low pitch with tie-beams on arched braces and quite frequently a little tracery in the spandrels of the braces or above the tie-beam, so many in fact that they are generally not mentioned at all in this book. There are also a larger number of TILES than can find mention, introduced by the fine C13 pieces, perhaps from Chertsey Abbey, at Little Kimble. There is a little STAINED GLASS of the C13 at Aston Sandford and Chetwode, there are whole C14 figures at Hitcham and Weston Underwood and early C16 scenes at Hillesden. WALL PAINTINGS are numerous and date from all 19a Gothic centuries, but nearly all of them are too badly preserved to make an aesthetic impact. Professor Tristram's reconstruction of the earliest of them can be seen in his volumes. The only ones of these wall paintings which can claim a leading position in the whole of English painting of this time are those of Eton 18 College, done in c. 1479–88 by *William Baker* and a certain *Gilbert*.

Eton College was of course the principal secular job in Bucking- 33a &b hamshire in the C15 and early C16. The buildings were from the beginning on a scale preceded only by those of Winchester College. They comprised a quadrangle for the college proper and a detached range W of it for the school. Their main accent is Lupton's Tower added in 1517. Lupton's Tower as well as the 34 C15 buildings of Eton are of BRICK. This in itself is an interesting fact; for England had been very slow in taking to brick. Bucks has little of brick in churches – only half a dozen instances before the C18 (the W towers of Dorney and Hitcham, the Hastings Chapel of c. 1560 at Stoke Poges, the W tower of Langley Marish and the tower top at Colnbrook, both early C17, and the Kederminster Chapel and Library also at Langley Marish and also early C17).*

The original Hall at Eton College survives. It is one of several 35a pre-Reformation halls. The others are at Savehay Farm, Denham, of the early C14 and with scanty remains of former aisles, at Huntercombe Manor, Burnham, also C14, and at Dorney Court, C15. The Old Parsonage, Marlow, has two big straight-headed mid-C14 stone windows with reticulation work in the tracery, and they are supposed to belong to the former hall. The King's Head Hotel at Aylesbury has a large ten-light window of wood 35b with arched lights and a transom, and this also belonged of course to the hall. The history of the planning of manor houses

---

* TIMBER in churches – except of course for roofs and furnishings – is even rarer. The only piece worth a mention here is the fine C14 S porch at Stoke Poges.

with the hall and the service quarters on one side, the parlour and
solar on the other, is intricate and can only be reconstructed from
fragmentary evidence. Buckinghamshire is not the best county
to try it, and no attempt is made in this book. It must in fact be
confessed that the medieval and c16 farmhouses, houses, etc.,
mentioned here are largely included for picturesque rather than
scholarly reasons. The perfected type has service wing and solar
wing projecting to the l. and r. and cross-gabled, as it can now be
seen e.g. at Savehay Farm. The wings at the Old Rectory, Beaconsfield, are so long that they enclose a proper forecourt. An occasional variation is to reduce the projection of the wings to very
little and run the eaves of the roof through flush, in which case
curved braces in front of the centre and rising in an outward
direction help to support them (Chalfont St Giles, Haddenham,
etc.). This type is known as the Wealden type.

The only memory of a stone-built castle in the county is
Boarstall Tower, a very substantial gatehouse of the early c14,
made more comfortable in the early c17. The Manor at Long Crendon also has a stone gatehouse, though on a more domestic scale.
Three detached domestic chapels still exist, one of the c12, the
others of the c13, at Creslow Manor, Great Hundridge Manor,
Chesham, and at Widmere, Marlow. The latter has a vaulted
undercroft, and a more elaborately vaulted undercroft of the c14,
with tierceron vaulting, remains at Creslow Manor but not in connexion with the chapel. It lies under part of the former solar
range. Brick appears at Chenies Manor House at about the same
time as at Eton. This early range at Chenies, with stepped gables,
an oriel on a brick corbel, and polygonal brick finials, is similar to
c15 and early c16 mansions in Essex. To it a long and imposing
wing was added about 1530.

By that time the RENAISSANCE had made an inconspicuous
appearance in the county. The earliest signs are the delightful
panels in Hambleden Church said to have belonged to The Vyne,
Hampshire (arms of Cardinal Wolsey and Bishop Fox of Winchester, and hence before 1526), the beautiful ceiling and wall
36a decoration in a room at Nether Winchendon House, the friezes,
fireplaces, etc., at Doddershall House, and the monument to
Margaret Giffard † 1539 at Middle Claydon. It is highly significant that from the moment of the inception of the Renaissance
secular jobs take precedence over ecclesiastical, and funeral monuments in churches over other church furnishings and church
buildings.

Of ELIZABETHAN and JACOBEAN houses Buckinghamshire

has little to offer, of funeral monuments much. Among HOUSES
easily the best is Gayhurst of 1597, stone-built on the well-known 37a
E-plan with 'extruded corners', and of the squareness which
more than anything distinguishes English from Continental mansions. Dorton of *c.* 1626, a brick house, has the same plan, Hartwell 36b
House, built of stone, the unusual feature of three big oriel 37b
windows on big corbels. The staircase of Hartwell House is
worthy of admiration. So are those of Dorton and Radclive Manor 38a
House. Hoggeston Manor House is of brick and has giant pilaster-
strips up its front in no understandable rhythm.

The series of Elizabethan and Jacobean MONUMENTS starts
with one chronologically a little pre-Elizabethan, the Dormer
monument at Wing of 1552, which is the most nobly and purely 22a
classical monument of its date in England. Its style belongs to the
circle of patrons round Lord Protector Somerset and the Duke of
Northumberland. It depends on the North Italian monuments
of Giulio Romano and Sammicheli and perhaps the adaptation
of this same style in France, e.g. at Ecouen. It has no effigy or any
other figures. Several others among the best Early Elizabethan
monuments are purely architectural: Hambleden († 1572),
Hillesden († 1576, specially good), Shenley Church End († 1577).
The type continues later at Ickford († 1595) and Chesham († 1617).
Continued from the Middle Ages without any compositional innovation is the type with a free-standing tomb-chest and one or
two recumbent effigies on it. This is the type of the first Earl of
Bedford † 1555 at Chenies, the earliest of the monuments in the 21b
Bedford Chapel, that storehouse of English monumental sculpture. Of the same type an Early Elizabethan piece at Hillesden
(† 1560), one at Denham († 1564), and one at Lillingstone Dayrell
(1571). The type also continues into the C17 at Chenies: † 1611,
also † 1600 with two large kneeling figures on the ground to the l.
and r., also † 1614 with four putti standing on the corners of the
lid, also erected 1619 with heraldic back-plate.*

The same type is often given a more spectacular setting by 22b
placing the tomb-chest against the wall and providing it with an
architectural surround, usually with columns, a flat or a deep
coffered arch, an entablature, and some cresting. The earliest of
these in Bucks is at Wing (1590), most of them are Jacobean or
even later: Chilton † 1608, Hitcham † 1624, where two soldiers

* In connexion with this medieval type, the perseverance of the cadaver
in a monument at so late a date as 1576 (Chicheley) ought to be mentioned,
and also the Hughenden forgeries, Elizabethan attempts at making up
medieval effigies.

hold a curtain open, Long Crendon † 1626 (?), Fulmer † 1631, Fawley † 1632, and later still the fourth Earl of Bedford † 1641 at Chenies.

Perhaps the most frequent Elizabethan type is that with two kneeling figures facing one another across a prayer desk. There are however not many of them in Bucks. A large example is at Dorney († 1607). At Langley Marish (1599) there are two couples, at Hambleden († 1633) the kneeling children crowd round the parents on the same level, not as usual smaller and somewhat below. A development beyond the recumbent effigy was the effigy stiffly placed on its side, and instances of this can be seen in Buckinghamshire at Shenley Church End († 1607), Chenies († 1623), and Ellesborough († 1638).

The bust occurs rarely before the second third of the C17, and then becomes fashionable for a while. Two stiff, formal busts of vicars can be named as early: Burnham († 1594) and Chesham († 1623). A bust also is the centre of the more ambitious monument to Provost Murray at Eton (†1623). The later busts are more elegant and appear less incarcerated in their niches. In three monuments at Datchet they stand entirely free above cartouches († 1626, 1633, 1636). At Marlow a monument has two busts and to the l. and r. small figures keeping curtains open († 1636). At Middle Claydon a monument by *Edward Marshall* has busts in oval niches in two tiers (1653). At Burnham a monument has two frontal demi-figures instead of busts († 1657).*

Finally, Sir William Drake at Amersham († 1654) appears in his shroud in a devout attitude and surrounded by a big, ambitious setting. The fashion for effigies in shrouds goes back to Nicholas Stone's Dr Donne of 1631 at St Paul's Cathedral. Buckinghamshire has two more examples: Mrs Salter rising in her shroud out of her black coffin († 1631, at Iver), and Henry 23a Curwen, at Amersham († 1636), standing in a kind of upright shrine the doors of which are held open by two angels. This is by *Edward Marshall*.‡ By *Epiphanius Evesham* is the curious monument † 1618 at Marsworth which bristles with allegorical conceits. This also was a passion of these years, as we know from literature. Among Bucks monuments, one at Beachampton (†1598) and one at Tingewick († 1608) illustrate it.

* But there is still a bust above an inscription plate at Wing in *c*. 1695; *William Stanton* has two busts in the same position at Quainton *c*. 1673, and 23b *Thomas Burman* two busts in oval medallions at Walton in 1672.

‡ In the original design by *Burman* for the Verney Monument († 1642) at Middle Claydon, Lady Verney was to be represented upright in her shroud.

The most revolutionary piece of the years under consideration is at Chenies, the monument to Lady Frances Bourchier † 1612, which has no effigy and consists of two black marble slabs connected by four white marble columns. Here one feels the approach of the new classical and courtly world of Inigo Jones, Nicholas Stone, and van Dyck. A tablet by *Stone* at Great Missenden of 1638 is indeed purely classical in its design, and so are two anonymous ones, one of *c.* 1634 at Great Hampden, the other also of *c.* 1634 (or even of *c.* 1620) at Chalfont St Giles.

The next step in the development of style must be watched in houses rather than monuments. DOMESTIC ARCHITECTURE UNDER CHARLES II has much of national interest concentrated in Buckinghamshire. Earlier c 17 types, still preserved as late as *c.* 1675 in the almshouses of Langley Marish with their Dutch gables, and as late as 1687 in the almshouses at Quainton, even with shaped gables, now give way to the new type with a hipped roof and upright windows, usually with a cross of one mullion and one transom. Quoins occur, and in the mid c 17 also occasionally superimposed orders of pilasters and a cupola or belvedere on the roof. Hall Barn of *c.* 1660 is a perfect example. The articulation 40a here is by coupled pilasters in three orders, a unique arrangement. There was a cupola, but it has disappeared. The quadrant link to a projecting range is a Palladian motif, introduced in England at the time of Inigo Jones at Stoke Bruerne and *de rigueur* in the Palladian c 18. Princes Risborough Manor House of *c.* 1670 is as characteristic as Hall Barn. It has two orders of pilasters and a staircase with a balustrade of twisted openwork rings. This can be 38b compared to the earlier staircase at Radclive of 1621 with open- 38a work squares and ovals. At Bradenham Manor House of *c.* 1670 the staircase has still the vertically symmetrical balusters of the earlier c 17, but the house belongs all the same to this group. Instead of pilasters there is a complicated system of layers in 40b depth by means of raised window-frames and sunk panels. At Doddershall House in *c.* 1689 the staircase has the sturdy twisted balusters typical of the Wren period, which we have now reached. At Tythrop there is instead an openwork balustrade of lush 39 foliage, a specially successful type to be found here and there from the sixties to the eighties (Eltham Lodge, London, Dunster Castle, Somerset, etc.).

The Wren type is represented in Buckinghamshire by one of the few houses which for good reasons can be attributed to *Wren* himself, Winslow Hall, where he certainly checked the bills, if he 43 did no more. The house is dated 1700 and has the simplest exterior: seven bays, a basement and two-and-a-half storeys, and a hipped roof. Quoins and a three-bay pediment complete this picture of undemonstrative prosperity. Wren may also have supervised Upper School at Eton, designed by *Matthew Bankes* and completed in 1694. The staircase here has dumb-bell balusters. The type of Winslow is also that of the H-shaped Fawley Court (1684), for which participation by *Wren* is probable, of the very perfect Great Hundridge Manor, Chesham, of 1696*, and of the bigger, also H-shaped Denham Place (1688–1701). Denham Place has some gay, rather rustic stucco friezes with 41 figures in landscape, Fawley Court a plaster ceiling of a boldness and finesse of modelling not exceeded anywhere in England. The 42a shell-hood of Stoke House, Stoke Mandeville, of about 1700, is in terms of wood carving of the same superb quality. Another good shell-hood is at Western House, Marlow, dated 1699. This type of house goes on to the Castle House, Buckingham, of 1708, and the Brewhouse at Eton built in 1714. Even the cross-windows survive here.

In terms of CHURCHES the exact counterpart to Winslow Hall 8a is Willen church designed by Wren's friend and colleague *Robert Hooke* in 1679. Its furnishings have been preserved gratifyingly complete. Church work between the Reformation and the late C17 is so rare and relatively insignificant in the county that it deserves no more than a few lines. For the Elizabethan Age the only fact worth recording is the sudden rush to replace PLATE melted down in the time of trouble. 1569 is the year of most purchases. The Royal Commission records it for fifty cups. Many more pieces were bought shortly after 1569, very few before (c. 1550 Winslow, 1565 Aston Abbots, Turville). Of the first half of the 17b C17 we have many PULPITS, some with their testers – the most lavish is at Ivinghoe. Dated examples are Langley Marish 1609, and Shabbington 1626. There are also the two dated FONT COVERS of 1631 at Dorton and 1640 at North Crawley, and there are the two SCREENS at Long Crendon and Langley Marish. Langley Marish is the most interesting church in the county for this period. The Kederminster Chapel, for which the money was left in 1613, has a six-light mullioned and transomed brick 19b window‡ and a gay and somewhat rustic painted screen with a strapwork top, and the wooden arcade of 1630 between nave and N aisle has Tuscan columns instead of Perp piers. Yet there is all

---

* The specially narrow windows here, close to the door, are typical of c. 1700.

‡ Swanbourne in 1630 still kept to Perp windows with arched lights.

the difference in the world between these experiments and the complete command of the classical (Dutch) vocabulary at Willen. While this may lack imagination in terms of architecture proper, the same cannot be said of the decoration that goes with it and its style and culminates in Wren's City churches. A reminder of these is the Pulpit at Wavendon which was originally in Wren's St Dunstan-in-the-West.

Wren's style in his old age changed in the direction of a peculiar ENGLISH BAROQUE, and younger men followed him (or perhaps even encouraged him) in this. One of them was *Thomas Archer*. There are two houses in Buckinghamshire which on account of their Borrominesque leanings have been attributed to him: Chicheley Hall of 1698 etc., with its giant pilasters, its 44a rising parapet, the odd ears of its windows, and the odd pediment over its door; and Marlow Place of *c.* 1720 where the door sur- 45a round is yet odder – the pilasters are placed at an angle – and the capitals of the giant pilasters have the most fantastic details. The entrance hall is grand and operatic in a Vanbrughian sense. Vanbrughian also is the eminently strange three-bay front of the Bradenham Rectory. There may even be a major domestic piece by *Vanbrugh* himself in the county, the N portico of Stowe with its 46 giant columns and pillars, which Mr Whistler attributes to him. It possesses enough of his ponderous grandeur to make the attribution convincing. What else Vanbrugh did at Stowe must occupy us in another context. Domestic architecture of these years used giant pilasters quite generally (e.g. Wotton Underwood 44b 1704–14, Iver Grove 1722, Hambleden Rectory 1724). Parapets are often met, partly hiding the hipped roofs, windows are often segment-headed (The Bury, Chesham, 1712; the Brewhouse, Eton College, 1714; Godolphin's Almshouses, Eton, 1714; Forty Green Farmhouse, Bledlow, 1718; Gawcott, 1720; Iver Grove, 1722; Temple Square, Aylesbury, 1739) and are sometimes given aprons or some other decorative brick enrichment.

The term Baroque, which can only with qualifications be applied to the majority of English buildings of the early C18, applies with far greater ease to the MONUMENTS that were erected in the churches. Here, under French, Netherlandish, and of course Italian influence, developments took place which broke all those iconographic restrictions still valid up to the Restoration. The first monument of the new order in Buckinghamshire is probably the Tyrril Monument of *c.* 1671 at Castlethorpe, where one 24a figure is seated, the other semi-reclining, and a convincing intimate group is created. The sculptor is not known. This is

25 followed by the grandiose monument to the first Earl of Nottingham at Ravenstone. He died in 1682 and is shown as a white, comfortably and elegantly semi-reclining figure on a black marble
slab under a canopy of marble columns. Similar semi-reclining
figures are on the Longueville monument of c. 1685 at Old
24b Wolverton and on the Winwood monument of c. 1689 at Quainton
which is by *Stayner*. A comparable ease, and even an element of
sensuality, appears in the life-size young caryatids of the West
monument of c. 1684 at Bradenham. With this we have reached
26b the most swagger monument in the county, that to the fifth Earl
and first Duke of Bedford at Chenies, which is of c. 1700 and
attributed, not entirely convincingly, to *Francis Bird*. It has two
seated figures under a looped-up baldacchino and coupled
columns l. and r. and fills the w wall of the Bedford Chapel almost
completely. More likely to be by Bird is one of the Dashwood
ladies in the West Wycombe Mausoleum. The two ladies died in
1710 and 1719. They both kneel, as do the two Bents in the
extremely awkward monument at Amersham († 1714). Other
monuments whose sculptors are known are one by *Gibbons* at
Soulbury without effigy († 1690), one with a bust in front of a
fine bouquet of military trophies at St Leonards by *Bigée* († 1712),
and a very large and noble one, also without effigy, at Amersham
by *Andrew Carpenter*. The date of death here is 1724, and the
monument might well have been designed not by a sculptor
but by one of the architects who led along the new Palladian
road.

This road had been opened for the English by Colen Campbell,
the architect, and Lord Burlington, the amateur-architect and
patron. *Lord Burlington* designed a house near Iver Heath (Round
Coppice) which does not survive,* and of *Campbell*'s Great Room
at Hall Barn there is only one narrow end and the Grand Entrance
preserved. Palladianism begins here. To it belong *Leoni*'s garden
buildings at Cliveden (c. 1735) and *Kent*'s and others at Stowe.
But to these we must turn later. Palladian also, in a quiet conservative way that shows the continuity from the domestic style
of Wren, is the stone front of Biddlesden Park of 1731 (the staircase here also harks back to Wren), and conservatism is the domi-
nant quality of the big brick mansion of Chilton, built c. 1740 on
the model of Buckingham House in London, which dated from
1705. One of the finest Palladian interiors is the Library of Eton
College, built in 1725–9 by *Thomas Rowland*. 1755 is the date of
1b Harleyford Manor near Marlow, designed by the Palladian *Sir*

* Mr John Harris kindly drew my attention to this.

Robert Taylor. It has a compact brick exterior and inside a saloon with splendid stucco trophies etc. Claydon House of *c.* 1752–*c.* 90 also is externally compact and far from eloquent and contains splendid stucco work and woodwork inside. One can indeed say without hesitation that for Rococo decoration, whether in the French Rocaille, the English Kentian, or the Chinese or the Gothick fashion, there is no house in England to surpass Claydon. Comparisons abroad can only be with Germany and Austria; France has hardly anything so exuberant. Comparisons with much interior decoration of the Dixhuitième can be made comfortably without leaving the county, thanks to the inspired collecting of Baron Meyer and Baron Ferdinand de Rothschild, who accumulated at Mentmore and at Waddesdon treasures sold willingly by impoverished French noblemen. At Cliveden also there is an original French room. Claydon is only one wing of a mansion so giddily grandiose that two-thirds of it were pulled down before the c18 was over. This accounts perhaps for the extreme plainness of the exterior. On the other hand exterior simplicity pleased the Palladian patrons. Three examples are the external alterations of *c.* 1750 at Gayhurst (which went with good new Kentian interiors) and the two houses designed about the same time by *Stiff Leadbetter*, Langley Park and Shardeloes, both decidedly uneventful. Langley Park was given more drama in the mid c19, Shardeloes more elegance in the 1760s by *Robert Adam*.

Adam also designed the Market Hall at High Wycombe, standing at r. angles to *Henry Keene*'s slightly earlier, more substantial and more handsome Guildhall. Buckinghamshire being a county of small towns, there are many pre-Victorian town halls left, though none very grand or architecturally distinguished. They start with the Amersham Town Hall of 1682 and the Buckingham Town Hall (with a façade of the 1780s). This is followed by the County Hall at Aylesbury of 1723, with handsome and interesting interiors, by the new High Wycombe buildings of 1757 and 1761, the Chesham Town Hall, the Marlow Town Hall of 1807, and the modest Princes Risborough Town Hall of 1824. The function of these buildings, with their open ground-floor arcades, was always a mixture of market hall and meeting room. Only at Wycombe the Adam building was a separate one. But Adam's principal work in Buckinghamshire is the s front of Stowe, even if in the execution modified by *Borra*, a festive composition with many details which tell more of Adam than of Palladio.

But Stowe is more than a grand mansion. The grounds are at

least as important as the house, and the whole as an ensemble is unmatched in England. Palladian architecture runs parallel with PICTURESQUE GARDENING. This surprising fact must by now be accepted. As soon as Palladian architecture starts, picturesque gardening starts. Pope defended the one and practised the other, Lord Burlington promoted both. The reasons for this parallel of the formal and the informal, of cube and serpentine, are manifold and complex. They cannot here be set out, but it must be stated that to understand the meaning of the Palladian house in this island as against the Veneto it is necessary always to visualize it in a landscape setting. At Stowe all the great creators of landscape gardening have been active, first *Charles Bridgeman* (*c.* 1720–5), who still tried to combine straight axes and radiating avenues with asymmetrically composed wildernesses, then *William Kent* (*c.* 1730–48) 'who jumped the fence and saw that all nature was a garden' (H. Walpole) and who created the Elysian Fields and the Grecian Valley, and after him *Capability Brown*, to whom we owe the final scale of the Stowe landscape. There are two aims in English C18 landscape gardening. It was intended to be 'natural', and it was intended to be suggestive. The two aims sometimes clashed. The second, associative or evocative, called for buildings, some just to fix view-points (i.e. alcoves, umbrellos, etc.), others to kindle moods. The latter accounts for most of the BUILDINGS IN THE GROUNDS of Stowe and other C18 houses in Bucks and other counties. There were more at Stowe than anywhere else, and still are more, although e.g. of *Vanbrugh*'s build-
48a ings only the Rotondo and the Bourbon Tower remain and six, including a large pyramid said to be the earliest in England, have been pulled down. Apart from Vanbrugh, *Kent* designed for Lord Cobham, and *Gibbs*. The buildings are fully discussed in the
47a text. Most of them are classical, several porticoed. There are also the indispensable memorial obelisk and memorial column, and the equally indispensable knick-knacks, such as the cascade, the pebble alcove, and the shell bridge. Historically specially interest-
48b ing is the Temple of British Worthies with busts including Bacon, Hampden, Milton, Locke, and Newton. But from the point of view of architectural history perhaps the most significant is the
47b Gothic Temple, designed – one is surprised to hear – by *Gibbs*. Its approximate date is 1740–5. It belongs to the incunabula of the Gothic Revival, and we shall have to revert to it presently. Meanwhile Pope's plea in his Epistle to Lord Burlington to emulate Lord Cobham and also to create 'A Work to wonder at – perhaps a STOW' had been listened to by many, and picturesque gardens

with picturesque furnishings appeared everywhere. Buckinghamshire is unusually rich in these. Sir Francis Dashwood's West
Wycombe must be given second place. Here an early C18 house
had been made grander by a spectacular two-storeyed colonnade 56
along its S front, the work of *John Donovell, c.* 1750–60, it seems,
and by the deep porticoes across its short ends, built by *Revett,
c.* 1771. Splendid interiors were also created, and at the same time
a number of temples and more utilitarian, but equally picturesque-
looking, buildings erected in the grounds. They culminated
aesthetically *c.* 1780 in the poetical Island Temple by *Revett,* but
structurally in the quarter-mile-long cave of 1750–2 which was 50b
dug below the steep and sudden hill on which the church was at
the same time rebuilt. A connexion of this cave with the deeds
of the Hell-Fire Club cannot be established. For memories of the
activities of this one ought to go to Sir Francis Dashwood's other
house, Medmenham Abbey, where a Gothic colonnade and a
ruined Gothic tower were built about 1760. The many garden
furnishings of Wotton Underwood are derelict,* those of Weston
Underwood described by Cowper have all gone. At The Wilderness, Upper Winchendon, where the Duke of Chandos had laid
out a princely garden, there survives a Vanbrughian Summer
House, at the Stanhopes' neighbouring Eythrope again nothing.
At Cliveden, about 1735, *Leoni* built for Lord Orkney a substantial Gazebo with a beautiful view over the Thames valley and
a Blenheim Temple to commemorate a battle in which Lord
Orkney had commanded a brigade. On a hill at Hedsor is Lord
Boston's Folly, a sham castle front with three towers which must
be one of the most substantial follies in England. Fawley Court
preserves a Serlian Watergate, a domed ruin, the dome decorated
inside with knuckle-bones, and a chapel-like Dairy with an
original, re-set Norman doorway. At Stoke Court, Stoke Poges, is
Gray's Gothic Alcove, at Hall Barn a rotunda and an obelisk.
Dropmore's Greek Doric temple fronts are made of wooden
trellis-work, and the extensive trellises of Dropmore are altogether a delightful sight, interrupted by a tall iron Aviary 59b
decorated with green Chinese procelain panels.

Chinoiserie and Gothiquerie celebrate triumphs in adjoining
rooms at Claydon House. The Gothic Room is the most exuberant 54
example of the GOTHICK FASHION in the county, but only one
of many. Buckinghamshire as a matter of fact has more early
examples of the Gothic Revival left than any other county. The
earliest example, though included with reservation, is *Vanbrugh's*

* At the time of writing.

Bourbon Tower at Stowe of *c.* 1720–5, medieval but not Gothic. This is followed by a small house in Bull Lane, High Wycombe, which carries a date 1729. But the few Gothic motifs here may 47b well be due to alteration. After that, *Gibbs*'s Gothic Temple at Stowe, as has been said, is of *c.* 1740–5, the Gaol at Buckingham of 1748, and Stowe Castle, near Stowe, of before 1750. But while all these are follies, the Gothic Revival at this moment also began to invade the house itself and embroider its exterior and interior in that playful way practised so successfully by Horace Walpole at Strawberry Hill. His Gothic conversions there started in 1749. To his Committee on Taste belonged his friends *John Chute* and *Richard Bentley*. Both were busy in the mid fifties gothicizing Chalfont House, Chalfont St Peter. However, what is now visible of gothicism there can be no earlier than the 1830s. On the other 50a hand, Hampden House, Great Hampden, was certainly in the process of gothicizing as early as 1751. The designer was *Thomas Iremonger*. In the remodelling of the stairs there is a touch of Jacobeanism too, a rare variant of C18 revivalism. The garden side of the small and pretty Drayton Parslow Rectory is Gothic too and has a date 1754. After that examples multiply: the castellated Liscombe Park of 1774, the castellated Missenden Abbey of *c.* 1800, *James Wyatt*'s castellated Wycombe Abbey of 1785 etc., and his castellated Vicarage at Stoke Poges of 1802, and *William Atkinson*'s castellated Ditton Park of 1813–17.

The Gothic Revival appears early in Bucks churches too. Of GEORGIAN CHURCHES little need be said. The work was mostly minor. The church built at the inspiration of Browne Willis at Fenny Stratford in 1724–30, the church by the house at Gayhurst of 1728, the church of 1731 forming an externally indistinguishable part of the stables at Biddlesden Park, the chancel of Fawley rebuilt in 1748, the little church of 1788 at Loudwater and the church of Gawcott designed in 1827 by the incumbent, the Rev. *Thomas Scott*, Sir G. G. Scott's father, are all small fry. What makes one remember them is more the completeness of their C18 FURNISHINGS than their architectural qualities. At Fawley the furnishings were bought from the sale of the Duke of Chandos's palace at Canons. Again, more distinctive inside than outside, though in a very different, humble and honest, way, is the 14a Friends' Meeting House at Jordans built in 1688. This, the equally modest Baptist Chapel at Winslow of 1695, and the much bigger and more self-assured Baptist Church at Amersham of 1783 are the only NONCONFORMIST CHAPELS to be recorded here. The only really remarkable mid-C18 churches are West Wycombe and Hartwell. West Wycombe was largely rebuilt by Sir Francis Dashwood. It was completed in 1763. It is prominent, as one approaches it from High Wycombe and London, with its golden ball on top of the tower, and it is beautifully decorated and equipped inside. The pulpit and lectern and the font are amongst 20a the strangest of post-Reformation CHURCH FURNISHINGS in &b England, the former being comfortable chairs, the latter not allowing within its ring of pretty doves more space for the baptizing bowl than a porringer would take. Equally strange is the large hexagonal Mausoleum built to the E of the church and left open to the sky. This dates from 1763–4.

While West Wycombe is classical, Hartwell is Gothic. It was 8b &13 built in 1753–5. It is octagonal in plan and has two towers, again an odd conceit. The church is by *Henry Keene*, a convinced Gothicist, even if he could build classical as well (e.g. in the High Wycombe Guildhall). Hartwell, lying close to the house, was a gem, and it is a great shame that it has been allowed to fall into ruin. By *Keene* also is the top of the tower of High Wycombe parish church (1755) and the delicious family pew of the Shelburnes now kept at Wycombe Abbey School.* Mid-Georgian churches are at Stony Stratford (1776 by *F. Hiorne*) and at Buckingham (1777–81; almost completely altered by *Scott*). Of the end of the century is the charming screen at the entrance to the Kederminster Chapel at Langley Marish. This was erected in 1792 and is made of *Coade* stone.

Coade stone is more frequently seen in sculpture than in architecture, and to GEORGIAN SCULPTURE we must now turn for a moment. A few monuments not in churches must first be mentioned; for Bucks is uncommonly rich in them. There are *Bird*'s Henry VI at Eton of 1719, the equestrian lead statue of George I at Stowe of 1727, the other equestrian lead statue, which is a Frederick Prince of Wales at Hartwell and dates from 1757, the lead statue of Heroic Beauty on a column at Stowe of 1747, the statue of Queen Caroline on a clustered column at Stowe of *c*. 1730 (a work by *Rysbrack*), the Lord Cobham at Stowe of 1747 on a pillar 115 ft high (the statue does not exist any longer), the George II on a column at Hartwell of 1757, the Henry VI by *Bacon* in Eton Chapel of 1786, and the Sir Edward Coke by *Rossi* at Stoke Park of 1800.

Of FUNERAL MONUMENTS there are hundreds in the county. Simple tablets are not mentioned in the gazetteer. Nor are head-

* From the same church the monumental altar painting by *J. H. Mortimer*, now in the Guildhall.

stones in churchyards, although many of them are interesting.*
This applies especially to the work of Cowper's friend *James
Andrews* of Olney (1735–1817), who also did one major church
monument, that to Alexander Small † 1752 at Clifton Reynes,
where the bust however is a terracotta by *Scheemakers*. The brief
survey of major monuments which is all that can be attempted
here can start with Scheemakers. His monument to Montague
Drake † 1728 at Amersham was designed by *Gibbs*. Architects
indeed did design monuments quite frequently. The most
familiar example is Kent's design of the Newton Monument in
Westminster Abbey. At Quainton there is a monument without
figures designed and signed by *Leoni*. The Drake at Amersham
has the deceased seated on the sarcophagus and a female figure
seated at his feet. This kind of free grouping, which started in
England with Bushnell and Gibbons in the time of Charles II
and in Buckinghamshire with the monument at Castlethorpe
already referred to, became characteristic of the more ambitious
Early Georgian monuments. The Dormer monument at Quain-
27a ton, e.g., of *c*. 1728, has the kneeling mother and the dead son. Mrs
Esdaile attributed it to *Roubiliac*, but that cannot be so, either on
stylistic or on historical grounds. Roubiliac probably did not
arrive in England until *c*. 1732. That also rules out his name for
28 the Wright monument at Gayhurst of *c*. 1728, again given to him
by Mrs Esdaile. This, with its two standing figures in their
normal clothes, is rather the work of one of the masters of the
early C18 such as Green of Camberwell. For the monument at
Quainton even an approximate attribution is lacking. The other
two *Scheemakers* monuments are later: the Pigott at Grendon
30a Underwood † 1751 and the spectacular Shelburne at High
Wycombe, erected 1754. In both cases the deceased wears
Roman dress, a convention favoured by Scheemakers (but
followed already by the Longueville at Old Wolverton † 1685).
The Pigott is represented in a seated position, the Lord Shelburne semi-reclining. To his l. and r. are groups with large standing figures. The only *Rysbrack* in the county has no effigy, only a
putto by a broken column.‡ *Sir Henry Cheere* is well represented
by the agitated little relief of the monument to John Hampden
at Great Hampden (1743), while his monument at Hillesden
(† 1733) with two busts is of less interest. A good piece by a
27b lesser sculptor is *William Woodman*'s Lord Newhaven of *c*. 1730

    * Special studies on them by Mr F. Burgess have been published in the
Monumental Journal, 1948, 1949, 1950.
    ‡ But cf. the statue of Queen Caroline, above p. 35.

at Drayton Beauchamp, again a semi-reclining and a seated figure, like the Scheemakers–Gibbs of *c.* 1728.

The change of style of *c.* 1760 is impressively illustrated by the Bedford monument at Chenies designed by *Sir William Chambers* and carved by *Joseph Wilton* in 1769. Its sculptural style is clearly of Roman descent, an outcome of the Roman 'Baroque Classicism' of the late C17 and early C18. The rest is a summary catalogue: *Carlini* at High Wycombe (†1771) with a standing figure, several fine *Bacons* (especially Burnham 1792 and Amersham † 1801 and † 1802), several *Nollekens*, a very good figure of *Coade* stone (Langley Marish † 1788; another at Soulbury 30b † 1786), one *Flaxman* (1816, Stoke Poges), several *Westmacotts*, several *Chantreys*, and an outstandingly fine *John Gibson* 31 († 1833).

In this context the Freeman Mausoleum of 1752 at Fawley, an impressively large and noble Palladian building, and the Gray Sarcophagus near Stoke Poges parish church, designed by *James Wyatt* and erected in 1799, ought to be referred to. James Wyatt had good connexions in the county. He did the library at Shardeloes in 1771, was responsible for decorations at Fawley Court in the same year and for decorations at Wilton Park. He also, by additions and alterations, probably of *c.* 1800–8, made Stoke Park the most impressive of all LATE GEORGIAN HOUSES 58b in Buckinghamshire. Its Greek Doric columns are a sign of progressiveness considering the fact that Greek Doric columns had only been introduced into English architecture about 1790, the date when Bonomi used them at Great Packington church, and its later tall dome on a drum is an unusual and successful feature. *Soane* was specially fond of Greek Doric and introduced it in several of his jobs in the 1790s. In 1796, e.g., he designed a Mausoleum for Tyringham which was intended to have Greek Doric columns. The Entrance Hall of the house also had them. The Gateway, however, his principal remaining piece at Tyringham, 58a is not Grecian: it is Soanian and nothing else in its thin, linear, rigid rectangularity, and his one room at Stowe (1803–6) is 57b Gothic.

The ambivalence of Gothic and Classical is typical of the late C18 and early C19. Soon more styles were admitted as sources of inspiration, until by Queen Victoria's ascent to the throne the stage was set for the fancy-dress ball of historicism. In Buckinghamshire the NORMAN REVIVAL begins exceptionally early. While this short-lived fashion is usually characteristic of *c.* 1835–45, it appears at Old Wolverton in 1815 (*Hakewill*) and at Calverton in 1818–24.* Its belated culmination is the bleak Grand Hall of 1855 at Taplow Court.

The RENAISSANCE REVIVAL had been initiated in London by *Sir Charles Barry* just before 1830. Its first example in Bucks 61a is a late work of Barry's, Cliveden, where his pattern is the Genoese Cinquecento. This is a grand pattern but an orderly one. As soon as he had died, *Clutton* added the clock tower in a wild Italianate style of mixed and lushly transmogrified sources. Mixed indeed are the sources also of that white elephant, the 9a parish church of Gerrards Cross, by *Sir William Tite*. The church was built in 1859 and its style can only be described as Byzantine-cum-Italian-Romanesque-cum-Baroque. So bold a mixture almost amounts to originality, and HIGH VICTORIAN originality at its most ruthless (and ugly) is the character of *E. B. Lamb*'s refronting of Hughenden Manor for Disraeli in 1862. *Lamb* also designed a church in Bucks (Prestwood), and that also is self-assertive and unbeautiful.

But when it comes to self-assertiveness and an intrepid mixing of sources, there is nothing in England to beat Baron Ferdinand 61b de Rothschild's Waddesdon of *c.* 1875–80 and Baron Lionel's, or rather Baron Alfred's, Halton, completed in 1884. Waddesdon is by a French architect, *Destailleur*; the architect of Halton is un- 62 known. Halton has a sumptuous hall inside too, at Waddesdon the interiors, as far as they are not of the French C18, are remark- ably restrained. The scale of Waddesdon had been surpassed already twenty years before by Baron Meyer de Rothschild's 60 Mentmore, designed by *Sir Joseph Paxton*, or rather his son-in- law *Stokes*, and built in 1852–4. It is a variation on the theme of Wollaton Hall – an Elizabethan 'prodigy house' out-prodigied by the Victorian one. These three are not the only Rothschild houses in the neighbourhood. There are also Lord Rothschild's Tring, a much simpler house, Sir Anthony's Aston Clinton, bought in 1851 and recently demolished, and Mr Leopold de Rothschild's Ascott, enlarged after 1874 in the Old English half- timbered mode by *Devey*. Devey also built the so-called Pavilion by the lake at Eythrope, near Waddesdon, for Baron Ferdinand's sister, Alice de Rothschild, in 1883 and other houses in the county for other clients.‡ The Rothschild contribution is the most con- spicuous and significant aspect of Victorian architecture in Buckinghamshire.§ The only other Victorian work of a character

* Norman also was the former church of Slough, built in 1835.
‡ A house of a similar type is Warren House, Iver Heath, by *Edis*, 1881.
§ This being so, it may be useful to append (opposite) an abridged genealogy of the Rothschilds in question.

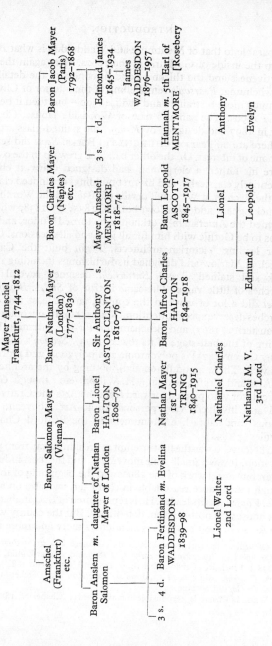

PART OF THE ROTHSCHILD FAMILY TREE

comparable to that of Mentmore and Waddesdon is what *Burges* did to the inside of Gayhurst in the 1860s. Here again the self-assertiveness and the thickness and heaviness of the details are overwhelming. *Pearson*'s remodelling of the interior of Cliveden is a much more restrained and civilized job – but then it belongs to the 1890s. The same is true of Woodside House, Chenies, built in 1897 and designed by *Kempe*, the stained-glass artist.

There are no Pearson CHURCHES in Bucks. *Scott* did several, but none of interest. On the other hand, he grew up in the county, where his father, a clergyman, had designed Gawcott church, still entirely classically, and his first buildings are indeed classical too, the Rectory at Weston Turville of 1838 and the Workhouses at Buckingham and Winslow, both of 1835. By 1838, when he designed the Amersham Workhouse, he turned Tudor, and soon it was to be Gothic with him for all jobs and all occasions. Of the other leading Victorian architects, *Pugin* built the Catholic church at Marlow and designed its furnishings including metal-work and stained glass.* *Butterfield* designed several small churches of little value. The same is true of *Sir A. Blomfield*.‡ *Street* did a lot of work in the county, and at least two of his churches deserve special attention, Westcott for its uncompromising austerity (1867) and Beachampton for the charming balus-trading of the bell-stage of its tower (1873). *Seddon*'s chancel of Lacey Green (1871) is polychrome and polygonal and represents him well. There is, oddly enough, nothing by the architects of the Arts and Crafts, Sedding, H. Wilson, etc., though *Gilbert*, the sculptor who pushed forward from the Arts and Crafts into a wild and involved, very personal proto-Art Nouveau, did a curious candelabra-like Monument in the Bedford Chapel at Chenies († 1892).

Art Nouveau was the first attempt at breaking away from period imitation. It was a small-scale movement, and the most independent architectural work of the 1890s and the beginning of the C20, though much more reasonable in character, was also on a small scale. *Voysey* was its leader. He is represented in Buckinghamshire by a house at Knotty Green, dated 1907. But the county was too rich for so modest a style. As Londoners more and more settled

* Of other VICTORIAN STAINED GLASS there is a great quantity by *Kempe*, specially interesting the earliest, of 1877 and 1882 at Upton, Slough, of 1878 at Linslade, of 1880 at Frieth, of 1882 at Horton, and 1884 at Coln-brook. *O'Connor* did sets of windows at Wavendon and Datchet (1860–5). *Morris & Co.* did nothing.

‡ Who, however, is responsible for the Lower Chapel of 1889–91 at Eton.

down in Bucks, more and more big, proud, prosperous houses were asked for and built. They were no longer as showy as the High Victorian Rothschild houses had been. They were more genteel, more subdued in their detailing, and tried to be more convincingly period. The biggest jobs were the neighbouring Danesfield and Medmenham Abbey, both by *Romaine Walker* and both of *c.* 1900, the latter a conversion and addition, the former a completely new stone-built neo-Gothic job with later elements. It has two courtyards and three big towers among other things. Other mansions went on with half-timbering and Tudor gables. A really good neo-Tudor design is *Lorimer*'s Barton Hartshorn of 1903–9. In the average rich houses of those years, and even more in those built between the two wars, much old timber was used, and often old brick too, in order to convince. The style was also popular for the smaller house, and the Abbots Brook Estate at Bourne End, of the nineties, is a perfect example of cosy make-believe. A trout-stream flows through it. Among the more serious architectural efforts, *Sir Reginald Blomfield*'s Wittington, Medmenham, of 1898, must be given first place. It is an uncommonly good example of the William-and-Mary revival. *Lutyens*'s Nashdom of 1910 shows him more conventionally neo-Georgian than he usually chose to be. The size here is again astonishing, even if not as astonishing as Lutyens's display of three formal pools and two full-dress pavilions at Tyringham, laid out and built in 1926.*

The style of the TWENTIETH CENTURY came to Buckinghamshire in two forms: as Expressionism, and as bogus streamlining. Expressionist to a degree very rare in the whole country are the stained glass windows at the w end of the Slough parish church. They are by *A. A. Wolmark* and were done as early as 1915 – an abstract design in strong colours, comparable in England only with what Wyndham Lewis did at the same time in 'Blast'. Bogus streamlining is the only appropriate term to be applied to the monumental gateway and the early factories of the Slough Trading Estate. This was created in 1920 and began to build new factories in 1927. It is highly interesting as an early experiment in planned industrial layout, including a Community Centre with clubs, etc. Meanwhile the International Style, created just before the First World War and established by 1925–6 in Germany say in Gropius's Bauhaus and in France in Le Corbusier's early villas, had also begun to make converts. It was

* The disastrous frenchifying of Soane's house had taken place earlier: in 1909. The architect responsible was called *Rees*.

to the latter that *Amyas Connell* turned for inspiration in his High and Over, a prominently placed villa above Old Amersham, and the first villa in the new style in England. The date of its design is 1929. It was followed by four more Corbusiesque villas on the same estate, designed by Connell's partner *Basil Ward* in 1934. Then, in 1934–7 more supporters of the new style received com-
63b missions in the county: *Mendelsohn* and *Chermayeff* at Chalfont St Giles, *F. R. S. Yorke* at Eton and Iver, *Val Harding (Tecton)* at Farnham Common, *Christopher Nicholson* at Fawley. *Gropius* himself, i.e. during his short English years *Gropius & Fry*, de-
64a signed a large laboratory for a film company at Denham in 1936.

The less exacting mode of after the Second World War can also be studied in Buckinghamshire. Good domestic examples are *Lionel Brett*'s Taidswood, Iver Heath, and *John G. Fryman*'s Portals at Medmenham. But most of the work in this style is due to the County Architect *F. B. Pooley* and his team. There are
64b attractive schools in many places, and there are the tall, well designed and proportioned blocks of the College of Further Education at Slough. Nearly all the modern buildings of the last twenty-five years in the county have been illustrated and discussed in the *Architectural Review* and the *Architects' Journal*.

One more note must now be appended. It is to deal with the new YORKSHIRE AND BIRMINGHAM MOTORWAY, the C20 version of the Roman Watling Street, called in the matter-of-fact C20 way M1. No more than 55 miles of it exist at the time of going to press; not much compared with the German *Autobahnen* or even Italian *autostrade*, and moreover started remarkably (and very Englishly) late. However, it must be admitted that the soil of England is so closely and intimately worked and so subtly landscaped that the intrusion of the motorway was bound to be specially violent. It was for this reason that opposition to it remained victorious for so long. The motorway enters Buckinghamshire NE of Broughton, runs W of Newport Pagnell and Gayhurst, and leaves for Northamptonshire W of Salcey Forest. *Sir Owen Williams & Partners* were briefed in 1951, the decision to go ahead was made in 1955, and work started in 1958 and was completed in 1959 – quite an achievement, considering that e.g. more than 130 BRIDGES had to be built. They are of six standard types. The bigger ones are of mass concrete with the simplest reinforcements, and impress by a cyclopean rudeness rather than by elegance. Especially surprising are the supports between the traffic lanes in the N and S directions: a kind of elementary columns, without base and capital, but with an abacus – a curious period suggestion, not called for in this forward-looking job. Sir Owen Williams evidently wanted to impress permanence on us, and permanence is a doubtful quality in devices connected with vehicles and means of transport. Elegance, lightness, and resilience might have been preferable, an elegance achieved so spectacularly already in Swiss concrete bridges before the First World War and – with the aid of the more recent device of pre-stressing – often since in other countries. On the motorway elegance was arrived at only in the foot-bridges. Even retaining walls, revetments, etc., are of concrete blocks. The motorway has three traffic lanes in either direction, as against the two of the *Autobahnen* and the four of some American highways. The total width of the motorway is 105 ft. The centre strip is 13 ft wide and so far unlandscaped, which must be the next job to be contemplated and carried out in consultation with landscape architects.

In conclusion and briefly 'Further Reading'. For everything prior to the early C18 the two volumes of the *Royal Commission on Historical Monuments* (1912) ought to be consulted. They are on the whole still valid. The *Victoria County History* has also completed its work in Buckinghamshire. It is published in four volumes with a fifth for the indices (1905–28). For Prehistory J. F. Head: *Early Man in South Buckinghamshire* (1955) offers not only a fully documented gazetteer, but also a useful summary to the end of the Pagan Saxon period. For houses, especially of the C18, *Country Life* is of course indispensable. In addition the *Records of Buckinghamshire* are extremely useful. They contain for instance Mrs Esdaile's account of Baroque monuments (vol. XV, 1947 etc.). Equally useful are the old county histories by Lipscomb (4 vols., 1847) and Sheahan (1862), and of course Kelly's *Directory* which, like all its companions, has the most surprising wealth of Victorian information. The most enjoyable book on the buildings of Buckinghamshire is John Betjeman and John Piper: *Murray's Buckinghamshire Architectural Guide*, London, 1948. On Eton College the standard book is H. C. Maxwell Lyte: *A History of Eton College*, 4th ed., 1911, but there is also the remarkably complete *Illustrated Guide to the Buildings of Eton College* by R. A. Austen Leigh (first ed., 1904; several editions since). For Stowe one needs Mr Laurence Whistler's excellent guide, sold at Stowe, and his *The Imagination of Vanbrugh*, London, 1954, and in addition the volume of *English Homes* by H. Avray Tipping and Christopher Hussey, which deals with Vanbrugh's work (Period 4, vol. II, 1928), and *Country Life*, vols. CII (1947) and CVIII (1950).

BUCKINGHAMSHIRE

*

ADDINGTON

ST MARY. Externally all of the restoration by *Street*, 1859. However, the W tower, the arcades with the rare peculiarity of piers continued into the arches without any capital or other caesura, and the chancel arch are original C14 work. – STAINED GLASS. A large number of Netherlandish panels, round and otherwise, of the C16 to C17. The ornamented glass in the clerestory windows was made by *Powells* to *Street*'s design. – PAINTING. Good Italian Baroque sketch of a scene with saints and angels on clouds. – MONUMENTS. Sir John Busby † 1700. Good cartouche with trophies and a portrait bust at the top. – Thomas Busby, signed and dated by *Rysbrack*, 1753. Standing wallmonument with a putto standing by a broken column and holding a snake which is biting its own tail. – Anne Busby † 1798. Standing wall-monument. Kneeling woman by an urn.

OLD MANOR HOUSE, N of the church. A fragment of a much larger house. What remains seems late C17, brick with quoins. Some furnishings of the house were transferred to Addington Manor (*see* below). A big BARN by the house is assigned to the late C16. The STABLES, with a seven-bay front and a pediment above the central archway, have a date 1642, but their present appearance is clearly later, probably again of the late C17.

ADDINGTON MANOR. 1928–9, by *Michael Waterhouse*. Brick with stone dressings. Nine bays and two storeys. Pedimented centre with tall, freely Late Georgian Ionic pilasters.

ADSTOCK

ST CECILIA. Fragmentary Norman N and S doorways. On the N no more than re-used bits of an arch. The S doorway has one order of shafts with foliage capitals and foliage in the abaci. The arch is of the C14. Chancel of *c.* 1300 – see the windows. One of them is a 'low side' window and has a transom. Perp W tower and nave windows. – STAINED GLASS. W window by *Powell & Sons*, 1875, not at all bad. – PLATE. Cup and Cover Paten of 1569.

7030
AKELEY

ST JAMES. By *J. Tarring*, 1854 (GR). With a S tower with spirelet on the higher stair-turret. – STAINED GLASS. E window by *Mayer & Co.* of Munich and London, 1884.

HOUSE, ¼ m. SW. By *H. J. Richards*, 1956. One-storeyed, of brick and rubble, with much glass. Beautifully placed under old trees and nicely spreading, making in its planning the best use of a fine situation.

AKELEYWOOD. By *Devey*, who was paid his fees in 1867–8. Large, with stable range and lodge. All with plenty of gabling and half-timbering, highly asymmetrical and picturesque.

9090
AMERSHAM

ST MARY. Externally all Victorian (restoration of 1890). W tower with higher stair-turret and spirelet on this. S view and N view very varied, with transepts and additions to their E. Transepts C13; see the N transept E lancet and the S transept cusped W lancet. W tower and N chapel Perp. Big N window in the chapel with four-centred arch and panel tracery. Perp also the handsome tierceron-vault of the S porch with its foliage bosses. Arcades of the C14: four bays with octagonal piers and double-chamfered arches. – STAINED GLASS. E window, C17, foreign, with some whole large figures and more small ones in the tracery lights. The glass was brought in 1760 from Lamer, Hertfordshire. – N chapel E by *Kempe & Tower*, 1908. – MONUMENTS. Amersham is richer in noteworthy monuments than any other church in the county (except of course for Chenies and its Bedford Chapel), thanks primarily to the monuments of the Drake family and its successors. Most of these are in the Drake chapel on the N side (abbreviated D.C. – usually locked). The monuments will here be described in chronological order. Brass to Henry Brudenell † 1430 and wife (chancel N), 19 in. figures. – Brass to Thomas Carbonell † 1439 and wife (N aisle), 3 ft 2 in. figures. – Headless civilian, *c.* 1440, 3 ft 1 in. (N aisle W). – Brass to John de la Penne † 1537 and wife, 2 ft 1 in. (N
23a   aisle). – Henry Curwen † 1636, by *Edward Marshall*, of alabaster. A very beautiful hanging monument, still Mannerist in style. Upright figure in shroud, in the twisted stance of Michelangelo's Christ at S. Maria sopra Minerva. He stands in an arched shrine whose doors are kept open by two slender angels with fat Mannerist faces. Putti in the spandrels of the arch. Small figures on the open segmental pediment (chancel N). –

Sir William Drake † 1654. Big standing monument. The effigy relatively small, a frontal bust in shroud, one hand on his heart, the other raised. The surround has columns, and a strange pediment. Much ornamental enrichment, rather added together than integrated (chancel N). – George Bent † 1714 and his mother † 1730. Two figures kneeling frontally, but placed so awkwardly and ignorantly in the surround that their legs had to be cut off to fit into the available depth. He appears in contemporary dress, she as a Roman matron. A thin column stands between them on which she rests her elbow. Pilasters on the sides ending in volutes, segmental top. A bad piece of design (chancel S). – Montague Drake † 1724. Signed by *Andrew Carpenter*. Noble architectural background with unfluted Ionic columns and a segmental pediment with two putti. Big dark grey sarcophagus and above it against the back wall two oval portrait medallions (chancel S). – Montague Gerrard Drake † 1728. Signed by *Scheemakers*, but illustrated in *James Gibbs*'s 'Architecture' as designed by him. Big white and grey marble sarcophagus with a cartouche on which are allegorical female figures. On it the deceased sitting up and clothed in Roman dress. Behind him a sarcophagus. His wife seated on the l. with a book. Corinthian pilasters, segmental pediment, its centre recessed. – Mrs Elizabeth Drake † 1757. By *Sir Henry Cheere*. White, grey, and pink marble. Exceedingly elegant, especially the relief of a kneeling mother with six children. This is placed inside a frame. Below a sarcophagus. Above a broken pediment on brackets. On the base two seated putti and an inscription telling us 29

> Of God's mercie above Satan's malice
> Of his wonders in casting downe his Children y
>   hee may raise them up
> Of the truth of his praises in refreshing the
>   weary soule
> Of the force of faythful prayer
> Of the powers of God's saving truth
> Of the gaine of Godliness even in this life

(D.C., S Wall). – William Drake † 1795. Simple tablet, signed *John de Vaere* (D.C., S). – Elizabeth Tyrwhitt-Drake † 1801 in her seventeenth year and two children who died aged two years and aged seven days. By *Bacon Jun*. Three urns, one with the Signs of the Passion, the other two with initials. Above them three portraits in clouds. Obelisk-like background with double-curved outline l. and r. (D.C., S). – William Drake, by *Bacon*,

Jun. 1802. Hanging monument with a beautiful female figure, kneeling, her head on the base of an urn. Obelisk background (D.C., E). – Thomas Tyrwhitt Drake † 1810. By *Bacon Jun.* Hanging monument with two small figures against a big obelisk. They are the deceased, reclining half-naked on a Grecian bed, and Faith by his head pointing upward (D.C., E). – George Tyrwhitt Drake Clerk † 1840. By *Manning.* Tablet with sarcophagus with relief and weeping willows to the l. and r. (D.C., S). – Thomas Tyrwhitt Drake. By *Weekes,* 1854. Standing monument with the deceased in his dressing gown, semi-reclining. He holds an open book. To the l. and r. of the back plate two floral shapes on long stalks (D.C., N). – In addition a large number of plain tablets and several more with female figures, urns, sarcophagi, etc.

PUBLIC BUILDINGS. *See* Perambulation.

PERAMBULATION

The main part is a walk along the main street. There are one or two side-streets, but beyond that no more than some appendices. The main street is entered from London, and starts with one Georgian brick house of two storeys across the street facing E. Opposite, the end of Outer London, the big LONDON TRANSPORT GARAGE by *Wallis Gilbert & Partners,* 1935; and then, rather deplorably, the gasometer. After that the character of the street is established. It is first called BROADWAY, then High Street. No. 12 on the S side, which lies back, is of *c.* 1700, built of vitreous and red brick. It is three bays wide and has a gable and aprons to the first-floor windows. No. 15 has a nice shop front; the GRIFFIN HOTEL of the early C18, with a five-bay front of chequered brick, has three storeys. But two storeys are the rule at Amersham. Opposite now the churchyard. Then on the l. off into WHIELDEN STREET with plenty of nice minor houses. Towards the end on the W side, the FRIENDS' MEETING HOUSE of 1685, part of a cottage of 1624 and very unpretentious. The cottage is on the l., the meeting house on the r. Late C18 extension. The street leads to the former WORKHOUSE, now Hospital, built in 1838 by *Sir G. G. Scott* in the Tudor style. Flint and red brick. On the E-plan. Then buildings of interest become more concentrated. Across the middle stands the town hall.

TOWN HALL. Built in 1682 by Sir William Drake of Shardeloes. Red brick and stone dressings. Six by two bays with a hipped roof. Wooden bell-turret with lantern facing w. Ground floor open with broad pillars carrying arches. On the upper floor cross-windows.

To the s of the town hall the CROWN HOTEL with a pretty porch across the pavement. Wooden fluted columns built up, it seems, on the cooper's principle. To the N into CHURCH STREET. Here, past the church, the premises of a former Brewery and opposite a pretty range, perhaps former stables. The N side is weather-boarded, the short E side, towards the street, has flint walls with rubble forming pointed blank arches on two storeys; the back has a row of the same blank arches, but is of brick and flint. Then follows a Gothic flint cottage with pointed windows and then a white house of three storeys with pretty Grecian friezes. Opposite, more two-storeyed Georgian brick, especially BADMINTON HOUSE of grey and red brick with five bays. Projecting panels below the first-floor windows. Parapet. The date is probably the early C18. This sequence ends with the RECTORY, on the hill, facing s. This was built in 1732–5 and is of two storeys above a basement, five bays wide, of yellow brick. Centre with blank giant arch and broken pediment. Doorway with fluted Ionic pilasters.

Now on into HIGH STREET. On the N side THE GABLES, C17 with two big shaped gables and two canted bay windows below. Mullioned and transomed windows.* Opposite, minor half-timbered work and, lying back from the street, APSLEY HOUSE, late C17 and late C18, with quoins and a pretty roundel in the middle of the front. Then No. 47, an interesting C15 house with the wings projecting at the back. To the street three gables. In the centre was the Hall, in the w wing parts of a traceried Hall Screen, probably not *in situ*. The RED LION opposite is Grecian and white. Next to the King's Head a narrow passage leads to the BAPTIST CHURCH of 1783, of red brick, five bays and two storeys with arched windows. Those on the ground floor have keystones, all with the same female head. Truncated pyramid roof and glazed diagonal lantern. Then the biggest house in Amersham, ELMODESHAM HOUSE. This is of the early C18, eleven bays wide and two-and-a-half storeys high, of purple and red brick. The first five bays and the last four have rusticated brick quoins. Between these are two slightly recessed bays, and in them is the stately tripartite doorway with Roman Doric columns, a triglyph frieze, and a

* Inside elaborate chimneypiece of *c.* 1640 with pilasters and caryatids (RCHM).

straight entablature. (In No. 61 a room on the ground floor with C17 paintings of the Nine Worthies against landscape backgrounds. F. W. Reader, *Rec. of Bucks.* XII.)

After a while on the same side SIR WILLIAM DRAKE'S ALMSHOUSES, established in 1657. A modest one-storey composition with two gables to the street and a wall between with doorway. This is arched and flanked by pilasters, and the same motif is repeated blank below the gables. In the centre at the back a gable. The windows are mullioned and have arched lights. Even beyond this stage the fine Georgian houses continue. PIERS PLACE has a rain-water head with the date 173?. It is of five bays and two storeys and has a parapet. Doorway with attached Tuscan columns and broken pediment. MINTON HOUSE is similar, but the pediment of the doorway is on brackets. THE MILL on the N side must date from before 1700. Chequered brick, cross-windows, seven bays and two storeys with two very narrow outer bays. Finally, LITTLE SHARDE-LOES, again on the S, of the C17, with brick gables.

The first of the appendices is HIGH AND OVER, built on the hill E of Station Road in 1929–31 by *A. D. Connell* and one of the first in this country to accept the style of Le Corbusier's early villas. The bare concrete walls, the sharply cut-in horizontal windows, the meeting of unrelieved cubic shapes, the fully glazed staircase, all these are now familiar features – they were shockingly new in England then. The concrete water-tank on the highest point of the site is a shock still – a circular pole with a large circular cistern like a millstone high up. The plan of the house is a hexagonal centre and three radial wings, completely symmetrical, but varied in height so that no formality appears in the elevations. Only one wing runs up to full height, and this has a one-storeyed addition at its end; the other two have only one upper floor but roof canopies on this. Sir Howard Robertson, then a young man, wrote enthusiastically about High and Over in 1930. Below it, by the road, *Basil Ward*, Connell's partner, in 1934 built four smaller houses in the same style. The whole group is a monument to the International Style of the thirties, but it cannot be denied that it still looks alien now. Why is that? The answer lies in the renewed change of style of *c.* 1945–50. Since 1950 much has gone up in the changed idiom of the mid century, and these new houses have succeeded in becoming part of the English scene. They could, because they have never had any intention of hitting as hard as the Connell and Ward houses. So these remain very valuable documents of the courage and boldness of a client and his architects.*

AMERSHAM-ON-THE-HILL is Outer London, shopping streets of familiar character without any civic accent. From this centre WOODSIDE ROAD runs sw towards Little Chalfont. On the l. between MITCHELL WALK and RAANS ROAD several COUNTY SCHOOLS, Infant, Junior, and Secondary. All these are of good architectural quality and represent their various functions nicely. They are by the County Architect, *F. B. Pooley*. At the end of Raans Road RAANS FARM, with a mid-C16 porch, gabled and with mullioned windows whose lights are still arched. Brick doorway. Remains of more windows in other parts of the buildings. The continuation of Woodside Road is WHITE LION ROAD, where the Atomic Energy Commission is building its new RADIO CHEMICAL CENTRE. The architect is *E. D. Jefferiss Mathews*. It is a clear, logical job, concrete-framed and with much curtain walling, partly one-, partly two-storeyed. After that, at the corner of Finch Lane the entrance to BEEL HOUSE, early C19, of two storeys and five bays, cemented. The centre bay projects. Roman Doric porch. On the two sides bow windows with pilasters on the ground floor, also a canted bay window.

RUSHYMEAD, s of Old Amersham. Large, neo-Georgian, with gables; good. By *Smith & Brewer*, c. 1924.

(WOODROW HIGH HOUSE, 1½ m. sw, has a GROTTO cut into the side of a dingle. It is a domed octagon, 10 ft across, with bold patterns in pebbles. B. Jones)

SHARDELOES, *see* p. 233.

ASCOTT

8020

A timber-framed house with a date 1606 recorded above the front door was considerably enlarged in the same style by *Devey* after Leopold de Rothschild had bought it in 1874. Another extension dates from *c.* 1938. The old part forms the centre of the front; the extension by Devey, which contains the principal rooms, is to the r., the extension of 1938 to the l. The whole is picturesque and irregular. In the gardens a large bronze FOUNTAIN of Venus with cherubs on a chariot drawn by sea-horses. This is by *Waldo Story*, the American sculptor who lived in Rome (cf. Cliveden).

* In the same part of Amersham, in BATCHELOR'S WAY, in the garden of a house called QUANTOCKS, a STATUE of Neptune, C18, from Bassetsbury, High Wycombe. It came originally from Kent House, Richmond.

7010
ASHENDON

ST MARY. Norman masonry visible on the N side, also a blocked
Norman doorway. Lengthening to the w of the Norman nave
c. 1200, see the lancet window. The same is visible inside, where
the Norman nave must have had an aisle which is now represented by the C14 arcade of two bays. The details of this arcade
in its C14 form correspond to those of the blocked arch to the
former N transept. The preceding Norman s side of the church
was also lengthened *c.* 1200. The lengthened part was cut by a
fine C13 bay with one big pointed arch with a slight chamfer on
simple imposts. Perp w tower, short Perp clerestory, the
windows with pretty embattled sills inside. Chancel early C19.
– FONT COVER. Jacobean, plain. – PULPIT. Of *c.* 1700, plain. –
MONUMENT. Effigy of a Knight, cross-legged, defaced, late
C13.

9000
ASHLEY GREEN

ST JOHN EVANGELIST. By *Street*, 1875. Chancel with lancet
windows in blank arcading. No tower. Bellcote over the E end of
the nave. The nave windows are pairs or triplets of lancets.
Nothing of interest inside. The usual Streetian low stone
SCREEN and stone PULPIT.

GROVE FARM, 1 m. SE. A barn belonging to the farm is a fragment of a C15 or early C16 domestic building. Flint with a two-
light NE window under a gable, and a doorway in a lower r.
annexe. (Almost opposite the barn to the E are the bases of two
polygonal towers, probably of a gatehouse, and parts of the
curtain wall. MHLG) The barn stands in a partly preserved
moat and the house and outbuildings to its s in a moat including
as its NW quarter the w and N sides of the other, older moat.

WHELPLEY HILL. 1½ m. SE by E of the church a single-rampart
IRON AGE HILL-FORT. Much denuded and roughly circular,
it encloses some 4½ acres; the original entrance appears to
have been to the SE.

8020
ASTON ABBOTS

ST JAMES. By *Street*, 1865–6, except for the Perp w tower. The
latter has an oblong stair-projection on the s side. The church
is of no interest. – PLATE. Cup and Cover Paten of 1565.

8010
ASTON CLINTON

ST MICHAEL. Of flint. Externally the chancel is early C14, the
rest is Perp, and all is much restored. The upper storey of the

porch is C19. Inside the S arcade is C13, the N C14. Both have
alternating octagonal and circular piers, but the arches of the S
arcade are double-chamfered with little half-pyramids at the
springers, the arches of the N arcade have two sunk quadrant
mouldings. C14 also the circular clerestory windows, the
chancel with its chancel arch, and the very ornately crocketed
Sedilia and Piscina and the recess opposite. All these have ogee
arches. C14 finally the tower arch, though the rest of the tower
was built in 1800. – WALL PAINTING. C14. Fragment of a
draped figure (chancel, S side). – STAINED GLASS. E window
of 1855. – PLATE. Stem of a Cup, Elizabethan.

RECTORY. 1850, by *E. B. Lamb*, but quite harmless externally,
brick and stone, Elizabethan.

Aston Clinton is a Rothschild village. The mansion, built probably in the 1840s and acquired by Sir Anthony de Rothschild
in 1851, has been pulled down, but the Gothic SCHOOLS, facing
each other in the main road, close to the church, are Rothschild
gifts (1856 and 1862, by *Gotto* of Tring), and so is ANTHONY
HALL of 1884.

GRIM'S DITCH. *See* p. 148.

ASTON SANDFORD

ST MICHAEL. Tiny, with a weather-boarded bell-tower. Inside
remains of a C13 chancel arch, much altered. – STAINED
GLASS. Small seated Christ, C13, in green and yellow (E window). – PLATE. Cup and Cover Paten, 1661.

Sir G. G. Scott built a house here (D. Cole). It is probably the one
to the NW of the church.

ASTWOOD

ST PETER. Perp W tower, chancel, and clerestory. Dec S aisle
with an arcade of low quatrefoil piers and double-chamfered
arches. The W tower cuts into the W arch of the arcade. –
BENCH ENDS. Straight-topped with buttresses. – PLATE. Stem
of a Cup *c.* 1570; Knife and Fork, probably late C17. – MONU-
MENTS. Brass of Thomas Chirwale † 1534 and two wives.
Figures of 2 ft 3 in. length. – William Lowndes † 1775. Signed
Vidler. Tablet of white and brown marble. Portrait relief in
oval medallion at the top.

(BURY FARM, ½ m. N. C17. Timber and brick. VCH)

(DOVE HOUSE. Octagonal, converted into a house. NBR)

AUSTIN'S FARM see CHALFONT ST GILES

AYLESBURY

Aylesbury is the county town, but it has only just over 24,000 inhabitants, and the county offices are not prominent in the pattern of streets and open spaces. The impression is of a market town, prosperous in the C18 – and that is what Aylesbury indeed was – see e.g. Defoe's description. The centre of Aylesbury is compact, with an intricate and interesting sequence of squares, and the church in its churchyard lies away from them. There are plenty of enjoyable buildings, Georgian, just pre-Georgian, and just post-Georgian, but nothing of the first order.

St Mary. A large cruciform church of the C13 and early C14 with Perp alterations, but so recklessly restored by *Sir George Gilbert Scott* in 1850–69 that exterior and interior look mostly Victorian. The chancel for instance is a fine, noble E.E. piece, but the whole E wall and the whole S wall are C19. Only the N wall is genuine. It has three tall shafted lancet windows set in shafted arcading inside. The shafting outside has shaft-rings and carries stiff-leaf capitals. Inside below the arcading an Easter Sepulchre. The arch is very depressed two-centred and starts with short vertical pieces on top of the short shafts l. and r. The single-framed roof with ashlar struts and straight braces up to a collar, that is a heptagonal appearance, is supposed to be of the C13 too. The crossing tower and transept seem also to be of the C13, but of its end. Here again most of the detail is C19, especially the various arches from the transepts to E and W, except for that from the N transept to the organ chamber which has shafts and much dog-tooth. Genuine and similar the arch from the same transept to the N aisle. The crossing tower has double-chamfered arches to all four sides and above them a triforium of twin two-lights to each side. The spandrel of each two-light unit is pierced with a lozenge. Externally a tower rises above this triforium stage, with renewed lancet bell-openings. Perp panelled battlements and a higher NW stone turret. Behind the battlements rises a recessed, square, lead-covered clock-stage, and on this a spirelet or spike – a pretty C19 copy of a C17 original. The nave and arches seem of the same date as the crossing. Six bays, quatrefoil piers with moulded capitals, double-chamfered arches. In the aisles the C13 appears only towards the W end, especially in the SW window, a small deeply-splayed lancet, and in the S porch with blank arcading along the E and W walls and an entrance arch with continuous mouldings. The latter could be later than 1300. The W doorways and the S and N doorways are all imitation. The early C14 added the Lady Chapel to the S transept. The windows are of the restoration, but look convincing. Below the Lady Chapel a bone-hole. Early C14 also the widening of the E parts of the N aisle – see the tomb recesses with finely moulded arches. Many Perp additions, namely the clerestory, the big W window, the odd four-centred transverse arches across the aisles (this last an attempt at buttressing the clerestory wall), and the widening of the E parts of the aisles into chapels. The S chapel is nearly square and has one central pier of timber carrying four-way arched braces up to the ceiling. The transept roofs are Perp too, of very low pitch and with tie-beams on traceried arched braces. Tracery also above the tie-beams. In the upper floor of the Perp NE vestry a small two-light lancet window of the late C13 has been re-used. Very curious is the way in which a straight-headed three-light Perp window pierces the blocking of the arch from the S transept to the E.

FURNISHINGS. FONT. Late C12. A beautiful, restrained, and civilized piece. Circular on a square base. The base is treated as a reversed two-scallop capital. The lunettes of the scallops have scroll and leaf decoration, and some spurs of leaf jut forward from the stem on to the base. Short stem, banded. Bowl with spiral fluting and, above, a band of foliage scrolls. – PULPIT. From the Scott restoration (by *W. W. Thompson*). – STALLS. Four MISERICORDS with a monster, a small animal, a human head, and a human figure. Also two ends with poppy-heads. – VESTMENT PRESS (S transept), a great rarity. C15. Of wardrobe shape with a set of swinging arms for the vestments. Strongly moulded top cornice. – SCULPTURE. Two figures l. and r. of the high altar, given by Scott, carved by *Farmer & Brindley c.* 1870. – STAINED GLASS. Much Victorian glass, but nothing of distinction. The best is the grisaille glass of the E lancets with a few pointed oblong medallions showing single figures on a deep blue ground. By *Willement, c.* 1855–60. – The chancel N and S windows by *Oliphant*, 1858. – By *O'Connor* the windows of the S aisle chapel (1870–5) and the crowded W window, premiated at the International Exhibition of 1862. – Lady Chapel E by *Burlison & Grylls*, 1868; by the same N aisle chapel W. – The middle N window of the chapel is of *c.* 1855 by *J. G. Waller*. – Finally, in the S aisle the second from the W is signed by *C. Gibbs* and dates from *c.* 1861. – MONUMENTS.

Knight, late C14, alabaster, very badly preserved (N transept N). Found near the Aylesbury Greyfriars. – Lady Lee
† 1584 and children. Alabaster, with two columns of touch
carrying a straight entablature. Two large kneeling figures
facing in the same direction. – Many tablets, e.g. Thomas
Farrer † 1703. By *Edward Stanton*, cartouche with scrolls and
flowers. – Anne Barker Bell † 1749. Standing wall-monument.
All white. With tall obelisk between two urns. No figures.
Attributed by Mrs Esdaile to *Scheemakers*.

ST JOHN, Cambridge Street. By *J. P. St Aubyn*. 1881–3, chancel
1894. Red brick, tall, simple, with lancet windows. No tower.
Good serious interior.

CONGREGATIONAL CHURCH, High Street. E.E. by *Rowland
Plumbe*, 1874. Asymmetrical façade. No piers inside.

METHODIST CHURCH, Buckingham Street. Terrible Italianate
style, by *James Weir*, 1893. The former Wesleyan Chapel is in
Friarage Passage (*see* p. 59).

PUBLIC BUILDINGS

COUNTY HALL. Plans were submitted by *Thomas Harris* and
Mr Brandon. These plans were judged by *Vanbrugh*. Harris's
were chosen, and it is not known whether Vanbrugh made any
alterations to them. In spite of the date 1723 on a rain-water
head, the building was not completed until 1740. Red-brick
front towards the Market Square of seven bays and two storeys.
The three middle bays are emphasized and carry a pediment.
The ground-floor windows are arched, the upper windows
pedimented. The ground floor up to the arches is ashlar-faced.
The upper middle window is arched and flanked by pilasters.
Internally the ground floor was mostly modernized recently
(and very nicely) by the County Architect. The r. entrance
leads to the stately staircase. Open well, balusters with twisted
fluting on the bulbous foot-piece. The centre hall upstairs
altered, by *D. Brandon c.* 1850. Against the back wall of the hall
fine big two-bay panelling with giant pilasters surrounding two
big arched entrances. These lead into the Court Room, a per-
45b   fectly preserved C18 room with 'box pews', galleries, the
raised judge's seat, etc. The style of all this is rather 1700 than
1725. Old panelling and raised seat with columns and open
pediment also in the larger (Council) room. It is noteworthy
that the upper hall is not in axis with the court room, nor is
either in axis with the façade. Behind much additional building,
including the new County Offices.

COUNTY OFFICES, towards Walton Street. Neo-Georgian by *C. Riley*, the then County Architect, 1929 and 1939. Seventeen bays, three storeys, brick and stone dressings.

CORN EXCHANGE (former), now part of the Municipal Offices, Market Place, by the County Hall on the E. 1865 by *D. Brandon*. Brick and stone dressings. Upper room with mullioned and transomed windows above a tripartite arched passage like a triumphal arch below. Not a bad design.

MUSEUM, *see* Perambulation, p. 58.

ROYAL BUCKINGHAMSHIRE HOSPITAL, Buckingham Road and Bicester Road. By *Brandon*, 1861 etc. Italianate and restrained; rather dull. Brick and stone. The present appearance is no more than a remodelling of the Infirmary as first built in 1832–3.

TINDAL HOSPITAL (former WORKHOUSE), Bicester Road. By *Parker*, 1844–5. Red brick, gabled, dull.

BORSTAL INSTITUTION (former GAOL), Bicester Road. Red brick and stone dressings. The big entrance arch is dated 1845. By *Major J. Jebb*. (Gibbs mentions the spacious and elegantly built chapel.)

TELEPHONE EXCHANGE, New Street. By *T. F. Winterburn*, 1953. A straightforward modern building.

OAK GREEN PRIMARY SCHOOL, completed in 1950. By *F. B. Pooley*, the County Architect. For 480 children. Steel-frame with brick and timber infilling.

THE GRANGE SECONDARY MODERN SCHOOL. Similar, and by the same architect, but more recent. For 600 children.

QUARRENDON COUNTY SECONDARY SCHOOL. By the same architect. For 600 children. Completed in 1959, after a construction period of only twelve months. The teaching block is linked by the cloakrooms etc. to the administration block and Hall, Dining Hall, and Kitchen. Free-standing laboratory block. Load-bearing brick walls.

PERAMBULATION

It may be best to start by the church. Round the churchyard houses so designed and accidentally so grouped that they form a setting which suits the church everywhere, and occasionally heightens its impressiveness. On the N side the only house worth singling out is the DERBY ARMS, built as a private house in the Early Georgian decades. Vitreous and red brick, five bays, two and half storeys. Ground-floor windows segment-headed, upper windows with characteristic aprons. Doorway

with pediment on Ionic pilasters. On the w side the church
faces the PREBENDAL SCHOOL, formerly Prebendal House,
i.e. Rectory. Big, stuccoed, rather grey C18 house of five bays
and three storeys. Doorway with Gibbs surround hidden by a
porch with Ionic columns. (Fine Kentian chimneypiece.) Nice
Late Georgian staircase with slim twisted balusters. The
garden front was altered probably at the same time.* The
Gate Arch, which is of brick, partly brick-rusticated, also seems
Early Georgian. This goes into PARSON'S FEE, a street in
which, adjoining the Gate Arch, a fine group of the C17–18.
This was the Prebendal Farm and is now ST OSYTHS. The
house is of five bays and two storeys and has windows with
wooden crosses. (Contemporary fireplaces inside. MHLG) The
buildings along the street are timber-framed.

Back to the churchyard, called ST MARY'S SQUARE.
Against its s side (still Parson's Fee) a terrace of timber-framed
houses with oversailing upper storey. Then the opening into
Church Street flanked by HICKMAN'S ALMSHOUSES of 1871
and, opposite, the former GRAMMAR SCHOOL, now MUSEUM.
It was built out of a bequest of 1714 and opened in 1720. Its
architect is unknown. Its front turns N towards the church. It
is of nine bays and two storeys. Vitreous and red brick. The
two slightly projecting two-bay wings were masters' houses.
The recessed five-bay centre contained the schoolrooms. Tall
arched windows and a blank attic storey over with a circular and
an oblong panel and two niches. Good doorcase with open
segmental pediment. Another towards Church Street. Both
were carved in 1718. To the E, adjoining the Museum, is the
CHURCH HOUSE, Victorian, red brick, with two gables.

CHURCH STREET is the best street in Aylesbury. In it, No. 7
(CEELY HOUSE), now also part of the Museum. This is also
early C18, red brick, of five bays, with a projecting one-bay
centre. Fine porch of unfluted Corinthian columns with pediment. Opposite, first No. 10, C18, of six bays and simple, and
then THE CHANTRY. Charming front of c. 1840 with three
bargeboarded gables and all windows carrying hood-moulds.
At the back C16 brickwork. (Inside an original fireplace with
oak lintel forming a four-centred head to the fire opening.
RCHM) More good houses further s in Church Street, especially
No. 1, partly facing TEMPLE SQUARE. This is dated 1739.
Vitreous and red brick, segment-headed windows, doorway
with pediment on attached Tuscan columns. (C16 interior

* (Large BARN with queenpost roof. MHLG)

features, e.g. moulded ceiling beams. RCHM) In Temple
Square more nice quiet Georgian houses, especially No. 10
(W side).

From Temple Square, Castle Street runs W and links up with
Parson's Fee, and RICKFORDS HILL runs S with a hook to the
E at its end. In Rickfords Hill at the corner GREEN END
HOUSE, handsome and apparently of *c*. 1700, but much remodelled Early Victorian. Seven bays, two storeys. Tuscan
porch against rusticated back facing. Above this an arched
window flanked by columns. S of this THE FRIARAGE, irregular, C18. The name commemorates the house of the Franciscans
or Greyfriars at Aylesbury, founded in 1386. All that is left of
it is some pieces of walling in the garden and along FRIARAGE
PASSAGE. In this lane also the former WESLEYAN CHAPEL,
now Ex-Services Club, 1837, red brick, three bays, two
storeys, with big pediment. The windows are segment-
headed, and there is segment-headed giant blank arcading.

Back to Temple Square and down TEMPLE STREET, in continuation of Church Street. Nice C18 name-plates of street and
square at the corner. In Temple Street No. 28 has an extremely
handsome doorcase with richly carved capitals and brackets.
No. 26 also a good Georgian house. From the S end of Temple
Street turn E into MARKET STREET. On its S side the DARK
LANTERN INN, irregular, C16–17, partly timber-framed.

At the E end of Market Street lies the MARKET SQUARE.
This is oblong but diversified by a step back in its W side so as to
appear almost L-shaped. In the Market Square the CLOCK
TOWER, 1876 by *Brandon*, insipid Gothic with spire. To its S
MONUMENT to Lord Chesham by *J. Tweed*, 1910 (to the l. and
r. on separate bases two recumbent lions). To the N of the
Clock Tower MONUMENT to John Hampden by *H. C. Fehr*,
1912. Of houses, apart from the County Hall, there is not much
to report, but it is a fact worth recording that none do harm to
the Market Square. On the E side BARCLAYS BANK, early C18,
of seven bays and two storeys, red brick, with giant pilasters
and three dormer windows in the roof, two with steep triangular
pediments, one with a steep segmental one. Doorway with
pediment and a blank arch above. Nice house of one bay to the
S of this. A little further N the BULL'S HEAD HOTEL, recessed, and externally all Victorian half-timbered. But inside
some original features. On the N side the most interesting house
also lies back, the KING'S HEAD HOTEL. This was built in 35b
the C15, but has been much altered. It has three gables, and to

the l. of the archway into the yard the big hall window of ten lights divided into five plus five by a stronger mullion. One sturdy transom. The lights are arched.

The HIGH STREET starts from the NE corner of the Market Square and runs E. Nothing of note. From the same corner KINGSBURY runs N and opens almost at once into an irregularly triangular space which to the perambulating visitor appears to be one with the Market Square. The moment of the strange spreading is stressed by LLOYDS BANK, classical to Italianate with imitation ashlar rustication on the ground floor, and segmental pediments to all first-floor windows. This long, broken façade dates from 1853 and the 1920s. On the N side of Kingsbury No. 40, a house with a fine doorcase, Ionic pilasters and carved brackets carrying a straight hood. A detour along Buckingham Street to its N end, where, across in Whitehall Street, are the grounds of ARDENHAM HOUSE. This was built in the late C18 for the sister-in-law of Nollekens, the sculptor. Tall three-bay front of three storeys. Elegant Tuscan porch, above this tripartite window, and above that tripartite lunette window; top balustrade. (Contemporary decoration inside. MHLG) In the garden a five-light Perp window of unknown provenance. N of Buckingham Street in BICESTER ROAD the new premises of Messrs ANTIFERENCE, by *E. H. Eames*.

The perambulation is concluded from the SW corner of the Market Square. To the W in GREAT WESTERN STREET the RAILWAY HOTEL of 1898, an engaging little horror with a turret, gables, big blank arches with alternating rustication, and a tripartite coach entrance. To the S WALTON STREET leads to Walton. In it, opposite the new County Offices, some minor but by no means small, stuccoed Georgian houses. Further S the AYLESBURY BREWERY, early C19, red brick, a variety of buildings, and later, S of the Brewery, WALTON TERRACE, an irregular group of Georgian houses, one with a veranda along the street. At the S end of Walton Street the triangular WALTON GREEN and to the E in WALTON ROAD No. 26, a last good Early Georgian house. Vitreous and red brick, five bays. Doorway with Roman pilasters, and narrow windows to its l. and r.

QUARRENDON, *see* p. 229.

BARTON HARTSHORN

ST JAMES. Small, with bellcote, mostly C19. – PLATE. Cup of 1570, with band of ornament round the bowl.

MANOR HOUSE. At the NE end a fragment of a C17 house. It bears the date 1635. In 1903 *Sir Robert Lorimer* was called in and added much. In 1908 he added yet more. The result is picturesque and entirely successful. Lorimer carried on the Tudor style of the house of 1635. He composed his addition into an L-shape with an old walnut tree in the focal position between the two arms.

(OLD MANOR COTTAGE, 200 yds W. Gabled, with mullioned windows with arched lights and hood-moulds. NBR)

BEACHAMPTON   *7030*

ASSUMPTION. The best part is *Street*'s W tower, or rather his upper part of a C14 tower. This upper part is unbuttressed and ends in a low bell-stage consisting entirely of balusters, and a shingled spire starting as a pyramid roof and then rising at a steeper pitch. The effect is pretty and decidedly Late, not High, Victorian. The date is 1873–4. The medieval work in the church is mostly of *c.* 1300. Various windows with Y-tracery. Arcades of three bays with quatrefoil piers and double-chamfered arches. They start from the W and E imposts on corbels, one being a head. The chancel arch has one head and one leaf corbel. Arcade hood-moulds on leaf stops. – MONUMENTS. Mathew Pigot † 1598 (chancel S). Tablet with shrouded figure holding a skull. Extremely primitive stone surround with skull, bones, and many inscriptions. – Simon Benet † 1682. 26a Splendid standing monument. Inscription plate framed by volutes with garlands. Back wall with flanking demi-columns and a scrolly open pediment with achievement. The centre is an excellent bust with wig and lace jabot, the face probably from a death mask. It is said in the literature that the monument was erected by University College, Oxford, in 1759, or even later. But the bust is certainly of 1680–90 in style and not of 1760.

HALL FARM, N of the church. Gabled; early C17, of stone. On the E side canted bay window of seven lights with transom. A curious door surround inside with a kind of belated billet motif. (In the outbuildings materials from a preceding house of *c.* 1500. RCHM)

THE GRANGE, at the end of a lane, ½ m. SE. Timber-framed on a stone base. Plastered infillings. Eminently picturesque, with its irregular gables and the little pedimented oriel window in the two-storeyed porch. In the pediment the date 1629. The ground floor of the porch has to the l. and r. open balustrading. Did this give Street the idea for his bell-stage?

ELMER SCHOOL, opposite The Grange. Founded in 1652. Stone, two storeys, of five wide bays. The windows, altered, were originally of three, two, two, three lights. In the middle a two-storeyed gabled porch. The lantern looks *c.* 1800.

9090

BEACONSFIELD

ST MARY AND ALL SAINTS, almost entirely of the C19. Perp part of the tower and the W parts of the arcades (octagonal piers, double-chamfered arches). In the Victorian extension the W tower is most prominent. It has polygonal and clasping buttresses faced with flint and stone squares.* Big polygonal pinnacles, a decorated parapet, battlements, and a higher stair-turret with a spirelet. – SCREEN. Of one-bay divisions with flat ogee arches (between chancel and S chapel). – CHEST (N aisle), C17 with small painted landscapes. – MONUMENTS. In the chancel N wall tomb recess, early C16. Tomb-chest with shields in richly cusped quatrefoils. Recess with flat pointed arch, tracery panelling in the spandrels, and elaborate cusping. – Tomb-chest behind chancel and S aisle, with two shields in quatrefoils. – In the churchyard monument to Edmund Waller, the poet, † 1687 (*see* Hall Barn, p. 150). Oblong, box-like tomb-chest, half draped with hanging stone cloth. On the corners four urns. In the middle tall obelisk, really like a four-sided needle-spire. According to Le Neve by *William Stanton*.

ST MICHAEL, New Town. 1914 by *Fellowes Prynne*.

COUNCIL CHAMBERS, New Town, 1935–6 by *C. H. Watson* and *A. A. Stewart*. Neo-Georgian, of pale purple brick. Two-bay centre with stiffly free-classical clock-turret, lower three-bay wings.

BRANCH LIBRARY, Reynolds Road, New Town. Pretty in the 1950 way, with low-pitched roof, much glass, and timber slatting. By the County Architect, *F. B. Pooley*, 1955–6. Friendly interior.

Beaconsfield falls into two parts, separated by nearly a mile of open country, gradually filled in by wealthy houses. The NEW TOWN is Metroland, shopping terraces of between the wars and well-to-do suburban housing. Many desirable properties N of the town.

The old town deserves a detailed PERAMBULATION. It ought to start from the church. To its W the OLD RECTORY, an

* The buttresses with their chequerboard pattern are part of the original Perp work.

important house of *c.* 1500. Two-storeyed and built round three sides of a courtyard. Brick below with blue brick diapering and timber-framed upper storey. Brick wall to the E and, also to the E, gables on the two projecting wings. Here curved timbers are used. Hall in the recessed centre. This and other rooms have original fireplaces. (Also two good mid-C18 fireplaces. NBR) Through a passage and past a picturesque timber-framed house with brick infilling of the so-called Wealden type, that is with a recessed centre above which the eaves of the roof run without recession, supported on curved braces. At the end of the passage one is at the hub of Old Beaconsfield – a roundabout, but one which does no harm visually, because the four main streets are so wide as to submerge it; so wide indeed that the Market Place, which adjoins it to the N, is no wider. They are characteristically called Wycombe End, Windsor End, London End, and – past the Market Place – Aylesbury End. The inspection must go in one direction after the other, and first to the W.

In WYCOMBE END by the roundabout on the S side, LLOYDS BANK, etc., original timber-framing and overhang, but much restored. Then the RECTORY, a grand mid-C18 house lying back from the street, with nice iron gates. Five bays and two storeys, red brick, hipped roof. Doorway with Tuscan pilasters, metope frieze, and pediment. WYCOMBE END HOUSE is also mid-C18. It has two canted bay windows to the street and to the W four Venetian windows in its two storeys. Much minor Georgian brickwork. Outside the built-up area on the S side WIGGINTON, Early Georgian, of three storeys and five bays with segment-headed windows. Doorway with Tuscan pilasters and pediment. By the side an exceptionally large araucaria.

Secondly, WINDSOR END, so wide that in the middle a line of trees runs down it. Particularly fine the old pollarded elms. Of the houses only one worth singling out, the one at the very end looking into the Hall Barn estate: LITTLE HALL BARN. Purple brick and red brick. Five bays of unusually slender windows, two storeys, doorway with attached Tuscan columns and pediment. Picturesque red brick outbuildings.

Thirdly the MARKET PLACE. Here the former LOCK-UP, across its end: three bays and two storeys, the middle bay emphasized by brick-rusticated quoins.

LONDON END has most to offer. That the start is the 3b SARACEN'S HEAD, that is an essentially modern imitation

half-timbering job, is a reminder of the imminent danger of
Beaconsfield becoming Outer London, like the Chalfonts
and Gerrards Cross. But then the genuine houses start. A
pretty shopfront on the N side, and after that the KING's
HEAD, with 1713 on a rain-water head, of five bays and a
panelled parapet which continues on the neighbouring house.
This neighbouring house is HIGHWAY HOUSE, of four bays,
with a specially finely detailed doorway. Then, opposite, Nos
14–16, Early Georgian, of four bays, low, and also with a
panelled parapet. After that BURKE HOUSE, a plastered C17
house with five canted bay windows. Mullioned and transomed
windows with pretty octagonal C18 glazing bars. Top parapet.
Two C18 doorways, one with Tuscan columns, the other with a
Tuscan porch. Opposite the MALT HOUSE, once more of five
bays and two storeys. The doorway here has attached Tuscan
columns and a broken pediment. Then a later Georgian house
of three storeys, THE YEWS. Widely spaced fenestration.
Five bays. The end is LONDON END HOUSE, formerly an inn.
Of C16 origin, refronted in the C18. The next item would be
Wilton Park (*see* p. 294), whose gates stand across the end of
London End.

FAR CORNER, Woodside Avenue. The Lodge at the back is by
June Park, 1946. Oblong, of brick; an attractive design.

EDITH EDWARDS CHILDREN'S HOME, 1¼ m. NW. Built as a
private house *c.* 1937 by *John Campbell*. Of a strange, informal,
rural monumentality. Brick, whitewashed, in simple gabled
shapes of various heights interlocked in an unexpected way. The
openings also of various and unexpected forms, many arched
(without any mouldings), others horizontal or in horizontal
bands. The dining room is circular and in a tower with conical
roof. It is connected with the drawing room by a long corridor
with a tunnel-vault of alternating longitudinal, not transverse,
stripes of brick and plaster.

HOLLY MOUNT, Amersham Road, Knotty Green. By *Voysey*,
1906–7, in his unmistakable idiom, used very simply here.

WINDMILL. A tower mill, built in 1811, but only the shell remains.

WILTON PARK. There is an undated TUMULUS known as 'The
Mount' about ½ m. NE of the church.

BIDDLESDEN

BIDDLESDEN PARK. Rain-water head 1731. Stone, with a very
quiet nine-bay S front overlooking a lake. Seven-bay centre.

Two-bay wings somewhat projecting. Two storeys, parapet, hipped roof. Porch with Tuscan columns and pediment. Staircase with balusters decorated with foliage at their feet. In the NW corner room a splendidly carved fireplace with flowers and two young caryatids. To the l. and r. of the façade pieces of low brick wall, each with a doorway which has a segmental pediment on Tuscan pilasters. On the r. follows a one-storeyed brick wing (not repeated on the l.) and then at r. angles the STABLES. Seven bays with a big blank archway in the middle and a lantern. No one would expect that the last two windows on the r. belong to the church.

ST MARGARET. Part of the stables of the house. Brick with generous stone dressings. s façade of five bays with middle entrance. This has a pediment; the windows are arched. They and the entrance have big Gibbs surrounds. Quoins, hipped roof. Completely preserved interior. WEST GALLERY in two storeys, with Roman Doric and Ionic columns. The upper part for the family of the house. – BENCHES of unusual shape, with gently double-curved tops. – FONT. An elaborate baluster with much gadrooning. – PULPIT, three-sided COMMUNION RAIL, BOARDS with Creed, Lord's Prayer, Commandments, etc. – PLATE. Parcel-gilt Cup given in 1702. – MONUMENT. George Morgan † 1847. By *Grimsley* of Oxford. Mourning woman bent over a sarcophagus.

BIERTON

ST JAMES. Early C14 with a crossing tower. The style is consistent throughout except for the strange 'clerestory' windows of the aisles, introduced when flat Perp roofs replaced the higher pitch of the C14, or in the C17 to light galleries which might then have been put in. Typical of the early C14 are the tall 11b arcades with their quatrefoil piers and many-moulded capitals. In the diagonals are groups of three thin shafts each, the middle one with a fillet and the whole group without a capital. The crossing arches are of the same type. The doorways also correspond. Low-pitched nave roof Perp. – FONT. Norman, circular, with simple rope bands. – TILES. Some of the C14–15 in various places. – PLATE. Paten of the C14, with the face of Christ in a sunk quatrefoil. – MONUMENT. Samuel Bosse, 1621, with small kneeling figures.

BLACKWELL GRANGE FARM *see* CHESHAM

BLEDLOW

HOLY TRINITY. A flint church in a good position, with a wooded ravine to the E. Evidence of the Norman church the plain N doorway and plain blocked chancel S doorway. This Norman church received aisles about 1200. The arcades are of four bays with circular piers, low, small capitals with the early type of upright stiff-leaf, octagonal abaci, and pointed arches with a single-step moulding. Responds with stiff-leaf too. Later C13 W tower. The bell-openings have bar tracery, two lights and an unencircled quatrefoil. Of the same time the S doorway, which has a finely moulded arch on two orders of colonnettes with stiff-leaf capitals. Then, c. 1300-10, the chancel windows (the E window is of three stepped lancets under one arch) and the splendid transeptal S window which is of four stepped lights, cusped and with pointed quatrefoils in the tops of the lights. Inside, below this window, two low tomb recesses. Early C14 S porch. Inside the chancel a string-course with a little ornamented turret on the place to the S and N where it rises a step. – FONT. Norman, cup-shaped. The lower half fluted, a band of almond-shapes above filled with big leaf motifs. The base is like a recessed two-scallop capital with the lunettes decorated. – REREDOS. S aisle, originally in the chancel, C18, by *John Gwynn*, with a painting by *Samuel Wale* (Colvin). – CANDLE-STICK. S aisle, on a window sill. C18, of wood, with a sham flame of wood. – SOUTH DOOR. C13 or early C14, the hinges at the back. – WALL PAINTINGS. Many C13 fragments, especially St Christopher (N wall). – (Adam and Eve, over the S doorway; C14. Foliage in three colours in the arcade spandrels.) – Many C17 texts. – PLATE. Cup 1569; Paten on foot C17; Flagon 1672; large Paten 1689. – MONUMENT. Brass to William Hern † 1525, vicar, an 18 in. figure (chancel N).

To the SE of the church the MANOR HOUSE, early C18, of very pale brick, five bays and two storeys, hipped roof. The building extends far back and may have more of interest. Behind a ten-bay BARN, weather-boarded. To the SW of the church MANOR COTTAGE and another house, both very picturesque, timber-framed with brick-nogging.

OLD MILL, Pitch Green, at the junction of the B4009 road and the road to Radnage. C16, timber-framed with brick-nogging.

FORTY GREEN FARMHOUSE, 1¼ m. NW. Dated 1718. The front of brown and red brick, of two storeys and five bays.

Segment-headed windows on the ground floor; on the first they have curly top framing.

BLEDLOW CROSS. This is cut in the solid chalk on the slopes of WAIN HILL, about 1 m. SSW of the village. It measures 75 ft transversely and has arms about 15 ft in breadth. Like its counterpart, Whiteleaf Cross, Monks Risborough (*see* p. 211), it may not be earlier than the C17.

THE COP, on the N slopes of Wain Hill, marks the remains of a BARROW excavated in 1937 and revealing Beaker sherds together with finds dating from the later Bronze Age to the Saxon period.

VILLA. Between the county boundary of the Cuttle Brook and the branch line below Wain Hill is the site first noted in 1918 of a Romano-British villa, marked by a surface scatter of tile and potsherds. Coins of C2 date have also been found.

On WARNES HILL at the N end of Bledlow Ridge a kidney-shaped mound may represent a similar structure to that on Whiteleaf Hill (*see* Introduction, p. 15).

BLETCHLEY

8030

ST MARY. The arch of the S doorway is Norman, with big beakheads and a face of Christ at the top. It is re-set and was no doubt originally round, not pointed. Of the C13 the chancel – see the arch of two chamfers on corbels and the Sedilia and Piscina with their shafts. Then follows the S aisle. This is early C14, see the flowing tracery of the E window and the arcade of four bays. Octagonal piers, double-chamfered arches. Circular clerestory windows above the spandrels, not the apexes. Of the early C14 also the N chapel with an octagonal pier with a little ballflower decoration. The double-chamfered arches have little half-pyramids at the foot. Then the N aisle arcade with octagonal piers and triple-chamfered arches. The E respond has a head-corbel. The W bay of the aisle is C15. Impressive contemporary roof on big arched braces which rest on heads. The chapel roof is panelled and has leaf bosses. Perp also the nave clerestory and the W tower with a higher stair-turret and a big four-light W window. – POORBOX. Dated 1637. On a sturdy baluster. – STAINED GLASS. In the S aisle a window by *Powell & Sons* of 1868, designed by *Holiday*. Characteristic Pre-Raphaelite faces. – PLATE. Paten on foot of 1698, silver gilt. – MONUMENTS. Probably Richard, Lord Grey de Wilton, † 1442. Alabaster on tomb-chest with shields on quatrefoils. Re-cut, especially the face, in 1704 (*see* Gunnis, p. 429). –

Thomas Sparke † 1616. Alabaster slab with arabesque ornament and brass plate. Bust, children and members of the con-
gregation to the l. and r., allegories of death and fame above,
with many inscriptions. Attributed by Mrs Esdaile to *R. Haydock* (cf. Tingewick). – Thomas Willis † 1699 and wife, the
parents of Browne Willis, the antiquary. Two plain slabs in the
chancel floor. Browne Willis did not want to spend money on
' Marble statues or fine Embellishments, whilst the other part
of God's house in which they lay wanted a requisite Decency
and Convenience'. So he restored the church instead. It was
restored again in 1867–8.

GRAMMAR SCHOOL, Bletchley Park, w of the station. 1955–6 by
the County Architect, *F. B. Pooley*. Good.

WILTON COUNTY SECONDARY SCHOOL, Rickley Lane, ½ m.
NW of Bletchley Park. Also recent and also by *F. B. Pooley* and
his department.

STATION. 1881. Jacobean, big and varied.

There is no perambulation needed of Bletchley. A few cottages
remain s of the church, and no Victorian buildings need singling
out, apart from the public buildings already mentioned. Bletchley Road connects Bletchley and Fenny Stratford, with Victorian, between-the-wars, and after-the-second-war contributions. On WATER EATON GREEN a nice five-bay Georgian
house of vitreous and red brick with pedimented doorway, and
several other old houses.

6010   BOARSTALL

ST JAMES. Built in 1818 and gothicized in 1884. Nave and chancel
with bellcote over their junction. – PULPIT. C17, with still
Jacobean or Laudian motifs, but probably later. – STAINED
GLASS. In the w window bits of Late Georgian heraldic glass.
In the E window glass by *A. Gibbs*. – PLATE. Large silver-gilt
Cup with panels of Annunciation and Nativity and strapwork
decoration, early C17; silver-gilt Paten on foot, 1615. – MONU-
MENTS. Tomb-chest of the late C15, with three shields in big
elaborately cusped quatrefoils. Above neo-Gothic wall-monu-
ment of *Coade* stone, 1815, and opposite a similar one of 1826.
They and the other monuments in the chancel are to members
of the Aubrey family. Also a tablet to Sir Thomas Digby
Aubrey, 1854 by *Bedford*, Gothic too.

BOARSTALL TOWER. The gatehouse of a large house for which
licence to crenellate was obtained in 1312 and which has disappeared. The gatehouse is also of the C14, although much

changed in the C17. Two big polygonal turrets flank the entrance. They have cross-shaped arrow-slits and battlements. The centre has above the original entrance arch of segmental shape a C17 bay window carried by a round arch which forms a kind of porch for the entrance. Top balustrade. Balustrading also on the sides where there are handsome canted bay windows. The side towards the former courtyard has slimmer turrets and mullioned and transomed windows. To the s of the approach to the gatehouse a range of STABLES, now a farmhouse. This is of the later C17. Brick, of two storeys, with six widely-spaced mullioned two-light windows, and a hipped roof. (Some original stalls with supports in the form of Doric columns. MHLG)

BOTOLPH CLAYDON 7020

BOTOLPH HOUSE. Built c. 1712. Very accomplished brick house of five bays and two storeys with a doorway with Ionic columns and a window with simple side curves above this. Three-bay pediment. The house was built for a steward of the Verneys of Claydon and became a dower-house. Fence to the street in Chippendale style, openwork, of wood, with ogee quatrefoils, some fretwork, and similar motifs. (Interior: Central Hall with arcaded walls and vault. Venetian archway to the staircase. This has three balusters to the tread.)

BOURNE END 9080

ST MARK. By *Blomfield*, 1889, i.e. no longer in his 'hard' early style. Nave and chancel in one. Even red brick. Long and low with lancet windows. Bell-turret on the nave above the place where the s porch comes out. Apse. The brick is exposed inside.

CORES END HOUSE, ½ m. ENE. Chequer brick. Five bays, two storeys, hipped roof. Early C18.

ABBOTS BROOK ESTATE. Laid out c. 1895 with half-timbered houses along the course of a trout stream. The arrangement is picturesque indeed, and the estate is secluded – a subtopian fairy world.

BOVENEY 9070

ST MARY MAGDALEN. All on its own, close to the river, in one of its least overcrowded places. The chapel is reached along a footpath from Boveney Court. Built of rubble. Nave and chancel in one. Weatherboarded bell-turret. Norman w window. Simple double-chamfered s and N doorways. – SCREEN. Made up of C15 and C17 pieces. – SCULPTURE.

Fragments of figures probably from a former reredos. Assumption, Crucifixion, Resurrection, etc.

BOVENEY COURT. Timber-framed with brick-nogging. Half-H plan, much restored.

BOW BRICKHILL

ALL SAINTS. In a very picturesque isolated position, in the woods along the scarp towards Bedfordshire and Woburn. From the church a wide view over the plain to the W; from the plain the church appears against a fringe of forest trees. Of ironstone. Mostly C19. Perp arcades of standard detail. Perp W tower. The chancel E wall rebuilt of brick when Browne Willis restored the disused church in 1756. – FONT. Perp, octagonal, with quatrefoil, trefoil, and tracery panels. – PULPIT. C15, of wood, with two blank arches with crocketed ogee gables to each side. – PLATE. Cup and Paten of 1626.

MAGIOVINIUM. *See* Little Brickhill, p. 189.

BRADENHAM

As one arrives on the spacious Green one sees ahead at an angle the grey flint church and the red brick Manor House, a group not easily forgotten, and the houses of the village lined up along the street.

ST BOTOLPH. Of modest size and externally all Victorian (1865, *Street*). Perp W tower, nave, and chancel. The S doorway is Norman with certain elements still oddly Anglo-Saxon. The shafts l. and r. are not at the angles of the jambs, but some way away from them, demi-shafts against the wall surface continued not in an arch but in a semi-roll again on the wall surface. The capitals are short and have a rope necking. The lintel stands on shapeless corbels and is decorated with diapers. – COMMUNION RAIL. By *Canon Staley* (cf. Brill and Ickford). – STAINED GLASS. W window by *Kempe*, 1887. – Some C18 heraldic glass in the N chapel E window.* – In this chapel also the most interesting MONUMENT. Charles West † 1684. Inscription flanked by the life-size caryatid figures of a youth and a maiden, both standing gracefully cross-legged. Big complex frieze and open scrolly segmental pediment. Below large altar-like base flanked by big volutes. This part is dedicated to Mrs West † 1713.‡ –

* Mr Frank West kindly pointed out to me that the crest of Thomas Lord Windsor is one of the earliest examples of enamelled glass in existence.

‡ Mr West attributes the monument to *William Kidwell* on the strength of its great similarity to the Coventry monument at Mortlake, Surrey.

In the chancel brass to Richard Redberd, rector in 1513–21, a 21 in. figure.

MANOR HOUSE. An impressive brick front nine bays wide with a 40b r. hand addition, and a building extremely characteristic of its date. The RCHM in 1912 still regarded it as later than 1714, the date at which their inventorizing terminated. We can see now without difficulty that it must belong to about 1670. It has already the fenestration and the hipped roof typical of the classical houses of the late C17 and the C18, but the treatment of the details is still pre-classical and still connected with what Sir John Summerson calls Artisan Mannerism. The windows have plain raised frames; their straight architraves on the ground floor mark a plane yet a little further forward, but the windows are separated from each other by sunk panels, opening a plane further back. Very simple rusticated door surround with segmental arch (altered). Inside only the staircase survives from the original decoration. Strong vertically symmetrical balusters. Painted ceiling with putti in a blue sky and a feigned stone balustrade along the sides. Inside the arch from the entrance Hall to the staircase two painted allegorical figures. In front of the house a front garden closed towards the Green by a wall with gatepiers and an iron GATE, also still clearly of the C17.

Of the houses in the village street the only one to deserve singling out is the WHITE HOUSE, cemented and at the time of writing a greenish grey. Five bays, C18 Gothick, castellated, with four-centred arches to the windows and the middle bay projecting like a porch or tower. On top of its raised top a crowning chimneystack.

Outside the village, ¼ m. SW, the RECTORY, a curious, somewhat Vanbrughian house of flint and brick. The central motif of the tall, narrow front is hard to describe. It is flanked by two big chimney-breasts quoined by flint strips and has a pediment above an arched window so high that small windows in two storeys accompany it l. and r. The arched window is again flint-framed.

GRIM'S DITCH. See p. 148.

BRADWELL

ST LAURENCE. W tower with saddleback roof. In the S aisle a round-headed simple doorway, perhaps older than the building of the S aisle. The date of this is recognizable by the S arcade. Three bays, short circular piers, square abaci. One capital with a head and leaves, just pre-stiff-leaf, the other with broad upright leaves. Pointed arches with one slight chamfer. All this points to c. 1200. Chancel arch of the same date with two slight chamfers. There are two incomplete inscriptions on the chancel arch. That on the l. reads VIGINTI : DIES : RELAXATIONIS, that on the r., IS : ECCLIA : DEDICATA : E : IN : HONORE : SCI : LAURECII : XI ... – PAINTING. On the altar triptych by *Westlake*. – STAINED GLASS. By *Clayton & Bell* the w window (*c.* 1869), E window (*c.* 1876), s aisle E, chancel N, nave NE; by *Powell & Sons* chancel SW (1868). – PLATE. Large Flagon and Paten on foot of 1688.

CASTLE, 100 yds NE of the church. Remains of a motte and one bailey, no more than ½ acre in size.

BRADWELL ABBEY. A Benedictine priory was founded at Bradwell c. 1155. It is likely that the outbuilding N of Abbey Farm, ¼ m. w of the church, incorporates fragments from the church. They are of the C14 and include two doorways, one with ballflower decoration, a window with reticulated tracery, two straight-headed two-light windows, and a frieze of quatrefoils.

HOUSE, ¼ m. NE. Early Georgian, of red brick. Five bays and two storeys, with giant pilasters and segment-headed windows. Two more bays to the r. again ending in a giant pilaster.

₆₀₁₀ BRILL

ALL SAINTS. Largely rebuilt in 1888 by *J. Oldrid Scott*. Traces of Norman work in the N and s doorways with one order of shafts. Norman chancel with one blocked N window. Extended to the E in 1888. The E window of *c.* 1400 put up above the new E window. C13 chancel arch. The N aisle was added in 1839, the s aisle by *J. Oldrid Scott* in 1888, but the fine N aisle E window of *c.* 1275 is original. Four lights, or rather two separate two-light windows each with an unfoiled circle in bar tracery, and across the two (or four) one large unfoiled circle. Short Perp w tower with spike. Handsome C17 roof. – FONT. Heptagonal with quatrefoil panels; Perp. – FONT COVER. By Canon *Vernon Staley*, *c.* 1918–20. He was rector of Ickford (*see* p. 175). – PLATE. Two Cups and Cover Patens, one of 1569, the other of 1689; Flagon 1751.

Brill is magnificently placed on its hill with far views in all directions. The lay-out of the village is happy too, with the Green s of the church (which is not strong enough to dominate it) and the Square a little further w.

In THE GREEN several good houses, especially BRILL HOUSE

on the S side at the end of a drive. This is of vitreous brick with red brick dressings. This combination is characteristic of a number of houses at Brill, e.g. one immediately SE of the churchyard. Brill House has a doorcase with Doric pilasters and a pediment. On the W side of the Green humble WESLEYAN CHAPEL of 1841 and humble ALMSHOUSES of 1842.

THE SQUARE is widest at its N end and then funnels in to the S. At its S end a group of old trees and to their r. the MANOR HOUSE. Elizabethan, of red brick. Front of E-shape with gables to the three projections. The original windows mullioned, but most of the windows sashed. By the side handsome STABLES of c. 1700 with horizontally oval windows. In the garden a square C18 SUMMER HOUSE. Along the sides of the square modest terraces of brick cottages. At the N end the VICARAGE, vitreous brick with red brick dressings, especially rhythmically arranged vertical bands. Three bays, two storeys. Another such house to the N (BERNWODE HOUSE) in the HIGH STREET, yet another further NW in WINDMILL STREET, on the way to the WINDMILL. This was built in the 1680s. Low round-house of brick, weatherboarded post-mill, complete with sails.

BROUGHTON   8040

ST LAWRENCE. Perp W tower. Early C14 nave and chancel with pretty two-light openings to W and E. – WALL PAINTINGS. C14 to C15. Restored by Professor Tristram. On the S wall, very large, St George, the Dragon, and, much smaller, in the costume of c. 1400, the Princess. Opposite C15 Doom. On the N wall further E the most interesting piece: a Pietà surrounded by 19a young men carrying Christ's heart, feet, bones, etc. Below, two men quarrelling over a backgammon board. It is a sermon against swearing by God's wounds, etc. The approximate date is 1400. On the S wall, E of the St George, St Helena and St Eloy (?). Below, tools of the farriers whose patron saint St Eloy is. – STAINED GLASS. Chancel E 1894 by *Kempe*. By him also chancel S. – By *A. Gibbs*, 1864, a nave S window.

BUCKINGHAM   6030

ST PETER AND ST PAUL. On the motte of the former castle, away from the main traffic of the town. Built in 1777–81 but so much altered by *Sir G. G. Scott* from 1862 onwards that only the tall outline remains of the C18 building. The chancel is entirely rebuilt by Scott, and all the windows are his, except for the bell-openings of the commanding w tower. This is crowned by a stone spire. The aisles are of the same height as the nave, and their narrowly-set buttressing might be c18, as is no doubt the fact, awkward for Scott, that the windows along the aisles were in two tiers, no doubt on account of the c18 galleries. Entirely by Scott the s porch with the heavily picturesque turret. The style is Late Geometrical throughout, Scott's favourite. The interior is vaulted in timber, an effect being obtained similar to that of the chancel of the Temple Church in London except that the piers are an improvement of Scott on the c13. They alternate between polished black granite circular, and compound in beige stone. – BENCHES (S aisle E). Some with rich tracery, early c16; one of 1626 with a shield surrounded by scrolls. – CHANDELIER. Of brass, large, given in 1705.

PUBLIC BUILDINGS. See Perambulation.

PERAMBULATION

We start in the MARKET SQUARE. Its s side is taken by the TOWN HALL, late c17, with a staircase of that date (dumb-bell balusters), but a red brick façade of the 1780s. Very simple. Five bays, two storeys, the ground-floor windows under blank segmental arches. Clock-turret with golden swan. Along the e side of the Market Square first the WHITE HART with an Early Victorian front. Deep Tuscan porch across the pavement. Then a townish terrace of Late Georgian brick houses with giant pilasters. No. 8 has a good shop-front. Along the w side of the Market Square pleasing mixture of houses. Nos 15–12 again with giant pilasters. No. 12 with another Late Georgian shop-front. The Market Square is continued in MARKET HILL. This is wider than the Market Square and has a most successful island of two low cottages of even roofs in the middle. Off the s w corner a little to the s the CHANTRY CHAPEL of St John, later LATIN SCHOOL, an oblong of 1475, much restored by *Scott* in 1875. Norman s doorway with one order of shafts and zigzag in the arch. Curious inner arch moulding of something like pointed arches. On the e side of Market Hill, No. 1 looks unpromising from outside but is a c16 timber-framed house with inside some ornamental wall-painting and some good panelling, both of the early c17. No. 2 is a handsome Georgian house of five bays and three storeys, plastered. Three-bay pediment. Doorway with unfluted Ionic columns carrying a pediment. Opposite on the w side Nos 12–11 is also Georgian and has two nice canted bay windows whose ground floors are treated with the Venetian-window motif. Then, across the N side of Market Hill, the OLD GAOL, built by Lord Cobham in 1748 in the form of a mock castle. Crenellations and angle turrets, trefoil windows and others. The S front was added in the same style by young *George Gilbert Scott* in 1839. It is semi-circular and provided the gaoler's house. From here the street or square is called HIGH STREET. This is as wide as Market Hill, and has rows of lopped trees in the middle and a space for the cattle market. The houses are minor, the best No. 1 at the SW corner, timber-framed with oversailing upper floor. Just off this corner, in MAIDS MORETON ROAD, the premises of the SALVATION ARMY, former Baptist Chapel, with coupled giant pilasters, arched windows, and pediment. It was built in 1842. At the N end of the town in STRATFORD ROAD, the former WORKHOUSE, built in 1835 and still entirely in the classical style. Yet the architect was *George Gilbert Scott*. Stone. Centre of five bays with three-bay pediment.

We must now return to the Town Hall and fan out in three directions. First for a moment to the E, down Bridge Street. Both corners to Market Square are successfully rounded here. From Bridge Street WELL STREET turns S. On the r. a former CHAPEL, not detached. Three bays, the lower windows arched, the upper segment-headed. No pediment. Then nice minor Georgian houses. Well Street in the end links up with Church Street. If one continues from Bridge Street across the bridge, one arrives at the junction of London Road and Chandos Road. At the far end of London Road lies ST BERNARDINE'S COLLEGE, red brick, of 1892–4, by *Pugin & Pugin*, not of any architectural merit. CHANDOS ROAD was formed in 1861 to lead to the station. In it villas in gardens, notably CHANDOS LODGE in the Italianate style of the mid C19 with asymmetrically-placed tower.

WEST STREET, leading off the S end of Market Square to the W, is the most interesting street of Buckingham. We start with No. 31 on the S, with a pretty Gothic shop-front. Opposite, No. 1, detached, Georgian, of five bays and two storeys, cemented. Ionic porch with pediment. Quoins. A Venetian window at the back. No. 3 is also of five bays and two storeys, cemented, but has a three-bay pediment. The ground floor is entirely altered. No. 5 is of vitreous and red brick and has a charming doorcase with fluted Ionic pilasters, a pulvinated frieze, and a pediment. Further on, still on the N side, CASTLE HOUSE, by far the

most important house in the town. The s front is of 1708, very
stately. Eight bays and two storeys, with four-bay centre and
somewhat projecting two-bay wings. Brick and stone dressings.
Quoins, good window surrounds, hipped roof with the steep
dormers used some fifty or thirty years earlier. The centre is of
four bays so that the doorway could not be placed centrally.
It is tall and has a segmental pediment high up. This is for
symmetry's sake repeated for the adjoining window. This
Queen Anne front hides a house structurally of pre-Reformation date. It was built round a courtyard then. The N range,
however, has not survived. The oldest part, now the w front,
where there are two-light straight-headed Perp windows with
panel tracery, is not wholly convincing-looking. Inside, below
these windows, the Parlour with a lavish fireplace dated 1619.
A date 1623 outside the N wall.

Now s from the NW corner of the Town Hall up CASTLE STREET.
There was a disastrous fire at Buckingham in 1725, and especially in Castle Street nearly all houses had to be rebuilt. There
are several good-looking ones, the best being TROLLY HALL.
This is of five bays and three storeys with a parapet. Brick and
stucco in imitation of stone. Above the plain doorway an arched
window, and above this a circular one. To the l. No. 17, with
an Early Victorian plastered front and a very handsome door.
It has a big circular centre with concentric grooves. The middle
is a lion's head. On the other side of the street, first the SWAN
AND CASTLE HOTEL with an attractive white Early Victorian
front with trim painted black. The windows very wide and
tripartite, flanked by pilasters. From the apparent end of
Castle Street straight up to the church. On the r. No. 8 Castle
Street, Early Georgian, narrow, red brick, three bays with two
arched windows one above the other, the upper in the steep
broken pediment. Then past the church and still straight on
down CHURCH STREET. Here, No. 20 is of the C16 and C17
and interesting. Then the VICARAGE, of the same time, but
altered, and after that the MANOR HOUSE, built as a Prebendal
House. Early Tudor, but also altered. Picturesque front, of
L-shape. Stone base, upper floor timber-framed and partly
plastered, partly with brick infilling. At the N end of the s wing
a very oddly twisted chimneyshaft.

From the w end of Church Street to the w in HUNTER STREET
lies YEOMANRY HOUSE, Early Georgian, of five bays and
three storeys, cemented. Early C19 porch. To the E Nelson
Street and off this at the very start of TINGEWICK ROAD the

handsome miller's house of the former Castle Mill: Late Georgian, red brick, of three bays, with giant pilasters. Arched doorway and window above it. Off to the s in ST RUMBOLD'S LANE on the l. at the NW corner of a house a timber angle-post of pre-Reformation date with quatrefoil decoration. From the E end of Nelson Street, Bride Hill comes up and joins Castle Street.

BUCKLAND 8010

ALL SAINTS. Externally mostly Victorian. Late C13 N arcade with circular piers and alternately octagonal and circular abaci. Double-chamfered arches. C14 S doorway (over-restored) with fleurons in the arch. – FONT. C13, of cup shape. With a band of foliage. – PLATE. Small C16 Cup.

GRIM'S DITCH. See p. 148.

BULSTRODE PARK 9080

1862 by *Ferrey*. Brick and stone, two-storeyed with a big square tower and plenty of gables. The garden front is symmetrical except for a piquant turret – a typical Victorian irregularity. The details of the colonnade along this front are also typically Victorian, a debased version of whatever style was the point of departure. The grounds were laid out by *Repton* – see his 'Theory' of 1803. (Of garden furnishings the MHLG lists a GOTHIC TOWER, of brick, three-storeyed with tall open arches, corner turrets and battlements, a SWISS COTTAGE with a rustic porch, a good early C18 GATE of wrought iron to the kitchen garden, and a DOVECOTE converted into a cottage.)

IRON AGE HILL-FORT, *see* Gerrards Cross, p. 141.

BURNHAM 9080

ST PETER. Of flint. Of the C13 the S transept tower (top stage and recessed spire 1891), the unmoulded single-step arches from it to nave and S aisle, the N transept and the tomb recess in it, and the aisle arcades (N circular piers and abaci and double-chamfered arches, S octagonal piers and abaci and double-chamfered arches). The wall PANELLING in the N transept was collected abroad. – COMMUNION RAIL. With openwork acanthus panels, of *c.* 1680 (cf. staircases of the same years). – MONUMENTS. Brass to Gyles Eyre and wife, early C16, 12 in. figures (N aisle, floor). – Two Brasses to Elizabethan members of the Eyre family (nave, w) are palimpsests of Flemish brasses of the C14 to late C15 (*Rec. of Bucks.*, XIII). – John Wright, vicar, † 1594, frontal bust in niche. – George Evelyn † 1657. Black and

white marble. Two frontal demi-figures. Columns l. and r. –
Bridget Freind † 1721. With a draped coffin and on it cushion
and skull. – Mr Justice Willes. By *Bacon*, 1792. Elegantly
carved seated figure in profile holding a medallion with profile
portrait (s aisle).

BURNHAM ABBEY. A house of Augustinian canonesses founded
in 1266. Of the buildings more survives than of any other monastic house in Buckinghamshire. After the Dissolution they
came to the Wentworth family. They are now part of an Angli-
can nunnery. The E range of the cloister exists, with the finely
moulded C13 doorway to the CHAPTER HOUSE and the room
itself with lancet windows at its E end to E, N, and S (recently
rebuilt further to the E than originally). The lancets have external mouldings of two small quarter-hollows and internal
rere-arches with two hollow chamfers. To the s the SACRISTY,
also C13. To the S of this was the church, which does not stand
above ground. The doorway from Sacristy to church exists
however. In the spandrel a sexfoiled circle and three trefoils.
Excavations have shown that the church was 108 ft long and had
no aisles. The E range stands to the height of the Dormitory,
which ran along its upper floor. To the N of the range the FUEL
HOUSE with two W lancets. Above it was the Reredorter (or
lavatories). Of the N range, the Refectory range, the S and a short
fragment of the N wall remain. After the Dissolution Paul
Wentworth put on to this part a big chimney, the breast of
which appears on the S side. The fireplace is of stone. Close to it
on the upper floor a brick fireplace. To the NE of the Chapter
House the INFIRMARY, also standing up and also with brick alterations (two windows of Paul Wentworth's). Moreover to the
E the stone PRECINCT WALL can still be seen over a long stretch.

HUNTERCOMBE MANOR, Huntercombe Lane South, N of Burnham Abbey. A picturesque rambling exterior which appears
essentially early and late C19 and does not prepare for the interesting and beautiful interior. Hall of the C14 with one truss
with big arched braces supporting a strongly-cambered tie-
beam. Also traces of the C14 office and kitchen wing to the W of
the Hall. In addition three rooms with excellent ceilings of *c.*
1675, going back to a remodelling by George Evelyn, cousin of
John. One of them is on the first floor. They have all three
painted centres, ascribed convincingly to *Verrio*. The paintings
are surrounded by wreaths of stucco and divers stucco panels of
great richness. The staircase rises round an open square well
and has characteristic twisted balusters with only two twists on

cup-shaped lower parts of the balusters. In the upstairs room a splendid overmantel with carved garlands, a flower vase, etc. The Victorian additions are considerable and date from 1887.

BURNHAM PRIORY. Built in 1824 but apparently altered later. With a picturesque tower and battlements. The S front has mullioned and transomed windows.

HOUSE OF PRAYER (Convent). The CHAPEL is by *Comper*, 1935.

DORNEYWOOD, 1½ m. NE. The house is of *c.* 1920 in a simple Tudor style with Georgian-type windows. In the inner porch decorations by *Rex Whistler* (*Country Life*, vol. 110).

BRITWELL ESTATE, S of East Burnham Park. Not yet fully completed. Planned for about 3,000 dwellings, mostly in two-storeyed houses. Also some three- and four-storeyed flats and one-storeyed houses for old people.

ENCLOSURE. At the S end of Burnham Beeches, on a plateau above the lane through East Burnham Common lies an undated oval enclosure of some 3 acres, much damaged to the E by clay-pit diggings.

IRON AGE SITE. N of POYLE'S FARM, just 70 yds N of a disused brickworks, is a habitation site of the Belgic Iron Age, as indicated by sherds picked up within the confines.

HARLEQUIN'S CASTLE (or Hardicanute's Castle), an enclosure, is variously considered medieval or of the C17.

CADMORE END
1½ m. NW of Lane End

7090

ST MARY-LE-MOOR. 1851 by *Rhode Hawkins*. Of no architectural interest. – STAINED GLASS. E window by *Hardman*, 1855.

CALVERTON

7030

ALL SAINTS. 1818–24, perhaps by *Hakewill* (*see* Old Wolverton). Neo-Norman W tower. The higher stair-turret has a conical spirelet. The chancel of 1818 has windows with intersected tracery. The S aisle was beautified by the then Rector, the Hon. and Rev. *C. G. Perceval*, rector from 1820 to 1858. Here the Gothic is more florid and rises to a rose window at the E end, to an openwork parapet, and to a chancel chapel with crazy cross-gabling. Inside certain medieval materials were kept or re-used, cf. the arcade piers, and the tower and chancel arches. The interior is partly of Perceval's time, notably the whole of the STAINED GLASS (which Mr Betjeman and Mr Piper assign to *O'Connor* and the year 1859) and the curious stamped plaster decoration of the chancel, and partly of *c.* 1870 when *E. H. Swinfen Harris* of Stony Stratford added the painted decoration of the chancel arch, the polychroming of the stone pulpit, and the Venetian mosaic-work of the reredos. – In the churchyard ornate CROSS of *c.* 1873 with the Signs of the Four Evangelists at the corners of the base.

MANOR HOUSE, to the N. Core of *c.* 1500, see one original window on the w side. Late C16 additions, and more decisive alterations in 1659 (date on the porch). These comprise the two tall dormers and the two-storeyed gabled porch, also the gabled s wing.

7040   CASTLETHORPE

ST SIMON AND ST JUDE. N tower built after its predecessor had fallen in 1729. Round-arched doorway and windows. Above the w window a C14 head of a saint or Christ. Short nave with C15 clerestory and higher chancel with an odd w gable. The earliest feature of the church is the N arcade of two bays. Circular pier, square abacus, capitals with feathery upright leaves. Pointed arches with one slight chamfer. This evidence points to *c.* 1200. Dec chancel with characteristic three-light E window, not flowing. The s doorway has a head made of a two-light window head. Perp s aisle. – PULPIT. Nice simple piece of *c.*
24a   1800 (cf. Hanslope). – MONUMENT. Sir Thomas Tyrril † 1671. Broad standing wall-monument of alabaster and touch. Two columns, a big segmental pediment, and looped-up curtains to reveal Lady Tyrril seated and her husband semi-reclining with his head in her lap. A true and intimate conceit, which was still quite exceptional at that moment.

CASTLE. The church is in the SE corner of the site of a motte-and-bailey castle which extends to the N and NW. The motte or mount stands to the W of the church and rises to a height of 36 ft. The inner bailey is 4 acres in size and well preserved. The outer bailey has on its W side a straight rampart and ditch with a small barbican mount. The ditches of the castle are up to 60 ft wide.

(CASTLE YARD, W of the church and the castle mount. A fine big C17 farmhouse of stone. RCHM)

9090   CHALFONT ST GILES

ST GILES. Flint with a Perp w tower. Externally all Victorian. The chancel dates from the C13, see the one s lancet and the Double Piscina with a detached shaft. Of the three-bay arcades (octagonal piers, double-chamfered arches) the two E bays on the N side are, judging by their details, also C13. The others are Perp. Early C14 S aisle with cusped and enriched Y-windows and a pretty doorway with continuous mouldings. In one moulding ballflower and fleurons. Inside the aisle a low tomb recess. – FONT. C13. Of Purbeck marble. The table-type on five supports. Blank arches along the sides of the square top have perhaps been chiselled away. – BENCHES. Some with simple fleur-de-lis poppy-heads are C15 or early C16. – COMMUNION RAIL. With opulent openwork acanthus foliage in the panels. Probably of c. 1700, and perhaps foreign. – WALL PAINTINGS. Above the chancel arch a curious architectural, battlemented design of c. 1400. In the S aisle much of c. 1330. Apparently scenes from the Life of the Virgin, from Genesis, and from the Life of Christ. – STAINED GLASS. N aisle E by H. Hughes, 1864; terrible. By the same no doubt two windows in the S aisle. – By Kempe N aisle N 1891 and two much later; S aisle W 1894; chancel E 1900. – PLATE. Large engraved Cup of 1569; Paten on foot of 1637; both formerly gilt. Also large Paten of 1718, Flagon of 1721, and Almsdish of 1803–4. – MONUMENTS. Brasses in the chancel to the N to a Priest, late C15, 13 in. figure, in the tomb recess in the S aisle to a Civilian and two wives, c. 1530, 1 ft 10 in. figures.* – In the S aisle at the E end a tomb-chest with brasses to William Gardyner † 1558. – In the chancel tomb-chest to members of the Fleetwood family; with three circular panels with shields; C16. – Near by tablet with Brasses of Thomas Fleetwoode † 1570 and family, kneeling. – Sir George Fleetwoode † 1620 and wife † 1634 (chancel S), a very remarkable hanging wall-monument, remarkable because at so early a date so entirely un-Jacobean. At the foot a fox's skin with the head hanging down in the middle and a shield on it. The inscription is framed by black Corinthian pilasters and volutes with thick garlands. Top an open scrolly pediment with crest and drapery. – Sir Hugh Palliser † 1796. With urn in front of a steep pyramid.

The centre of the village is a small Green with cottages, timber-framed or of brick, but nearly all now invaded by shops to cater for the London population of the mile around. To the S W of the church the RECTORY, red and vitreous brick, of c. 1700, seven bays, two storeys, with hipped roof. Doorway with carved

* Mr H. Adams Clarke mentioned to me two more Brasses to be fixed in the S aisle: Lady, 18½ in. figure, early C16, and three Boys, 6 in. figures, also early C16.

brackets. The Roman Doric columns probably a later addition. A little further on, MILTON'S COTTAGE, C17, where Milton, the poet, lived; timber-framed with brick infilling.

THE STONE, ¼ m. NE. 1810, with shallow bows and a Tuscan porch.

THE VACHE, ¼ m. NE. Elizabethan, with the gables at the ends of the front. Much altered. On the front now Venetian windows. At the back C19 Jacobean windows. Opposite the back, a little distance away, the MONUMENT to Captain Cook, erected by Sir Hugh Palliser in the late C18. Flint and red brick. Arch with globe on a pedestal.

ROUGHWOOD FARM, to the SW of the grounds of Roughwood Park, 1½ m. NE. The N wing was added by *Voysey* in 1902. Very typical of him, with its pebble-dash, mullioned windows, and parapet curving up to the chimneystack.

63b SHRUB'S WOOD, ¾ m. ENE. By *Mendelsohn & Chermayeff*, 1934–5. Beautifully placed among the trees of an old estate. The house is larger than modern houses of the thirties usually were. One long range running E–W so that all rooms have S light. The entrance is on the N, and here the continuity of the range is broken by the glazed quadrant curve of the staircase. The part W of it with Hall, Living Room, Nurseries, etc., is recessed; the part E of it with cloaks and garage lies further forward. In elevation the garage is low, the rest two-storeyed. Well balanced contrast between the E part with window bands on two floors and the long W part with only one band of windows on the upper floor. To the S it is different. Here the contrast is bolder. The W wing has two long bands, the centre projects and is partly windowless, the garage lies back and does not much enter into the picture. The house is of reinforced concrete, plastered white, as was more or less *de rigueur* among the most progressive architects of the thirties.

NEWLANDS PARK. Early C19 (before 1807?). Five bays, two storeys, white. Greek Doric portico of six columns in the rhythm 1-2-2-1 or 1-1, 1-1, 1-1. Lower three-bay wings with Soanian sunk panels. The interior quite altered.

AUSTIN'S FARM, 1 m. SW. C16, timber-framed with brick infilling. The front is of Wealden type, i.e. the centre recedes but the eaves of the roof remain even and are carried on a coved cornice.

DIBDIN HILL, ½ m. S. Here P. H. J. Baume, the French-born socialist, built in 1846 two houses, two two-storeyed cottages, and eight one-storeyed ones. Much of the interesting colony survives. The one-storeyed cottages have a middle door and one window l. and r.

CHALFONT ST PETER

ST PETER. A church of 1726, savagely gothicized by *Street* in 1857. Red-brick W tower with quoins and round-arched W window. Plain higher stair-turret. Nave windows altered. Chancel of red and black brick. – STAINED GLASS. By *Kempe* chancel S 1888, nave N 1893; by *Capronnier* S chapel SW 1869. – BRASSES. William Whappelode † 1398 and wife; William Whappelode † 1446 and wife, two very similar pairs, with 2 ft 7 in. figures. – Priest, *c.* 1500, 1 ft 4 in. – Nice IRON RAILINGS and GATES to the churchyard, *c.* 1800.

RECTORY, NW. Built in 1728, but refronted by *John Sanderson* in 1780. Red brick, two storeys, three bays, with one-bay pediment.

Round the church much remains of the old village centre. The most handsome house is the GREYHOUND INN, red brick, five bays, with carriageway in.

LODGE to The Grange, 250 yds S. Yellow brick, with four Tuscan columns carrying a pediment.

The area of Chalfont St Peter still includes three Commons, Chalfont Common on the extreme NE, Goldhill Common, and Austinwood Common. But between them all is recent housing, closely or loosely distributed. To the E of Austinwood Common in OVAL WAY the church of

ALL SAINTS by *Temple Moore*, designed in 1912 and still without nave and tower, only an ambitious N aisle. The details inside are interesting, especially the shape of the piers and the odd 3 ft-high wall-passage inside the N aisle well below the windows.

To the NW of Goldhill Common in GROVE LANE a new COUNTY SECONDARY SCHOOL, by *F. B. Pooley*.

CHALFONT HOUSE, the principal mansion, lies along the high road to Gerrards Cross. It was designed about 1755 in the new Gothic fashion for Horace Walpole's brother-in-law, General Churchill, by Horace Walpole's friend *John Chute*. The stables, also Gothic, are by Walpole's other friend *Richard Bentley*. The present house is also Gothic, but its heavy detail must be attributed to the activity of *Salvin* in 1836. The crenellations especially are Victorian in their fussiness. In the Entrance Hall a Jacobean chimneypiece with scenic reliefs.

HILL HOUSE, Guard Hill and Copthall Lane, 300 yds N of the church. Georgian, with a canted bay window.

WELDERS, Welders Lane, 1 m. W. Red brick, Jacobean, with three big shaped gables. By *Macartney, c.* 1899.

PASSMORE EDWARDS COLONY, 1 m. NNE. For epileptics. By *Maurice Adams.* Begun in 1895. Brick and half-timbered houses, gabled. No big blocks. At the entrance to the Colony, OBELISK, erected in 1785 to serve as a beacon and milestone. Of flint rubble, which is highly unusual.

CHALVEY *see* SLOUGH, p. 237

7010   CHEARSLEY

ST NICHOLAS. C13 nave and chancel (see lancet windows and see also the doorways) and Perp W tower. Rough tie-beam roof. – Simple BOX PEWS and WEST GALLERY. The latter is of 1761 (Lipscomb). – FONT of cauldron shape, Norman. The lower part of the bowl fluted, above a frieze of upright three-lobed leaves. – BRASS to John Frankelyn † 1462 and wife. The figures are 14 in. long.

LOWER GREEN FARMHOUSE, NE of the church. C15–16. Of stone, H-shaped, with massive chimneybreasts.

9010   CHEDDINGTON

ST GILES. Of the Norman church decorative fragments in the S porch. The church is small, with a broad W tower of the C15. C15 also the N aisle. Octagonal piers. Chancel arch mid-C14. –
17b PULPIT. Jacobean, with back panel and tester, richly carved, also book-rest on brackets. – REREDOS. By *Powell & Sons,* 1870; of glass mosaic.

LYNCHETS. A series of lynchets lies on the slopes of Westend and Southend Hills, the latter group being the most imposing in the county.

8020   CHELMSCOTE MANOR
                                 1 m. E of Soulbury

The large house appears mostly C20 from outside, but the S side is the surprisingly complete survival of a C14 chapel. The W wall remains, and the W window, the SW buttress, the S wall with the marks of the roof and arch of the S porch, the marks of the arch of a S transept, the complete squint from the transept into the chancel, the arch and squint of the N transept, and the piscina of the chancel. All this is now part of a modern, comfortable house.

CHENIES

ST MICHAEL. Entirely rebuilt in the C15, and almost entirely
gone over in the C19 (1861, 1887). Flint. W tower with higher
stair-turret. Nave and lower chancel, S aisle with pier of four
shafts and four hollows, carrying four-centred arches and with
Late Perp four-light windows without tracery. Chancel arch of
the same type. Victorian hammerbeam roofs. The Bedford
Chapel was added in 1556 and has since been rebuilt. The
quatrefoil piers inside the chapel are of beautiful grey mottled
marble. – FONT. Cup-shaped, Norman, the lower half fluted,
above a band of wavy trails framing regular almond-shaped
medallions, and in these symmetrical leaf motifs. – STAINED
GLASS. In the E window an early C16 figure of a kneeling donor.
– PLATE. Paten on foot of 1634 (?). – MONUMENTS. Brasses to
Lady Cheyne and her second husband † 1484 (S aisle W, 2 ft 5 in.
figures under a double canopy), to Richard Newland, rector
† 1494 (nave W, to the S, 9 in.), to Lady Phelip † 1510 (S aisle W,
3 ft 6 in. figure holding her heart from which two scrolls issue;
canopy), to Agnes Johnson † 1511 (nave W, 1 ft 6 in.), and to
Elizabeth Broughton † 1524 (nave W, 1 ft 8 in.).

BEDFORD CHAPEL. The Bedford Chapel is the richest
single storehouse of funeral monuments in any parish church of
England. As the monuments are not generally seen by the public, they are here described chronologically rather than topo-
graphically. The STAINED GLASS in the chapel is all by *Kempe*
and dates from 1895–8. – SCULPTURE. Two saints, the RCHM
says from Le Royal, but what can that mean?* The RCHM also
says early C16, but the extremely good St Andrew must be
considerably earlier – of the late C14 probably. – The earliest
monument is one to a Cheyne and his wife, late C14 effigies, his
for some reason never completed and left entirely in the rough
block (N aisle E). – Then the Bedford series begins. John
Russell, first Earl, † 1555, and wife † 1559, alabaster, tomb-
chest with shields in broad flat frames decorated with such
Venetian Renaissance motifs as circles and lozenges, also quatrefoils. Excellent large-featured effigies, boldly and broadly
carved (chancel). – Lady Bridget, second wife of the second
Earl, † 1600 (transferred from Watford parish church). High
tomb-chest with flat vertical pilaster-strips and shields. Recumbent effigy. To the l. and r. of the tomb-chest, on little

* La Réole?

stands, two kneeling male figures both facing w (middle row, third from w). – Anne Countess of Warwick † 1604 (daughter of the second Earl). Alabaster. Tomb-chest and in front of its angles four black columns. They carry the lid on whose corners four putti with shields. Effigy recumbent (E of the previous). – Elizabeth Lady Russell † 1611, wife of the second son of the second Earl. High tomb-chest with columns and shields. Beautiful effigy reminiscent of Mary Queen of Scots in Westminster Abbey. Also from Watford parish church (w of Lady Bridget). – Lady Frances Bourchier † 1612 (a grand-daughter of the second Earl). Very noble. No effigy at all. Black slab with three shields. Four short white columns and a perfectly uncarved black top slab. – Second Earl † 1565, but erected in 1619. By *William Cure II*. He was paid £226. 13s. 4d. for it. Alabaster. Big tomb-chest with pilasters and shields. Two recumbent effigies. A back plate rises behind their heads carrying an achievement (s wall, E). – Lady Chandos † 1623, mother of the fourth Earl, carried out after 1641. Semi-reclining alabaster effigy on a base. Is it complete ? (s wall, w of the following). – Fourth Earl † 1641 and his wife † 1653. Alabaster. Still of the same Late Elizabethan and Jacobean type. Big tomb-chest with recumbent effigies. Pilasters and shields on the tomb-chest. Back wall with two arches. Under one a little girl half-sitting up, under the other a baby on its back. Big open pediment (s wall, w of second Earl). By 1640 Nicholas Stone had changed the style of English funeral sculpture, and the monument to the fourth Earl was a little out of date when it was made. The chapel, however, contains no evidence of the style of the next fifty years. – Then comes the most swagger of all monuments in 26b   Buckinghamshire: fifth Earl (and first Duke) † 1700 and his wife. It fills the whole w wall of the chapel. White and some grey marble. Pairs of Corinthian columns and between them four oval medallions with portraits on the l., four on the r. Two life-size seated figures, he in his normal clothes, she as a Roman matron. Both lean outwards. A helmet lies between them. A ninth oval medallion above them. Looped grey baldacchino above this. Putti below the top. The monument is consistently ascribed to *Bird*; but there seems no documentary evidence. – Then again nothing for sixty years, and then *Joseph Wilton*'s early masterpiece, the second Duke and Duchess, made in 1769. The monument was designed by *Sir William Chambers*. All white alabaster. Above base and sarcophagus life-size kneeling figures of a half-naked youth and a maiden, he with open hands. Clouds between them and a cloud even hanging on the base. Putti and the divine triangle above. The execution is in the English tradition but strongly influenced by the 'classical Baroque' of c18 Rome. Wilton had indeed spent eight years in Rome and returned (with Chambers) only in 1755 (s wall, near w end). – Of the later c19 the following: Georgiana, daughter of the fourth Duke of Gordon, † 1858, by the younger *R. West-macott*. Gothic arch with knobbly foliage. Praying lady in profile. Good (N wall, near E end). – First Earl Russell † 1878, the Prime Minister. Almost a copy of the monument to Lady Bourchier, but a coronet on the low slab (free-standing in the N aisle). – Odo Baron Ampthill † 1884. By *Boehm*. Tablet with profile in roundel (N aisle w wall). – Ninth Duke † 1891, designed by *G. E. Fox*. An alabaster imitation of Jacobean monuments. No effigy (N wall). – Lord Arthur Russell † 1892. By *Gilbert*, eminently typical of his Baroque, crustaceous brand of proto-Art Nouveau. A bronze candelabrum, with figures of Love, Truth, Courage, and Faith.

MANOR HOUSE. Beautifully mellow under the trees by the church, and archaeologically a fascinating puzzle. Special research ought to be devoted to this house, which now consists of two wings joined by a surprisingly thin link, the w range short and picturesque, the range running from its s end to the E long and of even design. Both are probably Early Tudor, though the w range could be a little earlier. Leland writes of the house that it has been 'so translated by Mylord Russell that little or nothing of it in a manner remains untranslated and a great deal . . . is even newly set up made of brick and timber, and fine lodgings be new erected in the garden'. The latter remark points to the s range and would date it *c.* 1530. Both ranges are of brick. The w range has two stepped gables to the E and a higher tower between in which the staircase runs up. Thin polygonal angle buttresses and brick finials – similar all this to contemporary brick mansions in East Anglia, and especially in Essex. The back of the range has been refaced, probably *c.* 1802–5 when much reconditioning took place, and again altered about 1860. It is in this direction, where there is, e.g., a detached small Tudor building still upright, that one may have to look for former extensions. As it is, the plan of this range remains obscure. The long wing, on the other hand, consists simply of a range of chambers in a row. The back, i.e. s, side is most impressive. It has six (and had seven) projections like enormous chimney-breasts, and indeed crowned by ranges of two to four shafts.

These are of the most elaborate Early Tudor patterns. But behind the flues in these chimney-like projections lie closets every time whose functions vary and are mostly not clear. In one was a garderobe or privy, in another a baking oven, in a third a staircase. The s windows are tripartite and transomed and cannot be as they were c. 1530. Also there are four corbelled-out oriels along the N façade identical with the one oriel in the w range to the E. Originally a second W–E range ran along from the N side of the W range. Part of its E wall is now visible from the church as a normal boundary wall.

WOODSIDE HOUSE. To the N, in trees, overlooking the river Chess. Built for Adelina Duchess of Bedford in 1897 by *Kempe*, the glass painter.* Red brick, picturesquely irregular, and clearly aware of the changes brought to English domestic architecture by Norman Shaw and his generation. (GARDENS by *Lutyens*.)

THE VILLAGE. The interest of the village lies in the Bedford Estate housing, red brick mostly but also timber-framed and plastered white. The brick houses, many semi-detached, look as if they might be of c. 1870 or later, and yet carry dates of about 1850 and even a little earlier. Their design lacks all Early Victorian fancies. Late Georgian estate housing also survives with dates c. 1828–9.

SCHOOL. The village school by the picturesque triangular green s of the avenue to the house has recently acquired a new additional building. The Hall, with the low-pitched roof typical of 1950–60, has large windows divided by strips of wall which are faced with alternating squares of flint and red brick. By *F. B. Pooley*, the County Architect.

ROMAN VILLA. At DELL FARM, and partly covered by it and the road to Chesham on the s bank of the Chess, is the site of a Roman villa found in 1834 and excavated in 1863–4 and 1909. Although the complete plan was unrecoverable, it could be seen that the building was of the courtyard type. The central area measured 65 by 140 ft and contained a corridor with two divisions, six or seven rooms to the SE, portions of an E wing, and perhaps another under the road. The central area was paved with coloured tiles, and some walls bore fragments of frescoed designs. Four coins and the associated pottery gave a C3–4 date.

* Information given to my former assistant Mrs S. Michaelson by the late W. E. Tower, Kempe's partner and successor.

CHEQUERS

8000

According to a C17 estate map the house then consisted of a N range preceded by an apparently independent S range of offices, etc., through which the house was approached. The N range is essentially intact as far as the exterior is concerned. It is of brick and has a date 1565. The N front is eight bays wide, if the canted bay windows are counted as one bay each. There are two storeys and in addition five gables separated by parts of a parapet. The windows are of four lights with two transoms. To the r. of the centre is a small doorway with a four-centred head. The main entrance must have been to the S where the original courtyard between the two ranges was covered over in 1909–12, i.e. at the time of Lord Lee of Fareham's reconditioning and re-modelling of the house. His architect was *Sir Reginald Blomfield*. He very much remodelled the S range, whose S side is in its brickwork mostly original and in its windows, etc., not. Lord Lee placed the principal rooms here and converted the N range, which had held the principal apartments until then, into more and smaller rooms. To the W a Victorian addition and then the low, neatly detached, prettily cupolaed kitchen range of Lord Lee. Behind this however a lobby with an original stone doorway to the E room of the N range and a staircase with a window to the W (now looking into the Hall) and turned balusters of strong profile which also seem original, though they may not be *in situ*. In the N range on the first floor the Great Parlour and the Long Gallery, the former with fine panelling with pilasters and a fine chimneypiece brought in from a house at Ipswich (from which also a wooden oriel window survives inside the house and overlooking a small courtyard W of the Hall), the latter with another good fireplace surround. On the second floor the Prison Room, where Lady Jane Grey was kept for two years. Pretty walled S garden with SW and SE summerhouses.

RAGPIT HILL. *See* Great Kimble.

CHESHAM

9000

ST MARY. Large with a crossing tower with battlements and a recessed lead spire. Externally all C19-looking (restoration *Scott*, 1869), but the chancel Dec, the S transept E Dec, S Perp, the N transept N Perp, and Perp also the S aisle, two-storeyed S porch, and the W front with its W doorway and large windows. The porch has a tierceron-vault. Inside more of interest. Part

of a C12 window in the S wall of the N transept is reported by the
RCHM, but now hidden by the organ. Arcades of five bays with
octagonal piers and arches with two slight hollow chamfers and
little half-pyramids at their springing. It is all very baffling. The
elements seem C13, as the RCHM suggests, yet the flatness and
thinness of the whole look later. Late C13 E arch of the crossing.
The other arches Dec. – DOOR. The W door is of the C15.
Traceried. – WALL PAINTING. S wall, large St Christopher
wading through water; small figures of a fisherman and a her-
mit. – MONUMENTS. John Cavendishe † 1617, son of the Earl
of Devonshire. Sarcophagus, flanked by coupled black columns
carrying obelisks. Scaled double-curved roof in the middle,
and on it achievement in strapwork surround. No figures. –
Richard Woodcoke † 1623, vicar. Stately bust, frontal, in a
niche with pointed frame. – Nicholas Skottowe, by *John Bacon
Jun.*, 1800. Mourning woman kneeling over a sarcophagus; the
interpretation of remarkable tenderness. – More Late Georgian
tablets. – In the churchyard ashlar-built, unadorned and pedimented MAUSOLEUM to the Lowndes family.

CHRISTCHURCH, Waterside. 1864 by *Raphael Brandon*. By the
river. Flint, without a tower. Lancets, quatrefoil clerestory
windows.

PERAMBULATION

The perambulation starts from the churchyard. Immediately to
its E the VICARAGE, Later Georgian, red brick, of three bays
with one-bay pediment, the ground-floor windows under blank
arches and a Tuscan porch. Then down CHURCH STREET to
the SW. At once on the l. Nos 54 and 56, which is a C14 house.
One front window and one blocked W window have original
wooden tracery. Inside No. 54 one roof-truss with kingpost
and fourway struts. Next to this No. 58, mid-Georgian, brick,
with two giant pilasters and a parapet. Opposite, the two Lodges
to THE BURY, a fine preparation for the only grand house at
Chesham. The date is 1712 (rain-water heads). The house was
built for William Lowndes, Secretary to the Treasury. The
Lodges are one-storeyed with rusticated brick quoins and parapets. The Tuscan porches are later. The house has its façade to
the S. This S front was originally narrower than it is now. It had
no more than five bays. The wide bays to the l. and r. with their
low Venetian windows on the upper floor are a Late Georgian
addition. The original windows are segment-headed. Quoins,
parapet, hipped roof. In the SW room good door surrounds,

fireplace, and plasterwork. Similar decoration in the SE room. The staircase has a plaster ceiling with an oval wreath. Large addition to the W of 1853–64. Further later additions behind.

Church Street ends with a number of minor Georgian cottages. Then to the E along Wey Lane to FULLER'S HILL. Here, a little S, GERMAINS, with a timber-framed, pre-Reformation wing and a handsome mid-C18 addition of four bays. Porch with Ionic columns and a broken pediment. Further S LITTLE GERMAINS, of five bays and two storeys. Then down GERMAIN STREET to the N, where on the S Nos 35–7, Early Georgian, with a parapet curving up from the angles. Four very widely-set bays. Red and vitreous brick. Further S and higher up in AMERSHAM ROAD lies CHESHAM BOIS MANOR, Gothic, of 1880, by J. Wallis Chapman (loggia and hall 1908).

Now the MARKET SQUARE, with the TOWN HALL, built partly in the C18 and partly in 1856. Red brick and vitreous brick. Arcading for the market stalls, now closed. One upper storey. Hipped roof and handsome clock-turret with lantern. Nothing else in the Market Place. In the HIGH STREET, the GEORGE INN with some wall-paintings of c. 1715. Then on the r. an early C18 brick house with plain Venetian windows and a parapet raised pediment-wise above an arched upper window. Then the POST OFFICE, partly timber-framed with oversailing upper floor. Very big chimney with polygonal stacks. (Good C17 fireplace inside.) After that, on the other side, THE LIMES and BEVERLEY HOUSE, both Early Georgian, one of three the other of two storeys, both with similar Late Georgian doorcases.

WATERSIDE. Nice river scenery with MILLS.

VALE FARM, 1¼ m. NNW. C16 and later. Timber-framed with brick infilling and gabled, with oversailing upper floor. Chimneys square, set diagonally. Weatherboarded outbuildings. A good group.

(CODMORE FARM, 1 m. NE. With C15 roof trusses. RCHM)

BLACKWELL GRANGE FARM, 2 m. SE. Timber-framed with narrowly placed posts and later brick infilling. The core is of the C15. Hall roof partly preserved with moulded wall plates and purlins and with curved wind-braces. Double tie-beams, one above the other. Original doorway to the Hall, C16 mullioned windows.

GREAT HUNDRIDGE MANOR, 1½ m. W. Dated 1696 and a perfect example of its date. Built for an apothecary of London. Flush front, projecting wings at the back. The front is of seven bays and two storeys, the bays near to the doorway much narrower than the others. The doorway has carved brackets and a pediment. The windows have wooden crosses, the roof is hipped. Staircase with twisted balusters. (Also a rather flamboyant fireplace with circular opening. This is not, as one might think, of *c.* 1850, but of 1827, *see Country Life*, vol. 89, 1941, 147.) Behind the house a flint-built C13 CHAPEL with some lancet windows and a Perp E window.

9090   CHESHAM BOIS

St Leonard. Mostly of 1884. The arch of the s entrance to the churchyard must be part of the medieval church. – PULPIT. Early C17 with strapwork and arabesque panels. Strapwork so prominently displayed is not usual on pulpits. – MONUMENTS. Brasses to Elizabeth Cheyne † 1516 and her husband † 1552, in armour of *c.* 1530, the figures about 2 ft 10 in. long. – Brass to Benedict Lee, *c.* 1520, a chrysom baby. – John Cheyne † 1585. Tomb-chest with three shields in wreaths. Inscription tablet separate on the wall.

6020   CHETWODE

St Mary and St Nicholas. The remains of the church of an Augustinian Priory founded in 1245. This became a parish church *c.* 1480, when the narrow W tower was added which has now a pyramid roof. Behind this, and much broader than it, remains the long chancel of the priory church. Its E part is earlier and aesthetically much finer than its W part, the parish nave. The E part has a splendid group of five stepped lancets at the E end and groups of three stepped lancets on the N and S. They are all abundantly shafted inside, with foliated capitals. Group of Sedilia and chancel doorway with stiff-leaf and dogtooth. An odd and enjoyable trick of moulding in the apexes of the arches, where a length of roll moulding appears out of a hollow and disappears into it again. Later than this E end the two nave S windows with bar tracery (trefoiled circles), and yet later the N window with fine late C13 shafts with small naturalistic foliage capitals and a much later lintel. Of the same date the (re-set) W window with Y-tracery. – Painted TRIPTYCH with verses from the Bible in cartouches. Dated 1696. – STAINED GLASS. In the chancel SE lancets some beautiful early glass: two figures in almond-shaped panels of *c.* 1250 and others of the C14, especially one under a canopy. – The E window, glazed in the same style, very successfully, by *William Holland* of Warwick

in 1842. – MONUMENTS. (Sir John Giffard, C14 slab with incised cross and inscription in French. RCHM) – Mary Risley
† 1668. Tablet with, l. and r., two little weeping girls.

MANOR HOUSE, ½ m. ENE. A composite group, the W end the
earliest – of the Jacobean period – the E end the most recent.
The W front is of red brick with black diapering and has two
gabled dormers and original chimneystacks. Inside, the staircase has flat balusters, and a panelled room on the first floor has
a big fireplace with bulgy Tuscan columns flanking the opening
and Corinthian columns flanking the overmantel.

CHICHELEY

9040

ST LAURENCE. With a Perp central tower. In it an uncommonly
large S window. Pairs of two-light bell-openings with transom.
Most windows Perp. Earlier the N arcade inside. This is early
C14, as its short quatrefoil piers show. Double-chamfered
arches. Probably early C14 also the nave W window. About 1708
(rain-water head) the chancel was rebuilt. Fine Corinthian
angle pilasters. To the S two tall windows with segmental pediments. The Y-tracery is probably later. A doorway with scrolly
open pediment on brackets between. To the E instead of
windows two tall niches. Crowning pediment. The chancel
furnishings are all of c. 1710 and good. Plaster ceiling with oval
flower wreath in the centre. – REREDOS of stone. Three arches
on pilasters and a broad frieze of foliage. – SCREEN of Tuscan
columns carrying arches. – GATE of wrought iron. – CEILING
under the crossing with upper gallery. On this incidentally an
early ROOD by *Comper*, 1904. – In the nave BOX PEWS. At the
W end they are partly raised amphitheatrically. – MONU-
MENTS (N chapel). Anthony Cave and his wife, erected 1576,
by *Thomas Kirby*. Sarcophagus with his naked cadaver on it.
To the l. and r. tall free-standing caryatids carrying a pediment.
An interesting monument, out of the ordinary in composition
and execution. – Sir Anthony Chester † 1635 and his wife. Two
kneeling figures facing each other. Two columns and a big
superstructure. Well carved.

CHICHELEY HALL. Chicheley Hall was built for Sir John 44a
Chester c. 1698–1703. The architect in all probability was
Thomas Archer. The reasons for the attribution are stylistic; for
though the house belongs to a group typical of a variety of architects and all characterized by giant pilasters and attic storeys
above the main cornice, it has certain details peculiarly characteristic of Archer and lacking in such houses as Buckingham

House, London, of 1705 by Winde, Cound in Shropshire
of 1704 by Price, and The Ven in Somerset of 1698. The most
prominent such motif is the frieze above the capitals of the
giant pilasters, curving up in the centre, allowing for a complete
cornice here, and carrying the whole attic storey with it. The
aprons below the first-floor windows are found in other Archer
houses too, and Archerish in its Borrominesque licence also is
the pediment above the main entrance, curving outward to
carry the segmental top. The house is of brick with stone dressings, as are the others of the group. It is nine bays wide and
two-and-a-half storeys high. The articulation by giant pilasters
is odd. They appear at the angles, between the second and third
and the seventh and eighth bays, and they flank the three-bay
centre, where, by its projection, they appear as square pillars.
They are all fluted and have richly carved Corinthian capitals.
The frieze in the centre is also richly carved. This centre has
arched windows with oddly stepped and curved frames, even
in the attic. The top looks abrupt above them. On the side the
cornice and attic do not rise, the pilasters are unfluted, and the
door has a simpler, even if also an odd, pediment. At the back
there is an unexpected rhythm. There are only eight bays, the
centre four being recessed and the centre two, behind which
lies the staircase, very tall and arched. Between bays one and
two and seven and eight blank arched niches on all storeys.

Fine Entrance Hall, more like Kent than like Archer,
panelled, with a classical ceiling, a Greek-key frieze along the
wall, a fine Corinthian aedicule round the doorway, and a screen
of three arches on grey marble columns to connect it with the
staircase. This has three balusters to the step, one fluted, the
other two twisted in different ways, and carved tread-ends.
Good fireplaces, etc., in other rooms as well. Those in the
Drawing Room and Billiard Room are flanked by giant Corinthian pilasters. The elaboration is the same right to the top of
the house. In the attic storey is indeed a Library with all shelves
behind doors which look like panelling. In one room a crude
Jacobean overmantel with little termini caryatids remains from
the old house, in others some panelling.

From the house a quadrant link runs to the OFFICES. The
STABLES are at r. angles to the entrance side and call for a companion. What was the plan originally? Links to four service
buildings or only to two? The Offices are of brick, eleven
bays long, with angle rustication in brick and strange aprons
immediately below the eaves as if a third storey had been

projected. The centre has a pediment and below it an arched window and two arched niches. Big arched recess on the ground floor.

CHILTON

ST MARY. The distinguishing feature of the exterior is the short transeptal N tower with a higher stair-turret. The earliest part of the church is the chancel with single lancets and three stepped lancets under an arch at the E end. Of the same date the S transept, see the S window, similar to the chancel E window but with a hood-mould. The N tower is Dec with flowing window tracery and a triple-chamfered arch to the nave. Perp nave, S chancel chapel, and N porch. The porch is two-storeyed and has a four-centred tunnel-vault with transverse ribs. The nave in the C15 rebuilding took up the space of the former nave and S aisle; hence the lopsided position of the chancel. At the E end of the former nave a Perp double recess in which the former rood-stair must have started to run up. The E wall of the S transept is confused by the later access through the C13 wall into the Perp S chapel. This has a Perp arcade to the chancel, but a few details indicate the existence of a no doubt smaller earlier chapel in the same place. – SCREEN. Between chancel and S chapel, with Perp Flamboyant tracery but with Jacobean turned balusters. – STALLS. Made up from panels from a screen and poppy-heads. – ORGAN. C18, from Chilton House. The second organ is a copy of the first. – PLATE. Cup and Cover, 1569. – MONUMENTS. In the S Chapel Sir John Croke † 1608 and wife. Big alabaster structure. Two recumbent effigies. Against the front of the tomb-chest kneeling figures, detached, not in relief. Coffered arch. Back wall with inscription and strapwork. Two black columns and two obelisks outside them. Big superstructure. Good quality. – Elizabeth Tyrrell † 1631 (also S chapel). Small kneeling figure between columns. – Chief Justice Carter † 1755. Erected by him before he died (W wall). Tripartite screen of white and grey marble. Outer pilasters, inner columns, and open pediment. No figures at all, but palm-fronds and cherubs' heads in the frieze.

The church lies surrounded by excellent houses, a group not easily matched. To the N at the back of a big lawn TOWNHILL FARMHOUSE, early C18. Stone with giant brick pilaster-strips. Two storeys, hipped roof. Horizontal oval window above the plain doorway. To the W a C16 cottage of timber-framing with brick infilling and with an oversailing upper floor. Then the road bends to the W, to the gatepiers of Chilton House. Just outside them to the E GATEHOUSE, late C17, of brick, six bays and two storeys, hipped roof, two big red chimneys, windows with wooden crosses.

CHILTON HOUSE. Built c. 1740 by Chief Justice Carter 'after a reduced model' of Buckingham House in London. This was built by William Winde in 1705 and is one of a group of similar houses of about 1700 (cf. Chicheley, p. 93). Chilton has not much in common with it except the giant pilasters. The main façade is the entrance side. It faces E and enjoys a view over a spacious forecourt and distant rolling fields. The *cour d'honneur* is closed by brick piers and iron railings and a gate. To the l. and r. square stables with entrances from the E and blank arcaded walls to the court. Lantern turrets. Low brick walls connect these with the house. The house is of brick with stone dressings and has a nine-bay front. The height is of a basement (rusticated), two storeys and a half storey, and a panelled parapet. Giant Tuscan pilasters at the angles and the angles of the five middle bays. All ground-floor and the five middle windows on the first floor have surrounds of rustication of alternating size. Stairs up to the doorway, which is pedimented. Unfluted Ionic columns. The back to the church has symmetrical windows except for bays three and seven, where there is a Venetian window on the ground floor and an arched one on the upper floor. While all this corresponds to the date of the house, the N side reveals the fact that the whole was only a remodelling of an earlier building. Here there is a Tudor chimneybreast with diagonally placed stacks. From the NE corner a wall runs N in which there are two Perp doorways. The interior of the house has less to offer. Entrance Hall with pilasters and pedimented doorcases. Staircase with three twisted balusters to the tread and carved tread-ends. NE room with a marble chimneypiece and a stucco ceiling.

CHIPPS'S FARM *see* WEST WYCOMBE

CHOLESBURY

9000

ST LAURENCE. Drastically restored in 1873. Original N and windows. Original also the good S doorway, early C13, with one order of shafts and rolls in the arch mouldings. Nice wooden bell-turret with saddleback roof of before 1710, or a copy of the one appearing in a reproduction of 1710.* – PLATE. Cup of 1577.

* Information kindly given by Major R. C. Money.

WINDMILL, Cholesbury Common. Also known as Hawridge
Mill. The original smock-mill was built in 1863. In 1884 the
timber structure was found to be unsafe and the mill was rebuilt as a tower-mill, using the existing cap, fan-tail, and
machinery, but new sails. Now converted into a dwelling-house.

CHOLESBURY CAMP. An IRON AGE HILL-FORT on the
summit of the Chiltern ridge, comprising some 15 acres, the
parish church being contained at the s w end. To the E there is
a triple rampart, elsewhere double, with to the N w a triangular
outwork and possibly the original entrance. Excavations in
1932 revealed seven hearths in the central area and pottery
ranging from C2 B.C. Early Iron Age forms to Romano-British
coarse ware. The main occupation was clearly Belgic with
forms paralleled at Wheathampstead (see The Buildings of
England, Hertfordshire), but a joint occupation by native and
later Belgic elements is quite possible. The enigmatic cross-
dyke is undated.

CIPPENHAM see SLOUGH, pp. 238, 240

CLAPTON REVEL see WOOBURN

CLIFTON REYNES

ST MARY. An embattled church, even to the extent of the nave
and chancel E gables. This embellishment is Perp, the church is
much older. Unbuttressed Norman W tower (see the E window,
now inside the church). The tower top is C14. Of the C13 the
s aisle w window. The N aisle with its characteristic large windows with intersected tracery was rebuilt in 1801. This motif is
originally one of the late C13 and early C14, and of that date
there is indeed much in the church. Chancel and Sedilia and
Piscina, arcades of three bays with quatrefoil piers with slim
additional shafts in the diagonals, octagonal capitals, arches of
two sunk quadrants, N chapel of two bays with octagonal piers
and many-moulded arches. The tower arch may be a little
later. – FONT. C14. Octagonal, with figures of the Virgin, the
Trinity, and Saints. – PLATE. Cup and (undated) Paten of
1692. – MONUMENTS. Knight and Lady, of oak, c. 1300. –
Knight and Lady, of oak, c. 1300. The knights are in all probability members of the Reynes family. The one couple lies now
(not in situ) in a recess of c. 1300, the other on an uncommonly
good late C13 tomb-chest with shields in elongated quatrefoils.
– Knight and Lady, of stone, on a tomb-chest with eight

21a

9050

mourners against each of the long sides. They stand below ogee arches. Badly preserved, and never of very fine quality. The date probably *c.* 1380. – Brass to Sir John Reynes † 1428 (2 ft 8 in.). – Brasses of a man and a woman in shrouds, *c.* 1500 (20 in.). – Alexander Small † 1752. Bust in front of obelisk. The monument is signed by *James Andrews* of Olney, who did innumerable tombstones in graveyards in this part of Buckinghamshire. But the bust is by *Scheemakers*. It is of terracotta.

9080

CLIVEDEN

61a One of *Sir Charles Barry*'s best mansions, designed in 1850 when he was fifty-five. The house lies in a superb position above the Thames, by a bend, so that the main vista is not across but along the river. There was a house here built *c.* 1665–80 by *William Winde* for the Duke of Buckingham. It was on the same site and had the same dimensions and general layout. The balustrade in front of the present house survives from it. The balustrade below comes from the S forecourt of the Villa Borghese in Rome. It was bought by Viscount Astor, who had acquired the house from the Duke of Westminster in 1893, but Barry's mansion was not built for him either. The owner before him who was Barry's client was the Duke of Sutherland. He had bought it in 1849 and it had been burned immediately after. Sir Charles Barry's house is remarkably restrained, as mid-C19 mansions go, or indeed as Victorian mansions in Buckinghamshire go. It is in the Cinquecento style, and reminiscent of the villas of Genoese noblemen. The front to the river is nine bays long and two-and-a-half storeys high with one-bay, one-storey appendices. They and the house itself are finished with balustrades. The ground floor is rusticated, and the only motif here which is Georgian rather than Genoese is the Gibbs surrounds of the arches. Giant Ionic pilasters above this ground floor. The first-floor windows are all pedimented. To the N a porte-cochère of Tuscan columns set in pairs one behind the other. Low quadrant links with attached Tuscan columns and side wings at r. angles to the centre. The links are structurally a survival of colonnades which *Thomas Archer* had built for Lord Orkney, the then owner, about 1720. The side wings are seven bays long and two storeys high. So far all is chastity. But then, shortly after Barry's death, *Henry Clutton* added, asymmetrically, a tall CLOCK TOWER of restless many-stepped outline at the top. Four separate balconies below the clock-faces. Victorian flamboyance and assertiveness could not be defeated.

An avenue to the N leads to a sumptuous very French FOUN-TAIN with nudes and a huge cockleshell. This was made for Lord Astor by *Ralph Waldo Story*. To the s below the balus-trades a formal parterre with short box hedges and a bronze group of the Rape of Persephone after *Giovanni da Bologna*. To the r. of the parterre and hidden a GAZEBO by *Giacomo Leoni*, built for Lord Orkney about the year 1740. It is octagonal, and enjoys a beautiful view over the Thames valley. Lord Astor converted it into a chapel, and he is buried in it. (Mosaics by *Clayton & Bell*, designed by *J. L. Pearson*.) Also by *Leoni* the BLENHEIM PAVILION in the NW corner of the garden. This is a handsome building with an arched opening on coupled Ionic pilasters in the middle and lower rusticated one-bay wings. To the l. and r. of the arch garlands in the spandrels. Pediment with trophies. The alcove or open room inside has giant Ionic pilasters, and the lower side parts are open towards it. In the middle now a statue of Marlborough by *Story*, 1897. Lord Orkney had been commander of a brigade at the Battle of Blenheim.

The interior of Barry's mansion is no longer in the state which he gave it. It was redecorated by *John L. Pearson* for Lord Astor in the 1890s. Large hall with wooden Corinthian pilasters open on the r. to the staircase, which has as finials groups con-nected with Cliveden throughout its history. They are by *W. S. Frith*. The ceiling painting is by *A. L. Hervier*. The large François-Premier fireplace in the Hall is an original work from the time of that king (see the salamander). The Dining Room has genuine French Rococo panelling from the château of Asnières near Paris, built in 1751 for the Marquis d'Argenson (Hautecoeur). The Large Library, six bays long, is light in colour and has coupled Corinthian pilasters. The Small Lib-rary has brown panelling and an Adamish fireplace. These are the State Rooms.

CODMORE FARM *see* CHESHAM

COLD BRAYFIELD

9050

St MARY. Norman window in the nave wall above the doorway, Norman shafts in the C19 chancel arch. Scalloped capitals. One shaft is decorated with horizontal zigzag. C13 chancel with low-side lancets, C13 tower with low, only slightly chamfered arch towards the nave and single lancets as bell-openings, late C13 N porch (see the entrance arch). – PLATE. Late C16 Cup.

BRAYFIELD HOUSE. Late Georgian, of eight bays and two
storeys, with an iron veranda along the s front. This front over-
looks the river Ouse.

COLESHILL

ALL SAINTS. By *Street*, 1861. Small with lancet windows and
two quatrefoil circular windows in the chancel on the s side.
Weatherboarded bell-turret with steep, shingled pyramid roof.

BOTTLE COTTAGES, N of the church. Dated 1809. Flint and
brick. On the first floor bottle bottoms used ornamentally, as is
indeed not so rare in Buckinghamshire.

STOCK GROVE COTTAGE, 300 yds SW. Three bays, two storeys.
Brick with vertical bands of vitreous brick stretchers alternating
with headers. The windows are wider than they are high. In the
middle of the first floor a big oval cartouche with the date 1692.

COLESHILL HOUSE, 600 yds NE. Georgian and apparently enlarged and remodelled *c.* 1850. Four-bay centre with pitched
roof and l. and r. tall two-bay wings with flat roofs. Plastered
white.

(RUSHYMEAD, 1 m. from the church on the road towards
Amersham. By *Smith & Brewer*, illustrated in 1924.
Georgian with shutters to the windows, but gabled. On the SE
side a veranda on simple pillars. Classical interiors.)

WINDMILL. A derelict tower-mill, built in 1856.

COLNBROOK

ST THOMAS. By *Ferrey*, 1849–52 (GR). Flint. Nave and chancel
and bellcote. – SCREEN. By *Basil Champneys*, 1886 (GR). With
Flamboyant tracery. – STAINED GLASS. All the glass in the
chancel by *Kempe*, 1884.

VICARAGE and probably also SCHOOL by *Street* (D. Cole).
Yellow and red brick. Slight.

Colnbrook is half in Middlesex and half in Buckinghamshire. The
bridge across the Colne connects the two parts, which are vir-
tually one High Street. On the Middlesex side KING JOHN'S
PALACE, of *c.* 1600, plastered front and a tall carriageway.
TAN HOUSE FARM, N of the High Street, just E of the bridge,
is a pretty whitewashed brick group by the mill-stream.

On the Bucks side the GEORGE INN, a nice composition of three
plus three bays separated by an arched carriageway. Above this
a pediment. The angle bays of both side parts have tripartite
windows. Then on the other side the timber-framed OSTRICH
INN, with oversailing upper floor.

CRESLOW

1 m. NE of Whitchurch

MANOR HOUSE. Early C14, but much altered, even after the publication of the volume of the RCHM. What remains now is the general masonry of the Great Hall (l., i.e. the N half of the house), the solar wing placed at r. angles, i.e. across the present house in its centre, and a tower at the r. corner, i.e. the SW. This has a higher stair-turret and some early C17 windows. Of the original windows very few survive now, and none of special beauty. A little tracery in a tower window on its N side. Below the W half of the solar, with entry from the garden, a crypt, beautifully vaulted with a tierceron-star-vault and five leaf bosses. NW of the house a detached CHAPEL. The N doorway has re-used parts of a Norman arch with zigzag and billet motifs. The windows are Dec and Perp. (Inside one elaborate fireplace of the C17 and in the same room a deeply coffered ceiling. In an upper room C17 plaster decoration. MHLG)

CUBLINGTON

ST NICHOLAS. Perp. The W tower has some unusual details, such as the blank tracery of the S bell-openings and the deeply-chamfered outer splays of the W window. Chancel arch on corbels with a man and a monkey. L. and r. of the E window castellated niches. – Humble WEST GALLERY. – PLATE. Cup and Cover Paten, 1692.

THE BEACON. Mount of a Norman castle, about 20 ft high, 500 yds W of the church.

MANOR HOUSE. Of the former Manor House, NW of the church, the stately C18 stable-block survives, of brick, with a big hipped roof, and the GRAIN STORE on a low arcaded basement.

NEAL'S FARM, E of the former. Of c. 1600. H-plan. Timber-framing and brick infilling, with two symmetrical gables l. and r. of the centre. The S front was refaced with brick in the C18.

CUDDINGTON

ST NICHOLAS. A complicated building history, fully discussed by the RCHM. The arcades inside are witness of it. Three bays (originally four) on the N side, four on the S. All details of the late C12 to C13, but otherwise many differences. The earliest mouldings seem to be those of the chancel arch. In the arcades of the nave occur circular and octagonal piers. The NE arch corresponds to the chancel arch and may at that time have led into a transept (semi-octagonal responds, double-chamfered arch). On the other hand the capital of the circular pier on the N side and that of the first circular pier from the W on the S side have capitals with trumpet scalloping. They must therefore be of the late C12 and were probably re-used when the aisles were rebuilt in the course of the C13. The C13 mouldings are chiefly of two hollow chamfers. A curious irregularity is the transverse arch across the S aisle, just E of the S entry. The S doorway is of the later C13. It has plenty of dog-tooth decoration and fillets to the roll mouldings. Yet later in the century, say c. 1290, the S chapel E window (intersected tracery uncusped), and perhaps once more later by ten years or so the E windows of the chancel and the N chapel (intersected cusped). Other windows Dec and Perp. Perp W tower with higher stair-turret. The church was restored by *Street* in 1857. Designed by him is the STAINED GLASS in the E window (made by *Powell*), with strong blue, red, and green. – In the S aisle E window two small original C14 figures of angels. – By *Street* no doubt the design of the stone PULPIT. – FONT. C12, tub-shaped with tapering sides. Decorated with tall, thin, blank arches.

TYRINGHAM HOUSE, NW of the church. Dated 1609 inside. Of stone; asymmetrical, tall front with a two-storeyed bay window.

Many picturesque cottages, notably at LOWER GREEN one that is called THREE COTTAGES. Timber-framed with white-washed infilling. A big stone chimneybreast.

DANCER'S END HOUSE *see* DRAYTON BEAUCHAMP

9070   DATCHET

ST MARY. By *Raphael Brandon*, 1858–60, with an ornate octagonal NE tower standing on the oddest substructure and continued in the oddest cross-gabled N transept and outer N aisle. – STAINED GLASS. Almost completely by *O'Connor*, 1860–5, and interesting to those who choose to study the art of Victorian glass-painters. – MONUMENTS. Tablet to Christopher Barker † 1599 'qui typographiam Anglicanam lateritiam invenit, marmoream reliquit'. – Three remarkable tablets, with cartouches, all different, and busts on top: Mary Wheeler † 1626, Hanbury Wheeler † 1633, John Wheeler † 1636. Mrs Esdaile suggested an assistant of Le Sueur.

Datchet is not engulfed yet in suburban developments. It has still its Green and it has the short HIGH STREET leading to the Thames. Along the street a terrace of small three-bay Georgian red-brick houses, then a few semi-detached Early Victorian yellow-brick houses, and then on the r. DATCHET LODGE, red, three-storeyed, and in two parts, and on the l. OLD BRIDGE HOUSE, three storeys, with pebbledash and, towards the river, a bow with a cast-iron veranda. Nice Gothick door-case.

On the HORTON ROAD about $\frac{1}{4}$ m. E THE LAWN, red brick, two-storeyed, with a Venetian window to the E.

SECONDARY MODERN SCHOOL. 1958–9, by the County Architect, *F. B. Pooley*. A handsome group with load-bearing brick walls. Three-, two-, and one-storeyed.

DENHAM

0080

ST MARY. The unbuttressed W tower may well be Norman. On the bell-stage there are, to the l. and r. of the later big openings, two small round-headed ones. The exterior is all renewed, but the lancets in the chancel point to the C13 and the rest to the C15. Perp arcades inside, three bays, the piers with four shafts and four hollows. Clerestory. Perp also the arch between tower and nave. – FONT. Of Purbeck marble. C13. Bowl of table-top type, octagonal, each side with two shallow blank pointed arches. – PAINTING. Much-defaced C15 Doom above the S doorway. At the bottom the unusual scene of the sea giving up her dead. Bottom l. kneeling lady, probably the donor. – STAINED GLASS. E window, 1876, by *Dixon, Frampton & Hean* (TK). – PLATE. Cup of 1673. – MONUMENTS. Brasses to Amphillis Pekham † 1545 (chancel S; 15 in. figure), palimpsest of a mid-C15 figure; to Walter Duredent † 1494 and two wives (chancel floor, 2 ft 2 in. figures); to Agnes Jordan, last abbess of Syon, Middlesex, † 1544 (chancel floor, 3 ft figure). – Low tomb-chest with triangular panels with cusped pointed trefoils (chancel S). On it stood originally a wooden canopy in Renaissance forms with Corinthian pillars carrying an entablature with a decorated frieze and eighteen fluted flower pots with flowers of silk and leaves of lead (Lipscomb IV, 450). The monument was to Elizabeth Micklow, *c.* 1550. – Sir Edmund Peckham † 1564 and wife (chancel N). Tomb-chest with short columns; two recumbent stone effigies. – Sir Roger Hill † 1729 (N aisle). With bust on a roguish plinth. Fluted pilasters, baldacchino with looped-up curtains. By *Thomas Bull*. – William Bowyer † 1745 (S aisle). With a relief at the foot showing a ship and nautical tools.

Denham is one of the most attractive villages in the county, and
one of the most attractive ones in any direction near London.
It is essentially of the mellow red of old brick. The village is a
main street leading from the church to a little Green and the
little bridge across the river Misbourne. We start by the church.
To the N of the churchyard the CHARITY SCHOOL, 1721, of
grey and red brick, three bays only, hipped roof. The ground-
floor windows Venetian (later?) with an additional arch over
all three parts. Then the street proper starts with HILL
HOUSE, later C17, with four gables, alternatingly shaped and
stepped. The r. stepped gable is smaller and a later addition.
After that a cottage with an end gable of truncated ogee shape
and decorated by a big blank Venetian window. Many more
houses and cottages nice to look at, e.g. WRANGO, Later
Georgian, stretching back from the road and having five bays
and two storeys, then a cottage with oversailing upper floor.
Here the street bends and approaches the triangular Green. The
FALCON INN, on the r., has again five bays and two storeys,
and BLACKSMITH'S COTTAGE is quite large, of timber with
brick infilling, and has in the centre the two big curved wind-
braces which usually indicate that the centre recedes, but the
eaves were even (Wealden type). Finally, across the bridge,
MISBOURNE COTTAGE, also timber-frame and brick infilling.
At the Green and opposite Misbourne Cottage, the long brick
garden wall of Denham Place.
DENHAM PLACE. Built in 1688–1701 for Sir Roger Hill, and a
very good if somewhat conservative example of its date. The
architect probably was *William Stanton*, better known as a
sculptor, but a trained mason and master-mason at Belton
House, Lincolnshire, earlier in the eighties. Belton is indeed
very similar in style to Denham Place. The latter is of H-shape
with an eleven-bay front and back of two storeys and hipped
roof. Five-bay centre and three-bay wings projecting one bay.
Sides of five bays. Dormers in the roof. The chimneys square
with oblong sunk panels. The eaves with a swagger egg-and-
dart frieze. The broad main doorway on the E side (originally
on the W side) is swagger too; it is also of an odd design. The
Ionic columns stand further away from the doorway than usual
and allow space for raised panels. The pediment thus has two
horizontal parts before it rises into an open scrolly triangular
shape. This part stands on extra brackets. Busts on the pediment and the horizontal parts. The house underwent alterations
shortly after 1771. The slender shape of the windows and their

glazing belong to that date. Originally they were shorter and had thicker glazing bars. Also the dormers had alternating steep triangular and semicircular pediments. In addition there was a balustrade and a cupola on the roof – all elements introduced in England as early as *c.* 1650 and a little past their day by the time Denham Place was begun.

Entrance Hall, converted after 1771 from being the Saloon. The main Staircase to the r. dates from the same time. Subsidiary staircase to the l. The latter has the original dumb-bell balusters. Of the former only the ceiling is original. It is the first of a number of excellent ceilings which distinguish the interior. Centre panel in the shape of a barbed quatrefoil. To the r. the Chapel, with a window with Y-tracery, not apparent as such outside. The chapel is a later conversion and contains materials brought in from outside, it is said from the Hills' ancestral Poundesford in Somerset. But there is also evidence that fittings of the chapel at Bulstrode went to Denham. Screen of three-light divisions with panel tracery, high linenfold Panelling, Bench Ends in a C17 Gothic mode, Pew with ornate linenfold panelling, etc. The front of the Gallery with thick acanthus framing to the middle opening. Plasterwork behind on the upper floor. A simple panel similar to those in other rooms. Date 1692. The main N room and the NW room (Drawing Room) have in the coving of the ceiling big plaster friezes of landscapes with figures and sporting pursuits, done in a lively, rustic manner. The panels of the ceilings are beautifully and much more urbanely composed. One of the ceilings has the date 1693. The other has as the centre an arrangement of musical instruments, and in the surrounding panels birds and four cupids in roundels. *William Parker* was paid for plasterwork the sum of £274. 11s. 0d. in 1691. What did he do? The panels and the friezes can hardly be by the same hand. The Library on the W side and its Lobby have prettily framed wood panelling of the 1690s. On the first floor also rooms of the same date. In one room re-used Jacobean panelling with blank-arched panels. 42b

The Stables date from after 1771. In the garden to the S a Lake. The landscaping is due to *Capability Brown*. Originally the garden was of course formal. At the W end of the garden very fine wrought-iron Screen and Gates of the 1690s.

DENHAM COURT, E of the church, along a long straight avenue. The house is large and obviously much pulled about. The S front probably of the early C18 with late C18 bows added l. and

r. Yellow brick with red dressings. Late C18 porch of paired Tuscan columns. A lower wing at the back towards the w seems late C17.

DENHAM MOUNT, 1¼ m. WSW. Early Victorian house, rendered white. With pretty wooden trellis porch and verandas.

SAVEHAY FARM (THE SAVOY), ⅝ m. NE. A C14 hall house of which much survives. Timber-framing and brick infilling. The Hall was aisled, and traces of the posts and arches of the E aisle are still accessible. Posts with shafts set in the angles. The Hall probably extended further N originally, and the wing here was added c. 1500. C15 the S (Solar) wing.

64a RANK LABORATORIES, on the A412 road, less than ¼ m. NW of the Savoy. By *Gropius & Maxwell Fry*, 1936. Long front with parts of various heights, the l. one with long balconies of corrugated iron on two floors. Then a raised bit and a r. part with windows on three storeys. Doorway with canopy on thin shafts, a motif often repeated since. The building is relatively unknown.

DIBDIN HILL see CHALFONT ST GILES

7010 ## DINTON

ST PETER AND ST PAUL. The church has an outstandingly
4b elaborate Norman S doorway. One order of shafts, twisted in the Cosmati, not the Durham, etc., way. One of the capitals has a bird. Continuous outer zigzag and billet mouldings. On the lintel a dragon ready to devour a tiny St Michael holding out horizontally a cross rather than a spear. Tympanum with the Tree of Life and two lions. Inscription:

> Praemia pro meritis si qis despet habenda
> Audiat hic preepta sibique sit retinenda

It would be tempting to connect the building to which this belonged with that which the English Bishop Egino, when he founded Lund Cathedral in Sweden in 1072, wished his English architect Donatus to copy. He referred explicitly to Dinton. However, the story is far from well documented, and furthermore the doorway is clearly later than 1072, and nothing else either Saxon or Norman remains.* C13 chancel with lancet

* Dr Erik Cinthio of Lund has however pointed out to me in a recent letter that, although Donatus belongs to the C12 cathedral, archaeological investigations have revealed a late C11 cathedral which was small and of Anglo-Saxon or Anglo-Norman type.

windows (the E window is of 1868). S arcade of five bays with standard details also C13. The rest mostly Perp. – FONT. Cup-shaped. The fluted lower part of the bowl could be Norman, the upper with arch-heads and quatrefoils C14 or C15. – PULPIT. Jacobean, with one row of blank arches and one of panels with arabesque decoration. – STAINED GLASS. Chancel windows and S aisle E window by *O'Connor*, done with the advice of *Lady Eastlake*. – PLATE. Large Cup and Cover Paten of 1569; Salver given in 1721; two Flagons given in 1772. – MONUMENTS. Brass to John Compton and wife † 1424 (19 in. figures). – Brass to William Lea † 1486 and wife (20½ in. figures). – Brasses to Thomas Grenewey † 1538 and wife (22½ in. figures), and Richard Grenewey † 1551 and wife (2 ft figures), both palimpsest from the same large late C15 figure of a Cleric. – Brass to Francis Lee † 1558 and wife (13 in. figures), also palimpsest. One fragment comes from a very fine Flemish brass of *c.* 1380. All these brasses are in the chancel floor. – Elizabeth Vanhattem † 1764. Tablet by *King* of Bath (nave NE).

DINTON HALL. The building history of Dinton Hall is obscure. The house is large and varied with its many gables and chimneys. It consists of three parts, that to the W being the oldest. This alone is of stone. In its basement it has a very curious stone support for a former major chimneypiece above. It consists of four tall corbels connected by three horizontal shelves. The tops of the corbels are moulded. The whole piece has been attributed to the C14, but may well be of *c.* 1500. The centre of the house has undergone many alterations. The S front was sashed in the C18 and received cross-windows in the C19, when it was probably also refaced. The N front is very puzzling. It has windows with arched lights of a kind usual under Henry VIII but not with the proportions of that time. Moreover they are flanked on the first floor by very broad flat pilasters with waist bands round a very low waist. These could be Elizabethan, and the windows then might be a historically wrong C19 adaptation to the Elizabethan style of sashed windows like those of the S side. This N front is gabled. Above the centre of the centre block a battery of chimneyshafts in a row. The E part of the house is also gabled and also at least partly original. It certainly existed in the C18 (see a painting in the house), and the brickwork of the SW gable seems to be C17. Fragments of C18 furnishing in the W range. C17 Gatepiers, and nearby a circular stone Dovecote.

DINTON CASTLE, on the main road, N of the Hall. Built as an eye-catcher or folly by Sir John Vanhattem in 1769. Hexagon with two towers, now in decay.

VICARAGE, E of the church. By *Sir G. G. Scott*, built, according to his *Secular and Domestic Architecture*, p. 140, of cob.

THE SUMMERS. Picturesque group S of the church, two houses but originally one. Timber-framed with brick-nogging. Lower wing at the back in the same technique.

0070

DITTON PARK

Built by *William Atkinson* in 1813–17 in the place of a medieval house refronted about 1700. Atkinson's design is castellated, and his embattled and turreted ranges are cement-rendered. In the middle of the S front a three-storeyed canted bay rising above the rest of the façade. Behind this a tower with higher stair-turret, a visual reminiscence, it seems, of the C14 tower, preserved behind the William and Mary front. Atkinson's entrance side has first a Gatehouse, then Stables and Offices in separate blocks to the l. and r., and then a five-bay front with projecting three-bay centre. Interiors also Gothic, none spectacular, the best perhaps the Staircase which runs up through two storeys and has a Gothic cast-iron balustrade. In the Gallery (with wall-shafts and a canted ribbed ceiling) a number of C14 TILES are displayed which have been found on the site. There is a MOAT round the house, and outside the Moat to the SW stands a CHAPEL, built in 1817. This is also Gothic and has also a ribbed canted ceiling. Chancel and nave are not structurally divided.

7020

DODDERSHALL HOUSE
2 m. W of Quainton

A U-shaped house surrounded by a moat. The oldest part is the E range. Here lies the Hall with its E and W porches. The detail of the Hall is as far as recognizable rather *c.* 1525 than before, see e.g. the medallions outside and the (re-set ?) frieze of foliage and grotesques inside. Fine chimney to the original Hall. The W side, i.e. the side towards the courtyard, has much early C19 alteration; much was done inside at that time too. But to the N of the W porch a Jacobean staircase remains. The main staircase lies in the S wing, which was remodelled *c.* 1689 (rain-water heads). It belongs to this remodelling. Strong twisted balusters. A fine three-bay room with panelling W of the staircase. This has a Renaissance entablature above a four-centred fireplace opening. Octagonal stacks on a base decorated by brick rustication of three courses height for each imitation-ashlar block.

DORNEY

Court and church are in a delightfully secluded spot close to Dorney Reach and mercifully far from suburban developments.

ST JAMES. Stone and flint, nave and lower chancel. Remains of a Norman s window in the chancel. W tower of brick Early Tudor, s porch of brick dated 1661. In the early C17 the Garrard Chapel was added to the church. It has mullioned windows with straight tops. The nave windows are probably C18. The interior has great charm, thanks to its modest and fairly complete old furnishings. – FONT. Tub-shaped, Norman, with ornamental decoration in big motifs. – PULPIT. Mid-C17, with two tiers of panels with four raised L-shaped pieces round a raised oblong centre. – SCREEN. Remains of the traceried dado. – STALL FRONTS. Traceried and perhaps not *in situ*. – BENCHES. Plain, with moulded tops; C16. – WEST GALLERY. Dated 1634. Three-sided, with typical balusters. – FAMILY PEW. C18. – PAINTING. In the arch to the N chapel two figures of the Annunciation were discovered in 1932. They are of the C14. – MONUMENT. Sir William Garrard † 1607 and wife. Alabaster. Large standing monument with kneeling figures facing each other. The children kneeling against the base. Outside two obelisks.

DORNEY COURT. A house of *c.* 1500, the history of which is obscured by C19 and C20 restorations and alterations. Originally it seems to have been L-shaped with the Hall in the larger arm and the parlour and solar in the shorter, projecting N at the E end. The Hall is still there, with a fine roof with thin arched braces and wind-braces. The fine fireplace with big tracery about the opening was brought in from an unknown place, the linenfold panelling from Faversham Abbey in Kent. The main entrance now, however, is at r. angles to it in the E front, and this is almost entirely a reconstruction, achieved by renewing an C18 brick façade. The middle oriel is supposed to have been brought from elsewhere. One of the chimneys, however, of bold star-shape, is supposed to be original. Original also the N return of the E arm and the extremely pretty gabled W half of the N front, timber-framed with brick infilling. The wall continues the N wall of the Hall. Behind this gabled front the kitchen and offices and a small enclosed courtyard. Some original fireplaces.

In the Parlour good wooden overmantel of *c*. 1600. – North-east
GATES, classical, of cast iron, *c*. 1830.

THE HERMITAGE. A former Lodge or a Folly. Stone and flint,
one-storeyed, with an octagonal tower. Some patterning with
bottle-bottoms.

At Dorney and around much phoney half-timbering in C20
houses.

DORNEYWOOD *see* BURNHAM

DORTON

6010

ST JOHN BAPTIST. In the nave a C13 lancet. Chancel Perp, s
aisle Dec, attached to the Perp s porch. Weatherboarded bell-
turret on pretty timber supports. It dates from *c*. 1630. – SOUTH
DOOR. With C13 iron hinges. – FONT COVER. With strapwork.
Dated 1631. – COMMUNION RAIL. Of the same time. – PLATE.
Small Cup and Cover Paten of 1568.

DORTON HOUSE. Large Jacobean mansion of red brick. E front
with two far-projecting wings and two one-bay projections in
the inner corners. The fenestration mostly altered *c*. 1784. Five-
bay centre with broad pedimented Tuscan porch. Windows on
the ground floor altered from the original mullioned and transomed ones. On the upper floor four Venetian windows and an
arched one. At the end of the wings Venetian windows too. The
s side has all mullioned and transomed windows, much renewed. Small stone porch with decorated round arches. To its
l. and r. pairs of big three-light windows with two transoms.
Irregular w front. Symmetrical N front, flat with two canted bay
windows in the first and last bays and a small square porch. All
much renewed.

Inside there is a good deal of interest. Hall Screen, ornate
with strapwork crestings. Hall fireplace with a big plaster
cartouche above. Big staircase in the N corner projection and
extending N beyond it. Vertically symmetrical balusters.
Stucco decoration with broad bands on the underside and the
ceiling of the part projecting into the N wing. The staircase
starts there by passing through a two-bay screen with Ionic,
somewhat baluster-shaped, columns. The date 1626 appears in
the stucco work. A minor staircase with flat balusters in the s
wing, evidently altered. It is reached from the Hall by a passage
with two round stone arches. In the s wing four-centred door-
heads, apparently earlier. On the first floor, two rooms with
36b   elaborate coved plaster ceilings of the same style. In one of

these also a big fireplace. In the N wing on the first floor a plain
Long Gallery.

DORTON SPA. The Grecian buildings of the Chalybeate Spring,
built *c.* 1840, have disappeared. The pump room had a semicircular portico of eight columns, and eight giant columns
inside.

DRAYTON BEAUCHAMP   9010

ST MARY. A very pretty church in a pretty situation outside the
village and below the Chilterns. Flint with square stone blocks,
the chancel of ashlar with bands of ironstone. W tower. The
church is battlemented throughout. All windows Late Perp. Inside arcades of four bays, according to the convincing suggestion of the RCHM re-used C13 as well as C14 parts. Of the late
C13 the tower arch. In the S aisle below the E window a quatrefoil frieze, probably belonging to a former REREDOS. – FONT.
Cylindrical, Norman, with tall blank arcading. – STAINED
GLASS. The E window with ten complete C15 figures, in the W
window two much restored figures. – MONUMENTS. Good
Brasses to two Knights, chancel S and N, the latter William
Cheyne † 1375, the former probably Thomas Cheyne † 1368,
both figures about 4 ft 9 in. long. – Brass to a Priest, perhaps
Henry Fazakyrley, † 1531 (10½ in.). – Lord and Lady Newhaven 27b
† 1728 and 1732. By *William Woodman*. A large, important
piece, and no doubt this sculptor's *chef d'œuvre*. Reredos background with Corinthian columns and an open scrolly pediment.
Semi-reclining figure on a grey sarcophagus against a grey
obelisk. The seated figure of the Lady was added only after her
death, and without her the monument would have much more
balance. She is seated below, at his feet, on the high white base,
a figure rather too big for her position. To the l. the coronet.
Both figures in contemporary dress, he wearing a wig.

DANCER'S END HOUSE, 1¼ m. SE. Early C18, red and vitreous
brick, five bays and two storeys, segment-headed windows.

GRIM'S DITCH. *See* p. 148.

DRAYTON PARSLOW   8020

HOLY TRINITY. Small and part Dec, part Perp, with simple W
tower, nave, and chancel. – FONT. Octagonal, Dec, with niches
against the stem whose nodding ogee arches reach up against
the bowl. Castellated top. – GLASS. Bits of the original glass in
N and S windows. – LOCKER. In the chancel S wall, with wooden
door; Jacobean. – PLATE. Cup and Cover Paten, 1569.

RECTORY. 1754. The street front looks one generation older. Five

bays with a one-bay broken pediment or dormer, into which an
arched window rises. Vitreous and red brick, the windows
vertically laced in red brick. The garden side is one of the most
charming pieces of early domestic Gothicism in the county. L.
and r. canted bays, the centre with a tripartite doorway carrying
an odd pediment with a trefoil. Two ogee-headed windows
above and a top pediment with a quatrefoiled circle.

9080   DROPMORE

ST ANNE, Littleworth Common. By *Butterfield*, 1866. Small, of
flint with brick bands and with a tile-hung bell-turret with
wooden top. The w gable is timber-framed and painted *sang-
de-bœuf*. It has bargeboards too. S porch at the w end of the
nave. Inside a frieze of red and black vitreous bricks. The N
transept was added in 1877 ('almost certainly by Butterfield'
GR). Scissor-braced nave roof. – STAINED GLASS. E window by
A. Gibbs, c. 1866. – PULPIT. With Early Renaissance panels
with heads in roundels. Are they Flemish?

VICARAGE. Also by *Butterfield*, it seems.

DROPMORE HOUSE. Built for Lord Grenville, Prime Minister
to George III, shortly after 1792, and attributed by Mr
Hussey to *Samuel Wyatt*. The N front and the w end of the S
front probably additions of c. 1810. Long, white, and delightfully unassuming. Towards the grounds, with their uncommonly splendid trees, three bow windows, and all along wooden
trellis work, a conservatory between the bow windows on the
r., a veranda between those on the l. This front continues

59b   beyond the house on the l. in a veritable orgy of trellis, including
Greek Doric temple fronts with single and coupled columns.
In the centre of these long pergolas an AVIARY of iron and green
Chinese pottery panels. The entrance front has a hexastyle
one-storeyed portico with Tuscan columns, to its l. and r. behind raised from two to three storeys and provided on the
ground floor with tripartite windows with blank segmental
arches over. The same windows on the two-bay E side. Entrance
Hall with a screen of columns at the back. Good plaster ceilings
and fireplaces in several rooms. The daintiest details are in the
Long Library, the largest S room. On the first floor above the
centre room with its bow is a circular room. Below the house by
the Lake a re-erected ALCOVE from the London Bridge preceding Rennie's.*

* Others at Guy's Hospital, London, and in Victoria Park, Hackney,
London.

In the NE corner of the estate a LODGE, built on the pattern of
that of Hall Barn, probably in the second half of the C19. Of
timber, with all kinds of bits and pieces re-used from various
sources: twisted columns, Early Renaissance panels, perhaps
from church benches, perhaps from bedsteads. Also a number
of panels made specially for the Lodge – more than at Hall
Barn (*see* p. 152).

DROPSHORT *see* LITTLE BRICKHILL

DRY LEYS *see* QUAINTON

DUNTON   8020

ST MARTIN. Norman nave of fine large squared stones with an
original N doorway. Zigzag arch, panels l. and r. of the lintel
decorated with figures. Three human figures on the l. (one
standing, the second kneeling before the third which may be
Christ or a Bishop), a horse on the r. The nave S windows are
of the C18, arched. Chancel of the C13 with lancet windows.
The chancel arch is in confusion. The big shafts l. and r. probably come from the Norman chancel arch. Plain Perp W tower. –
WEST GALLERY. Late C18, humble, with many inscriptions,
including two in Greek. – BOX PEWS. – BRASSES. Couple of
c. 1420, inscription scrolls from their mouths, 12 in. figures. –
Lady, *c.* 1510, 12 in. figure.

EAST CLAYDON   7020

ST MARY. Except for the Perp W tower nearly all Victorian
(restoration 1871 by *Scott*). Inside, one arch from the nave to a
S chapel is early C13. Pointed unmoulded arch on moulded imposts. Hood-mould with a small zigzag frieze at r. angles to the
wall surface. This also is much renewed. The chancel arch and
the chancel N doorway and one chancel N window are Dec. The
arch rests on corbels with grotesques and monsters. The doorway has fleuron decoration. The window has flowing tracery. N
arcade of 1871. – PLATE. Cup and silver-gilt Cover Paten, 1569;
Paten, 1826.
Many nice cottages. The most interesting house is the WHITE
HOUSE, NW of the church. This has a porch with a Victorian
date 1662. It looks rather earlier. The entrance still has a four-
centred head. Flanking pilasters. Front garden with C18 brick
wall.

EDGCOTT

6020

ST MICHAEL. Perp w tower and Perp s window. C14 chancel arch, much restored. – FONT. Probably of *c.* 1660. Polygonal with sunk panels. – BENCHES. Some fragments of C16 benches. – PLATE. Cup and Cover Paten 1569; Paten on foot 1718.

EDLESBOROUGH

9010

ST MARY. Very prominently placed on an isolated hill, a big all-embattled church with a broad w tower. The oldest part of the church is the four-bay arcades with octagonal piers and double-chamfered arches. This is of the C13. It seems to have been built in two campaigns. The strip of wall converting one pier on each side into two responds represents the junction with the original w wall (of a Norman church?). The Dec w tower was built into the w end of the C13 nave. It has a tall w lancet and bell-openings with simple Dec tracery. Higher stair-turret. Before the tower was built, the chancel had been rebuilt and received a gorgeous E window of five lights with free Geometrical tracery, unfortunately heavily restored. The tracery consists of two two-light side parts with trefoils, a higher middle lancet light, and three foiled top circles. This looks *c.* 1290. Of about the same date the N doorway. In the N wall near the w end C15 figure of a Pilgrim. Perp most windows, also the transverse arches across the aisles (cf. Aylesbury). The N chapel of one bay was built between 1342 and 1350 and enlarged and remodelled in the C15. Fine figured brackets on the E wall. – FONT. Perp, octagonal, simple. – PULPIT. Perp, much restored, with the very rare feature of a tall, four-tier canopy. – SCREEN. Tall, of three-light divisions (cf. Wing), with the ribbed E coving preserved. – STALLS. With MISERICORDS, e.g. an owl, a mermaid, a bat. – PAINTING. In the nave painted decoration in red lines, by *Bell* of London, 1867. – STAINED GLASS. Chancel s. By *Kempe*, 1901, with his trade-mark, the wheatsheaf. – Nave w, by *Ward & Hughes*, 1867. – TILES. C14, in various places. – PLATE. Cup and Cover Paten, 1607; large Cup and Paten on foot, 1636. – MONUMENTS. John de Swynstede † 1395, the figure 4 ft 9 in. long. – John Killingworth † 1412. With a rose, like that of a rose window, 14 in. across. – John Rufford † 1540 and three wives. Palimpsest of a Lady of the early C15. (All three in the N aisle.)

CHURCH FARM, NE of the church. With a BARN, 180 ft long.

6a

17a

Mid-c16, timber-framed with brick infilling. Nine roof trusses.

WINDMILL. A derelict tower-mill.

LYNCHETS. There is an ill-defined series of lynchets s of the church.

ELLESBOROUGH   8000

ST PETER AND ST PAUL. Big, of flint, externally all Victorian (1854–71). In a prominent position N of Cymbeline's Mount and with a wide view to the N. The SW tower is tall and has a taller stair-turret. Tall S arcade of four bays, probably late c14. Octagonal piers, arches with sunk quadrant mouldings. The tower arches of the same type. – STAINED GLASS. Fragments in the Vestry windows. – PLATE. Large Cup and Cover Paten of 1569. – MONUMENTS. Brass of a Knight, 1 ft 8 in. figure (s wall). – Bridget Croke † 1638. Of alabaster. Stiffly semi-reclining on her side. Coffered arch on black columns. The monument does not seem to be *in situ*.

CYMBELINE'S MOUNT, in Chequers Park. Motte-and-bailey castle. Circular mound, c. 22 ft high, and two small baileys. Surface finds of Iron Age and Romano-British wares have been made in the vicinity.

ALMSHOUSES. 1746. Humble one-storeyed group s of the church.

CHEQUERS, see p. 89.

TERRICK HOUSE, 1 m. NNE. Built in 1702. Five-bay front of two storeys, with cross-windows.

BEACON HILL. The MOUND used as a beacon may be mentioned as a possible prehistoric barrow.

EMBERTON   8040

ALL SAINTS. An excellent, essentially Dec church, closely related to Olney. Only the W tower is Perp. Most windows with flowing tracery. The E window of five lights one of the best in that style in Buckinghamshire. The chancel NW and SW windows are of the low side variety, with transoms. Five-bay arcades with quatrefoil piers and arches with two sunk quadrant mouldings. Clerestory with quatrefoil windows. The chancel arch has a different moulding. In the chancel moulded courses along the walls, with stops. Sedilia and Piscina with ogee arches on moulded shafts and ballflower in the arches. Everything much restored. – FONT. Octagonal, Perp, with crisply detailed blank arches and tracery. – SCREEN. Remains in the chancel, N side. Three one-light divisions. – PLATE. Cup and Cover

Paten of the earlier C17; large Salver of 1671. – MONUMENTS. Brass to John Mordon alias Andrew † 1410, a priest. The figure is 2 ft 6 in. long. – War Memorial, a life-size angel of alabaster, free-standing. Signed by *Farmer & Brindley*, the well-known firm of church sculptors. Well-meaning.

CLOCK TOWER. In the centre of the village. Erected in 1846 by a rector in memory of his wife. E.E., with three lancets each side as bell-openings. Rather depressing.

To the SE of the church a four-bay Georgian house, to the NW of the clock tower one which is gabled, but has a Georgian five-bay front.

9070

ETON

Eton to the world is Eton College, but there is also a town of 3,250 inhabitants. Eton College is the old buildings and the vast expansion of the C19 and C20 from about 300 to 500 boys in the C18 to about 1,200 now. As luck would have it this has not spoiled Eton. Arriving from Windsor one finds oneself still in a little town with its High Street and nothing unusual. Only at its end one takes in Eton College, but still as a college in the self-contained precinctual sense of a Cambridge college. Only the Hall and Library opposite the entrance gates suggest something new and big. All the rest is tucked away behind to the w.

ETON COLLEGE

33a INTRODUCTION. Eton College was founded by Henry VI in 1440, when the King was only twenty years old. As he bought the advowson of the parish church two years earlier, he must have had the idea already then. He was guided in its execution by Winchester College, which he visited in 1440. Winchester College was created by William of Wykeham as a counterpart to New College, Oxford. In the same way Henry created King's College, Cambridge, as a counterpart to Eton College. The foundation at Eton was called 'The King's College of Our Lady of Eton beside Windsor' and was to consist of a Provost, ten Fellows, four Clerks, six Choristers, a Schoolmaster, twenty-four poor and indigent Scholars, and twenty-four poor and infirm Men. Shortly after, the number of scholars was increased to seventy and an Usher, ten chaplains, and ten more choristers were added to the staff. The idea of the almshouses for poor men was given up within the first thirty years of the existence of the college, but the idea of the college in the sense of a collegiate establishment of secular priests remained as

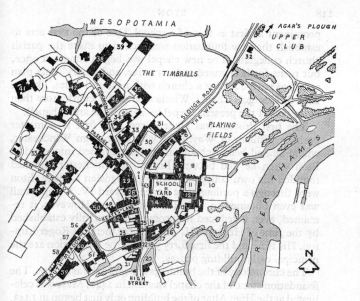

PLAN OF ETON COLLEGE

1 Burning Bush	23 Jourdelay's	45 Common Lane
2 Savile House	24 Old St Christopher's	House
3 Lower School	25 Hodgson House	46 Holland House
4 Weston's Yard	26 Carter House	47 Godolphin House
5 Lupton's Range	27 Hawtrey's	48 Manor House
6 Weston's	28 Durnford House	49 Ballards
7 New Buildings	29 School Hall	50 Keate House
8 Provost's Garden	30 New Schools	51 Waynflete
9 Provost's Lodge	31 Angelo's	52 Westbury
10 College Garden	32 Old Cricket Pavilion	53 Cotton Hall House
11 Cloister Court	33 The Hopgarden	54 Mustians
12 College Hall	34 Warre Schools	55 Walpole House
13 Brewhouse Yard	35 Wotton House	56 Montague James
14 Chapel	36 Gymnasium	School
15 Baldwin's End	37 Caxton Schools	57 Music School
16 Baldwin's Bec	38 Alington Schools	58 Science Schools
17 Baldwin's Shore	39 Drawing Schools	59 South Lawn
18 Bekynton	40 Babylon	60 Lower Chapel
19 Corner House	41 Villiers House	61 Queen's Schools
20 Barnes Pool	42 Warre House	62 Evans's
21 Gullivers	43 Farrer House	63 Upper School
22 St Christopher's	44 Penn House	

prominent at first as that of a school. One of the first acts to establish the new foundation was indeed to make the parish church collegiate. The new chapel was begun almost at once, but plans for it changed at least twice, and Henry's last plan seems to have been for a church with nave and aisles, like the later St George's Chapel, Windsor, and of a length more than twice that of the present chapel (as against the ante-chapel).

The first Provost was Henry Sever, the first Headmaster perhaps William of Waynflete, who came from Winchester, where he had been Schoolmaster. He remained interested in Eton when he had become Bishop of Winchester and had founded his own college at Oxford, Magdalen College. Eton went through a perilous time under Edward IV. A papal bull was even obtained in 1463 for its abolition. However, it remained, even if reduced in income, and was fully established by the time of Henry VIII. The provost then was Roger Lupton. His time and the first forty years of the foundation are the principal early building phases.

The chronology of the buildings appears to be as follows. The foundation stone of the chapel was laid in 1441. Mass was celebrated at the High Altar of the building only just begun in 1443. In 1443 a contract was made for the Cloister Buildings, mentioning the hall, the cloisters, the chambers (for fellows), and seven towers. Only the hall was begun in stone; the rest is of brick, a material by then not yet much appreciated in England (cf., however, the contemporary Tattershall Castle in Lincolnshire and Caister Castle in Norfolk). The Hall, though probably unfinished, was in use in 1449. The chapel went up quickly, but it looks as if, in 1449, what had been built was again pulled down to be replaced by something more ambitious. After the deposition of Henry VI work naturally slowed down, and the ante-chapel was not begun until 1479. It was finished in 1482, and the paintings in the chapel were executed between 1479 and 1488. The school was at first a detached brick range running w from the NW end of the cloister quadrangle and was built at the same time. It is the Long Chamber and Lower School of today. Only under Lupton was the w range of the cloisters with the big gate-house built. It was begun in 1517. There are Lupton bricks also at the upper w end of the Hall; so there also final completion had to wait for his time. In Lupton's w range were the Provost's Lodge and the Library.

There is no clear evidence on the masons, let alone the designers. Henry VI's master mason during the years in question was *Robert Westerley* (1439–61), but he seems to have been under a cloud in 1449–51, i.e. just at the time when the chapel was re-planned and re-started. In 1449 *James Woodrofe* of Norwich was paid for two visits to Eton. In 1448 *John Smyth* is called master mason at Eton, in 1449 *Robert Jenyns* warden of the masons. So we have the choice, and, as so often, the recorded names do not lift the essential anonymity of the work. Similarly Lupton's work seems to have been designed and supervised by *William Virtue*, King's Master Mason, *Henry Redman*, Master Mason of Westminster Abbey, and *Humphrey Coke*, later King's Master Carpenter.

After Lupton's time nothing important was built until about 1670, when Provost Allestree gave a range to close the w wide of School Yard between Lower School and Chapel. The building was badly executed and had to be rebuilt, or at least thoroughly remodelled, about 1690. The work may have been supervised by *Wren*, but was certainly carried out and probably designed by *Matthew Bankes*, Master Carpenter to the Royal Works. It was completed in 1694. The range is known as Upper School. Of C18 additions the Brewhouse of 1714 and the College Library of 1725–9 are the most notable.

Those receiving schooling at Eton are divided into scholars and oppidans. The oppidans boarded in town. This is, e.g., known of William Paston in 1479. He speaks of his 'hostess'. In 1580 Bess of Hardwick's son boarded first at an inn and then privately. As the numbers of oppidans grew, such haphazard arrangements were no longer admissible, and a system established itself of proper boarding-houses for boys, managed by dames. The term was clearly established when Horace Walpole used it in 1746.* In 1766 there were thirteen of these dames' houses. In the course of the C18 the building of boarding-houses was also undertaken by masters (e.g. the former Headmaster Andrew Snape, who built Godolphin House and Jourdelay's) and some former college servants. The system went on till in 1845 the first houses were built by the Provost and Fellows (Hawtrey and Durnford Houses). Gradually the College obtained possession of the older houses. Meanwhile conditions in College had also changed. They were abominable right through the C18 and the first third of the C19. No one can have said with conviction that Long Chamber, the dormitory above Lower School, was a suitable home during the major part of the year for fifty-two boys. Originally the Headmaster and the Usher had

* Yale Edition, IX, 1941, p. 43, to George Montagu.

slept adjoining its two ends, but that had long changed and
what cruelty and sexual aberrations went on in Long Chamber
one reads with horror and incredulity. Perhaps one ought to
temper that; for the flogging entertainments of Dr Keate, Headmaster from 1809 to 1834, are their exact counterpart. Humane
education is a recent growth. It came to Eton with Dr Hawtrey,
who in 1843 provided a new building for the collegers. New
Schools was built in 1861–3, Queen's Schools in 1889–91,
Lower Chapel in 1889–91, Warre Schools in 1904, the School
Hall and School Library in 1906–8. Meanwhile buildings for
science had begun with the Chemistry Laboratory of 1869. The
Mathematical Schools followed in 1877, the Science Schools in
1881, and all the time new boarding-houses were being opened.
They are still being built in this century, and one of them (by
Sir William Holford) is not yet complete at the time of writing.

SCHOOL YARD

The entrance is through an archway in the middle of the w range
or UPPER SCHOOL, the range which was erected *c.* 1670 and
largely rebuilt in 1689–94. It was built by *Matthew Bankes* (*see
above, p. 119*). It was damaged in the second World War and
has since been restored by *Seely & Paget*. It makes the most
undemonstrative entrance to such an establishment as Eton.
Dark brick with stone dressings. Only two storeys. The width
is eleven bays. The windows are of the cross-type and of wood,
but there are stone quoins. The roof is hidden by a stone balustrade. The entrance arch is segment-headed and has a flat rusticated stone surround. All windows have straight entablatures.
The elevation repeats to the E, i.e. to School Yard, except that
the ground floor is an open arcade, exactly as at Pembroke College, Cambridge, where entrance range and chapel are in the
same relative positions and the chapel was designed by Wren in
1663. The arcade is of solid piers with attached coupled Tuscan
columns and a metope frieze. The arches are round except for
the wider middle bay, which has a depressed rounded arch – an
awkward solution. There is a slight three-bay projection in the
centre of the E elevation. Inside, Upper School is a plain room
with windows high up and panelling below (re-done recently).
The ceiling is plain and never had much plaster enrichment.
To its N is the Headmaster's Room, which became this, i.e. the
Headmaster's form-room, in 1834. To the s of this is the spacious STAIRCASE with fat dumb-bell balusters.

In the middle of School Yard is the MONUMENT to Henry

VI. The statue is by *Francis Bird*, who was paid £443 17s. 11d. in 1719.

Along the N side runs the range known as LONG CHAMBER and LOWER SCHOOL. This is of brick, two-storeyed, long, low, and embattled. The windows are of two lights and have hoodmoulds. The oriel window at the E end is a C19 addition. On the ground floor of Lower School is the schoolroom itself, to its W the original Headmaster's Room (in which he slept as well as worked), and to its E the apartment of the Master in College, successor to the original Usher. Formerly the rooms were called Lower Chambers and used as dormitories in addition to Long Chamber. Lower School has two rows of posts to divide it into a nave and aisles. These are of *c.* 1630. They are connected longitudinally by segmental wooden arches with pendants. Midway down is a low balustrade from the posts to the wall. It has a wavy top polished to perfection by generations of bottoms. The forms also of *c.* 1630. – ORGAN. By *Snetzler*. Made for George III in 1760. Went to Eton in 1926. Very pretty.

Above is LONG CHAMBER, the dormitory of most collegers up to 1844. It is a completely plain room. The N elevation of Lower School, as seen from WESTON'S YARD, has closely-set two-light windows with transoms for Lower School proper and a more irregular fenestration further E. There are two stair towers with a third set diagonally at the NW, i.e. the Headmaster's end, from which he could reach Long Chamber.

Attached to the E end and running N is NEW BUILDINGS, Provost Hodgson's new and improved accommodation for the collegers. This was designed by *John Shaw* and built in 1844–6. It is three-storeyed, of red brick with stone diapering, and in an appropriate Tudor style. There is nothing much for or against it. Weston's Yard is triangular. At its N end, placed SW to NE, was the Jacobean Savile House. This was severely damaged in the second World War and replaced by a range of masters' houses by *Seely & Paget*. However, the impressive back, with its big chimneybreasts, survives and flanks most promisingly one side of the approach from Slough. WESTON'S, the house from which the yard received its name, stands beyond its NE corner, a mixed building of red brick with C16 and C17 parts and C18 re-fronting. It faces the Playing Fields, and the brick wall which starts from Weston's and separates the Playing Fields from the Slough Road is the scene of the Wall Game. Close to Weston's is the MEMORIAL GARDEN of King

Prajadhipok of Siam, laid out in 1929. In it a bronze STATUE of
Perseus by *Lajos Strobl*.

34   Back now into School Yard, as we came. The E range is LUP-
TON'S RANGE, dominated by the commanding Gatehouse. The
range was built of brick in 1517–*c*. 20. The gatehouse has four
storeys, the polygonal turrets five plus open crowning lead
cupolas, probably of the C18, the rest of the range two. In the
middle of the gatehouse is a two-storeyed stone oriel with large
transomed windows. Immediately above the archway two
angels holding a heraldic shield. Higher up small medallion of
the Assumption. On the l. side of the oriel picked out in black
brick the lily-pot of the Annunciation. Below the archway inside, a very fan-like lierne-vault with panels left without arches
or cusping. The l. hand upper windows are very closely-set, and
that, in the college tradition, represents library fenestration.
The r. hand fenestration is different. There are here two transomed four-light windows. At the s end is a square tower.

THE CHAPEL

7   The chapel is not attached to Lupton's range. It stands free to the
E with a small walled churchyard below its E and S windows. The
chapel consists of the choir and the ante-chapel, as do such
Oxford college chapels as that of New College and Merton
College. New College may be its immediate pattern, although
the older Merton Chapel represents more closely the situation
as it was at Eton. Merton had been intended to have a nave to
the W of a crossing and transepts. The nave was not built, and the
transept became the ante-chapel, an ideal plan for the special
job of a college. At Eton also, at least for a short time, a nave was
meant to continue the chancel. The chapel itself was built from
1449 to *c*. 1460 and from *c*. 1469 to *c*. 1475, and the ante-chapel
was added *c*. 1479–82. The chapel and ante-chapel are just
under 190 ft long inside. This compares with 290 ft for King's,
Cambridge, begun in 1446, with 230 ft for St George's Windsor,
begun in 1474, and with 130 ft for Henry VII's Chapel at Westminster Abbey, begun *c*. 1503 – i.e. the other great royal chapels
of the later Perp style which are amongst the most lavish and
most characteristic buildings of their time in England. Eton
Chapel proper is eight bays long with tall transomed windows
under four-centred heads. The E window has nine lights and its
arch shows a change of plan from a steep to a (stylistically later)
less steep slope – a change which is probably connected with the
break between *c*. 1460 and *c*. 1470. The E front is flanked by

polygonal turrets, as are the ends of King's and St George's. The side windows start above a high bare dado and are of five lights in an intersected three-plus-three rhythm. Pinnacles crown the buttresses. The stairs up to the N porch are of 1694–5. The ante-chapel is lower than the chapel proper and has seven-light windows to N and S and five-light windows to the W, i.e. the street. Big S porch S of the W end built as the entrance for townspeople. Stone staircase of 1624 corresponding to the N staircase mentioned above in connexion with Upper School.

The interior achieves greatness by means of uncompromising 12 consistency. The whole is the outcome of a single thought. There is no variety, there are no surprises, or at least there were none until recently; for now there is *Sir William Holford*'s simplified fan-vault. The vault is no doubt visually satisfactory, and that is perhaps all that should matter. Structurally it is not a fan-vault in the Tudor sense. The roof construction is of steel and the panels of the fan-vault are of light-weight concrete, stone-faced and set in T-section steel framing. The ribs are attached to the framing too. So the vault is really suspended, not carrying. But then, all art is make-believe, and the gospel of strict structural honesty is less than two hundred years old. If one is worried by doubts in looking up into the vault, the reasons are different. Should the Eton College authorities have interfered with their venerable chapel at all? Should they not have regarded it as complete, even if completed only by a roof which, in its state of 1950, dated only from 1699? My own answer would be the same as that which they gave. The roof was neither original Tudor work, nor worthy of the chapel. It could be replaced by a roof or vault worthy of it, and of course worthy of the century that chose to erect it. But can the answer then be a fan-vault, that is essentially an imitation of an Early Tudor vault? Sir William Holford's vault is visually different from vaults put up under Henry VII and Henry VIII only in so far as the panels which decorate the fans (and justify the name) have neither arches nor cusps, but even for that there was the precedent at Eton of the vault inside Lupton's gatehouse. So the layman must be considered right who even now looks at the new vault as an ancient vault. To justify a period piece it would in my opinion be necessary to be able to prove that such a vault had been the intention of those who built or at least completed the chapel. The proof cannot be given. The buttresses outside indicate an intention to vault. The five shafts up the walls at the springing of each bay could point to a fan-vault (wall-arch, fan, transverse arch, fan, wall-arch, as Sir William Holford has done it), but as well to a lierne-vault. However, even if on this score one grants Sir William Holford the benefit of the doubt, the question yet remains as to whether this is the vault one would have expected from the designer of the precincts of St Paul's. At St Paul's, the problem was to combine a monument of venerable age with new elements whole-heartedly in the style of the C20. Was the situation at Eton not the same? Architects on the Continent, faced with buildings damaged in the second World War, have shown that a radical juxtaposition of old and new can come off. Basil Spence's vault for his cathedral at Coventry is designed to be of the C20 yet not out of sympathy with the Gothic past. Admittedly, a vault like that projected for Coventry would not have done for Eton. What should it then have looked like? The critic is in the enviable position of not having to give an answer. Sir William Holford's answer, coming from this particular architect, remains puzzling.

To return to the C15 work, the supports for the vault consist of five shafts. The four E bays have blank stone panelling to the ground. The rest has the wall paintings, on which *see* below. Off the N side the Porch, off this to the E Memorial Chapel (probably former Vestry), and off that to the E LUPTON'S CHAPEL, a chantry chapel erected by Provost Lupton *c.* 1510–15 and accessible also from the Presbytery. It has a fan-vault with a pendant boss, a five-light window, and a stone SCREEN with a four-centred arch to the chancel. To the Memorial Chapel the blank panelling of the chancel is simply opened, an effect similar to that of the side chapels at King's, Cambridge.

SCREEN between ante-chapel and chapel by *Street*, 1882. – ORGAN on the screen, huge, the case by *Pearson*, 1885–7. – DOOR from the NW porch original. – STALLS, 1849–50 by Mr *Deeson* and Mr *Rattee* (the latter of the future firm of Rattee & Kett of Cambridge). The canopies were removed in 1923 to expose the paintings. – LECTERN. Of brass; C15 with heavily moulded base on four lions, moulded stem, and double book-rest with pierced patterns. – SCULPTURE. Statue of Henry VI, by *John Bacon*, 1786. Of surprisingly Victorian sentiment. He holds a model of the chapel and looks up. – WALL PAINTINGS. In the chapel. *See* the paragraph below. In the ante-chapel handsome Victorian heraldic painting. – PAINTINGS. Adoration of the Lamb, Neapolitan School, C17 (Memorial Chapel, W wall). – Presentation in the Temple, by *Benjamin West*, about

9 by 6 ft (Lupton's Chapel, E wall). – Sir Galahad, by *G. F. Watts*; a replica painted by him (S wall, opposite the pulpit). – TAPESTRY. Star of Bethlehem, by *Morris & Co.*, designed by *Burne-Jones*, 1895. The side panels were added by Morris & Co., adapted from designs by Burne-Jones at Salisbury Cathedral (E wall, below the window). – STAINED GLASS. E window by *Evie Hone*, 1949–52. Last Supper, Crucifixion, and Old Testament figures. A triumph for the authorities of Eton, which refused to be satisfied with the anaemic glass put into so many churches of England before and after the second World War. Here is bold, vigorous design and strong, glowing colour. – N and S windows of the E bays designed by *John Piper* and made by *Reyntiens*. Only the first installed at the time of writing, a powerful, nearly abstract composition.

WALL PAINTINGS. Executed *c.* 1479–88 and paid for to at 18 least two painters, one *Gilbert*, the other *William Baker*. Baker is only mentioned in 1488. In 1483 a 'presbyter magister pictorum' appears in the documents. The paintings were done in two strips along the three W bays of the chapel proper. They were whitewashed in the C16, re-discovered in 1847, and uncovered in 1923 and restored by *Tristram*. The upper strips on both walls were found to have been destroyed beyond repair. Only one scene is here still recognizable. The bottom strips, however, survive, and are the most important remaining example of monumental C15 painting in England. The strips show scenes from the miracles of the Virgin interrupted by single figures of saints painted in imitation of sculpture. The scenes are in monochrome with touches of colour. The S strip tells the story of the empress falsely accused and the help given her by the Virgin, a story familiar from Chaucer. On the N side, first the miracle of the woman who died unconfessed, was restored to life, confessed, and died again; then the story of the woman whose son was a captive and who seized the child of a statue of the Virgin and was given back her son; then the story of the lady who had a vision of the Virgin present at Mass and woke up and found herself holding a candle from the visionary Mass; then the severely damaged story of Amoras selling his wife to the devil; and finally that of the man who threw a stone at an image of the Virgin and fell down dead when he saw blood gush forth from the child's body. The style is wholly Netherlandish, and nearest to that of Dirk and his son Albert Bouts.

MONUMENTS. BRASSES in the ante-chapel: Vice-Provost Barker † 1489 (15 in.). – Provost Bost † 1503 (4 ft, under a triple

canopy, the only outstanding one of the brasses). – Richard
Arden † 1509 (18 in.). – Early C16 Cleric (16 in.). – Early C16
Lady (2 ft). – Lord Grey † 1521 (19 in.). – William Boutrod
† 1522 (2 ft). – William Horman, Headmaster, † 1535 (16 in.). –
Vice-Provost Edgecomb † 1545 (three-quarter figure; 13 in.). –
Elizabeth Stokys † 1560. – Provost Lupton (Lupton Chapel),
made c. 1536 (37 in.). – Provost Murray † 1623, the biggest of
the monuments. Alabaster. Frontal bust in arched recess with
big scrolly volutes l. and r. This part of the monument stands
on a slab supported by a pillar and two female caryatid busts.
Behind the corpse of the provost, l. and r. of this centre, black
columns on high bases. Flat arch with inscription in strapwork
cartouche. Superstructure with arms, etc. – Provost Wotton,
i.e. Sir Henry Wotton, former Ambassador to Venice, † 1639.
Large floor slab of black marble. – Provost Allestree † 1680. By
William Stanton (attribution by Mrs Esdaile). – Provost
Godolphin † 1732. Two big architectural monuments without
effigy (N porch). – Earl Waldegrave, by *Bacon*, 1796 (N porch).
Tablet with a putto by an urn in front of an obelisk. – Edward
Tew † 1817. By *Whitelaw* (N porch). A fully clothed genius
with wings rising against a black slab. – Dr Hawtrey, Headmaster and Provost, † 1862. By *Nicholl*, designed by *Woodyer*.
Recumbent effigy in an arched recess. – Dr Balston, Headmaster. 1892 by *Farmer & Brindley*. Recumbent effigy on a
tomb-chest (S wall, fourth bay).

CLOISTER COURT

The ranges round Cloister Court were built between 1441 and c.
1460, although it is not known how much was actually finished
when Henry VI was deposed. Brick, of two storeys with stone
dressings. A second upper storey in the N and E ranges was
added by *Stiff Leadbetter* in 1759–62. Four cloister walks with
stair-turrets in the corners. That on the NW was enlarged and
made more comfortable in 1618. The passage through Lupton's Tower arrives close to the S end of the W range. The tower
here has two tiers of five-light windows with two transoms
instead of the W oriel. In the S range is the Hall with the C18
Library over. The N and E ranges were built for fellows' sets;
hence the numerous square stair and garderobe turrets on the
outer sides to the E and N. Ground floor arcaded, of stone, with
four-centred arches. Fine wrought-iron RAILINGS of the C18
in the arcade openings. Upper floor with four-light straight-
headed windows, the lights arched. Original doorways set in

pairs and original small ground-floor windows. On the E side of the E range the C18 storey seems to incorporate C15 windows. On the ground floor here some original windows with mullions and transoms. The N front of the S range towards the court was remodelled in 1729. Two-and-a-half storeys, seven bays with a three-bay projection crowned by a balustrade.

Of interiors around Cloister Court the following deserve special notice. In the W (Lupton's) range, which is part of the Provost's Lodge, at the N end the MAGNA PARLURA, with panelling of 1624 and a big mid-Victorian chimneypiece incorporating mid-C17 panels. The Parlour is followed by the ELECTION HALL, which has some original stained-glass medallions and a screen with bulgy Tuscan columns above a dado with bulgy pilasters. Can this screen be as early as 1549? Historically it is tempting to suggest such a date, as it is that of the conversion of the room into a private Dining Room by the first married Provost, Sir Thomas Smith (later of Hill Hall, Essex). After the Election Hall the ELECTION CHAMBER, where boys were elected not only as collegers for Eton but also from Eton to King's. The chamber lies in Lupton's Tower behind the oriel window. It has late C17 panelling. At the S end of the range a private door gives the Provost direct access to Hall. A new range to provide more spacious and commodious rooms was added to the Provost's Lodge in 1765–6. It projects N from the NE corner, i.e. lies immediately E of New Buildings (through which the entrance to the Lodge is now arranged). In the N range along the cloister, at its NW corner, on the ground floor, a Queen Anne room with an apsed recess (for a hand-basin?). Off the N range, near the E end, a Kitchen built for Lady Smith, now a lecture room.

In the S range is the COLLEGE HALL, accessible up a much-renewed staircase. The entrance arch to the staircase shows a remodelling by Lupton of the arch of the 1440s. The Hall has a 35a tall canted bay window to the S and three big fireplaces. They are said to have been found without flues. The canopy behind the High Table is of 1858. The stained glass here is also Victorian, as is the West Gallery. The usual three doorways from the screens passage to the offices. But here two now lead into the buttery, and the third to a staircase. The KITCHEN is a separate square brick building to the S. The brickwork looks C16 rather than C15. The upper part is octagonal. Wooden ribs; purlins with wind-braces; lantern. The transition from square to octagon by coving. Two big fireplaces.

Next to the Hall the COLLEGE LIBRARY, installed here from
its former position in 1729, when the work begun in 1725 t
Thomas Rowland's plan was complete. The room is perhaps th
finest in the college, except for the chapel. It is tripartite, of tw
square side parts and an oblong centre. In the plaster ceilin
(by *Worrall*) this is represented by two circles and an oval.
balcony runs round each part. The openings between th
parts, which are not in the middle of the walls, are set out with
fluted wooden columns, oddly of the Ionic order not only below
but also above. In the middle of the back wall of the centre par
a fireplace with pilasters. Above it the date 1736. The wood
work is by one *Richards*.

BREWHOUSE YARD

By passing through a passage in the E range, or more easily through
the gap in School Yard between Lupton's range and the chapel
one enters Brewhouse Yard, an irregular and picturesque back
yard, which gives, however, the best view of the C15 hall and it
big traceried bay window. C18 brick at the top, but at the W end
C16 brickwork. Pretty Gothic louvre, probably C19. Opposit
the Hall, facing W, the BREWHOUSE, built in 1714. This is o
seven bays and two storeys and has segment-headed window
and a hipped roof. By an archway from Brewhouse Yard on
can leave the precinct and start a perambulation of the town a
Baldwin's End (*see* p. 132 below).

THE WESTERN REACHES

More or less opposite Upper School is what might be called th
hub of Eton but is more commonly known as the BURNIN
BUSH, an ornate wrought-iron lamp standard put up in 1864
May it be steadfastly preserved. Opposite this to the W th
SCHOOL HALL and SCHOOL LIBRARY, built in 1906–8 to th
designs of *L. K. Hall*. As Austen-Leigh's invaluable guidebook
puts it, 'they carry on Wren's great English tradition'. Austen
Leigh continues: 'The ornament may be excessive.' He i
right in this. They are in fact the only buildings at Eton which
seriously jar. They are of brick with ample stone dressings. Th
library is a domed polygon and in its conception depends on th
Radcliffe Camera at Oxford, outdoing that model, however, i
ornamentation – an ornamentation as much indebted to th
French C18 (via Sir Reginald Blomfield?) as to the English
Internally the Library is preposterously impractical as regard
seating as well as shelving. Instead of better accommodation

(a) *Scenery:* The Chilterns. View from Hampden Bottom

(b) *Scenery:* The Thames and Harleyford Manor, by Sir
Robert Taylor, 1755 (*Copyright Country Life*)

I

Scenery: Fingest, with the Norman church

(a) *Townscape:* High Wycombe, with the Guildhall, by Henry Keene, 1757, and Market Hall, rebuilt by Robert Adam, 1761

(b) *Townscape:* Beaconsfield, London End

(b) *Norman Church Exteriors*: Dinton, south doorway

(a) *Saxon Church Exterior*: Wing, apse

4

Norman Church Exteriors: Water Stratford, south doorway

5

(a) *Early English Church Exteriors:* Edlesborough, east window

(b) *Decorated Church Exteriors:* Olney

Perpendicular Church Exteriors: Eton College Chapel, fifteenth century

(a) *Church Exteriors*: Willen, by Robert Hooke,
1679–80

(b) *Church Exteriors*: Hartwell, by Henry Keene,
1753–5

8

(b) *Norman Church Interiors*: Upton

(a) *Church Exteriors*: Gerrards Cross,
by Sir William Tite, 1859

9

(a) *Early English:* Ivinghoe, capital
of north arcade

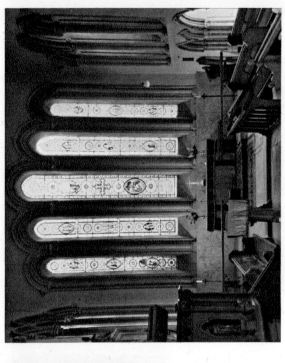

(b) *Early English Church Interiors:* Chetwode

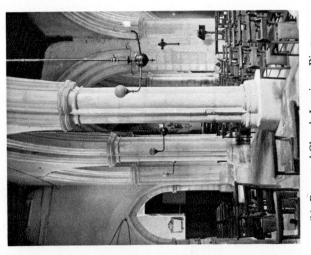

(a) *Early English Church Interiors:*
Princes Risborough

(b) *Decorated Church Interiors:* Bierton

11

Perpendicular Church Interiors: Eton College Chapel, fifteenth century. The fan-vault is by Sir William Holford, 1957

Church Interiors, Vaulting: Hartwell, by Henry Keene, 1753–5

(a) *Church Interiors and Furnishings:* Jordans, Friends'
Meeting House, 1688

(b) *Church Interiors and Furnishings:* Wotton Underwood,
with stone screen of 1867

14

Church Furnishings: Aylesbury, font, late twelfth century

Church Furnishings: Stone, font, Norman

(a) *Church Furnishings*: Edlesborough, pulpit canopy, Perpendicular

(b) *Church Furnishings*: Cheddington, pulpit, Jacobean

17

Church Furnishings: Eton College Chapel, wall paintings, by William Baker and Gilbert, *c.* 1479–88

(*Copyright Country Life*)

(a) *Church Furnishings*: Broughton, wall painting, c. 1400

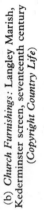

(b) *Church Furnishings*: Langley Marish, Kederminster screen, seventeenth century
(*Copyright Country Life*)

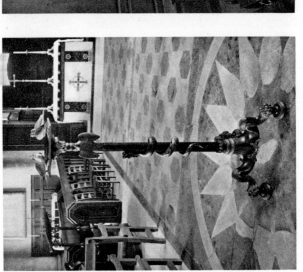

(a) *Church Furnishings*: West Wycombe, font, eighteenth century

(b) *Church Furnishings*: West Wycombe, lectern, eighteenth century

(b) *Church Monuments*: Chenies, monument to the first Earl of Bedford, † 1555, and wife

(a) *Church Monuments*: Clifton Reynes, tomb-chest, c. 1380

(a) *Church Monuments*: Wing, monument to
Sir Robert Dormer, 1552

(b) *Church Monuments*: Hardmead, monument
to Francis Catesby, † 1636

22

(a) *Church Monuments*: Amersham, monument to Henry Curwen, † 1636, by Edward Marshall

(b) *Church Monuments*: Walton, monument to Bartholomew Beale and wife, by Thomas Burman, 1672

(a) *Church Monuments:* Castlethorpe, monument to
Sir Thomas Tyrril, † 1671

(b) *Church Monuments:* Quainton, monument to Richard Winwood
and wife, by Thomas Stayner, 1689

Church Monuments: Ravenstone, monument to the
first Earl of Nottingham, † 1682

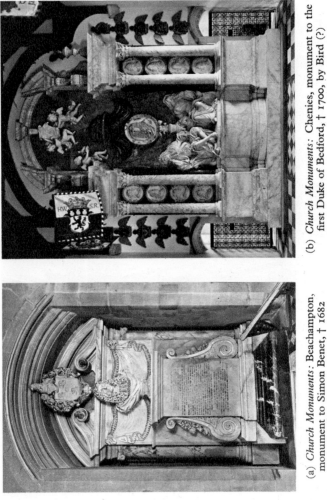

(a) *Church Monuments:* Beachampton, monument to Simon Benet, † 1682

(b) *Church Monuments:* Chenies, monument to the first Duke of Bedford, † 1700, by Bird (?)

(a) *Church Monuments*: Quainton, monument to Mr Justice Dormer, *c.* 1728–30

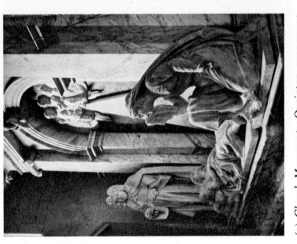

(b) *Church Monuments*: Drayton Beauchamp, monument to Lord Newhaven, † 1728, by William Woodman

Church Monuments: Gayhurst, monument to Sir Nathan Wright
and his son, *c.* 1728

Church Monuments: Amersham, monument to Mrs Elizabeth Drake,
† 1757, by Cheere

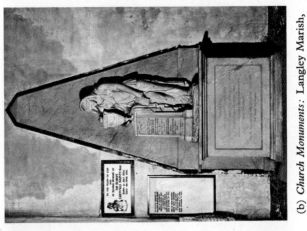

(a) *Church Monuments*: High Wycombe, monument to the Earl of Shelburne, by Scheemakers, *c.* 1754

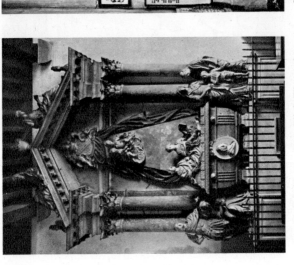

(b) *Church Monuments*: Langley Marish, monument to David Harvey, † 1788

30

Church Monuments: Whitchurch, monument to John Westcar, † 1833, by Gibson

Church Monuments: Chenies, monument to Lord Arthur Russell,
† 1892, by Gilbert

(a) Eton College, from the east, mid fifteenth century

(b) Eton College, Lower School, mid fifteenth century, posts *c.* 1630

Eton College, Lupton's Range, 1517–c. 20

(a) Eton College, Hall, bay window, fifteenth century (*Copyright Country Life*)

(b) Aylesbury, King's Head Hotel, fifteenth century

35

(a) Nether Winchendon House, panelling and decoration, *c.* 1530

(b) Dorton House, plaster ceiling and fireplace, *c.* 1620

36

(a) Gayhurst House, 1597 and early seventeenth century

(b) Hartwell House, Jacobean

(a) Radcliffe, manor house, staircase, c. 1631

(b) Princes Risborough, manor house, staircase, c. 1670 (*Copyright Country Life*)

Kingsey, Tythrop House, staircase, late seventeenth century

(a) Hall Barn, after 1651

(b) Bradenham, manor house, c. 1670

Fawley Court, plaster ceiling, 1691

(a) Stoke Mandeville, Stoke House, c. 1700

(b) Denham Place, room with stucco frieze in the coving, 1692 (*Copyright Country Life*)

Winslow Hall, by Sir Christopher Wren (?), 1700

(a) Chicheley Hall, by Thomas Archer (?), *c.* 1698–1703

(b) Wotton House, by Sir James Thornhill (?), 1704–14

(a) Marlow Place, by Thomas Archer (?), *c.* 1720

(b) Aylesbury, County Hall, Court Room, *c.* 1700

Stowe, north front, c. 1720-5. Portico by Sir John Vanbrugh (?)

(b) Stowe, Gothic Temple, by James Gibbs, c. 1740

(a) Stowe, Temple of Venus, by William Kent (?), before 1732

(a) Stowe, Rotondo, by Sir John Vanbrugh, *c.* 1719

(b) Stowe, Temple of British Worthies, by William Kent, 1733

Stowe, Hall, *c.* 1775 (*Copyright Country Life*)

50

(a) Great Hampden, Hampden House, gothicized by Thomas Iremonger, 1751

(b) West Wycombe, entrance to the caves, 1750–2

Nether Winchendon House, gothicized c. 1780

Middle Claydon, Claydon House, staircase hall, *c.* 1765
(*Copyright Country Life*)

Middle Claydon, Claydon House, North Hall, *c.* 1765

Middle Claydon, Claydon House, ceiling of Gothic Room, c. 1765 (*Copyright Country Life*)

Middle Claydon, Claydon House, Chinese Room, *c.* 1765

West Wycombe Park, south front, by John Donovell (?), c. 1760

(a) Shardeloes, by Stiff Leadbetter and Robert Adam, 1758–66

(b) Stowe, Gothic Library, by Sir John Soane, 1803–6

(a) Tyringham, gateway, by Sir John Soane, 1793–7

(b) Stoke Poges, Stoke Park, by Robert Nasmyth, wings, dome, and colonnade by James Wyatt, c. 1800–5 and after 1823 (?)

(a) Marlow, suspension bridge, by William Tierney Clark, 1831-6

(b) Dropmore House, aviary, early nineteenth century
(*Copyright Country Life*)

Mentmore House, by Sir Joseph Paxton and G. H. Stokes, 1852–4

(a) Cliveden, by Sir Charles Barry, 1850

(b) Waddesdon Manor, by H. A. G. W. Destailleur, completed 1883

Halton House, 1884, central hall

(a) Hall Barn, lodge

(b) Chalfont St Giles, Shrub's Wood, by Mendelsohn
& Chermayeff, 1934-5

(a) Denham, Rank Laboratories, by Gropius & Fry, 1936

(b) High Wycombe, High School for Girls, by
Denis Clarke Hall, 1955-6

it offers giant coupled columns set always to the immediate l.
and r. of an angle of the polygon, and stucco ornament in the
dome. The Hall is very large indeed and has a stuccoed tunnel-
vault on coupled Corinthian giant columns set against the wall.
The platform opening is a little narrower than the rest, and
again framed by giant columns. At the entrance end a gallery,
also tunnel-vaulted, and E of that a low ante-room with groin-
vaults on coupled unfluted Ionic columns. Between Hall and
Library was originally an open arcade. This is now closed, and
the resulting room has nice sky-lights.

From this hub of the C20 college to the N is NEW SCHOOLS,
designed by *Woodyer* and built in 1861–3. This is remarkably
successful for its date. The shape is of an L to the S, with a cloister. Red brick with dark diapering. The principal motif is a
sturdy square tower in the re-entrant angle. A wing was added
at the back in 1876–7, facing the SLOUGH ROAD. It contains the
MATHEMATICAL SCHOOLS. Opposite, the impressive range
of chimneybreasts of Savile House, *see* p. 121. N of the wing of
1876 THE TIMBRALLS of 1865. Across the bridge follow the
playing fields. The old CRICKET PAVILION is by the lodge to
Upper Club (1866 and 1876), the new on AGAR'S PLOUGH
(1901–2 by *Sir T. G. Jackson*).*

Back to the School Library and off to the N along COMMON
LANE. On the l. the MANOR HOUSE, white brick, utilitarian,
and then, set back a little, GODOLPHIN HOUSE, built as a
boarding-house in 1722. Six bays, red and vitreous brick, three
storeys, with a later fourth. Closed porch with two columns
between two pillars. To the r. of Godolphin House, facing down
the street towards the old buildings of the college, COMMON
LANE HOUSE, C18, low, of five bays and two storeys. Common
Lane House stands in a fork between Judy's Passage and the
continuation of Common Lane. Here on the r. WARRE
SCHOOLS, 1904, by *T. B. Carter*, red brick, plain, neo-later-
C17 with two gables. Recessed centre with three plain entrance
arches. Then, lying back and at r. angles, ANGELO'S, built as a
boarding-house c. 1790, red brick, of six bays and three storeys.
Much further back and facing The Timbralls, i.e. the large
playing fields, WOTTON HOUSE of 1903, designed by *T. E.
Collcutt*. This was much larger and more formal than any of
the boys' houses had been before. Utilitarian neo-Georgian,
brick with stone dressings, of eleven bays and four storeys with
a steep two-bay pediment to one side, a four-bay pediment to

* By *Jackson* also the CLUB-HOUSE on Queen's Eyot.

the other. Big hipped roof. Back into Common Lane and past
the GYMNASIUM of 1907 (by *T. B. Carter*; extension 1938)
with its gabled front, past PENN HOUSE opposite, a High
Victorian white-brick horror of 1860, partly a villa, partly a
four-storeyed addition to it, to CAXTON SCHOOLS, built for
the Savile Press in 1903–4 (by *T. B. Carter*), a handsome brick
building with gabled wings and recessed centre opened in four
big mullioned and triple-transomed windows with many
mouldings. Buttresses between them, and on the buttresses
crouching figures. Big arched window in the end wall of the l.
wing. Opposite, WARRE HOUSE, another High Victorian contribution, also of 1860. Down a passage by Caxton Schools are
the ALINGTON SCHOOLS, an L-shaped red-brick structure of
1926–7. By *W. A. Forsyth*, in a free neo-Tudor. The passage
leads into a large asphalted yard. At its end the DRAWING
SCHOOLS by *Forsyth* which were opened in 1930. This is a
pretty design with a central arcade with a raised centre and one-
bay one-storeyed pavilions l. and r. Behind the bare high brick
wall on the r. are the Fives Courts. In the NW corner of the yard
the DULEEP SINGH MEMORIAL GARDEN of 1928, by *Imrie
& Angell*. A little further NW ends Common Lane.

Now a new start must be made from the Burning Bush to the
s. Opposite Upper School and Chapel are two nearly identical,
rather bleak Tudor houses, one being HAWTREY'S. They date
from 1845. Turn then into KEATE'S LANE, although visually
it is more rewarding to walk up than down Keate's Lane. Only
in doing that does its gentle curve have the full effect of unroll-
ing the picture of the chapel. In Keate's Lane, first on the r. side
BALLARDS, C18, of two storeys with an (imported) very fine
Kentian doorcase. Then KEATE HOUSE, built *c.* 1785. This is
detached, of red brick, five bays wide and two-and-a-half
storeys high, with a hipped roof and a pedimented doorway.
After that again a fork. To the r. ETON WICK ROAD. On the l.
WALPOLE HOUSE of 1906 by *Collcutt*, big, three-storeyed, and
neo-Georgian, and the smaller, more domestic, also neo-
Georgian MUSTIANS of 1937 by *Sir Hubert Worthington*. Opposite, WAYNFLETE and WESTBURY, both big neo-Tudor,
and both of 1899–1900 by *Collcutt*, his first Eton jobs. Then a
footpath to FARRER HOUSE, a building by *Sir William Holford*, completed in 1959. It is for fifty boys, whose rooms are in
the gently curved s range. The range is of pre-cast concrete construction and faced with light brick. It has a low-pitched roof.
Behind it the Dressing Room, Common Room, etc., and at the

NW corner the housemaster's quarters, also gently curved.
Behind VILLIERS HOUSE, also by *Sir William Holford*, is going
up at the time of writing. It faces Farrer House across a garden
and is of similar materials but varied design. Villiers House
can be reached by Judy's Passage too (*see* p. 129). Eton Wick
Road continues with COTTON HALL HOUSE of 1869–70.
The road leads to Eton Wick and the College Sanatorium (*see*
p. 133).

At Keate House one can also turn l. The street is called
SOUTH MEADOW LANE. It has a range of schools and laboratories on the r., none of special interest (MONTAGUE JAMES
SCHOOL, 1956 by *Sir Hubert Worthington*; MUSIC SCHOOL,
1903; SCIENCE SCHOOLS, 1881, 1898, and 1958–9, the latter
extension by *Sir William Holford*), and on the l. the impressive
group of Lower Chapel and Queen's Schools. This was the next
conspicuous addition after New Schools. Both were designed
by *Sir Arthur Blomfield* and built in 1889–91 with a big addition
of 1903–5. LOWER CHAPEL is large, Perp, of stone, with a low
s aisle. It has no tower, but a stair-turret at the SW end. –
STAINED GLASS by *Kempe*, E window 1894, the rest gradually
to 1903. – PANELLING with Renaissance arches, surprising
but convincing. By *Tapper & Reynolds*. – TAPESTRIES. Designed by *Lady Chilston* and woven by *Morris & Co.*, *c.* 1920.
– The QUEEN'S SCHOOLS and MUSEUM adjoin the chapel in
a picturesque way. Red brick with dark diapering, Early Tudor
with cloister arcading of depressed pointed arches. The
cloister is reached from the street by an archway. SW of the
Queen's Schools SOUTH LAWN, a utilitarian-looking boys'
house of 1869 and 1904. Back to the High Street which must
now be walked properly.

THE HIGH STREET

We start s of Keate's Lane, with CARTER HOUSE, built as a
boarding-house in 1737. Red brick, five bays, four storeys, with
a doorcase with Tuscan columns. Then HODGSON HOUSE,
with an Elizabethan front of 1844 and an Early Georgian back;
OLD ST CHRISTOPHER'S, Early Georgian, of brick, formerly
three-storeyed (with the room of Pop, the Eton society, on the
ground floor) and ST CHRISTOPHER'S, two-storeyed, plastered white and dating from the early C19. Here an archway
leads through to JOURDELAY'S, a very handsome house of *c.*
1720, seven bays wide and originally two-and-a-half storeys
high, with a wing of 1864–6 coming forward on the l. Doorway

with attached unfluted Ionic columns, a decorated pulvinated frieze, and a pediment. The house was built as a boarding-house. Next to St Christopher's GULLIVERS, of red brick, also C18, and opposite CORNER HOUSE and BEKYNTON, three-storeyed, red, and of the late C17. The corner of Bekynton faces Barnes Pool and adjoins BALDWIN'S SHORE, a delightful gabled and plastered C17 house. It is the oldest surviving boarding-house, known to have been used as such in 1682. The lane ends by the archway into Brewhouse Yard (p. 128) and here, by the side of the archway, is BALDWIN'S END, a pretty neo-Tudor house of three bays and only two storeys, by Bodley's pupil *T. B. Carter*, 1908.

On in the High Street beyond Barnes Pool Bridge. The street now forgets the college and becomes the long, far from straight High Street of any small Bucks town.* Of houses the following – all minor – deserve a glance: No. 42 with a pretty shop-front of *c.* 1787, ETON SQUARE off to the l. with the former ALMS-HOUSES founded by Provost Godolphin in 1714, red-brick, two-storeyed, with hipped roof and segment-headed windows. Then in the High Street the COCKPIT CAFÉ, a timber-framed pre-Reformation house with an oversailing upper floor. Then No. 90 on the other side, early C18, a little more ambitious than the others. Red brick, four bays plus a narrower one at the end. The ground floor altered. The CROWN AND CUSHION is C17, of three storeys with an oriel on cast-iron columns. The end is friendly, casual, and undistinguished, as is by and large the whole street.

ST JOHN, High Street. Set back. With a S tower and W gable to the street. Interior big with tall, octagonal piers. Victorian stencilling on the aisle walls. By *B. Ferrey*, 1852–4. – STAINED GLASS. E window by *O'Connor*, 1865.

OUR LADY OF SORROWS (R.C.), Meadow Lane. 1914 by *Alfred Lord Braye*. Small, of stone, with a Continental Baroque front and no tower.

ETON WICK

ST JOHN BAPTIST. By *A. Blomfield*, 1867–9. Dark red and blue brick. Geometrical tracery. Nave and chancel in one, wilful

---

* A postscript to the college buildings is the pair of masters' houses built by *F. R. S. Yorke* in 1935 at Willowbrook. They are in the most progressive 'International Modern' of that moment, brick, cubic, with large horizontal windows.

bell-turret placed diagonally over their junction. s vestry. The
brick is exposed inside the church.

ETON COLLEGE SANATORIUM. Red brick with blue diapering,
with a number of shaped gables. Built in 1843, and enlarged in
1896.

(BELL FARM, ⅓ m. NW. Timber-framed with brick infilling. Of
the later c 14. The plan is still complete, though much has been
added. Hall in the centre, solar in the w wing, kitchen etc. in
the E wing. Both wings are gabled. A complete roof truss of the
Hall remains. RCHM)

EYTHROPE see UPPER WINCHENDON

FARNHAM COMMON   9080

ST JOHN EVANGELIST. 1907–8, by *C. Ford Whitcomb* (GR).
EGYPT END. 1936, by *Val Harding & Tecton*. Reinforced concrete. L-shaped. The larger arm is two-storeyed and faces s.
The short arm has only one storey, which contains one large
living room. The terrace above this is continued as a balcony
along the bedrooms on the upper floor of the long arm. An
inner staircase as well as an outer spiral staircase of iron. The
latter may well be termed the *leitmotif* of the most progressive
English architects of the thirties.

FARNHAM ROYAL   9080

ST MARY. By *Eden Nesfield*, 1867–9. The medieval chancel was
kept, see the blocked s doorway. Nesfield's building is big, of
flint, with irregular streaks of brick, w tower with pyramid roof.
The clock is placed asymmetrically in a somewhat perverse
position. Inside arcades with circular piers and double-
chamfered arches, and at their springing, instead of the small
half-pyramids which one finds sometimes in c 14 arcades,
grossly oversized half-cones. – STAINED GLASS. One s window
by *Kempe*, 1900. – PLATE. Cup and Cover Paten of 1569; c 17
Dutch Spoon.

FARNHAM PARK (Rehabilitation Centre). Built as Farnham
Royal House by *Nesfield*. The N side a c20 addition. To the s
picturesquely gabled and largely tile-hung façade.

FAWLEY

ST MARY. W tower of the C13 with corbel-table. The part above
Perp. The transepts are of 1883. The chancel, by far the most
interesting part of the church, was rebuilt in 1748 for John
Freeman of Fawley Court and refitted shortly after. The
fittings were bought from Canons, near Edgware, the Duke of
Chandos's palace. The chancel has an arched E window with a
blank framing by pilasters inside so as to give it the appearance
of a Venetian window. The pilaster motif is taken round the
corner on to the N and S walls and forms one more blank bay
there. Round chancel arch. – From Canons the FONT, the
STALLS, the PANELLING, the COMMUNION RAIL, the PUL-
PIT with beautiful carving including cherubs' heads, the
READER'S DESK, also carved, and the PEWS. – PLATE. Chalice
and Paten, presented in 1705. – MONUMENT. Sir James
Whitelock † 1632. Originally in a small burial ground of its own.
Two recumbent effigies, she lying a little higher and behind
him. Two attached columns, top with pedimental gable, two
small figures, and achievement. – FREEMAN MAUSOLEUM in
the churchyard, erected in 1750, now mostly hidden by yew-
trees, and moreover smothered by ivy. Octagonal ashlared
substructure, circular top part with dome, in ashlar rustication.
Domed interior. – MACKENZIE MAUSOLEUM, also in the
churchyard. Very heavy granite structure, in a cyclopic
Grecian style. Erected in 1862.

FAWLEY COURT. Built in 1684 for William Freeman, a typical
house of its date, but externally much smoothed over in 1771.
The type is the same as that of Denham Place. H-plan, two
storeys, hipped roof, red brick with stone quoins. Five-bay
centre and two-bay wings. The Ionic colonnade belongs to the
late C18. So do the details of the windows, as also does probably
the side elevation of seven bays with a slightly projecting three-
bay centre crowned by a pediment. Of the interior the Saloon
41   has the most splendid C17 plasterwork in the county. It is dated
1691. Oval centre with trail of grapes. Side panels with almost
completely detached garlands of fruit and flowers, small
animals, etc. The Library and the Museum have good late C18
stucco decoration. Of that time also several fireplaces. *James
Wyatt* worked at Fawley Court in 1771. He also designed the
ISLAND TEMPLE, the principal vista from the house. It lies
to the NE, but as the island is in Berkshire it cannot here be

described. About 1770 the gardens were also redesigned (by *Capability Brown*). In the gardens several more C18 furnishings. DAIRY to the N of the house. Flint, with a projecting centre in which a genuine Late Norman doorway is re-set. This came from a house in Hart Street, Henley. It has one order of columns and one with nook-shafts. Above these beakhead decoration, above the columns dog-tooth. Nearer the river to the SE the RUIN. It contains a domed room extremely prettily decorated with knuckle-bones and rises to a ruined wall with a genuine Perp window. To its E the WATERGATE. Tripartite, with pilasters, and blank side-pieces. The pilasters have intermittent coarse flint rustication.

KIT'S CLOSE, ¼ m. E of the church. By *Christopher Nicholson*, 1937. White and flat-roofed. L-shaped, with one arm two-storeyed, the other one-storeyed. Inside one very large living-cum-dining-room facing E. Above bedrooms with balcony in front. This and its cantilever canopy are of reinforced concrete. The rest is steel-framed with brick cladding. At the back the staircase projects with a curved, windowless wall.

(At FAWLEY BOTTOM a new house by *Brett, Boyd & Bosanquet*, 1958–9.)

FENNY STRATFORD

ST MARTIN. Built at the inspiration and with the financial help of Browne Willis, the antiquarian, who was one of the founders of the Society of Antiquaries. The money for the church other than that contributed by Browne Willis was raised by sub-scription, and the church erected in 1724–30. The builder was *Edward Wing*. Red brick. W tower with the date 1726. Arched doorway and windows. The N front of three bays is symmetri-cal, two windows and an arched doorway in the middle. The windows are Gothic in style, which is remarkable. About 1866 *William White* gothicized the rest of the church by adding a large nave on the S, thereby making Browne Willis's church into his N aisle. A further S aisle was added in 1908. The Victor-ian Gothic work is wildly patterned inside in red, white, and black brick. Of Browne Willis's internal features the ceiling survives, panelled and with, in the panels, the coats of arms of the subscribers. – STAINED GLASS. A heraldic window of *c*. 1730 in the N wall. Two fat angels hold two of the shields. – MONUMENT. In the E wall of the old part simple tombstone of Browne Willis, who died in 1760, a poor man.

Two characteristic CHAPELS in the Aylesbury Road, the Method-ists' of 1866 with a shaped Jacobean gable, and the Baptists' of 1892, much grander and in a thoroughly debased Italianate.

A few old houses at the church corner, but nothing of real note. The Aylesbury Road is the main shopping street. It connects by Bletchley Road with Bletchley, *see* p. 68. There is no divi-sion now between the two communities.

7090

FINGEST

2   ST BARTHOLOMEW. The Norman tower of Fingest is rightly famous. With its size of 27 ft each way externally, it seems ab-surdly mighty for the church appended to it, a Norman church as well – see the tiny N window in the nave. The tower has also such tiny windows below, but at the bell-stage on each side two big two-light openings, double-shafted and with roll mouldings in the arch. The whole is so big that it is covered by a much later (C17 ?) twin saddleback roof, an unexpected but not un-attractive ending. Sir Alfred Clapham suggested that the tower was used as a nave and the present nave as the chancel. C13 chancel with N lancets, W window in the tower of the later C13: three stepped cusped lancet lights under an arch with two quatrefoils in plate tracery. – FONT. Simple, octagonal, C14. – PLATE. Cup of baluster shape of 1639; Almsdish of 1819.

Round the churchyard several nice houses, timber-framed as well as of Georgian brick.

7010

FLEET MARSTON

ST MARY. Mostly of the date of *Scott*'s restoration, 1868. Nave and chancel. The gabled bell-turret and the W buttress no doubt by Scott. Early C14 chancel arch with ballflower on the capitals. C14 also the N doorway with a hood-mould on head-stops. – STAINED GLASS. E window by *Burlison & Grylls*, 1868.

ROMANO-BRITISH TOWNSHIP. A site has recently been noted 2 m. NW of Aylesbury on the original course of Akeman Street, where the Roman road departs from the A41 road, continuing W by NW across country on the line established by the modern route at Haydon Hill House just outside Ayles-bury. It is marked by a heavy scatter of Roman pottery.

FORTY GREEN FARMHOUSE *see* BLEDLOW

FOSCOTT

1 m. NE of Maids' Moreton

ST LEONARD. By the Green of a deserted village. Nave and chancel, no tower or bellcote. S doorway Transitional, simple but dignified. Early C14 chancel arch with three chamfers, two dying into the imposts, the third on corbels with ballflower decoration. – COMMUNION RAIL. C17. – PLATE. Cup and Cover Paten of 1632.

MANOR HOUSE. Much added to, but with an Elizabethan centre-piece, to the SE, of three wide bays, divided by super-imposed Tuscan pilasters. Mullioned and transomed windows.

ROMAN VILLA. ½ m. SE of the church, close to a minor tributary of the Ouse, is the site of a substantial Roman villa, excavated in 1837–40. Remains of a bath system and two tessellated pavements – one now in the Queen's Temple at Stowe Park (*see* p. 262) – were found. Coins dated the occupation to the early C4.

FOXCOTE *see* FOSCOTT

FRAMEWOOD MANOR *see* STOKE POGES

FRIETH

ST JOHN EVANGELIST. By *J. P. Harrison*, 1849, with a S aisle with oddly and somewhat demonstratively steep cross gables, 1872 by *Woodyer* ('probably' GR). Smallish church of nave and chancel. No tower or turret, not even a bellcote. – STAINED GLASS. The E window made by *Hardman* in 1849, according to Mrs Stanton's research, to *Pugin*'s design. Ornamented with stories in quatrefoils and elongated quatrefoils. – W window by *Hudson* of Pentonville (TK). – Other windows by *Kempe*, 1880 (St John), 1888 (King David?), 1901, 1905. The early one much more convincing. The wheatsheaf, Kempe's later signature, appears for the first time here in 1901.

FULMER

ST JAMES. The church was rebuilt by Sir Marmaduke Dayrell and consecrated in 1610. It was restored by *Street* in 1877–84, when the chancel was rebuilt and the S aisle added. Brick, with a brick W tower in which all the openings are in surrounds of brick too. – FONT COVER. Jacobean, recently restored and re-coloured. – STAINED GLASS. W window, signed by *G. Hoadley*,

London, 1844. Still of the C18 type of Reynolds's New College windows. – s and w, 1845, with three big figures, but of quite a different style. – s aisle c. 1886, no doubt by *Powell*. – MONU-MENT. Sir Marmaduke Dayrell † 1631 and wife. Large standing monument. Two recumbent effigies, she behind and a little above him. Deep arched and coffered recess. Two black columns with small figures on their architraves. The children kneeling in profile in front of the tomb-chest.

(FERNACRES. Plain, two-storeyed. Garden front with two bay windows. Built in 1815 by *P. F. Robinson*. No doubt altered later.)

6030   GAWCOTT

HOLY TRINITY. Designed in 1827 by the then incumbent, the Rev. *Thomas Scott*, father of *Sir George Gilbert Scott* who was born here in 1811. He was sixteen when the building went up. His Gothic leanings did not start from his paternal church; for this is in the classical Georgian style. Stone, with ashlar quoins. w tower, nave and lower polygonal apse. All windows arched. The tower ends in a parapet with ball finials. Original the BENCHES, PULPIT, ORGAN, etc., but alas not the ceilings.

WESTCOT HOUSE, in the main street, due E of the church. 1720. Chequered brick. Four bays, segment-headed windows. Modillion frieze.

(LENBOROUGH MANOR FARMHOUSE, 1 m. E. s front, dated 1772, flint with ashlar quoins, two storeys, five bays. C17 evidence behind this front. MHLG)

8040   GAYHURST

House, stables, and church form a very fine group as one enters.

GAYHURST HOUSE. Built on older foundations. (Doorway of *c.* 37a 1520 in the cellar. RCHM) The present house was begun for William Mulso in 1597 and completed by his son-in-law Sir Everard Digby in the early years of the C17. Many alterations under George Wright *c.* 1750 * and more, internally, under Lord Carrington in the 1860s. His architect was *William Burges*. The Late Elizabethan house has its entrance front to the s. Of stone, three-storeyed. Of the E-type but with bay windows in the re-entrant angles. Mullioned and transomed windows of six or four lights. The porch has two orders of attached columns, Tuscan and rather elongated Ionic. The wings end with un-relieved flat roofs, the recessed middle part has five small

* Before 1763, *see* Horace Walpole's *Journals*.

shaped gables, with double-curved sides and a flat top. To the
E far-projecting square porch on two heavy square piers with a
round arch between. L. and r. one bay and then a canted bay
window. That is all. To the N the wings also projected. But the
area between them was filled in c. 1750, and the front is now
mid-Georgian. In the wings, which again have unrelieved
flat roofs, are Venetian windows on the ground floor. The
centre of seven bays with windows with alternating pediments
on the first floor. Simple Doric porch. As one enters the house,
the Hall extends to the E of the main S porch. It was re-modelled
c. 1750, especially by putting up a big stone archway to the E.
Corinthian pilasters. The underside of the arch may be meant
to look Elizabethan. The staircase is of the same date. Large
open well. Twisted balusters, stucco on walls and ceiling. In
the filled-in part to the N, on the first floor, the mid-C18 Ballroom. Minor mid-C18 details in other rooms. Of Jacobean details there is, apart from some panelling, a strip of plaster in the
bay window of the NE room on the first floor. This has broad
decorated bands forming panels. *Burges*'s contributions are
grossly prominent. The SE room on the ground floor has a big
fireplace full of Burges's best, most playful detail. The walls are
panelled with extremely narrow panels all painted with naturalistic flowers, a veritable primer of English flowers. The room, of
its date, is extremely successful, and ought not to be tampered
with. In the room beneath the ballroom Burges introduced a
pair of big fireplaces with motifs from *Paradise Lost* and
Paradise Regained in the overmantels. The most extraordinary
piece of Burges's is the surround of the entrance to the so-called
Guard Room on the upper floor, with a male caryatid crouching
above the door and supporting an unexpected bit of staircase
that comes round. In Burges's kitchen there is an oriel for cook
to keep an eye on the doings of the wenches below.

STABLES. Two parallel ranges of five bays each, not completely in harmony now. Arched window in the middle, the
side windows with ovals above. To the S on the corner of the
kitchen garden a SUMMER HOUSE, square, with four gables,
which may well be original. The GATE LODGE is a crazy bit of
mock Elizabethan with two turrets. This was converted from a
mid-C18 one in 1882. The GROUNDS were laid out by *Capability Brown* before 1763 (*see* H. Walpole), and remodelled by
Repton before 1794 (*see* his 'Sketches').

CHURCH. Begun in 1728. The architect is unknown. W tower
with evenly rusticated angle pilasters below, tall thin pilasters

above. The bell-openings are round-arched with Y-tracery. Recessed lead cupola. The s side is the main front. Five bays, the angles with evenly rusticated pilasters, then Ionic pilasters, and then, for the centre bay, attached Ionic columns on high plinths, carrying a pediment. Arched windows. The chancel is lower and has at the E end a blank niche instead of a window. The chancel as well as the nave end in a pediment. On the N side the centre bay is completely rusticated and has two very odd pediments one on top of the other. White interior with giant pilasters and a plaster ceiling of rich but clearly divided detail. Tower arch and chancel arch are decorated identically. The chancel plastering is appropriately richer than that of the nave. The FURNISHINGS are complete: WALL PANELLING, BOX-PEWS, two-decker PULPIT with tester and a certain amount of marquetry, fine REREDOS, wrought-iron COMMUNION RAIL, tiny FONT on a polygonal pillar. The ROYAL ARMS, however, come from the previous church, as they are Stuart Arms.* –

28   MONUMENT. Sir Nathan Wright and his son. Erected c. 1728. Two standing figures in the clothes of the day and with wigs. Reredos background with Corinthian pilasters and an open segmental pediment. Above the two figures baldacchino with looped-up curtains. The attribution to *Roubiliac* is not based on evidence, and it is more likely that the monument is by Carter, or Green, or another of those mason-sculptors who occasionally produced work of such startlingly high quality. The Wright monument is certainly not only one of the grandest but also one of the most successful of its type in England.

0080

GERRARDS CROSS

9a ST JAMES. 1859 by *Sir William Tite*. Erected and endowed by the Misses Reid as a memorial to Major-General Reid. The style probably 'suggested by that modification of Byzantine found in the neighbourhood of Venice and Padua' (*Literary Gazetteer*, 17 Sep. 1859). Of white, yellow, and red brick. Nave with attached NW campanile, crossing, transepts, and straight-headed chancel. Over the crossing a lead-covered dome with dormers in which the *Rundbogenstil* breaks down and the High Victorian is triumphant. The nave has arched windows set in blank giant arches of white brick. The crossing is accompanied by four turrets whose roofs can only be called Chinese. Inside, the dome and its surroundings are treated in the Byzantine manner, i.e. the dome has squinches and the four pieces under

* Altered in Georgian times.

the turrets are narrow lower sub-centres. They are separated from the dome by mighty columns of scagliola. Don't be surprised that the capitals of the columns have E.E. stiff-leaf decoration.

The church lies by the Common, an open space with trees on the E side, a rough green on the W side, where to the S the BULL HOTEL, long, white, and rambling, and to the N a few surviving Georgian houses. Just SW of this green an Iron Age Hill-fort (*see* below).

Round the E periphery of the camp CAMP ROAD, a private estate developed with well-to-do houses in the last twenty years and very typical of such housing estates on the margins of large landscaped C18 estates (cf. e.g. Claremont, Esher). Of individual houses PORTLAND DENE, nice and new, is by *Peter Softley*, 1956–7. CAMP KEEP was built in 1937 with old materials. The gargoyles and heads came from a church in Scotland.

N of the Common all is Metroland, shopping for a large affluent population, and then, towards Chalfont St Peter, their villas, more or less sparsely set in the old trees.

BULSTRODE PARK. The oval IRON AGE HILL-FORT, overlooking the park to the SE and enclosing 22 acres, is the largest in the county. The rampart is double, with, to the W and NW, some damage to the outer ditch. To the NW there are signs of a flint revetting. Limited excavations in 1924 were inconclusive, but there can be no doubt as to the fort's Iron Age date.

GRANBOROUGH

7020

ST JOHN BAPTIST. Perp W tower, nave with an early C14 S doorway. Higher chancel, built between 1396 and 1401. Elaborate stencilled Victorian WALL DECORATION, said to have been done by a vicar as a pastime. – SCULPTURE. Nottingham alabaster panel of the Crucifixion; C15. – PLATE. Cup of 1569. – CHRISMATORY. Small, of pewter, on lions' feet with three cups, for wine, oil, and water.

GREAT BRICKHILL

9030

ST MARY. Of ironstone, with a central tower. This and the chancel are of the C13. The chancel lancets are shafted inside. The tower has very broad, heavy, semi-octagonal responds. In the S wall the upper part of a former C14 window. Perp S aisle with standard arcade. – (PAINTING. Traces of C13 painting in the N and S chancel windows.) – MONUMENTS. Several C18 tablets, one (of no special interest) by *Joseph Wilton* (Philip Barton † 1786). The best is that to John Barton † 1760, of white and brown marble with graceful decoration.

GREAT BRICKHILL MANOR by *E. B. Lamb* has been demolished. Several nice Georgian houses, S, E, and NE of the church.

8000

GREAT HAMPDEN

1a This is a part of the Chilterns which has so far resisted becoming Outer London. May its rural character be long preserved.

ST MARY MAGDALENE. Of flint. Externally mostly Perp, except for the plain C13 S doorway, the lower part of the SW tower, which looks *c.* 1300, and the Dec W window of the nave. Internally the N and S arcades (four and three bays, because of the tower) are Dec. Piers with four shafts and four wide hollows, arches with three sunk quadrant mouldings. The tower arches have the same type of mouldings. – FONT. Of cup shape. A Norman band at the foot, the top frieze C14 or C15. – BENCHES. Early Tudor, with linenfold panels. – STAINED GLASS. The bad E window signed *Thos. F. Curtis, Ward & Hughes,* 1898. – MONUMENTS. Brass to John Hampden † 1496 and wife. The figures *c.* 3 ft 6 in. long. – Brass to Sir John Hampden † 1553 and two wives. 2 ft 1 in. figures. – Elizabeth Hampden † 1634. Very tall inscription tablet with a fine classical open pediment at the top. – The great John Hampden, large hanging monument by *Sir Henry Cheere,* put up in 1743. Sarcophagus with two putti on it. Above an oval medallion with a family tree growing out of the battle scene of Hampden's death in 1643. – Thomas Kempthorne, 1759. Pink and white marble with a pair of oval medallions with portraits in profile. An urn with garlands at the top.

HAMPDEN HOUSE. Architecturally, the history of John Hampden's house stretches beyond his time forward as well as backward, forward to the C18, backward to the C14. The middle projection of the present S front, known as King John's Tower, has at least one detail which, if it does not reach as far as King John's time, reaches at least to a hundred years or a little more after it: the inner doorway between the tower and the Hall. The present Hall has indeed a medieval roof, but that is a recent import. It comes from the barn of Manor Farm, Great Kimble, a barn which probably was originally not a barn either but a church house or some secular hall. The gallery in the Hall may well be Hampden's, see the dumb-bell balusters. But the external appearance of Hampden House in general is Gothick, [50a] and documents prove it to be a very early case of Gothic Revival. Lipscomb gives the date 1754, but Mr Gunnis has found proof that *Thomas Iremonger* built the porch in 1751. That must refer to the w front, an eminently curious front of three bays with a deeply-recessed centre in which there is the prettiest Gothick doorcase. The side windows also with their ogee heads are characteristic of early Gothicism. Another almost equally pretty doorway, with a straight head on brackets, a little further N on the w side. The house is bigger on its NW and N sides than the principal front makes one expect. On the s front the medieval tower has machicolations. Everything received battlements about 1750, and the pretty pendant friezes below. Inside the most charming feature is the Staircase, always called Jacobean or thereabouts, but apparently also an ingenious conversion of *c.* 1750, and, as a sign of Jacobean sympathies at that date, of considerable interest.

STABLES to the s, nearer the church, also Gothick, also with a pendant frieze.*

RECTORY, 1 m. SE. A good Early Georgian house of five bays and two storeys, red brick, with hipped roof. The windows have segmental heads. Doric porch with pilasters and pediment. The house lies in the *point de vue* of one of the avenues of Hampden House.

Another, to the E, runs along the glade and ends in two one-storeyed LODGES.

MOUNDS. At the SE end of the stretch of Grim's Ditch (*see* p. 148) there are two undated mounds with causeways running NW–SE across their ditches. It is impossible without excavation to ascertain their age relative to the Ditch. DANES CAMP, a similar mound, lies ½ m. w in Hampden Park.

GREAT HORWOOD

7030

ST JAMES. Late C13 s doorway with three orders of shafts and many mouldings in the arch. Dec chancel with flowing tracery in the windows. The E window (of four lights) especially makes a fine display. Sedilia strangely arranged so that the arches and crocketed gables stand out detached in front of the SE window. On the E wall a head corbel. Early Perp w tower with higher

* According to H. C. Prince: *Landscape Gardens in the Chilterns*, unpublished M.A. thesis, University of London, 1953, which Mr Prince kindly allowed me to quote, a PINERY was provided in 1752, an ORANGERY in 1755–6, a GREENHOUSE in 1756, KENNELS also in 1756, and an ICE HOUSE in 1760.

stair-turret and an arch towards the nave still with Dec mouldings. Big Perp s windows, Perp arcades of tall octagonal piers and many-moulded arches. A pretty niche in the s aisle to the l. of the E window; shields below it. – FONT. Perp, octagonal, with tracery panels and shields in foils. – SCREEN. Perp, with two-light divisions. – SCULPTURE. Lower half of a wooden figure, C15, in the N aisle. – PLATE. Two Patens on foot, 1697.

In the village many attractive minor Georgian brick cottages, mostly built after a fire in 1781.

(MANOR FARM, ¼ m. NE. Early C17, remodelled c. 1700. Staircase with twisted balusters. MHLG)

GREAT HUNDRIDGE MANOR *see* CHESHAM

8000
GREAT KIMBLE

ST NICHOLAS. Of flint, externally all Victorian with its pattern of flint and stone squares in parapets and battlements. Inside C13 arcades with octagonal piers and double-chamfered arches starting with angle spurs. Early C14 chancel arch, square with three demi-shafts and with two small sunk quadrant mouldings. The chancel chapels were originally of the same time, but are now a rebuilding of 1876–81. C14 W tower, the tower arch partly on head corbels. – FONT. Norman, of cup-shape. Big and uncommonly beautiful. The lower half fluted, the upper with a band of beautiful symmetrical leaf-trail motifs. The base is a large reversed two-scallop capital with decorated lunettes. – STAINED GLASS. E window signed by *Sir R. F. Russell* and dated 1844, i.e. Sir Robert Frankland Russell. – PLATE. Cup with Elizabethan stem and Cover Paten of 1570.

VICARAGE. 1859 by *Lamb*. Red brick, Tudor.

RAGPIT HILL, Chequers Park, about 200 yds NE of the church. A small IRON AGE promontory HILL-FORT at the W end of a spur where there is a single rampart and ditch bisected by a small entrance. 300 yds E along the ridge is a second rampart and ditch with slight counterscarp bank. A third low bank to the N, apparently joining the two lines of fortification, is probably a modern boundary.

PULPIT HILL. ¾ m. SSE of Great Kimble church lies a second small IRON AGE FORT on the edge of the Chiltern escarpment. Sub-square, the rampart and ditch is double with, on the E, a noticeable platform behind the outer rampart. To the W the defences are less pronounced owing to the steep natural slope. To the SE there is an entrance 75 ft wide.

THE MOUND, W of the church between the road and the railway line, is probably a prehistoric BARROW, though of no known date.

GREAT LINFORD

Manor House, Almshouses, and Church are part of one picture which unfolds gradually.

ST ANDREW. Essentially c. 1300 to early C14. The tower comes first with lancet on the ground floor and the opening towards the nave with tripartite responds and a double-chamfered arch. The windows were mostly given bleak mullions and transoms when the chancel was rebuilt c. 1706–10. But in spite of this, there is plenty of evidence of the early C14. The best piece is the N chapel immediately attached to the N porch. The window frames here have external decoration with big fleurons, and the octagonal pier inside has small fleurons in the capital too. Double-chamfered arches. No E window. In the N porch a sexpartite vault with a good leaf-boss (cf. Newport Pagnell). S aisle of three bays. Also octagonal piers and also double-chamfered arches. The chancel arch was widened in the C18, but the tripartite responds were kept. – PANELLING, PULPIT, BOX PEWS, all very simple, and all Georgian. – STAINED GLASS. SE window by *Kempe*, 1904, S window by *Kempe & Tower*, c. 1910. – PLATE. Cup and Cover Paten of 1610; two Flagons of 1732; Dish of 1754. – MONUMENTS. Brass to Roger Hunt † 1473 and wife (nave), 19 in. figures. – Brass to Thomas Malyn † 1536 and wife (N aisle), 2 ft figures. – Two good tablets, instructive to compare: Sir William Prichard † 1704 and Thomas Uthwat † 1754.

ALMSHOUSES. Late C17. One-storey with raised centre. This has a doorway with plain shell-hood and wooden cross-windows. The four end gables of the higher and lower parts are all double-curved with a rounded top.

GREAT LINFORD MANOR. A very dignified Early Georgian stone house of five bays and two and a half storeys. Doorway with a fine segmental pediment on Corinthian pilasters. Passage across the house and by the exit the staircase with sturdy twisted balusters. The house is given added monumentality to a considerable degree by two symmetrical stable ranges set at a distance in front of the façade and framing a vista. They are only three bays wide, and look with their pedimented doorways and big hipped roofs like large lodges rather than stables. The house has plain lower wings l. and r. on the garden side, and on the entrance side on the l. a wall with ball-finial, partly a fragment of a former kitchen block.

GREAT MARLOW *see* MARLOW

GREAT MISSENDEN

8000

ST PETER AND ST PAUL. Outside the village against the hillside. Of flint, but the w tower of squared stone. Fenestration Perp, except for the Dec chancel s windows, s transept windows, N transept E window (straight head, flowing tracery), tower doorway and lower windows, and the N doorway. Four-bay arcades also Dec. Square with demi-shafts attached. The same mouldings for the transept and chancel arches. The tower was widened to the s in 1732. The arch towards the nave is triple-chamfered with the mouldings dying into the imposts. Very elaborate Dec details in the chancel, especially the extremely strange arcading in the N wall with detached shafts forming a kind of blank wall-passage. Steep-pitched crocketed gables. All extremely renewed. Also niches l. and r. of the E window, Sedilia, alas almost completely destroyed, and a Piscina with a nodding ogee over. Clerestory and nave roof are Perp, the arched braces on stone angels and with tracery in the spandrels. – FONT. With a Norman base in the form of a reversed one-scallop capital with decorated lunettes and a rope moulding. – STAINED GLASS. S aisle window W of the S transept by *Powell & Sons*, 1864. – MONUMENTS. Brass to a Lady, C15 (S transept), a 13 in. figure. – Brass of a helmet with crest including a delightful female bust, C15 (S transept). – Lady Boys, by *Nicholas Stone*, 1638 (N aisle near W end). An astonishingly pure piece of classical design. Framed tablet with open segmental pediment.

MISSENDEN ABBEY. Originally a house of Arroasian canons, founded in 1133. No systematic excavations have been undertaken. The present house lies on the site of the cloister, and two walls of it are brought out in the planning and decoration of the house. Also, in the E range, on the upper floor the C15 timber roof of the Dormitory survives. The estate itself was bought in 1787 by James Oldham Oldham, 'an opulent ironmonger of Holborn' (Sheahan). He is said (by *The Beauties of England and Wales*) to have built a house in the Venetian style. If so he must certainly soon have been converted to the Gothic fashion; for the house is now all Gothic. Cemented, castellated walls. Main front to the s, where the centre has a little castellated pediment.

To the l. and r. bay windows. Behind this front are the three main rooms, Entrance Hall with panelled ceiling and a miniature two-arm staircase at its back, Library to the E with Gothic book-cases and with Gothic ironwork in the fireplace, and Drawing Room to the W with apsed ends. The Cloister lies behind and connects with the porch on the W front. It is vaulted and the vault again has panelling.

The village is mainly one High Street and the branch to the church. There are no houses of special merit. What may be mentioned is two Gothick cottages, one white-plastered, at the E exit above the church, the other at the N end prettier, because its windows have flint surrounds and its angles vertical flint strips. In the village lying a little back from the High Street the BAPTIST CHURCH, of 1838 (MHLG), with a stuccoed three-bay front with Tuscan pilasters and a pediment. The wider centre bay is recessed.

RIGNALLS. By *Adams & Holden*, 1909. Uninhabited at the time of writing.

SECONDARY MODERN SCHOOL. By *F. B. Pooley*, the County Architect. Completed in 1955. For 300 children. Built in six months. The Assembly Hall, also used as a Community Centre, is steel-framed. The rest with load-bearing walls. African mahogany panels as cladding.

PRESTWOOD, *see* p. 225.

EARTHWORKS. Undated earthworks on FIRTH HILL, a furlong N of the church; apparently part of two enclosures.

GRIM'S DITCH, *see* p. 148.

GREAT PEDNOR *see* PEDNOR

GREAT WOOLSTONE
8030

HOLY TRINITY. 1839. Small and simple, of the Commissioners' type. Façade with two angle buttresses and turrets and a bell-cote. – PLATE. Cup of 1569.

To the NW a FARMHOUSE of *c.* 1700, three bays, but originally five. Two storeys, hipped roof. Vitreous and red brick. Quoins. Opposite another good house with projecting wings and a plain shell-hood.

GRENDON UNDERWOOD
6020

ST LEONARD. Fine mid-C13 S doorway. One capital with stiff-leaf, one hollow arch moulding with big openwork fleurons much decayed. Chancel late c 13, with windows with Y-tracery. Handsome Piscina with cusped arch and buttress shafts (one destroyed). Perp w tower with higher stair-turret. – PULPIT. Jacobean, with one tier of low blank arches and one of arabesque panels. – PLATE. Cup and Cover Paten of 1569. – MONUMENTS. John Pigott † 1751. Signed by *Scheemakers*. White marble. The deceased in a Roman toga seated on the base. A rather pedestrian sculptural treatment. Back wall with two fluted Corinthian pilasters carrying an open pediment. Between the pilasters grey marble background and a putto carrying a profile medallion of the son who died aged thirteen. – Viscount Say and Sele † 1781, Viscountess † 1789. Two good unsigned monuments of white, pink, and green marble. Nearly identical, except that on the first a mourning woman, on the second a genius stands beside an urn in front of an obelisk. Elegant and crisp execution of the ornamental parts.

RECTORY. 1762. Red brick. Ground floor of three bays with two Venetian windows, first floor of five bays. Hipped roof.

GRENDON HALL. Gabled neo-Elizabethan brick mansion. Built *c.* 1885, and designed by the Rev. *Randolphe Pigott* and his brother *Sir Digby Pigott*, the owner and his brother.*

SHAKESPEARE FARM, SE of the church. The gabled part on the l. is probably late c 16 (timber-framing and brick infilling), the brick range on the r. is late c 17. Shakespeare is said to have stayed here overnight on his way from London to Stratford and to have conceived that night the 'Midsummer Night's Dream'.

GRIM'S DITCH

Most likely of the Saxon period (*see* Introduction, p. 18). The best preserved stretches of this travelling earthwork, with its E-facing single rampart and ditch, are (1), the first section to appear in the w of the county. In Park Wood N of BRADENHAM it runs just w of N for about 1½ m., following the road most of the way to Lacey Green, where it turns to E of N for an almost straight run of 2 m. to the NW corner of Hampden Park. Here it makes a remarkable turn to the SE. At the turning is a presumably original gap, much used. This alignment is traceable through GREAT HAMPDEN to the two mounds mentioned on p. 143. A path continues the line w to the road by Lodge Wood. (2) A short section begins SW of Woodlands Park N of GREAT MISSENDEN and continues in a curve to the NW for about

* Information kindly given by Mrs Dawson.

700 yds. (3) The line of the ditch out of the county to the E is marked first of all by a track N from the corner of the lane E of Kingsash on the LEE–WENDOVER parish boundary. The line straightens to the NE and is visible for about a mile between Cock's Hill and Longcroft on the Hertfordshire border, the remainder of this line being marked by tracks.

GROVE

9020

ST MICHAEL. A pretty group with the canal, the hump bridge, and the lock-keeper's house. Tiny C14 chapel with C19 bell-turret. No N windows; W and E windows Dec, the E window flanked inside by two niches. S porch.

HADDENHAM

7000

ST MARY. C13 chancel, W tower and arcades. The chancel has original N and S lancets (the E window is Victorian), a double-chamfered chancel arch, and one-bay arches to chapels. The W tower is very impressive. Its bell-stage has five blank arcades on each side, holding lancets in the second and fourth bays. Plain parapet on the top. W doorway with three continuous chamfers, tower arch also of three chamfers, W window of three stepped lancets with chamfered surrounds under one shafted depressed arch with vertical pieces above the abaci. The arcades have circular piers and circular abaci (but tripartite responds) and double-chamfered arches with hood-moulds. No clerestory. The plastered ceiling is of the early C19. Dec and Perp windows, specially ambitious the Perp ones of the N chapel. The Piscina here must be re-set. It has a C13 trefoiled arch, decoration to the l. and r. of diaper and handsome foliage, and a round hood-mould with dog-tooth. A window of the same Perp type as those of the N chapel is in the S aisle. – FONT. Circular, Norman, with rough fluting on the bowl and above this rough frieze of leaf and dragons. – SCREENS. Perp Screen between N chapel and chancel. – A second Perp Screen, at the time of writing leaning against the W wall of the S aisle, a third under the tower arch. – STAINED GLASS. In the E window of the N chapel much original glass. Saints and angels in the tracery heads, three complete canopies, smaller fragments below. – BRASSES. In the N chapel. Thomas Nassh † 1428, rector (a 25 in. figure). – Demi-figure of a Priest, C15 (13 in.).
The church faces with its N side the Green, a happily rough, un-selfconscious Green. The village pond washes part of the

churchyard wall. To the w of the church MANOR FARMHOUSE
with a big C15 BARN, externally weatherboarded much later.
Six bays, aisles, tie-beams on braces, and diagonally set queen-
posts. To the E of the churchyard CHURCH FARMHOUSE. This
has an eminently picturesque stone frontage. Stone ground
floor, timber-framed upper floor of the Wealden type. The
sides project slightly, but the eaves run without a break, so that
the centre recedes a good deal below the eaves. They are here
carried by detached braces. Between them a small oriel window.
All this appears to be C15–16, but the stone parts are assumed
to be older. Adjoining on the E an C18 stone house of three
widely spaced bays. A little further E on the opposite side
GRENVILLE MANOR, an odd building with a Victorian date-
stone 1569. The carved bargeboarding of gables and porch
gable may not be *in situ*, and the wooden tracery of some windows could have formed part of the dado of a screen in the
church.

To the N of the Green up CHURCH LANE, facing s, CEDAR
COTTAGE with a big trimmed ilex and two trimmed yews. Up
CHURCH WAY, the DOLPHIN INN with an C18 front of three
bays, stone with brick dressings, and a nice wrought-iron sign.
Then on the other side the former BEEHIVE INN, early C18, of
brick, three bays with a steep one-bay pediment and, adjoining
the inn on the N, a pretty Georgian shop-front. HADDENHAM
HALL further N, on the same side, has handsome late C18 balcony railings of iron and wood with honeysuckle motifs. Further
N a main road is met, and along it to the w lies FORT END, with
more picturesque houses, especially OLD HADDEN on the s
side (timber-framing and brick-nogging). From here the HIGH
STREET returns to the Green. Here first on the w side DOVE
HOUSE with a big stone chimneybreast, then the BONE HOUSE,
dated 1807 with very rustic decoration all made of knuckle-
bones: e.g. two frontal heads in window lunettes, farm tools,
and beasts. The WESLEYAN CHAPEL of 1822 is entirely
standard: three bays, two storeys, arched windows, and a big
pediment across.

HALL BARN

40a The centre of the house was built for Edmund Waller, the poet
(cf. Beaconsfield, p. 62), some time after he returned from
France in 1651. The style makes a date before 1675 more likely
than after. It is of brick with stone dressings, three storeys high
and five bays wide. It was originally also five bays deep, and has

a hipped roof with a lantern – just like such houses as Ashdown, and just like a C 17 or C 18 doll's house. John Evelyn calls it Waller's town box. The decoration of the façade is most unusual. There are coupled pilasters at the angles and between the windows, and they are Ionic on the ground floor, Corinthian on the first, and composite on the second. Pretty lions' heads in the modillion frieze. The windows have mullion-and-transom crosses. The middle bay is emphasized by detached columns carrying pediments. The first-floor one is segmental, the other two are triangular, and the way columns have to be accommodated on the sloping sides of pediments is decidedly awkward. The ground floor is now covered by a porte-cochère added by *Devey*, probably before 1870, and the pediment is no longer visible. Moreover a careful drawing of 1821 shows no pediment on the second floor, and that is less easily explained. Three dormers are in the hipped roof, their pediments being steeply triangular–segmental–steeply triangular.

To this house belonged the quadrant wall on the r., which has rusticated brick pilasters and a doorway with intermittently rusticated Ionic pilasters and a pediment, and the stables wing. A corresponding wing was no doubt planned on the l. (cf. Stoke Bruerne, Northamptonshire, and the later Palladian houses). The stables however were altered in the Georgian period. They had seven cross-windows on two floors and have now five widely-spaced ones and a half-storey. Bell-turret on the top.

The most important C 18 addition however was *Colen Campbell*'s Great Room, illustrated in *Vitruvius Britannicus*. This was built for the then owner John Aislabie, stepfather of Waller's grandson, in 1724 and stood detached to the s w. All that remains of it is the s front of three bays with a (later) giant arch flanked by coupled Tuscan columns and (original) pedimented windows l. and r. with surrounds of intermittent rustication and a keystone head. The addition is seven bays wide with the ground-floor windows in blank arches and a top half-storey. After that *Devey* in 1883 added a Ballroom on the E side, keeping his architecture in perfect harmony with that of the original house.

Inside the house not much remains of the C 17 and C 18. Four fine Kentian doorcases with pulvinated friezes decorated with laurel, and the late C 18 staircase with simple, graceful, wrought-iron balustrade, are the best pieces.

To the s of the house a large LAKE, and at its end a

BOATHOUSE with four-column portico. Behind this the GROVE, in the middle of which a fine open rotunda, called the TEMPLE OF VENUS. It is domed, has unfluted Ionic columns and a frieze with garlands and ox-skulls, and inside the dome pretty stuccowork with dancing cherubs and garlands. Long straight walks through the Grove, the most spectacular the 1½-mile avenue from the s. On the edge of the Grove OBELISK behind a charming wrought-iron GATE with agricultural tools.

63a   LODGE at the entrance to the drive from Beaconsfield. Of timber, and Victorian no doubt. Its surfaces are encrusted with panels which originally formed Gothic bench ends, Early Renaissance panelling from walls or bedsteads, etc. There are also decorated barley-sugar columns and colonnettes. It strikes one as gratifyingly gay and irresponsible.

HALTON

ST MICHAEL. 1813 by *Henry Rhodes*, restored and remodelled in 1886–7. Built of squared blocks of grey stone with a mortar ornamentally studded with bits of flint (cf. Wycombe Abbey). w tower, nave and aisles, and short lower chancel, straight-ended outside but polygonal inside. The windows mostly lancets. The clerestory windows simply oblong. The w doorway pointed in an oblong frame. The aisles are probably an alteration of 1886, and the nave would originally have been much wider and provided with galleries. The arcades are in the style of *c.* 1190, but too slim. – PLATE. Cup and Cover Paten of 1569. – BRASS. Henry Bradschawe † 1553 and wife. Kneeling figures of 10 in. length.

HALTON HOUSE. Built in 1884 for Baron Alfred Charles de Rothschild, brother of the first Lord. His father, Baron Lionel, had bought Halton in 1853. An ambitious mansion in a free French château style, rather c 17 to c 18 than c 16 in origin. Two equal fronts with two canted bay windows and a raised centre, columns instead of pilasters in two orders, and preferably detached columns. Steep French slated pavilion roofs. The only difference between the entrance and the garden side is that the former has a deep porte-cochère like Waddesdon. On the garden side lower down in a pool a Fountain with figures. The w wing built for the Royal Air Force in 1935–7. It replaces the spectacular Winter Garden with its two large and nine smaller

62   domes. Inside a most sumptuous Central Hall in white and gold which goes through two storeys and has a huge chandelier.

White and gold also the Staircase Hall. The staircase has a bronze balustrade as usual in France. Other rooms equally sumptuously decorated. The establishment originally included a skating rink.

BODDINGTON HILL. On a spur in the SW corner of Halton Wood is a promontory FORT of uncertain date with a single rampart and ditch enclosing $17\frac{1}{2}$ acres. The strongest part across the neck of the spur has been destroyed, as has the ditch on the W. A break to the SW cannot be original. Surface finds of Iron Age sherds have been made on the bank.

HAMBLEDEN

7080

ST MARY. W tower of flint and red brick built in 1721, encased in flint and heightened (prettily) in 1883. The N side of the nave has Norman masonry. The Norman church had a central tower. It is known that this collapsed in 1703. The N transept is an early C13 addition or alteration. It has the unusually ambitious feature of an E aisle. Two bays. Circular pier with circular abacus. Double-chamfered arches. Much was clearly done early in the C14, though the C14 window tracery is mostly too much restored to be of value. Early C14 S doorway with continuous mouldings. Early C14 Sedilia and Piscina in the chancel. Crocketed ogee gables. The chancel arch and the chancel chapels are entirely Victorian. – FONT. Cylindrical, Norman, with big foliated cross motifs and similar motifs in lozenge-shaped and triangular panels. – PANELLING. Splendid Early Renaissance panels of *c.* 1525. On them the arms of Wolsey and of Bishop Fox of Winchester. The panels are said to come from The Vyne, near Basingstoke, Hampshire. They are intended to be used in conjunction with a new altar for the church. – SCULPTURE. Panel of the Adoration of the Child, C15, wood in the alabaster style (chancel N). – PAINTING. Virgen de la Faja by *Murillo*, on loan from Viscount Hambleden. – PLATE. Cup 1635; Paten on foot 1635 (?); Flagon and Paten 1705. – MONUMENTS. Brasses: kneeling Lady, $8\frac{1}{2}$ in. long; Priest, demi-figure, 7 in. long; Couple of *c.* 1520, 12 in. long. – C16 tomb-chest in an Easter Sepulchre recess. Shields in cusped quatrefoils against the chest. Recess with four-centred arch. The inscription runs: Liberaeme Domine de Morte Aeternae (*sic*). It is in Roman lettering (chancel N). – Ralph Scrope †1572. Low standing monument. Broad panel flanked by fluted Ionic colonnettes. The top a fanciful angular pediment. No

figures. – Sir Cope D'Oyley † 1633. Alabaster. Two kneeling
figures facing each other. They are surrounded in the most
engaging way by the crowd of their kneeling children. The
children, usually reduced to miniature size and banished to the
base of the monument, are here treated literally on the same
level as the parents. Architectural background. Mrs Esdaile
attributed the monument to *John Hargrave* (cf. Great Brington,
Northamptonshire). – Edward Marjoribanks † 1868. Tablet in
the C18 style (a rarity in High Victorian days) but with very
odd trees l. and r. – In the churchyard KENDRICK MAUSO-
LEUM, sketched (according to Betjeman and Piper) by Walpole
in his journal of visits to country houses *c.* 1750 at the latest.
Stone dome with urn on a square substructure with blind arches
framed by Tuscan pilasters.

The village is one of the most attractive in Bucks. The triangular
Green has along one side the churchyard, along the others flint
and brick or brick cottages. Above the roofs of some appear the
higher gables of the MANOR HOUSE, an early C17 building of
flint and red brick with four gables to the s, three to the w. In
the middle of the w side is the two-storeyed gabled porch. Mullioned and transomed windows. What a pity the church tower
was not left in its flint and brick garb. It would have added the
finishing touch to the *ensemble* of the Green.

THE RECTORY (also called KENDRICKS) lies NE of the Manor
House outside the village. It is of 1724 and has a front of red
and vitreous brick. Seven bays with three-bay projection. Parapet and hipped roof. Giant pilasters at the outer angles and
those of the three-bay centre.

At MILL END, 1 m. s, on the main road, YEWDEN MANOR (*see
also* below), and to its sw the delightful group of the MILL,
MILL HOUSE, and MILL END FARM.

GREENLANDS, to the w of Mill End, is essentially an Early
Victorian mansion in a sumptuous Italianate style with a square
tower. It dates from 1853 (Kelly) and was enlarged after 1871
(VCH) and again recently. The s front is of 1853 with l. and r.
bays of after 1871. The w (entrance) front was remodelled in
1936–8 by *P. Geddes Hyslop.*

YEWDEN MANOR. At MILL END, 400 yds N of the Thames, the
site of an extensive ROMANO-BRITISH VILLA was excavated
with adjacent buildings in 1911. A two-phase structure was
revealed above a primary Iron Age occupation. Finds included
C4 coinage, a mosaic floor, fourteen furnaces – perhaps connected with a corn-drying floor as at the Saunderton villa

(*see* p. 232) – and ninety-seven infant burials contained within the structure and immediate precincts.

FLINT FARM. Another building of Roman date has been noted at Flint Farm, $2\frac{1}{2}$ m. N.

HANSLOPE

8040

ST JAMES. The church has the finest steeple in Buckinghamshire. It is Perp throughout and was originally 200 ft high. It had to be rebuilt and is now a little lower. Tall pairs of two-light bell-openings. This top part has panelled clasping buttresses. On these, tall polygonal pinnacles connected by flying buttresses with the spire. The spire is recessed behind battlements and has three tiers of lucarnes in the principal directions. The tower hall inside has springers for an intended vault. The w window is a c 17 renewal. There is much else of great interest in the church. Late Norman chancel, externally articulated by strong demi-columns with blank arches up to the decorated corbel-table. Round-headed windows fairly high up. Priest's doorway with a kind of simplified beakhead no longer of an animal nature. The motif runs up the jambs and round the arch. Outer zigzag arch moulding. Hood-mould with oval beading. Inside, the chancel arch has four orders of shafts with decorated capitals and abaci. The aisles were both added in the early c 13, see the pair of lancets in the s aisle, shafted inside, and the single lancet in the N aisle with a hood-mould of small zigzag at r. angles to the wall. Both aisles are remarkably wide for their date, as was the Norman nave before the aisles existed. Of the c 13 also the recess in the s aisle, big pointed arches, cusped, with nailhead decoration, and the Sedilia and Piscina in the chancel. Late c 13 windows in the N aisle and N chapel. Perp rebuilding of the arcades. Piers with semi-octagonal projections, that towards the nave with a continuous moulding. Four bays but six clerestory windows. – PULPIT. Simple, of *c.* 1800 (cf. Castlethorpe). – WALL PAINTINGS. Bear with ragged staff (wall of the stair-turret). – PLATE. Cup of 1621.

RECTORY FARM, s of the church. With one big s gable with mullioned and mullioned and transomed windows. Stone.

The village street has many stone cottages, some with c 17 datestones. ALMSHOUSES, dated 1712, plain, of stone. BAPTIST CHAPEL, 1809, plain rectangle, the side with two arched windows and an arched doorway between. WESLEYAN CHAPEL, 1826, plain rectangle, the front with two arched windows and an arched doorway between. At the top of the main street, set across, the WATTS ARMS, Late Georgian, three bays, the first and third with giant blank arches.

HANSLOPE HOUSE. Big square plain Georgian house. The grounds were landscaped by *Repton* before 1794 (see his 'Sketches').

TATHALL END FARMHOUSE, 1 m. E. Date-stones 1602 and 1625. Of stone, gabled, with a square dovecote.

HARDMEAD

ST MARY. Unbuttressed C13 w tower. One bell-opening of two arches with a polygonal shaft between and a trefoil in plate tracery. s arcade and N arcade of two bays, both Dec, with quatrefoil piers and double-chamfered arches, but the extremely instructive differences in the mouldings of the capitals show that the s arcade was built earlier. Later Dec chancel, the windows with flowing tracery. Dec also the s porch, see the two-light side openings. Perp tower top and clerestory. – FONT. Perp, with elaborate tracery, rosette, etc. patterns, much re-cut. – BENCH ENDS. Straight-headed with buttresses. – ORGAN. Pretty Late Georgian piece in the Gothic taste. – STAINED GLASS. C14 fragments in a chancel N window. – PLATE. Salver of 1658; Cup and Cover Paten of 1692. – MONUMENTS. Francis Catesby † 1636. Miniature recumbent effigy (2 ft 3 in.). Three small, utterly arbitrarily placed kneeling figures above. Framing by two columns carrying a grotesquely oversized semicircular open pediment. What is the most engaging feature of this naive monument is that the background behind the columns and the surface below the effigy are closely patterned with what seems at first a grid, but is backs of books and foredges of books and the clasps of the bindings (cf. Dr Bodley, Merton College, Oxford, and Easton Maudit, Northamptonshire). – Robert Shedden † 1849. By *Gaffin*. He died in his sailing ship searching in the Arctic for Sir John Franklin. At the foot relief of the sailing ship.

HARDWICK

ST MARY. The N wall of the nave is Anglo-Saxon, see one window with deep double splay above the N doorway. Dec s aisle with fleuron decoration in the arch of the doorway, circular E window with a charming ogee four-petalled flower, and arcade of five bays. The piers are of an odd shape, quatrefoil but instead of the foils a broad flat front with ogee sides. Double-chamfered

arches, one circular clerestory window with quatrefoil. The w
tower also is Dec, see e.g. the bell-openings. Most windows
Perp. Wide nave with roof of low pitch and tie-beams with
tracery over. Chancel of 1872. – STAINED GLASS. Bits of original glass in the s aisle se window. – One n window by *H. Hughes*,
1878, terrible. – MONUMENTS. A number of minor tablets.

MANOR FARMHOUSE. Early C17. Timber-framed with brick
infilling. Staircase through two upper storeys; vertically symmetrical balusters.

RECTORY. To the l. of the mid-C18 front a wooden four-centred
doorhead with the date 1551. The front is of five bays and two
storeys with a three-bay pediment. Doorway and all windows,
including the circular one in the pediment, have frames of
stones of alternating sizes.

HARLEYFORD MANOR   8080
1½ m. sw of Marlow

Built in 1755 by *Sir Robert Taylor* for Sir William Clayton. Five 1b
by five bays, of brick. Basement, main storey, and half-storey.
Towards the river a generous three-bay bow window, towards
the e a canted bay, towards the entrance a three-bay projection
with arched main-floor windows and pediment. It is said that
there was here originally a portico, and that the columns were
removed for use around the rotunda in the grounds known as
the Temple of Vesta. This temple is now in decay. Inside the
house a splendid room behind the bow window with plaster
panels on the walls of the instruments of hunting, fishing, painting, music, etc. Fireplace with two bearded termini caryatids.
Fine overmantel also in the Library. Oak-leaves play round the
sides of the panel. The grounds are superb, landscaped according to tradition by *Capability Brown*. The river Thames is immediately down the front lawn of the house. In the grounds
STATUE to Sir William Clayton. (A duplicate on the terrace
above the house.)

HARTWELL   7010

HARTWELL HOUSE. The n front, though refaced in ashlar, is 37b
that of a major Jacobean mansion. Square central porch with
over-ornate tapering pilasters. Above it a bow window on an
over-elaborate bracket. To the l. and r. of the porch a canted
bay and one bay of windows. They are of several lights with two
transoms on ground floor and upper floor. Projecting end bays,
again with bow windows on the upper floor. The brackets are

simpler. The parapet with vases belongs to *c.* 1740. The Jacobean house had far-projecting wings to the s. The space between them was nearly all filled in the c18 and a new s front created. This has a wide three-bay centre with a curved porch on coupled Tuscan columns, fine tripartite arched windows on the ground floor, and niches between the windows above. To the l. and r. three narrowly-set arched windows representing the staircase and the former chapel, and then two projecting end bays with canted bay windows. Noble, well-proportioned c18 E front with two canted bay windows and a central Tuscan porch with coupled columns. The main upper windows have pediments and simple volutes down their sides.

Inside, the Jacobean age is chiefly represented by the Grand Staircase with a wide open well and figures on the newel posts. The balusters are in the form of small figures too. Also a number of very elaborate fireplaces on the ground floor and first floor. In the kitchen, to the w of the Hall, one Jacobean stone doorway. In the w wall re-done Jacobean windows. But mostly the interior was remodelled in the c18, apparently at two times, as the paving of the redecorated Hall was paid for in 1740 (Gunnis), but *Henry Keene* built the E front and did more in 1759–61 (Colvin). The Hall now has stucco panels, especially a large one with an allegorical figure over the fireplace, a stucco ceiling, again with an allegorical centre-piece, and a big fireplace with two male caryatids in profile. Also of the c18 the semicircular Vestibule s of the Hall and forming the centre of the house, the Library (s E corner) with the original bookcases and a Rococo fireplace, the room to the N of it which forms the centre of the E front (fireplace with two female caryatids), and the room to the N of this which is the N E corner room, more Rococo and livelier than the others. About 1830 an Observatory was added to the house. It projected E from the s E corner, but has since disappeared.

STABLES. c18 with an archway with Gibbsian decoration and three bays l. and r. The outer bays have Venetian windows.

8b
&13
CHURCH, NW of the house and a deliberate vista from it. 1753–5 by *Henry Keene*. It is one of the most important churches of the Early Gothic Revival, but has been allowed to fall into ruin. Octagonal centre with two identical towers, to E and W. In the s and N bays rose windows, in the sw, s E, NW, and N E bays tall three-light windows under crocketed ogee arches. Their detail is highly incorrect, e.g. transoms in the form of concave-sided octagons. In the attic-storey quatrefoil windows.

The extremely pretty plaster fan-vault inside has collapsed. GARDENS. The general layout of the gardens is due to *Capability Brown*, *c.* 1750. The long North Avenue was planted *c.* 1830. EQUESTRIAN STATUE of Frederick, Prince of Wales, lead, of 1757, an OBELISK without inscription s of the house, a COLUMN with a statue of George II E of the house, also erected in 1757. On the road to Lower Hartwell the so-called EGYPTIAN SPRING, which was built about 1830 and had the Greek inscription ' Ἄριστον μὲν ὕδωρ' along its top.

HAVERSHAM
8040

ST MARY. Norman nave, see the w window now looking into the tower. It has flat zigzag decoration round its frame. The w tower was added very soon after. Unbuttressed, with round-arched bell-openings. They are twin and have polygonal shafts between. Pointed tower arch, low, with one slight chamfer. Dec chancel E window and s window. Dec aisles, see several windows and the arcades. Both aisles have w lancets. The SE window has an angle piscina inside. Dec arcades. Octagonal piers, double-chamfered arches. The capitals of the N arcade earlier than those of the s arcade. Perp clerestory. – BENCHES. Some of the C16 with very elementary poppy-heads. – STAINED GLASS. N aisle E by *Powell & Sons*, designed by *Moberly*, 1860. Same style also chancel s. – PLATE. Cup and Cover Paten of 1569. – VAMPING HORN. To excite the choir to more lively singing. 4 ft 5 in. long. – MONUMENTS. Brass to Alicia Payn † 1427 (chancel s wall), a 20 in. figure. – Brass to John Maunsell † 1605 (chancel floor), a skeleton. – Lady of *c.* 1390. Alabaster. Angels by her pillow. Against the tomb-chest figures of angels and in the middle two mourners. Elaborate stone recess with openwork cusping and sub-cusping of the arch and an ogee gable. The recess probably earlier than the monument.

RECTORY. s of the church. Five-bay, two-storey brick house with hipped roof. Early C18. A later addition on the l.

HAVERSHAM GRANGE, ¼ m. NE. Gabled stone house with a date-stone 1628. Inserted a C14 doorway and two-light window.

HILL FARM, 1 m. NE. Gabled, of stone, C17, with a Perp doorway from Stantonbury.

HAWRIDGE
9000

ST MARY. 1856 by *William White*. Flint with bands of brick. Lancet windows. Wooden bell-turret. – FONT. C13, circular, with flowers, etc.

HAWRIDGE MILL see CHOLESBURY

9080

HEDGERLEY

ST MARK. By *Ferrey*, 1852. On an eminence a little away from
the village street. Flint. W tower, nave and chancel. – FONT.
Cylindrical, with eight small individual motifs carved on, a
shield, a rose, two fleurons, and four heads. Is it of the C15 or a
recutting of the C17? – PAINTING. The Ten Commandments,
surrounded by small scenes showing the fate of those who
broke them, e.g. 'Wicked Jezabel eaten with dogs for bearing
false witness against good Naboth', and in addition four scenes
from the life of Moses; 1664, rustic and enjoyable. – PLATE.
Small Paten on foot of 1634; Cup of 1700. – CLOTH. The piece
of red cloth on the chancel s wall is connected by tradition with
Charles I, who is said to have given a cloak for an altar frontal. –
BRASSES. Robert Fulmer † 1498 and wife, the figures *c.* 15 in.
long. – Margaret Bulstrode † 1540, a 1 ft 10 in. figure.

To the NW of the church along the road, facing one another,
VICTORIA COTTAGES, C16, timber-framed with overhang,
and the RECTORY, 1846, Tudor, brick with dark diapering and
two front gables side by side. A little further N SHELL HOUSE
of *c.* 1700, chequer brick, three by two bays with modern cross-
windows and a hipped roof. The doorway has carved brackets
which probably originally carried a shell-hood. The present
pilasters are later.

9080

HEDSOR

ST NICHOLAS. Small, of flint, nave and chancel and a bell-turret
with pyramid roof. Externally all renewed. The church, according to an inscription, was 're-edified' by Roland Hynd who
died in 1608. Restoration, i.e. re-gothicization, in 1862, when
the N aisle was added. In 1886 more alterations. – Victorian
FURNISHINGS, very complete: Reredos with mosaic and
marble, and corresponding Altar Surround. – Very Gothic
Chancel Stalls and Organ Case. – Tall wooden Screen, wide
open to see through. – Stone Pulpit.

HEDSOR HOUSE. 1862, of white brick, reticently Italianate with
bay windows.

HEDSOR PRIORY. The Italianate house incorporates part of the
walls of old Hedsor House. It seems to have received its present
form in 1844. In the grounds two modern cottages by *Eric
Janes.*

LORD BOSTON'S FOLLY. On the hill to the N of the church. Late C18. Remarkably substantial. Three flint towers, one of them circular, connected by curtain walling.

HIGH WYCOMBE

8090

With its 41,000 inhabitants, High Wycombe is the second largest town in Buckinghamshire. It is an industrial town too, but the furniture industry – to a considerable extent a C19 development incidentally – is not concentrated in a few vast establishments, but is split up in many small or medium-size units, and it is not a smoky industry. The town is neat, even where it is architecturally indifferent. It stretches for nearly five miles along the valley of the river Wye and has to its N and S, close to the centre, two lines of hills, which, though not high, are prominent. The main N–S roads have both to manage steep climbs.

CHURCHES

ALL SAINTS. A large church, and right in the middle of the town. The tower which dominates its centre is in its upper part a very pretty piece of early Gothic Revival – 1755 by *Henry Keene*, who built the classical Guildhall, but also the Gothic church of Hartwell. Below, the tower is Perp, of c. 1510–20. The vicar under whom it was built was later clerk of Cardinal Wolsey's work at Oxford. It has the polygonal clasping buttresses of the tower of Magdalen College, Oxford, a big W doorway, and large three light bell-openings with panel tracery. Keene's top has a graceful parapet with a frieze of openwork quatrefoils and an openwork cusping and banded obelisk pinnacles. The tower is stonefaced, the rest of the church is of flint. It seems externally all Victorian (restoration 1887–9 by *Oldrid Scott*, internal restoration 1873–5 by *Street*). The medieval church had a central tower which was taken down only in 1509–10. The transepts remain. Their fenestration (except for the N transept N window) represents original later C13 work – see the bar tracery with foiled circles; the same tracery occurs also in the aisles and the N chancel chapel. In a state nearer the later C13 original is the ground floor of the S porch: rib-vaulted with a fillet on the main roll moulding, blank pointed-trefoiled arcading on shafts along the side walls, and an inner doorway which is double-shafted and has a complexly-moulded arch. All shafts carry stiff-leaf capitals. Perp clerestory windows and Later Perp windows of the N and S chapels. The interior is spacious. Perp six-bay arcades plus the arches to the transepts. Tall piers with the

6—B.

familiar four-shafts-and-four-hollows section. Arches with a double-wave moulding. The tower arch is Perp too, but in front of it, seen from the nave, appears a taller shafted arch which must have belonged to a spectacular late C13 W window. The chancel chapels are of three bays, with piers of the same section as the nave piers, but with Late Perp four-centred arches. In the N aisle two (or rather one-and-a-half) low tomb recesses. – FURNISHINGS. FONT. By *Street*, executed by *Earp*. – SCREEN between S transept and S chapel. Of 1468, with an inscription referring to Richard Redehode. Much restored. – STAINED GLASS. E window by *Hardman*, 1872. – S aisle, two windows by *Kempe*, 1900; also chancel S, 1903. – MAYOR'S DESK (S transept), C18. – CHURCHYARD GATES. Wrought iron, 1762. From Wycombe Abbey. – PLATE. Cup of 1671; Cover Paten of 1686; larger Paten of 1684.

30a   MONUMENTS. In the N chapel Henry Petty, Earl of Shelburne, by *Peter Scheemakers*. Erected in 1754. A very large, ambitious piece with many figures. Reredos background with coupled columns, attached the outer, detached the inner. Broken pediment. In the middle, large sarcophagus with an oval medallion carrying the portrait bust of the famous C17 Sir William Petty. On the sarcophagus the semi-reclining figure of Lord Shelburne in Roman dress and behind him, sitting a little more upright, his wife. To the l. a Roman and his seated wife with a baby, to the r. two young standing women and a boy. – In the same chapel, Grecian tablet to Isaac King † 1832, with quarter Greek-Doric columns and on the l. the standing figure of Charity. By *Edward Physick*. – In the S chapel, Countess of Shelburne † 1771 by *Carlini*. Life-size standing figure with two children by an urn, the smaller nude and perched on the urn. Obelisk behind. – Also in the S chapel Mrs Shrimpton † 1784, by the elder *Richard Westmacott*. Obelisk at the back. Standing female figure with raised arm by a big urn and a portrait in an oval medallion. – In the S aisle Jacob Wheeler † 1621, a shoemaker. Modest tablet with a frame incorporating the shoemaker's tools.

ST ANNE, Wycombe Marsh. 1859 by *Street*. Flint. Small with a weeny bell-turret.

ST AUGUSTINE (R.C.), Amersham Hill. By *J. Sebastian Comper*, 1955–7. Externally in an anaemic neo-Gothic. Light brick. Very conventional inside too. Classical West Gallery, Early Christian altar canopy.

CHRIST CHURCH, Crendon Street. By *Arthur Vernon*, 1889–97.

(GR). Not on a detached site. Brick, Geometrical style with an entrance loggia and two higher bays, l. and r.; on the r., i.e. asymmetrically placed, a turret.

т FRANCIS, Terriers. By *Sir Giles Gilbert Scott*, consecrated in 1930. A remarkable church, among the best by Sir Giles Scott. Prominent from outside and sensitively planned inside. Tall central tower with tall paired bell-openings and concave-sided arches. Short altar space. No E window. Tall clerestory – not clear; for it is also without windows. No w window either. Low baptistery and low entrances in slightly higher side pieces of the w front. These side pieces have pyramid roofs kept well below the upper parts of the nave. Through these low entrances one enters the low aisles. The piers are oblong with rounded corners, and the arches die into them. They are of buff stone, the walls are whitewashed. Low arch to the Baptistery. After this relatively stark nave, the crossing is an excelsior. Very tall arches, lantern light from above, very tall transept windows, and very tall N and S windows of the short altar room. So a procession in terms of light is accomplished which is emotionally very effective.

т JAMES, Downley. By *Cecil Brown*. Built in 1938–9 and still only a fragment. But the fact is worth noting how active C20 High Wycombe has been in the building of new churches (*see also* below).

т JOHN, Desborough Road. By *Caröe*, 1901. Fiery red brick. Incomplete and externally unattractive. Inside, however, interesting, if somewhat confused. Piers without capitals, narrow, high aisle passages. Chancel with tall arch and then lower presbytery arch and yet lower arches to the chancel chapels.

т MARY AND ST GEORGE, Dashwood Avenue. By *Wellesley & Wills*, 1938. Large and ambitious. Reached up a high (and cheaply done) stair. Light brick with an octagonal crossing dome. Tall clerestory, incomplete w end with baptistery and bellcote, apse. Low aisle passages. All round-arched.

HOLY TRINITY, Hazlemere. Neo-Norman, of 1845. Yellow brick, with bellcote and apse. A new chancel was begun in 1958.

BAPTIST CHURCH. Easton Street. 1908 by *Thomas Thurlow*. A remarkably late case of the Baptist tradition of Italianate fronts with Cinquecento details and pediment.

PUBLIC BUILDINGS

GUILDHALL, 1757 by *Henry Keene*, the gift of Lord Shelburne. 3a A charming building, splendidly placed across the w end of the

High Street and effectively closing it. Open ground floor with
Tuscan arcading. Three-bay width, the centre bay projecting
and marked on the ground floor by columns two-deep. Middle
window with stone surround; pediment. Pretty cupola with
Tuscan colonnettes, projecting pieces of entablature and a little
dome. The upper front room has a platform with a rail (twisted
balusters) and a fine 'reredos'. In the back room a large painting, 'St Paul converting the Druids' by *J. H. Mortimer*, from
the parish church; one of his major paintings, competent and
with little of his inner wildness.

TOWN HALL, Queen Victoria Street. 1903 by *J. J. Bateman* and
C. E. & A. Hale. Red brick and stone dressings. Symmetrical
front. Pretty pediment over the entrance and a lively little
lantern.

MUNICIPAL OFFICES, Queen Victoria Street. 1932 by *R. G.
Brocklehurst & Cowles Voysey*. Neo-Georgian, of eleven bays
with a five-bay centre.

MUSEUM AND LIBRARY, Queen Victoria Street. Simple neo-
Georgian annexe to the Town Hall. By *R. G. Brocklehurst*
1935.

POST OFFICE, Queen Victoria Street. 1934. Careful neo-Georgian.

POLICE STATION, Queen Victoria Street. 1937 by *E. A. L.
Martyn*. Sedate neo-Georgian.

3a MARKET HALL, High Street. First built in the C17. Rebuilt by
Robert Adam in 1761, but not one of his masterpieces. Brick.
Canted projecting centre, rounded back. Low leaded dome and
lantern of *c*. 1900. Lower wings with half-pediments. The
ground floor open with arches on heavy pillars. On the string-
course of the centre the inscriptions on the SW To London 29
miles, on the SE To Oxford 25 miles – expressing the roaring
fate of High Wycombe today.

COLLEGE OF FURTHER EDUCATION, Lily's Walk, St Mary's
Road. 1955 by the County Architect's Department. Tall block
in the modern style. Nothing special.

ROYAL GRAMMAR SCHOOL, Amersham Road. 1914 by *A. S.
Vernon*. Stately neo-Georgian with projecting wings and a
clock-turret.

64b HIGH SCHOOL FOR GIRLS, Marlow Hill. 1955–6 by *Denis
Clarke Hall*. The school, which is for 720 girls, consists of three
parallel staggered blocks all facing E and W. The middle range
is the principal one. It is of three storeys and contains laboratories, classrooms, etc., and on the top floor staff-room, rest-room

and two long balconies. The short recessed w range is one-storeyed and holds the gymnasium. In the E range, which is connected with the middle range by a bridge, are the dining-hall and kitchens below, the two-storeyed assembly hall, a small hall, the library, etc. The building is mostly of steel-frame construction. The classroom range has curtain walling with asymmetrically-placed panels of blue, yellow, red, etc. The hall range has a recessed brick ground floor and a s end of concrete slabs without windows. Two open far-projecting staircases on the E and W sides, one on scissor supports. Interesting space-frame roof in the Assembly hall.

WYCOMBE ABBEY SCHOOL, Marlow Hill. The mansion of the Lords Shelburne, built by *James Wyatt* in 1795 (Lysons; Colvin: *c.* 1804). Large and heavily picturesque. Grey squared stone and mortar mixed with bits of flint. Castellated and with turrets. Asymmetrical fronts to N and E. The E front continued in an arcade and an Orangery, with pointed arches. Tall impressive Entrance Hall with empty stucco niches high up and a canted ceiling with indications of arched braces and hammerbeams. In the Assembly Hall the Family Pew of the Shelburne family from the parish church, a delightful Gothic piece by *Keene*. Canted centre with an ogee arch, charming carving. This pew had sash windows and, as *The Ecclesiologist*, vol. 11, says, 'carpets and rich velvet sofas of the most somniferous character'. The school was founded in 1896. Two houses along Marlow Hill were built in 1898–1902 to the designs of *Caröe*, and a third a little lower down followed immediately. They are in the style of Champneys's work at Newnham College, but the earlier ones rather restless in the detail. A further house to the SE by *Caröe* 1910. The chapel, also by *Caröe*, dates from 1926. Strange small front with small motifs, especially colonnading with Romanesque colonnettes. Middle gable. The chapel extends behind to the E. Splendid grounds up a wide valley, beautifully landscaped.

SECONDARY MODERN SCHOOL, Mill End Road. 1937 by *Thurlow & Lucas*. Neo-Georgian.

CHRIST CHURCH MEMORIAL SCHOOLS, Queen Victoria Street. 1926 by *T. Thurlow* in an indifferent Gothic. No longer a school.

SWIMMING POOL, Recreation Ground, s of London Road. 1957 by the Borough Architect's Department. Light brick, modern, in the 1930 way, that is the pre-curtain-wall way. A very large establishment for a town the size of High Wycombe.

The swimming pool marks the site of THE RYE, a large
Roman villa. In 1724 a circular figural mosaic was found, and
in 1862–3 another with female busts which may be of the early
C2 A.D. Excavations of 1954–5 showed the villa to be of medium
size and double-corridor type. They revealed another mosaic,
a large detached bath house (altered in the early C4), a boundary
wall with gatehouse, and a separate out-building. Pottery finds
below this indicated a Neolithic settlement (cf. p. 15). Some
building material appears to be incorporated in the Norman
hospital of St John the Baptist.

PERAMBULATION

3a The obvious place to start from is the Guildhall and the High
Street. In the C18, when this centre of High Wycombe was not
primarily a bottleneck, what a fine sight it must have been. The
Guildhall closes the vista from the London side, and there are
good houses all along the HIGH STREET, first on the l. the
Market Hall (see above), and opposite the MIDLAND BANK, of
chequered brick, three bays, the first-floor middle window
with a fine brick surround and a pediment. Then the CO-
OPERATIVE SOCIETY, with a doorway of Tuscan demi-
columns and a pediment, and the NATIONAL PROVINCIAL
BANK, an excellent six-bay house with a two-bay projection
with giant angle pilasters and a pediment. Doorway with Doric
pilasters and pediment. Opposite, the RED LION HOTEL,
three quiet four-bay houses. Porch on paired Roman Doric
columns. A big red lion on it. Then, again on the s side, the
WESTMINSTER BANK, the best house in the town. Five bays,
two and a half storeys, the half-storey above the main entablature. Giant angle pilasters. Segment-headed windows.
Projecting middle bay, the middle window with fluted pilasters
and a head in the keystone. All this points to c. 1720–30. Then a
five-bay house of knapped flint and brick. Egg-and-dart frieze
below the eaves. Doorway with Ionic demi-columns and a
broken pediment. The end on the s an eight-bay early C19 terrace of three storeys. Yellow brick with two-bay projections l.
and r. The ground floor has blank arcading round the windows.
Two plain arched doorways. Opposite, WHITE HOUSE
STUDIO. Late C17. Three storeys, with quoins and a doorway
with a flat rusticated surround and a pediment.

Here a short cross axis has been developed as a neo-Georgian
civic centre. For the public buildings in Queen Victoria Street
see above. In CRENDON STREET also there are neo-Georgian

buildings: shops and offices. Before turning off here, EASTON
STREET to the E should be follwed, where there are more Georgian houses and also No. 17, an interesting C17 house with three
gables, an oversailing upper floor, quoins, a rusticated ground
floor, mullioned and transomed windows, two canted oriels,
and a bit of balustrading at the sill of the middle window. Inside,
some minor Jacobean fireplaces. (In the garden SUMMER-
HOUSE, square, two-storeyed, with brick pilasters.) Then on
the S QUEEN ELIZABETH'S ALMSHOUSES, Tudor of 1856,
and opposite the former GRAMMAR SCHOOL, white and red
brick, asymmetrical, by *A. Vernon*, 1883. In the front garden
of this the bedraggled ruin of the HOSPITAL OF ST JOHN.
Arcades of two bays and a third pier. They probably belonged
to the infirmary hall. The date must be *c.* 1180–90. Round
piers, square abaci, unmoulded round arches. Low capitals
with decorated water-leaf, single-lobed upright leaves, etc.

In LONDON ROAD nice Georgian houses continue to No. 23.
Further on, off Bassetsbury Lane, BASSETSBURY MANOR,
an interesting later C17 brick house of seven bays and two
storeys with a hipped roof. Doorway with a surround with
pilasters placed wide apart. The aprons to the first-floor windows are recent (*see* below). The rain-water heads 1740 and
1743 cannot refer to the original building. The SW end is a
pretty addition of *c.* 1930. The two capitals come from a house
in the Market Place at Nottingham, the fine W balustrade of *c.*
1660–70 from Wokingham. Just before the Manor BASSETS-
BURY MILL, red brick, Late Georgian, with its wheel restored.
See p. 341.

Back now to the corner of Queen Victoria Street, down this, past
the public buildings and the wall of Wycombe Abbey, and up
N again, ST MARY'S STREET. At the NW end of the street
THE GABLES, five bays, of chequered brick, *c.* 1700, with a
centre gable, a doorway with shell-hood on carved brackets, and
a decorated brick window above with a straight hood on brackets. Now along Paul's Row to the corner of WHITE HART
STREET and Church Street. Gabled C17 house, timber-
framed. A little more to the W MURRAY'S STORE, gay and up-
to-date. In BULL LANE a very puzzling little house. Brick,
three bays, with tripartite windows l. and r., the three lights
arched and the whole window with a flat brick ogee surround.
In the middle a tablet in a surround with three Ionic pilasters
and the date 1729 in ornamental numerals. Can the side windows
also be so early? Mr Colvin believes so (*Rec. of Bucks.*, XIV). In

FROGMOOR, N of Bull Lane, a wide space, on the l. a nice
Early Georgian four-bay house with segment-headed windows,
recently continued to the r. The top windows have aprons. The
N continuation of Frogmoor is TEMPLE END, where Nos 45–
47 is another early C18 house: eight bays, segment-headed windows, dormers with alternating triangular and segmental pediments, doorway with segmental pediment on big upright volute
brackets.

We return by PRIORY AVENUE at the end of which, above the
railway, is CASTLE HILL HOUSE. In its grounds on the former
castle mount (which still stands to a height of approximately
30 ft) a castellated Folly, and N of the house a cottage with a
pretty thatched rustic veranda. Down the steps now and to
CASTLE STREET. Here, N of the church, a gabled C17 brick
house and the VICARAGE of 1756: five bays and two storeys,
vitreous and red brick, with a parapet. Central canted oriel
window on Tuscan columns. Finally, E of the church, the
OAKLEY MEMORIAL HALL of 1906, by *F. P. Oakley*, entirely in the Voysey style, i.e. with his curved parapets and
short finials and his pebble-dash.

A postscript on two outlying buildings: TERRIERS HOUSE, late
C17, in some ways comparable with Bradenham House. Of
seven bays and two storeys with hipped roof. Brick, plastered.
Rusticated ground floor. The middle bay projects and has on
the first floor pilasters l. and r. At the angles of the house broad
pilasters in two orders with sunk panels. Sunk panels also
between the windows. Entrance Hall arched at the end. The
staircase is Georgian. Further N, on the way to Hazlemere, in its
own grounds the new office building of the EQUITY AND LAW
LIFE ASSURANCE, sumptuous and neo-neo-classical, by
Brocklehurst, Cooper & Williamson.

On KEEP HILL, S of the Wye, a line of FORTIFICATIONS of uncertain date.

6020
HILLESDEN

ALL SAINTS. An uncommonly lavish, entirely Perp church. The
W tower comes first, and before the decision to spend so much
on the rebuilding. All the rest is shortly after 1493. Extremely
impressive exterior, especially from the N. Embattled N aisle
with large three-light windows, embattled tall N porch. Clerestory with a continuous band of lights not grouped into individual windows at all. Transept and N chapel also embattled, with
tall four-light windows. Two-storeyed N vestry with a stair-
turret carrying a delightful 'crown', i.e. an ogee-shaped top o

openwork flying buttresses. E side all embattled. Four-light N chapel window, four-light chancel E window with transom. This window has panel tracery, the others have none. S side also embattled, again with chancel chapel, transept and aisle, and with four- and three-light windows. One enters by the N porch, which has panelled sides and a fan-vault. The arcades have slender piers with an enriched version of the four-shafts-and-four-hollows section. In the chancel chapels there are eight shafts and eight hollows instead. Chancel arch of the same type. The display culminates in chancel and N chapel. The walls of both are panelled in stone, and the chancel has in addition a whole close row of stone angels below the ceiling. The church was thoroughly restored by *Sir George Gilbert Scott,* who at the age of fifteen had drawn it very competently (drawing in the Vestry). – ROOD SCREEN. Tall, of single-light divisions with traceried bands. Ribbed coving. – SCREEN to the N chapel with thin buttresses and linenfold panelling. – FAMILY PEW. Of *c.* 1660–75, good, especially the upper tier of cartouches. – BENCHES. With linenfold panelling, much restored. – DOOR (N aisle). Traces of carved sun, moon, and star on outer face. Late C15. – PAINTINGS. Moses and Aaron, crude, C18. – STAINED GLASS. In the S transept E window stories of St Nicholas, early C16. – The S window of the same transept in the same style by *Burlison & Grylls, c.* 1875. – In the chancel E window many saints in the tracery, late C15. – PLATE. Large Flagon of 1736; Cup of 1811. – MONUMENTS. Thomas Denton † 1560, of alabaster. Tomb-chest with shields separated by strips with balusters in relief. Two recumbent effigies. – Alexander Denton † 1576. No effigies at all. The centre is a tall narrow sarcophagus. Above it inscription plate with strapwork. L. and r. Roman Doric columns carrying an entablature. Above this another broad, sarcophagus-like shape, and then a crowning pediment. – Thomas Isham † 1676. Tablet with oval cartouche framed with odd gristly, sea-weedy, stylized foliage. Two cherubs' heads and a skull below, two cherubs and arms above. – Sir Alexander and Lady Denton, the latter † 1733. Signed by *Sir Henry Cheere.* Big white marble base. On it grey marble sarcophagus, and above this tall grey obelisks. To the l. and r. on bases freestanding busts, not very elegantly carved.

Hillesden is now a tiny hamlet. Of the mansion of the Dentons nothing remains, and the church is all the more impressive for its lone position.

WINDMILL. A post-mill.

HITCHAM

ST MARY. Tudor brick tower. Norman nave (N and S windows).
The chancel arch seems to date from *c.* 1190, i.e. the arch is
still round and simply one-stepped, but the shafts are keeled
and have capitals with upright leaves. The leaves on the l. are
broad and flat. The chancel itself has Dec windows, very
prettily shafted inside. The tiny capitals have foliage. A string-
course runs along the walls inside, and this ends in the NW with
a head. The SW head is not *in situ* and is re-tooled. The western-
most S window of the chancel is circular and contains a cusped
trefoil. – PULPIT with tester. C17 and the usual blank arches
below oblong panels. – STAINED GLASS. Interesting C14
remains in the chancel windows, including large figures of
angels on wheels. Smaller figures in the tracery heads. – TILES.
C14 and later; chancel floor. – PLATE. Cup and Cover Paten of
1684; Almsdish of 1694. – MONUMENTS. Roger Alford † 1580
and wife. Small, with the usual kneelers facing one another. –
Sir William Clarke † 1624. Of white marble. Recumbent effigy.
Two soldiers l. and r. hold curtains open. Superstructure with
obelisks. Children kneeling against the tomb-chest. Original
iron railings.

MANOR HOUSE. The building is gone, but the extensive C17
brick walling of the gardens survives, to the NE of the church,
including wrought-iron gates.

HITCHAM HOUSE, formerly Blythwood. Gothic, brick, with
stepped gables. By *T. Roger Smith*, 1870.

HITCHAM FARMHOUSE, E of the church. Early C17. The house
(N wing with brick-nogging and weatherboarding) and the
barns make a nice group with the church.

HOGGESTON

HOLY CROSS. Looks all new outside. Weatherboarded C16 bell-
turret over the W end of the N aisle, on heavy timbers inside.
Early C13 S aisle of two bays, circular pier, pointed arches with
no more moulding than a slight chamfer. C14 N aisle of three
bays with octagonal piers and double-chamfered arches. At the
same time a W bay was added to the S aisle. The former W wall
still recognizable. The double-chamfered arch dies into the
imposts. Some early C14 and Perp windows. – PULPIT.
Simple, of *c.* 1700. – STAINED GLASS. The E window by *Sir
Ninian Comper*, 1949. – PLATE. Cup with Cover Paten, 1569;

Paten on foot, C17; Flagon, 1683. – MONUMENTS. Recumbent stone effigy of a Civilian, holding a chapel in his hands; C14. – Elizabeth Mayne † 1599. Tomb-chest with shield surrounded by strap-work.

MANOR HOUSE, S of the church. Probably Jacobean. Brick with blue brick diapering. One shaped gable with a chimneystack right in front of it so that the chimneyshafts hide part of the gable. On the S as well as the N side broad giant brick pilaster-strips, not in any special arrangement. Staircase with fine dumb-bell balusters.

RECTORY. 1784. Three bays, tall ground floor with arched windows and doorway. Pediment right across with a broad white segmental fan motif. The wings are a C20 addition.

HORSENDEN

ST MICHAEL. The present church is no more than the chancel of the former. The nave was destroyed and replaced in 1765 by the short ashlar-faced W tower. The chancel windows are Perp and of three lights. – SCREEN. Of one-light divisions, but intersected blank arches binding them together in twos. Now against the W wall. – BENCHES. Arranged in the fashion of choir stalls, probably at the time of the restoration (1869). – PLATE. Cup on baluster stem, 1661 (1671 ?).

HORSENDEN HOUSE. Built in 1810. Cemented. Five bays to the N, three with a Venetian window to the S. Bow windows continue the five-bay front round the corner.

DOVECOTE, NW of the church. A delightful piece, with a ground floor used as a shed, with timber posts and arched braces, then a big truncated pyramid roof, and the nesting places on the weatherboarded upper floor. Little pyramid roof at the top.

HORTON

ST MICHAEL. A sumptuous Norman N doorway. It has one order of shafts and enriched scallop capitals, and in the arch zigzag at r. angles to the wall. Continuous outer mouldings, one of spools, the other of four zigzags. Transitional S arcade of three bays with very fat circular piers carrying circular capitals and square abaci. Unmoulded pointed arches with thin hood-moulds. Perp W tower with higher stair-turret. The top storey of both is of brick, of c. 1600. The church is of flint, but the chancel, which was rebuilt in 1875, is of stone. The S aisle walls also date from 1875. – FONT. Norman, tub-shaped. At the top, band of twisted

rope. – STAINED GLASS. Much by *Kempe*, e.g. the S aisle and
the chancel E of 1882–3. – PLATE. Cup and Cover of 1697.*

W of the church, past the Colnbrook road BROOKFIELD on the l.,
THE CEDARS on the r. The former is Late Georgian of red
brick with three bays and three storeys, the latter a little later,
of yellow brick with a cast-iron veranda. SE of the church HOR-
TON MANOR, also Late Georgian, with a porch of two pairs of
Doric columns.

MILDRIDGE FARM, ¾ m. N on the Colnbrook road, has a three-
bay front with a one-bay broken pediment. In it an oval window, and below it on ground floor and first floor Venetian windows.

8090

HUGHENDEN

ST MICHAEL. By *Sir Arthur Blomfield*, 1874–90, half-way up the
drive to the house. Flint, with a low W tower with pyramid roof.
Of the medieval church the N chapel of the C14 remains and the
early C16 arcade between it and the chancel. This is of two bays
with a smaller third to hold a monument (*see* below). – FONT.
Late C12 with blank arcading of thin shafts and trefoil arches. –
CHANCEL FITTINGS. Low metal Screen by *Shrivell* of London,
tiles designed by *E. Godwin*, paintings of the boarded roof by
Heaton & Butler. – STAINED GLASS. Chancel S window by
Willement, c. 1855. – Nave S window by *Clayton & Bell*, c. 1880.
– MONUMENTS (N chapel). Brass to Rolf Thurloe, vicar, 1483
(13 in. figure). – Effigy of a Knight, late C14 (window sill). –
Cadaver of the early C16. This lies in the arch between the
chancel and the chapel, and it can be assumed that it represents
the man who rebuilt the arcade. – Effigy of a Knight, cross-
legged, in a late C13 style. This lies now in a C14 recess in the
chapel, but clearly does not belong to it (the late C14 knight may
be the genuine inhabitant), nor does it belong to the late C13. It
has been exposed as without any doubt a fake of the time of
Henry VIII, made so that a member of the Wellesbourne
family, then lords of the manor, could prove their descent from
Simon de Montfort. To follow the fake in detail the heraldry
has to be studied. The genuine late C14 knight also received
a false coat of arms. In addition, faked deeds with faked seals
and a whole faked ancient parchment roll were fabricated.
Moreover, and this is of special interest to us, three whole sham
C15 effigies were made, one with visor drawn, the other two
with swords raised. They could not deceive anyone nowadays.

---

* Milton's mother is buried in the chancel.

The convincing suggestion has been made that the Welles-bournes came originally from Wellesbourne Montfort in Warwickshire and, after a century and more of life in Buckinghamshire, felt in need of an authentic pedigree. – Benjamin Disraeli, Lord Beaconsfield, erected by Queen Victoria, with the profile portrait by *R. C. Belt*. – Lady Beaconsfield † 1872 and others, outside the E end of the N chapel. Gothic triptych wall and grave in front of it.

ALMSHOUSES, SW of the church. Early C17, remodelled 1842. With six gables, l. and r. brick, the others timber-framed. Mullioned windows with hood-moulds.

HUGHENDEN MANOR. A plain, plastered, thirteen-bay brick house of the C18 of which six bays belong to two canted bay windows. This unassuming house was ruthlessly dramatized by *E. B. Lamb* for Benjamin Disraeli in 1862. He had bought the property in 1847. Lamb's details are excruciating, everything sharp, angular, aggressive. As much brickwork as possible set diagonally, the battlements stepped and with diagonally-placed pinnacles, the window-heads indescribable. Inside, most of the rooms with ribbed ceilings, even the underside of the quite small staircase. Only the Library has kept its late C18 fireplace and plaster ceiling.

MONUMENT, 1 m. to the W, on the edge of Great Tinkers Wood. Red granite pillar of florid forms erected to the memory of Isaac d'Israeli by his son. It is 50 ft high and was designed by *E. B. Lamb*. It was illustrated in *The Illustrated London News* in 1863.

MANOR FARM, ½ m. SW. Fine C18 house of six bays and two storeys. Chequered brick. Hipped roof. Doorway with pediment on upright carved brackets. (Inside, C18 paintings of mountains, lakes, fishing, hunting game, etc. *Rec. of Bucks.*, XIII.)

NORTH DEAN HOUSE, 1¾ m. NW. Good Early Georgian brick house of seven bays and two storeys with hipped roof. The middle window is flanked by rusticated brick strips.

UPLANDS, Kingshill. 1859. With pointed window arches and heavy castellation. It could be by *Lamb*, judging by the handling.

HULCOTT

ALL SAINTS. Small and close to an attractive green with old trees. Nave and chancel with S aisle. Weatherboarded bell-turret on strong, internally visible timbers. The E bay of the S aisle was originally a transept. Its arch is of the early C14. The w bay is late Perp. – MONUMENT. C16 tomb-chest with indents for brasses on the lid.

MANOR HOUSE, s of the church. The staircase with big vertically symmetrical balusters must be of the second third of the C17. On a wall of it some C17 WALL DRAWINGS of Leda and Hercules and arabesques.

7090   IBSTONE

ST NICHOLAS. Beautiful view to the s across the Turville valley. A picturesque and singular little church with a low weatherboarded bell-turret. Norman s doorway and Norman w window. The doorway is fragmentary. Lintel with three billet friezes, abaci with saltire crosses. Chancel E end C13, group of three lancets. – PULPIT. Perp, with buttress shafts at the angles and also to separate the two blank-arched panels on the outside. – PLATE. Cup of 1619 (?).

COTTAGES, near Ibstone House on the Fingest–Stokenchurch Road. By *Colin Penn*, 1948.

6000   ICKFORD

ST NICHOLAS. Essentially of the late C12 to early C13. Unbuttressed Norman w tower, see one round-arched window. Tall C13 w lancet, fine late C13 bell-openings to the w: twin lancets with trefoiled heads under blank pointed arches. The other bell-openings are Dec. Saddleback roof. In the N aisle also one Norman window. Others again C13, lancets and odd paired lancets. Especially odd the rere-arch of one which is trefoiled and has a kind of rosettes in the spandrels. There may well be some C16 or C17 re-working in the church. In the s aisle again lancets and also one large four-light window, perhaps of the time when Archbishop Sheldon was vicar of Ickford. Good s doorway with shafts with shaft-rings. One capital with upright leaves. Roll moulding, and, in addition, a continuous inner roll including the segmental inner arch. In the chancel N and s lancets too. The E window has Dec (reticulated) tracery. Inside, the earliest features are certain capitals, one in the s arcade with upright leaves like the buds of water plants, a similar one in the chancel arch, the other three of the Transitional type with trumpet-shaped scallops, and again Transitional capitals in the tower arch. The arches are all pointed, with roll mouldings in the chancel arch, double-chamfered in the arcades. The other s capitals and the N capitals are circular. – PULPIT. With a C17 tester. – FONT COVER. Made about the 1920s by Canon *Vernon Staley*, the then rector (cf. Brill). With thin balusters in various tiers, canopy-shaped. – COMMUNION RAIL. C18. – WEST GALLERY. Projecting on two columns. – STAINED GLASS. In several windows glass by *Comper*, 1919, 1934, 1947. – PLATE. Large Cup and Paten on foot, 1661. – MONUMENT. Thomas Tipping, 1595. No effigies, but the nine children kneeling small against the big tomb-chest. The initials of their Christian names are above their heads. Inscription plate with big strapwork surround. Thin black columns carrying a straight entablature. In the strapwork clamber figures and appear little heads with strange Red Indian head-dresses – a tradition of Flemish ornamental prints.

ICKFORD BRIDGE. Dated 1685. Two parts, one of one brick arch, the other of three stone arches. The bridge goes across the Oxfordshire border.

RECTORY. C16 and early C19. The timber-framed gabled wings l. and r. on the E side are C16, the piece between them is early C19. The future Archbishop Sheldon, when rector of Ickford, lived here.

LITTLE ICKFORD. A picturesque hamlet. The MANOR FARM of the C16 and C17 has a good staircase and arabesque wall painting below the later panelling of one room. THE CLOSE is of the C17 to early C18, timber-framed, but with one first-floor window in a rusticated surround.

ILMER 7000

ST PETER. Of stone. In pretty isolation, with only the smallest hamlet by it. Nave and chancel and a very attractive bell-turret. The church was restored in 1859–60 by *Street*, but the remarkable shingled spire on the tall weather-boarded bell-turret dates from 1890. It consists of a truncated pyramid with a needle-spire. In the nave a simple blocked C12 S doorway. The N doorway is pointed, also simple and of *c*. 1200. C13 chancel. – SCREEN. Of one-light divisions. The screen stands on a low stone wall. The tracery makes a relatively early date likely. – REREDOS of stone with inlaid cross of porphyry and marble. Of the 1860 restoration. – SCULPTURE. Small panels of the Trinity and St Christopher in the chancel N window. Of *c*. 1500. – PLATE. Cup and Cover Paten of 1569.

the chancel arch, double-chamfered in the arcades. The other s capitals and the N capitals are circular. – PULPIT. With a C17 tester. – FONT COVER. Made about the 1920s by Canon Vernon

IVER

ST PETER. Evidence of an Anglo-Saxon church one fragmentary N window. The frame towards the nave surrounded by a thin roll moulding and set into a small step. To this church a N aisle was added in the C12 by creating two unmoulded round-arched openings and setting the arches on big semicircular responds with many-scalloped capitals. The W tower follows, unbuttressed and with lancets and arch towards the nave of C13 shape. The top parts are Late Perp. Also of the C13 the S aisle. Three bays, circular piers with octagonal abaci, many-moulded (later?) pointed arches. Again C13 the chancel (chancel arch of many mouldings, also a S lancet). In it a fine (if over-restored) group of Sedilia and Double Piscina. From l. to r. two small pointed-trefoiled arches, one higher rounded-trefoiled one, and two pointed arches. C14 chancel N and S windows. Late Perp aisle windows. All external details much renewed. – FONT. Of Purbeck marble. Table-type, but with a kind of simple incised crenellation motif. Probably Norman. – PULPIT. Late C17, with cherubs' heads and garlands. – SCREEN. In the S aisle tall half-bay, probably a door-valve, of four lights and with tracery. The screen must have been unusually ambitious. – STAINED GLASS. By *Kempe* a N window in the chancel (1890), also the E window (1903). – MONUMENTS. Brass to Richard Blount † 1508 and wife, 3 ft 1 in. figures (chancel, N). – John King † 1604. Small, kneeling figure. Obelisks l. and r. Below, two oak trees and two hands joined together, with the motto: Inseparabiles Invulnerabiles. – Anna Melinge † 1610. Also with small kneeling figure (both S aisle). – Mary Salter † 1631. Attributed by Mrs Esdaile to *Gerard Christmas*. A very strange composition. The centre is a black coffin out of which the deceased woman in her shroud half-rises. Below, the inscription:

O death where is thy stinge
O grave where is thy victory

To the l. and r. of the coffin putti. Top pediments, too complex to be described. This whole upper part is supported by two black columns and a solid centre of weird shape. The children kneel small in between. – Henry Plant † 1784. Assigned by Mrs Esdaile for good reasons to *Sir Robert Taylor*. Unfluted Ionic columns with small flames on the shaft. Books at the foot to the

l. and r. – Edward Ward, 1838 by *Chantrey*. A portrait bust on a pedestal, a civic rather than a church memorial.

From the church to the NE BRIDGEFOOT HOUSE, a very fine Early Georgian house of five bays and two-and-a-half storeys with a hipped roof. Yellow brick with red brick dressings. The windows are vertically laced together in red brick. All front windows have heavy segmental heads. The windows of the half-storey in addition with aprons. Good railings, gate, and gatepiers. The architect *Bodley* lived here c. 1895–1905.

From the church to the W in the HIGH STREET No. 99 is an early house by *F. R. S. Yorke*, 1935. White, flat-roofed, with a terrace to the S, taking up one third of the ground-floor front. On the upper floor the terrace fills two-thirds of the front. The continuity of the concrete cube is however preserved by carrying the top beam as a frame along the front and back to the room behind the terrace. Very slim metal uprights. The side to the street (N) is frankly the back.

From the church to the N IVER LODGE, a handsome early C19 house of yellow brick. Three bays, the ground-floor side windows tripartite under shallow blank arches, the centre a canted bay in which the doorway is placed.

IVER GROVE, Wood Lane, at the corner of the B470 (Iver–Langley) road. Built in 1722, and one of the finest houses of Buckinghamshire in the Baroque style of that date. Brick, only five by three bays, but amply spaced. Two storeys with quoins. The centre of the W front has a three-bay pediment on giant Doric pilasters. The ground-floor windows are segment-headed. The middle window on the first floor is round-arched. So are the principal windows on the N and S sides. The W porch (pediment on Tuscan columns) is a later addition. On the N and S sides the centre bay is framed by a giant arch. Above it a short length of attic with a broken segmental pediment. This and the other features are typical of the style of the Wren office, i.e. the Office of Works, at the end of Wren's life, and connect Iver Grove with the work of Hawksmoor, Vanbrugh, and John James. Staircase with slender polygonal balusters and carved tread-ends. *See* p. 341.

About 1½ m. to the SW, THORNEY HOUSE, Georgian, of five bays and two storeys, with a hipped roof and a porch of two pairs of thin Tuscan columns.

(RICHING'S PARK, W of the above. Mr John Harris says that of the houses built c. 1790 a fragment of one wing remains, a pretty bridge, an ice-house, and the remains of a few cascades.)

0080   **IVER HEATH**

ST MARGARET. 1862 by *C. Reeks* (GR).

WARREN HOUSE. W of the church. By *R. W. Edis*, 1881. Picturesque Tudor, but with segment-headed windows on the brick
ground floor. Above harled plaster and half-timbered gables.
Inside a hall with gallery and glazed roof. The principal interior
fixtures were also designed by Edis.

DROMENAGH. Large, two-storeyed, of red brick, with a hipped
roof. 1910 by *Forsyth & Maule*.

TAIDSWOOD, 1 m. NE. By *Lionel Brett*, 1954. Delightfully
hidden in old trees with a view to the N. The contours allow for
a two-storeyed front and one-storeyed parts at the back. A
happy, informal composition. Yellow brick, weatherboarding,
and plaster.

9010   **IVINGHOE**

ST MARY. A big and noble church with a crossing tower. All embattled. The cruciform shape existed already in the C13,
although the crossing tower is of the early C14. Of the C13 the W
doorway with stiff-leaf capitals and deep arch moulding. Also
the five-bay arcades. They have octagonal piers with big,
10a   mature stiff-leaf capitals and double-chamfered arches. Above
the spandrels (not the apexes) of the arcade was a clerestory of
circular windows, fragments of which remain. The same windows preserved and restored with foiling of the circles in the W
walls of the transepts. Their E walls have somewhat later lancets
with pointed trefoils in the heads. The N transept N window is
of three lights, but its design is a variation on the same theme. In
the chancel N wall remains of the C13 fenestration too. The
crossing piers, however, must be later, as they cut into the nave
arcades and made some remodelling of the last bay necessary.
The details of the crossing look C14. C14 also the fine N doorway
with its fleuron decoration in one hollow. Perp W porch, good
Perp roofs with angel figures. The wall posts of the nave roof
have figures of the Apostles. The bay above the rood is panelled
and decorated with bosses. Perp clerestory and Perp tower top.
On the top a pretty lead spike. – PULPIT. Jacobean, with back
panel (on which a relief of the Resurrection) and tester. Very
ornate. – BENCH ENDS. With poppy-heads. – SCREEN. Bits re-
used in the Communion Rail. – PLATE. Large Salver of 1673. –
MONUMENTS. Very defaced C13 stone monument to a Priest.
The pillow is placed diagonally. – Brass to Richard Blackhed

† 1517 and wife. 16 in. figures. – Three later c16 brasses. – Henry Cooley. 1714 by *Edward Stanton*. A pretty tablet, with two cherubs' heads at the foot. – Deborah Heal † 1714. Convincingly ascribed to the same *Stanton* by Mrs Esdaile. – Outside the churchyard a formidable FIRE-HOOK to pull down burning thatch or timber.

To the W of the church in the main street first the YOUTH HOSTEL, later c18, of red brick, three bays wide, with an attenuated porch and arched windows over. The side windows are tripartite. Then the OLD TOWN HALL, attributed by the RCHM to the late c16. Of timber and brick. Sheahan says it was rebuilt in 1840, and the tall Gothic dormer windows with transoms and bargeboarded gables must indeed be Early Victorian in their present form.

PITSTONE GREEN MILL. Post-mill rebuilt from parts of an earlier mill. The timber is dated 1627, the earliest date connected with a windmill in the county.

RAILWAY WORKS. The railway cutting for the London–Birmingham line built from 1834 to 1838 was one of the great engineering feats of the age. The engineer in charge, as is well enough known, was *Robert Stephenson*. Smiles calls the cutting 'an immense chasm across the great chalk ridge'. It is 2½ m. long and for a quarter of a mile 57 ft deep. The one million and a half cubic yards of chalk and earth dug out were partly taken away, but partly also used to build up an embankment to the N of the cutting, nearly 6 m. long and 30 ft high.

IRON AGE HILL-FORT. On the top of Beacon Hill, 1 m. NE of the village, a triangular single-ditched contour hill-fort of the Iron Age enclosing 6 acres. The ground falls steeply on all sides except the E, the ditch having been thrown outwards to form a rampart. A 'bowl' BARROW, presumably of Bronze Age date, stands within the area of the fort. A second TUMULUS lies just E, a third about ⅓ m. due S of Beacon Hill.

JORDANS

9090

FRIENDS' MEETING HOUSE. The most famous of all Quaker meeting houses. Built in 1688 as such with a caretaker's dwelling under the same roof. Brick, recently renewed. Hipped roof. The meeting-part one-storeyed, the dwelling two-storeyed. Seats of the elders slightly raised. The wall panelling also rises 14a behind them. Plain balustrade in front. Gallery on the upper floor at the other end. In the graveyard the Penn and Pennington headstones.

STONE DEAN. Three wide bays, two storeys, hipped slate roof. Porch with paired columns.

DEAN'S FARM, W of the above. Timber-framing and brick-nogging.

OLD JORDANS FARM, N of the meeting house. C17 and later. Meetings were held here before the meeting house was built, at least as early as 1669. The house is now a hostel for Quakers and has been much restored and remodelled. The big Barn is said to be built with timber from the 'Mayflower'.

The village of Jordans was designed by *Fred Rowntree* before the First World War and begun in 1919. It follows the lines of the Hampstead Garden Suburb. Large oblong turfed main square with birch trees and Lombardy poplars. Red-brick houses with gables in a comfortable simplified Tudor. Several streets of such houses around.

7000

KINGSEY

ST NICHOLAS. 1892–3. – STAINED GLASS. E window, by *Kempe, c.* 1902. – MONUMENT. Tablet to Mrs Wykeham, 1823 by *Whitelaw* of London. With a weeping, kneeling woman, bent over an urn.

TYTHROP HOUSE. Late C17 house of two storeys. Brick, cemented. Very plain nine-bay front with a parapet and a doorway of unfluted detached Corinthian columns carrying a pediment. The window above has garlands and volutes. The side is also of nine bays. The middle three are three-storeyed. At the back two projecting wings. After this somewhat unpromising 39 exterior the interior is a surprise, especially the staircase, which is one of the finest in the county. Extremely luscious openwork foliage along the balustrade. Carving also along the string. Good upper doorcases. The plasterwork is later. Rococo ornament and full-length figures in relief. The Hall also has stucco of the same date. There are busts here of Milton, Newton, and two others. A wooden balcony runs around the hall. The house is supposed to have been built for a grandson of the fourth Earl of Pembroke (MHLG).

KNOTTY GREEN see BEACONSFIELD

8000

LACEY GREEN

ST JOHN EVANGELIST. 1826 by *J. Chadley*, chancel 1871 by *J. P. Seddon* (GR) – both parts interesting. The building of 1826 has centrally placed N and S projections with pedimental gables and large three-light mullioned and transomed windows of cast iron. Inside a West Gallery on cast-iron columns, twenty-nine shields of STAINED GLASS (by *Thomas Hills*), and a thin hammerbeam roof. Or is this roof a later alteration? If so, it can hardly have anything to do with Seddon. His chancel is typical of him: polygonal with, inside, restless yellow and red brick patterning. Steep chancel arch and a simple bold continuous moulding. Prominent TILING, in yellow and red and also green and blue.

WINDMILL. A derelict smock-mill. It was moved here from Chesham in 1821.

LANE END   *8090*

HOLY TRINITY. By *J. Oldrid Scott*, 1878 (GR). Tower heightened 1901 (GR). The tower is on the N side and has a pyramid roof. The interior is modest but not run-of-the-mill. Long nave with lancet windows which have cusped rere-arches. Small transept E of the tower continued in a two-bay chancel chapel. (The roof timbers come from a barn of Bisham Abbey.)*

MOOR FARM HOUSE, $\frac{1}{2}$ m. s. Late C17. The house has a five-bay front of two storeys, flint and red brick. The windows alas are altered, but the middle window on the first floor has cut brick-work at the top. The farmyard is accessible through a handsome brick GATEWAY with an arched entrance set in a rectangular frame and flanked by brick pilasters. A pair of shaped gables at the top, their semicircular top pierced by oval eyes.

CADMORE END, *see* p. 79.

LANGLEY MARISH   *0070*

ST MARY. One of the most rewarding churches of Buckingham-shire, a great surprise in the immediate neighbourhood of Slough. Norman masonry in the W front. Chancel and N chapel Dec. The windows much re-done externally, but originally shafted inside. The arcade to the chapel is of two bays with an octagonal pier and arches with sunk chamfer. In the chapel, head-corbels of 'green men'. In the chancel, Sedilia and Pis-cina, shafted, but not on the front – only towards the arches. Foliated spandrels. No gables. Then a number of brick addi-tions: the NW tower of 1609 with round-arched bell-openings and battlements, the gabled S transept or Kederminster Chapel with a large six-light transomed window, and the gabled

* Information received from the Rev. Hugh Crawford.

Kederminster Library to the w of the chapel fitted into the
s porch and a former chapel adjoining. A grant for the
Kederminster Chapel was obtained from the Dean and Chapter
of Windsor in 1613. The library was given in 1623 and housed in
1631, the date of Sir John Kederminster's will. In 1630 the
N aisle arcade was replaced by a wooden arcade of three bays
with six Tuscan columns set two-deep. – The church contains a
great wealth of furnishings, happily jumbled together. – FONT.
Perp, octagonal, with leaves, a head, etc., in quatrefoils. –
GALLERY in the tower to the s, with flat Jacobean balusters. –
GALLERY to the N aisle of the usual West Gallery type. – PUL-
PIT. With plain panels and strapwork on the posts. Dated 1609.
– SCREEN. Perp chancel screen with ogee-headed one-light
19b divisions. – SCREEN inside the Kederminster Chapel. Of wood,
painted. Inscription on the top frieze. Above this cut-out strapwork and openwork obelisks. – PAINTING. The chapel is
painted with fantastical architectural members. – SCREEN into
the Kederminster Chapel. Erected in 1792, after the chapel had
passed to the Harveys. Made of *Coade* stone. Of veranda type.
Three tall arches, slender quatrefoil piers. Vaulting inside. A
charming introduction to so curious a chapel. – Inside the
LIBRARY panelling, a frieze of landscapes with views of Eton,
Windsor, and some other buildings, and a late C17 chimneypiece. The panelling has an alternating rhythm of small vertical
and larger horizontal panels – a most successful arrangement. –
STAINED GLASS. C15 fragments in a N chapel N window. *See*
p. 341. – CHANDELIER. Of brass, C18. In the chancel. –
MONUMENTS. Kederminster family (chancel N), 1599. With
two pairs of kneeling figures facing one another and with their
30b children below, in the usual way. – David Harvey † 1788. Of
Coade stone. Slender and beautiful young woman standing by
a pedestal with an urn. The pedestal is placed at an angle.
Obelisk background. – Robert Gosling † 1794. Big standing
monument with obelisk, sarcophagus, and urn. No figures. Of
grey and white marble (N chapel). – Robert Bateson Harvey
† 1825. Very good unsigned monument. Seated figure of a
Grecian pilgrim with the Christian pilgrim's hat. – Robert
Harvey † 1863. Brass foliated cross on the floor of the Kederminster Chapel. – Robert Bateson Harvey † 1887. Brass with an
angel with widespread wings. Also on the floor of the chapel.
ALMSHOUSES. Of brick. The range s of the church founded in
1617 by Sir John Kederminster. Humble, of one storey with a
second in the gables. Four gables and a fifth over the central

porch. Brick doorways with pedimented gables. The range N
of the church is larger and was built between 1670 and 1680. It
is conservative for that date. Nine gables, including the one over
the porch, which is crowned by a pediment (a so-called Dutch
gable). The end gables have the same feature, which was
fashionable c. 1630–50. The porch and the doorways are
cement-rendered.

LANGLEY PARK. Built for the third Duke of Marlborough. Said
to be of c. 1740, but plans of c. 1755 exist and are by *Stiff Leadbetter*. The house is ashlar-faced and has seven by five bays. No
more decoration originally than a three-bay pediment to the
entrance and the lake, and a canted bay window to the garden.
Vigorous embellishments of c. 1850–60, especially on the entrance side, where, above a screen of one-storeyed columns,
walls were added ending in angle towers of Vanbrughian
character. Who was the architect? He was no doubt also responsible for the ORANGERY projecting to the S from the SW
angle. He also did much inside the house. Original chiefly the
Entrance Hall with a screen of four Tuscan columns at the
back. Staircase with Ionic columns on the first floor and an oval
glazed dome. On the first floor towards the S an octagonal room
in the centre. To the NW a large group of OUTBUILDINGS, of
red brick, including several ranges of Stables and an Orangery
with tall arched openings, seven bays, with a three-bay pediment. This may all be of the beginning of the C18.

Also to the NW, but further away, the COLUMN to the memory of
Robert Harvey, erected in 1805, a very oddly shaped and
decorated column with a kind of iron cage or pavilion on the
top.*

LANGLEY GRAMMAR SCHOOL. By the County Architect's Department (*F. B. Pooley*). Completed in 1956. For 600 children.
Pre-stressed concrete frame. The Assembly Hall is on the first
floor.

LATHBURY

ALL SAINTS. Of a Norman church two features remain, a handsome, if decidedly barbaric, tympanum (re-set at the NE corner
of the S aisle) with two beasts and the tree of life (plaited trunk,
very twisted branches), and an upper window to the l. of the E
bay of the S arcade. This arcade is of the late C12. Two broad
bays, pointed arch with one slight chamfer. Strong circular pier,
square abacus, capital with dragons. Leaves on the W and E

* This has recently been demolished.

responds. C13 w tower, unbuttressed. Bell-openings of twin arches with a polygonal shaft. Late C13 aisle fenestration: Y-tracery, intersected tracery, bar tracery with a circle. Y-tracery also in the N windows. To these belongs the N arcade: tall octagonal pier, double-chamfered arches. Dec chancel, see the Sedilia with ogee cusping and e.g. the s window with a circle with a wheel of three mouchettes in the tracery. – WALL PAINTINGS. Much of the C15: Doom (over the chancel arch), the Virgin weighing souls (nave N wall), Seven Sacraments (nave S wall). – PLATE. Cup of the mid C17; Flagon of c. 1680; Paten of 1683; Knife probably late C17.

LATHBURY PARK. 1801. Plain five-bay stone house, s of the church.

HOUSE of c. 1700, NE of the church. Five bays, two storeys, chequered brick. A later addition on the l.

LATIMER

CHURCH. By *E. Blore*, largely rebuilt by *Sir G. G. Scott* in 1867. Red brick, a small s turret with brick spire. By Scott the transepts and the apse, which is shafted outside. Inside chancel arch and apse arch with characteristically lavish naturalistic foliage. Alabaster altar surround. Canted wooden roof on corbels with wild-flower carving. – STAINED GLASS in the apse by *Clayton & Bell*. In the nave N side by *Powell & Sons* to *Holiday*'s designs, with N transept by the same to a design of *Wooldridge*'s. All of 1873. The designs are all good, but the execution leaves much to be desired. – In the s transept *Kempe*, c. 1892. – PLATE. Chalice, Paten, Flagon, Plate, all inscribed 1743.

LATIMERS. By *Blore*. Symmetrical red-brick front with mullioned and transomed windows and gables. Date above the porch 1863. Entrance Hall with Staircase behind. This is surrounded by a rib-vaulted passage. Rib-vaulted ceilings otherwise as well.*

RECTORY. C18, of vitreous and red brick. The red brick laces the windows vertically. Five bays, two storeys, with panelled parapet.

LAVENDON

ST MICHAEL. The earliest parts of the church are ascribed by the RCHM to the first half of the C11, i.e. the tall unbuttressed w tower (unmoulded tower arch; the top stage is Perp), the

---

* Mr Prince in his thesis quoted on p. 143 mentions plans by *Samuel Ware* for a rebuilding. They date from 1827.

nave (NW and SW corners, and one half-uncovered N window),
and the chancel (blocked S window-head). Late C12 to early
C13 three-bay arcades. Circular piers with square abaci and
unmoulded pointed arches. The S arcade comes first. Zigzag in
the hood-moulds, capitals with heads at the angles, high bases
with angle spurs. C13 and Perp windows in the chancel. C13
chancel arch, single-chamfered. Dec details in the N aisle, Dec
and Perp in the S aisle. Perp embattled N porch. – FONT. Perp,
with a variety of tracery patterns, also one panel with fleur-de-
lis, and one with leaf. – SCULPTURE. In the chancel C14 bracket
with a bearded head. – PLATE. Covered Cup of 1569; Paten on
foot, late C17.

CASTLE, ½ m. N of the church. Site of a motte-and-bailey castle.
It had three baileys.

LECKHAMPSTEAD   7030

ASSUMPTION. There are several Norman contributions, the
earliest probably the S tympanum, a wild composition of two
intertwined dragons with a small demon (?) below. This does
not fit into the Norman doorway and may well be older. The
doorway, the N doorway, and the (re-set) W window in the
tower could all be of c. 1150–70. The S doorway has one order
of shafts, decorated with scales (l.) and zigzag (r.). Capitals with
the unusual motif of a bird downwards with outstretched
wings. Thick roll moulding in the arch. The lintel has rows of
small saltire crosses, the space above the tympanum is pointed.
In the N doorway the principal motif is a zigzag on the hood-
mould with leaves in the spandrels. It starts on heads and the
apex is a head. The W window is shafted and also has a decorated
hood-mould. The W tower itself is of the C13, see the finely
moulded arch of the W doorway, and the bell-openings. Later
battlements and pyramid roof. But before the tower was built,
probably even before 1200, the C12 church had been enlarged
by a N aisle of four bays. The piers are simple square chunks of
wall left standing, their corners just slightly chamfered. Complexly moulded pointed arches. Hood-mould with an unusual
motif, a band with lunettes cut out along both edges; the effect
is like vertebrae. Dec chancel with renewed windows. – FONT.
Originally circular, made octagonal in the C14, with one
Norman panel of symmetrically arranged foliage, and seven
of the C14, including the Crucifixion, the Virgin seated, the Virgin of the Annunciation, and a Bishop. – PLATE. Parcel-gilt
Cup with band of elaborate ornament, 1569; Paten, 1789;

Flagon, 1793; beautiful Almsdish, probably foreign. – MONU-
MENTS. Stone effigy of a Knight, slender, *c.* 1325, not cross-
legged. – Brass to a Lady, early C16, 15 in. figure (nave, s wall).
– Brass to Reginald Tylney † 1506, 18 in. figure (N aisle).

(HOME FARM, South End. C17 and C18. Two mullioned windows, not *in situ.* Staircase with twisted balusters. VCH)

ENTRENCHMENT. About 200 yds S of the church, on top of a
hill, an undated line of entrenchment facing W and consisting
of a single rampart and ditch.

9020   LEDBURN

LEDBURN MANOR HOUSE. Early Georgian, of five bays and two
storeys, with parapet. Vitreous and red brick, the red brick also
used for a vertical 'lacing' of the windows. The doorway with
Doric pilasters and pediment is on the side of the house. The
back is older. Partly timber-framed.

FARMHOUSE, SW of the Manor House, Pretty, timber-framed
and gabled, mostly C16.

9000   LEE

ST JOHN BAPTIST. By *Augustus Frere*, 1867–9, quite simple, red
brick, with lancet windows. In 1910 *Fellowes Prynne* added to
the E end the vestry, transeptal short two-bay aisles, and the W
baptistery. Of that date also the internal decoration, especially
the woodwork. Provided by *Liberty's*. – PLATE. Set presented
in 1811.

OLD CHURCH, W of the new. Nave and chancel in one. C13 N and
s windows, E window of the late C13, three stepped lancet
lights under one arch. Of the same date the Sedilia and Piscina.
– MONUMENTS. Several Georgian tablets.

GRIM'S DITCH. *See* p. 149.

7030   LILLINGSTONE DAYRELL

ST NICHOLAS. An interesting church with a variety of elements.
The earliest evidence is the chancel arch, Early Norman, unmoulded, on the plainest imposts. Then the tower was begun.
Its arch into the nave is still round, but its windows are lancets
and its top is Dec – see the bell-openings. By that time a new
chancel was in evidence, a spectacular piece, apparently built
in the early C13 and lengthened fifty years later. To the earlier
date belong the lancet windows and the surprising wall arcading on the S side inside. The arches are of different width and

shape. A little nailhead in the abaci. To the later C13 belongs the E window, of three stepped lancet lights with three foiled circles over, and the delightfully dainty SE window which has two lights separated by a stone shaft with very fine dog-tooth behind it l. and r. The whole window has also a continuous roll moulding. An ornamented patera over. Late C13 again the curious Easter Sepulchre, in the chancel N wall. Two depressed arches under, and forming part of, a larger also depressed arch. The arches rest in the middle on a corbel, not a shaft. Arcades of the aisles of the late C13 too. Three bays, octagonal piers, double-chamfered arches. The responds are corbels. Of the same date the finely detailed s doorway. – HELMS. Two funeral helms and a piece of EMBROIDERY, dated 1669 (chancel N). – PLATE. Cup of 1604; Cup of 1617; Paten on foot of 1662. – MONUMENTS. Paul Dayrell † 1491 and wife. Two excellent brass figures, 2 ft 3 in. long, on a plain tomb-chest (chancel S). – Brass to Richard Blakysley, priest (headless; 11 in. long; chancel N). – Paul Dayrell and wife, 1571. Free-standing tomb-chest with, at the ends of the long sides, columns with bulbous lower parts. Small figures of the children between them. Recumbent effigies on the lid.

(CHAPEL, at Chapel Green, 2 m. NW. C15. Now cottages and partly rebuilt C17. W doorway and E window remain. RCHM)

(LILLINGSTONE HOUSE. Yellow brick. Six bays and two storeys. Greek Doric portico. MHLG)

MANOR HOUSE, ¼ m. NW. 1792. Of five bays and three storeys. Plain.

(OLD TILE HOUSE. Brick, still in English bond, though dated 1693 on the porch and 1697 on a rain-water head. Five bays, two storeys. RCHM and NBR)

TILE HOUSE. Big, neo-Elizabethan, of red brick, gabled, asymmetrical, and with one ogee-capped turret.

LILLINGSTONE LOVELL

ASSUMPTION. A handsome group with the former RECTORY close to the SW (Georgian, stone, five bays, two storeys). The church has an early C13 W tower, unbuttressed, with a steep, single-stepped tower arch towards the nave, on simply moulded imposts. Dec bell-openings; saddleback roof. Of the same date as the start of the tower the s doorway (re-set). Two orders, capitals of upright leaves with volutes and also water-leaf. Finely moulded arch. The rest mostly Dec, see the reticulated E window and the arcades of three bays with octagonal piers and double-chamfered arches. The details of the capitals differ characteristically. W responds on corbels with head. Chancel arch also double-chamfered and also on corbels. To the E of the arcades pieces of wall remain pierced by a window N and S. They now lead into the N and S chapels. Both of these have good piscinas with tracery. – REREDOS. Early C18. L. and r. of the altar, with Corinthian pilasters and Lord's Prayer and Creed. The Commandments are above the altar. – PULPIT. Elizabethan with two tiers of the familiar blank arches. – C18 COMMUNION RAIL. – C18 BOX PEWS. – PLATE. Cup and Cover Paten of *c.* 1570. – MONUMENTS. Brass to Thomas Clarell † 1471 and wife, 13 in. figures (chancel). – Brass to John Merstun, rector, † 1446. No effigy; only two hands holding a heart (chancel). – Brass to William Rysley † 1516 and wife, 18 in. figures (nave floor). – Mrs Wentworth † 1768, beautiful large hanging monument of white and pink marble, with an obelisk carrying an urn. – Mr Wentworth † 1784, similar, but more modest. – Col. J. Bugle Delap, by *E. Davis*, 1853. White marble. A half-naked genius holding an urn and pointing upwards.

LINSLADE

ST MARY, 1 m. N, close to the canal. Early C12 nave masonry. Of the same date the unmoulded chancel arch. C15 W tower, early C16 chancel. No aisles. Yellow limestone and ironstone. The nave is embattled. To the N of the chancel arch a Perp recess; to the S of the E side of the chancel arch a recessed early C13 SEAT, round arch, two stone arms – a very unusual piece. – FONT, late C12, circular, with a band of scrolls and beasts. – SCREEN. Remains of a C15 screen. – BRASS to a Civilian with three wives. 14 in. figures (W wall).

ST BARNABAS. In the New Town which is visually now part of Leighton Buzzard. By *Ferrey*, 1848, originally only with a S aisle. N aisle of 1913. Front with S W tower with pyramid roof. – STAINED GLASS. In two N aisle windows glass by *Kempe*, the Annunciation 1878, the other 1885. – PLATE. Cup of 1568.

MANOR FARMHOUSE, E of the old church. A fine early C18 house of five bays and two storeys, with one-bay additions. Vitreous and red brick. The centre bay is flanked by two sturdy giant pilasters. Doorway with pediment on rusticated Doric pilasters.

LISCOMBE PARK

8020

Large brick mansion, with a long N front and unusually long wings receding to the S from the E and W ends. All red brick. The front is probably of 1774 (rain-water heads) and is thus an early example of bold medievalism. Castellated, the centre with a castellated pediment flanked by two square turrets, the end portions with round turrets. This front was originally cemented. But the building behind this is older. At the back of the N range a rain-water head of 1639, and close to it a group of chimneys of the C17. The W front has stepped gables and shaped gables. The latter seem a late addition, but the stepped gables may well be as old as the C16 or early C17. At the S end of this wing group of circular, octagonal, and square chimneyshafts. The E wing in its S parts is stables, with typically early C18 details (brick rustication, blank niches, blank oval windows, etc.). The interior mostly altered. Most of the panelling and the fireplaces look Early Georgian.

CHAPEL. To the S. A small detached building of stone. The windows have characteristic early C14 forms but are renewed. In the W gable a foiled circular window.

LITTLE BRICKHILL

9030

ST MARY MAGDALENE. Of ironstone. Odd, very thin W tower, narrower than the nave. S aisle and S chapel with separate roof. They date from c. 1600, as does the S arcade of standard details (RCHM). To the N the blocked arch of a former transept. The details of this are Dec. Much of the rest over-restored in 1864. – STAINED GLASS. Chancel S by Kempe, 1887.

MAGIOVINIUM. At DROPSHORT, just S of Fenny Stratford on the N side of Watling Street and on the E bank of the Ousel, is the site of a documented Roman road station (see Introduction, p. 17). Finds of the period have been made since the C18, and the nature of the site confirmed by limited excavations in 1911. More recent work is as yet unpublished.

LITTLE HAMPDEN

8000

CHURCH. Small, the chancel C13 with the unusual motif of a 'low-side' lancet, i.e. a lancet with a transom. Fine, heavy, two-storeyed timber-framed C15 N porch. The upper storey for use as a belfry. Most other details Victorian. – WALL PAINTINGS. The chancel arch cuts into what must have been a row of standing figures under trefoiled arches. They seem to date from the early C13. On the N wall a Lion and two Saints of the mid C13. Above them a St Christopher. Also a mid-C13 St Christopher W of the N doorway. On the S wall traces of a C15 Doom. – SCULPTURE. A good small piece of later C12 sculpture in the chancel S wall. Bishop with Crozier.

Opposite the church MANOR FARM with weatherboarded barns.

DANES CAMP. *See* Great Hampden, p. 143.

LITTLE HORWOOD

7030

ST NICHOLAS. W tower Perp, of uncommonly large ashlar blocks. The rest externally all of the restoration of 1889 (*J. P. St Aubyn & Wadling*). S arcade of *c.* 1200. Three bays, circular piers with octagonal abaci. Double-chamfered arches. A shorter W bay was added later. Dec chancel arch. – PULPIT. With Jacobean panels of the familiar type with short blank arches. – WALL PAINTINGS. N wall. Most conspicuous the Seven Deadly Sins, large figure with six branches growing out of it, each ending in a monster's head. Early C16. Remains of a C13 St Nicholas. – PAINTING. Christ and the sheep. By a Spanish painter supposed to be called *Pobar*. – PLATE. Cup of 1562; Cover Paten of 1569.

HORWOOD HOUSE, 1 m. SE. By *Detmar Blow & Billerey*, 1912. Pale brick, simplified, rather conventional, symmetrical Elizabethan. Pretty Stable Yard by the side. Arched gatehouse at the end of an avenue to the N.

LITTLE HORWOOD MANOR, ¾ m. N. 1938. One of the last mansions built in England on such a Lutyenesque scale. The style also is a kind of watered-down Lutyens. Centre with pyramid roof. Diagonally projecting wings ending in pavilions with pyramid roofs. Further lodges with pyramid roofs. Big Gatehouse to the N.

EARTHWORK. About ½ m. E of the church an undated rectangular earthwork consisting of a single bank and ditch enclosing about 3 acres. To the SW an original entrance rampart and ditch turning outwards on each side.

LITTLE ICKFORD *see* ICKFORD

8000

LITTLE KIMBLE

ALL SAINTS, only ¼ m. N of Great Kimble church and ⅝ m. W of Ellesborough church. Of flint, small, with bellcote. In the chancel one 'low-side' lancet and another window of *c.* 1300, in the

nave Dec windows. The chancel arch C13. – PULPIT. With
Jacobean panels. – PAINTING. A remarkable series of c. 1300,
though poorly preserved. N wall E window St Francis preaching
to the Birds, Woman wearing a wimple. Then, large St George
and the Princess behind, then in the next window remains of
ornament and figures. Further W remains of a Doom. On the
S wall splendid figure of a Saint or Prophet, and over the S door
small Entombment of a female Saint. She is held by two angels.*
– TILES. In the chancel a number of excellent C13 tiles, of the
Chertsey Abbey type and, as Mr Hohler says, 'doubtless filched
from Chertsey'. Four tiles always make up one roundel with
figures.

To the E of the churchyard a little five-arch BRIDGE now all
covered with ivy, perhaps a romantic C18 conceit.

RAGPIT HILL, PULPIT HILL, THE MOUND. See pp. 144–5.

LITTLE LINFORD

8040

ST LEONARD AND ST ANDREW. Simple round-arched S doorway with decorated hood-moulds. Nave and chancel C13. The
nave has an original twin bellcote. The chancel E window of two
lights with a quatrefoil in plate tracery. C13 N arcade of two
bays. Circular pier, octagonal abacus, double-chamfered arches.
S arcade of the early C14. Three bays. Octagonal piers, double-
chamfered arches. Responds on corbels. E window with reticulated tracery. – PLATE. Cup of 1695. – MONUMENTS. Two
tablets by *Richard Westmacott Sen.* (1782, 1795).

LINFORD HALL. Late C17, with Georgian alterations. Front of
five bays with bare Venetian windows on the ground floor l. and
r. The three centre bays correspond to the Hall. In this a fireplace with an unexpectedly monumental overmantel. Large
trophy framed by Corinthian pilasters. The garden façade
with two canted bay windows.

LITTLE MARLOW

8080

ST JOHN BAPTIST. The earliest surviving parts are the arch
between the chancel and the S transept, which is round and
unmoulded, and the chancel arch, which is pointed and
unmoulded, the one C12, the other shortly before 1200. The
chancel windows have Geometrical tracery, two lights with a

---

* The Rev. John James tells me of further remains W of the main doorway.
They show scenes from the martyrdom of St Margaret.

sexfoiled circle, i.e. date from *c.* 1275. In the nave E wall is a re-set Piscina with pointed trefoiled head and a lot of dog-tooth. That also is late C13. E window Dec (reticulated tracery). C14 arcades, see the arch-mouldings, on the N side two sunk quadrants, on the S one and a hollow chamfer. The two dormers in the nave roof N and S are C20 replacements of C17 dormers. – STAINED GLASS. Fragments of the C15. – E window by *Heaton, Butler & Bayne*, 1866. – PLATE. Cup of 1569. – MONUMENTS. Brass to Lady Ledwitch † 1430 (1 ft 10 in. figure). – James Chase † 1721. Good standing monument of moderate size, purely architectural. The fluted pilasters carry a gable with concave sides and a segmental top.

MANOR HOUSE. C18 front of seven bays and two storeys and hipped roof. Behind it to the r. a gabled C17 part. (Inside Staircase with the newel-posts carried up through two storeys to the ceiling, and with arches between them which form a screen between staircase and Hall. RCHM)

SPADE OAK FARM, ¾ m. SE, by the river. C17, timber-frame with brick infilling. Picturesque group of barns, etc.

WESTHORPE HOUSE, ¾ m. SW. Late Georgian, of seven bays and three storeys, cemented and plain. The balustrade and the porch of four unfluted Ionic columns, each with its own piece of projecting entablature, seem to be later.

NUNNERY. At Abbey Farm, 1 m. E, the Benedictine nunnery was excavated in 1902. What was found was a cruciform C13 church with an added W tower and NE chapel, a C13 Cloister with the usual buildings around it (the Chapter-House not projecting further E than the chambers adjoining it to the S and the range ending as usual on the S with the Reredorter or lavatories), an added (or rebuilt) Kitchen SW of the refectory, and an Infirmary S of the refectory, kitchen, and dormitory.

LITTLE MISSENDEN

ST JOHN BAPTIST. The core of this interesting building is Anglo-Saxon, i.e. the nave with a blocked window in the S wall of the N aisle, and a chancel arch which is completely unmoulded and has flat imposts of Roman brick. Into this nave early in the C12 unmoulded arches were cut on the S side and a little later (nook-shafts!) on the N side. The S clerestory windows belonging to this campaign are now blocked. The chancel in its present form is E.E. – see the lancet windows and the beautiful E group of three lancets of even height, shafted inside and shafted again at a slight distance, as if of a wall-passage. Early C14 N chapel with low tomb recess, C15 timber porch and W tower with higher stair-turret. The exterior of the S aisle rebuilt in brick with two pointed windows in the C18. The pretty dormer window in the nave roof existed already in 1777.* – FONT. Cup-shaped, Norman, the lower half fluted, the upper half with horizontal three-lobed leaves. – SCULPTURE. Many architectural pieces in the N chapel. – WALL PAINTINGS. Although only very fragmentarily preserved, the wall paintings of Little Missenden are of uncommon quality and interest. Of before 1200 is the dado of which parts remain on the N and S walls of the nave. On the N wall, facing us as we enter, is a large, exquisite figure of St Christopher carrying the Child Christ. Fishes swim around St Christopher's feet. The figure is of the later C13. Of the same date further E five scenes from the Martyrdom of St Catherine. On the S wall scanty remains of the Passion of Christ, C13, and of the Seven Deadly Sins (Lechery), C15. Of the customary Doom above the chancel arch hardly anything is now recognizable. On the W and S walls of the chancel a drawn ashlar pattern. In the N chapel on the W wall a design of red roses, on the N wall fragments of a Nativity, and below, in the tomb recess, a mid-C14 Christ in Majesty with angels. Finally, on the W side of the first pier of the N arcade from the W a beautiful later C13 Crucifixion, and on the W respond facing the Crucifixion an Archangel Gabriel from the Annunciation. – STAINED GLASS. The E window and N chapel and S aisle E windows by *Heaton, Butler & Bayne*, 1880s. – PLATE. Cup and Paten on foot, 1639; Flagon, 1691.

MANOR HOUSE. E of the church. Jacobean, see two mullioned and transomed windows on the E side and the excellent stair-case, which has sturdy turned balusters and unusually tall, lively finials on the newel-posts. It goes through two storeys. S front late C17 or early C18; plain.

MISSENDEN HOUSE. Rain-water head 1729. Vitreous and red brick, front with two canted bay windows and a broad central doorway. Two storeys, parapet, hipped roof, no ornamental enrichments.

LITTLE MISSENDEN ABBEY, 1 m. NW. By *W. H. Seth-Smith*. With a very picturesque neo-Tudor entrance side, including a tower, a three-transomed Hall window, a gabled porch, and perhaps some older material re-used.

* Information given by the Rev. F. F. C. Roberts.

8030

LITTLE WOOLSTONE

HOLY TRINITY. Nave and chancel and bell-turret. Early C13 chancel arch on tripartite responds with a double-chamfered arch. Nave of the early C14 with big windows with reticulated tracery. – FONT. Norman, with intersected arches and a band of small zigzag at the top.

LITTLEWORTH COMMON *see* DROPMORE

6000

LONG CRENDON

ST MARY. Large, with a big and tall Perp crossing tower (cf. Thame across the border in Oxon.). Higher stair-turret, pairs of two-light bell-openings with transoms. Below these an odd two-light window with straight-sided arch (or triangular head) on each side. However, the prevailing style of the church is E.E., not Perp. E.E. the chancel (N and S lancets). E.E. the S doorway with one order of shafts and fine arch mouldings. E.E. the arcades of two wide bays, with a quatrefoil pier on the N side, an octagonal one on the S, and double-chamfered arches. E.E. also the crossing arches: triple-chamfered on squat octagonal responds. Only the chancel arch has a more complex arch moulding. The fleurons on the abaci may be a C17 re-cutting. A date 1632–3 for restoration of the tower piers is recorded. Dec, but with much still preserved from the E.E. style, is the spectacular N transept N window (copied in the C19 in the chancel E window). It has five ogee-headed lights, but above one large circle with a ten-spoke wheel. Dec N aisle windows and a fine tall niche inside the N aisle. This has a crocketed ogee arch and buttress shafts l. and r. Perp S aisle windows and transept, Perp W doorway and W porch. The window above it, however, appears C17 rather than pre-Reformation. Excellent Perp chancel roof. Collar-beams on arched braces, wind-braces, and a tracery frieze above the wall plate. – FONT. Octagonal, Perp. Against the foot, four seated lions and large single leaves in relief. Against the bowl, frontal heads in quatrefoils. The rim is supported by demi-figures of angels. – SCREENS. To the S transept, excellent strong piece of the mid C17. Three divisions, separated by Doric pilasters. Each division has its openings filled by strong vertically-symmetrical balusters. The intervals are seven, seven, and then four for the doorway. Simpler Jacobean Screen to the N transept. – COMMUNION RAIL. Jacobean. – MONUMENTS. Brass to John Canon † 1460 and wife (N transept). The

figures are 2 ft 6 in. long. – Sir John Dormer † 1626 (?) and wife.
Large standing monument in the s transept. Recumbent effigies,
she in front and a little below him. Black columns and black
obelisks l. and r. Shallow coffered arch. Lunette with strapwork decoration. Big superstructure.

A large and spreading village with many houses deserving some
mention. Immediately SE of the church, MANOR HOUSE, late
C17, of five bays and two storeys, with wooden cross-windows
and a hipped roof. Immediately w of the church, COURT
HOUSE, C15, stone base and oversailing upper floor of timber-
framing with brick infilling. The whole upper floor was built as
one long room with one small adjoining one. The big room has
an open queenpost roof. The house was well restored by *C. R.
Ashbee*. In the HIGH STREET, to single out only two, MADGES
with an C18 front of chequered brick and adjoining it a thatched
part with a large carriageway under the continuous roof, and
THOMSON'S FARM, partly timber-framing and brick and
partly stone (much restored). Past the Square, to the NW, on the
way to LOWER END the OLD VICARAGE, timber-framed (at
the corner of Carter's Lane), and at Lower End, facing s in an
impressive position, THE MOUND, with timber and brick
above a stone base, partly perhaps pre-Reformation, partly
Jacobean, partly C20 alterations.

Finally, from the Square s down FROGMORE LANE lies the most
important house in Long Crendon: LONG CRENDON MANOR.
It is reached by a C15 stone gatehouse, much altered in the C17
and C18. Buttresses to the street, NE stair-turret. The house
itself is partly of stone, partly timber-framed, its core also of
about the C15. The core contains the Hall of one roof truss and
E and W bays. The truss has two tie-beams and a collar-beam,
the lower tie-beam with heavy braces, the upper tie-beam with
a kingpost and struts up to the collar. The end bays are cut off
by framed walls with big upright timbers. To the E of the Hall a
wing which may be contemporary with the Hall. To the w a C16
wing with its own independent framing, and to the W of this
another, also with its own framing. However, the picturesque-
ness of the *ensemble* is due to *Philip Tilden*'s activity in the 1920s.
By him the central feature into the w bay of the Hall, the two
stair-turrets at the SW and SE angles of the courtyard, and the E
side and E half of the N side of the courtyard, including the oversailing upper floor. The Screen between screens passage and
hall with its embattled beam comes from a C15 house in Kent.
On the ground floor a fireplace with four-centred head and

foliage and shields in the spandrels. This comes from Chipping Norton. The small mullioned window at the extreme w end of the c16 part of the house is also imported.

LOUDWATER
1 m. E of High Wycombe

CHURCH. 1788, red brick, a plain rectangle with an open lantern and, on the N and S, hip-roofed extensions with three arched windows and three lunette windows over. They correspond to two of the three pretty galleries inside, which are happily preserved. They stand on columns and are connected by columns with the ceiling. The chancel an insensitive Gothic addition. By *G. H. Fellowes Prynne*, 1901–3.

LOUGHTON

ALL SAINTS. The tower is of the c14 below, see the arch with tripartite responds, and Perp above. Heavily buttressed, including a c19 buttress running right into the Perp w window. Good Perp s chapel with four-light windows and battlements. Octagonal piers, double-chamfered arches. Ceiling with moulded beams and bosses. – PAINTING. Christ at Emaus. c17. Said to be by *Gonzales* (which of the many?). – PLATE. Paten on foot of 1685; two Cups of 1685, remade 1865. – MONUMENT. Brass of Hugh Parke, demi-figure of priest, 10 in. long, early c16 (chancel N).

MANOR HOUSE. ¼ m. w. Partly of *c.* 1500 but mostly of *c.* 1580. Stone, gabled, with two-storeyed gabled porch. (Inside, in a first-floor room, some late c16 paintings of figures, grotesques, etc. On the same floor the roof trusses of the Hall of the original house. Queenposts. RCHM)

HOUSE, sw of the church. Handsome Late Georgian three-bay front of three storeys with a Tuscan porch.

LOWER WINCHENDON *see* NETHER WINCHENDON

LUDGERSHALL

ST MARY. Mostly Dec, and the phases not easily distinguished. What is certain is that the w tower, with its reticulated w window and its arches to E, N, and S, was built into the pre-existing nave and aisles. The arcades of these differ oddly in their detail. Two piers, one N, the other opposite, S, have capitals with big

busts of people, on the s side with interlocking arms.* The pier
w of this has a capital with human heads. All this is also Dec, if
a little clumsy. The other piers are octagonal. All arches are
double-chamfered. Good Dec s doorway with fine mouldings.
Typical early c14 chancel arch. Flowing tracery in the N aisle
E window. Perp the two-storeyed s porch and several windows.
– FONT. Norman, circular, the lower part of the bowl fluted
with foliage at the foot of the flutes. Rim with a narrow gadrooned band. – STAINED GLASS. C14 fragments in the N aisle
E window. – MONUMENT. Anne Englishe † 1565 and two other
women. Brasses on a completely plain tomb-chest.

RECTORY. W of the church, Georgian, with a hipped roof. Three
bays. Arched doorway with Tuscan pilasters and a metope
frieze.

MAIDS' MORETON

7030

ST EDMUND. Supposed to have been built by two maiden sisters
of the Peover family in the middle of the c15, and indeed a
church which looks the outcome of great zest and generosity. W
tower, aisleless nave with two porches, chancel. The nave is
short but wide and lit by very large three-light windows with
transoms. The effect of the glass cage is further heightened by
the chancel E window of five lights, which fills the upper part of
the wall entirely. Tall tower arch and four-light W window.
Fan-vault behind it, and the porches also both have fan-vaults.
The N porch had its entrance altered in 1637.‡ The N doorway
has a cusped and sub-cusped arch. But an even less familiar
effect is obtained by cusping in the tower. The second and the
bell-stage have pairs of simple cusped lancet lights. They are
separated vertically by a V-shaped buttress or shaft, and the
whole of the shafts and the openings are framed by a splayed
frame with a projecting giant arch with big crude cusping. In
the chancel elaborate Sedilia with canopies vaulted inside. –
FONT. Circular, Norman, with one band of symmetrical leaf
patterns. – SCREEN. With one-light divisions. – BREAD
BASKET (by the N door). Jacobean, with balusters. – DOORS. N
door with tracery; N porch door see above. – PAINTING. Last
Supper. Wall painting against the back wall of the Sedilia. Of
c.1600.–STAINED GLASS. C15 figures in the tracery heads of the
W window; canopies in the E window. – MONUMENT. Francis

---

* Cf. Hampton Poyle and Bloxham, Oxon., say John Betjeman and John
Piper.

‡ The DOOR is of that date.

Attenbury † 1685. Good, big tablet with columns and an open segmental pediment.

MORETON LODGE. In the main street. 1715. Three bays and two storeys. Stone. Doorway with big segmental pediment. The centre bay has in addition a pediment reaching into the roof.

MARLOW

8080

ALL SAINTS. 1832–5 by *C. F. Inwood*. Chancel 1875–6, arcades 1881–2, both by *Street*. The fine proud steeple with its fanciful spire added in 1898–9 by *J. Oldrid Scott*. The work of the 1830s is of white brick with tall Perp 'lancets' and three long, gaunt, undecorated w porches. – PULPIT. By *Street*, of stone, with open sides with closely-set polished marble colonnettes. – STAINED GLASS. In the chancel by *Burlison & Grylls*, 1876. – PLATE. Perforated Paten on foot, 1619; Cup and Paten on foot, 1629; two Patens with date 1629; Cup and Paten on foot, 1634. – MONUMENTS. Many, all minor. The oldest, of 1597 (s aisle), with the familiar small kneelers facing each other. – Of the others, noteworthy Sir Miles Hobart † 1636. Bust and two small figures keeping a curtain open. The monument was voted by Parliament and £500 were set aside for it. Sir Miles had been killed when his coach overturned just off Holborn, where the viaduct now avoids the valley. The accident appears on a relief below the bust. – Richard Davenport † 1799 by *Nollekens*. Tablet framed by two upturned torches. – Sir William Clayton † 1834 by *R. Westmacott Jun*. Circular medallion with seated draped woman reading.

HOLY TRINITY, off Dean Street. By *Sir G. G. Scott*, 1852 (GR). Nave and chancel and N aisle. Bell-turret. Of flint with Geometrical tracery. The chancel with painted and stencilled decoration. – Pretty, low metal SCREEN. – REREDOS of alabaster, stone, and mosaic.

ST PETER (R.C.), St Peter's Street. By *Pugin*, 1845–8. According to Mrs Stanton's unpublished researches, Pugin designed not only the church but also the stone SCREEN, made by *G. Myers*, the metalwork (that is, e.g., the hanging *coronae*) made by *Hardman*, and the STAINED GLASS, also made by *Hardman*. The architecture of the church is far from distinguished. Façade with a NW tower with broach-spire and a w gable not well in proportion to the tower. Lower chancel and N aisle. – PLATE and VESTMENTS. According to Mrs Stanton the church possesses the plate and vestments from the demolished chapel of

Scott Murray's house, Danesfield (*see* Medmenham, p. 204). –
MONUMENT. Augustin John Alphonso Scott Murray † 1871.
Whom is it by? Recess with cusped arch and crocketed ogee
gable. In the lunette Christ and two angels.

Pugin also designed the simple churchyard GATES and the
SCHOOL and MASTER'S HOUSE to the s. This is the most interesting design. Flint and red brick. Steep, bargeboarded gables,
to the w a group of three. This side is almost, but deliberately
not quite, symmetrical. The school lies behind the Master's
House and carries a spirelet.

METHODIST CHURCH, Spittal Street. 1901. In a mixture of
Gothic and Baroque, and still with an Italianate pediment over
the whole front.

PERAMBULATION

We start from that handsome if period-piece the SUSPENSION 59a
BRIDGE, which was built in 1831–6 to the designs of *William
Tierney Clark* and deserves a preservation order. To the l. a
small Green with a fine cedar tree, and behind it the houses of
the CAUSEWAY, notably *Street*'s Vicarage of *c.* 1865, red brick
and gabled, with Gothic windows, but two pretty oversailing
tile-hung gabled pieces, and the GEORGE AND DRAGON, C18,
red brick, of nine bays and two storeys with a three-bay pediment. To the r. a large recreation ground, and at its far end
COURT GARDEN, of *c.* 1760, with two canted bay windows and
a veranda.

Then STATION ROAD turns off to the r. In this is the most important house in Marlow, MARLOW PLACE, ascribed con- 45a
vincingly to *Archer* and regarded equally convincingly as the
pattern for a group of West-Country architects such as Cart-
wright, Ireson, and the Bastards. The house is supposed to have
been built in 1720 for the Prince of Wales, the future George II.
It was in fact built for John Wallop, later Earl of Portsmouth,
for whom Archer also built at Hurstbourne Priors. The house
has the oddest details on its façade, odder even than those of
Chicheley, of 1698, also attributed to Archer. It is of brick,
seven bays wide by six bays, and consists of a basement, a main
storey, and a half storey. The upper floors have giant angle
pilasters of brick with the strangest capitals. Their motif is as
likely as not three leeks, and that would confirm the traditional
connexion with the Prince of Wales.* The three-bay centre
also has giant angle pilasters. Their capitals are richer and

* Mr J. W. Jackson's observation.

rounder and have the inturned volutes which reappear in the
Bastard–Ireson group of houses. Three-bay pediment. There
is a ground-floor doorway, but the main entrance is up above
with a door surround hard to describe. It has framing pilasters
set at an angle. They carry a pediment, also partly canted. It has
a segmental centre. The window above is stressed by an elaborate stone frame. This motif repeats at the back, but the doorway
here is simpler, with fluted Doric pilasters, double-fluted in
their lower part. Inside the only room to continue the grandiose
and Baroque mood of the exterior is the Entrance Hall, which
is carried up through the half-storey, has giant Tuscan pilasters
a metope frieze, and above blank arcading of a strange tripartite
kind. Tripartite also the doorways, with the side-pieces blank.
Even the mouldings are in the same heavy and wilful mood.

Opposite Marlow Place starts St Peter's Street. The first
house on the l. is interesting and would deserve detailed study
It consists of two parts, the Old Parsonage and the Deanery. The former is long, irregular, and many-gabled. On its N
as well as its s side one big straight-headed stone window of the
early C14 with ogee reticulation. (These windows belong to the
C14 Hall. Of the same date the kingpost roof. RCHM) The
Deanery is attached to it, a three-bay house of three storeys, red
brick with stone cross-windows and a hipped roof. Several
attractive Georgian houses further s and then, at the end, facing
the river, Thames Lawn, early C19, white with a Tuscan
colonnade across the front. Opposite Thames Lawn, also facing
the river (and thus behind the church), Old Bridge House
of flint, brick, and stone, Victorian, tall with shaped gables. A
little lower down the river the Lock Mill, a charming
group of weatherboarded buildings.

Back to the end of the Causeway and now straight on along the
High Street. This starts at once on the l. with some nice
Georgian houses and their pedimented doorways. The best
houses in the street are No. 65, early C19, of yellow brick, three
widely-spaced bays with a porch of unfluted Ionic columns, and
the Post Office, a five-bay house of three storeys and a pedimented three-bay projection and a doorway with fluted Ionic
columns. The house is of vitreous brick with red brick dressings
and probably dates from the mid-Georgian decades. Then
New Court, 1877, red, big, and neo-Elizabethan, which lies
safely in its own grounds behind the High Street and is an-
nounced only by its tall gateway and lodge. At the end of the
High Street the triangular Market Place. As one approaches

it one has *en face* the former TOWN HALL, now Crown Hotel, built in 1807 by *Wyatt*, probably *Samuel*. Two storeys, the lower with pillars and segmental arches originally open, the upper with Tuscan pilasters, coupled at the ends. In the middle of the Market Place an OBELISK milestone, erected in 1822.

To the W runs WEST STREET, the street richest in Georgian houses. The following deserve singling out, all on the l. side: OLD HOUSE, of three bays with tripartite side windows under segmental arches and round-arched single middle windows, the top one with an odd trefoiled head. To the r. Nos 29–31 with rusticated brick quoins. No. 47 of vitreous and red brick is three bays wide with a blank half-storey and a three-bay pediment; Nos 81–83 is very similar, but has no half-storey. After that the continuous frontages stop and individual houses start. The first of them is REMNANTZ, a big early C18 house of yellow and red brick with canted bay windows and segment-headed windows. Doorway with unfluted Ionic pilasters and pediment. Good iron gates. The house has remarkably lavish Stables, a block parallel to the street of 13 or 15 bays, with a three- or five-bay centre and a tall clock-turret. The upper half-storey also has segment-headed windows. The Royal Military College started here in 1799 and stayed until it went to Sandhurst in 1811. Opposite, No. 104 etc., a terrace of charming two-storeyed cottages with Gothic windows. They are tripartite, and each part has an ogee head. Then the GRAMMAR SCHOOL, founded by Sir William Borlase in 1624. Flint and red brick, originally only three bays and two storeys, with a projecting three-storeyed, gabled porch. Mullioned windows under hood-moulds. C19 and C20 extensions in the same style. The end is WESTERN HOUSE, dated 1699, which has a very handsome shell-hood. The house is of chequered brick, only three bays wide. Brick wall to the street, and at its r. end a square Summer House with pyramid roof.

To the E of the Market Square there is much less. Nothing special in Spittal Street, and in its continuation CHAPEL STREET no more than the long low terrace of two-storeyed cottages, called BORLASE COTTAGES and dated 1788.

Only two outlying houses must be added, both to the N. The former WORKHOUSE lies at the end of the town on the lane to Munday Dean and is of red brick, with two projecting wings at the back and a hipped roof. Five bays, arched entrance. Off the road to Stokenchurch, 2¼ m. NW of the church, is WIDMERE, a farmhouse, part of which is a C13 to early C14 chapel with undercroft. The undercroft is of the C13, vaulted in twice four bays with three circular piers carrying octagonal abaci. The responds are demi-shafts. Segmental single-chamfered arches. Roughly domical vaults. Above, the remains of one N lancet and early C14 S and E windows. The former have cusped Y-tracery, the tracery of the latter has not survived.

HARLEYFORD MANOR, see p. 157.

6020   MARSH GIBBON

ST MARY. Mostly of the C13. Chancel with N and S lancets (inside a moulding runs along the wall and round their arches). Transepts with responds to their arches towards the crossing which have excellent big stiff-leaf capitals, one with grapes. In the N transept N wall two lancets. C13 also the nave S arcade. Octagonal piers, double-chamfered arches. The N aisle is of 1879–80, but the lancet on the W side is a re-used original window. Perp windows, especially those of the clerestory. Very big Perp S transept S window. Five lights, panel tracery. Perp W tower, rebuilt 1880. The pinnacles, unusual in Bucks, are probably of that time. – BENCHES. C17, simple. – PLATE. Large Cup and Cover Paten, 1674; Almsdish, 1720. – MONUMENT. C13 Coffin Lid with elaborate foliated cross.

MANOR HOUSE, SW of the church. Of stone, Elizabethan and Jacobean. The RCHM distinguishes a phase of c. 1560, to which the two-storeyed bay window and the big fireplace with a four-centred head in the Hall are attributed, from a phase of the early C17, to which the gables are assigned.

9010   MARSWORTH

ALL SAINTS. Over-restored in 1882–91. Of flint, clunch, and stone. The S aisle with a rough chequer of flint and stone, dating from the restoration. On the N side a pretty rood-stair turret. The original church was the present S aisle, the original chancel the present S chapel. The latter was re-built c. 1330 and a N aisle and chapel added (now nave and chancel). C15 W tower, with C13 materials (e.g. stiff-leaf capitals) re-used. The work of 1882–91 comprised a new E window, new decoration of the chancel, and much re-modelling of the S chapel. All this, in its proud and naive ostentatiousness, was due to the then vicar, *F. W. Ragg*, who did the designing himself and some of the handiwork with his wife. They also employed labourers, whom they trained. S arcade of three bays with octagonal piers, and similar two-bay arcade to the S chapel, both dated C14 by the

RCHM. – SCREENS. Made of old oak by the *Raggs*. – PULPIT. On a large C14 capital with angels and foliage. – STAINED GLASS. In the s chapel E window by *Kempe & Tower*, 1910. – PLATE. Salver of 1685; Flagon of 1697. – MONUMENTS. Edward West † 1618. Tomb-chest with allegorical reliefs of skulls, wheat-ears, etc., also single figures of Christ risen, a Skeleton, and two pilgrims (?). Above one skull Memento Mori, above the others Respice Finem. Against the N side brass plate with reclining effigy and kneeling figures, signed by *Epiphanius Evesham*. – Brass to Nicholas West † 1586 and wife. Palimpsest of a large late C15 German brass of a priest in richly detailed robes.

Marsworth lies where the Grand Union Canal meets the river Ousel. Good 'canalscape'.

(RUSSELL FARM, SW of the church. Probably of the early C16. Timber-framing and brick. The Hall horizontally divided, but the original roof trusses with queenposts remain. RCHM)

ROMANO-BRITISH SETTLEMENT. Just below the road bridge over the canal on the W bank there appears to be the site of a Romano-British settlement.

MEADLE 8000

WOOSTER'S FARM. A barn of this farm is of cruck construction, a rarity in the county.

(THE SPRINGS, close to the entrance to Wooster's Farm. Dated 1627. Of that time a very crude wall painting of Adam and Eve and the serpent. F. W. Reader, *Rec. of Bucks.*, XII.)

MEDMENHAM 8080

ST PETER. Built of a mixture of flint and chalk. Remains of a Transitional church are the s and the blocked N doorway, round-arched with a single chamfer. Perp W tower. The N transept is C20 work, but the arch into it bears witness to the existence of a C13 transept or chantry. – STAINED GLASS. In the chancel by *Willement*, 1845. – PLATE. Silver-gilt Cup and Paten on foot of 1637. – MONUMENTS. Robert Scott † 1808. Simple tablet with urn, signed by *R. Westmacott*. – J. M. T. Ritchie † 1940. Bronze plaque with portrait head by *K. Scott*.

The cottages and the Manor House near the church form a pleasant setting, dominated, as one approaches from the ferry, by LODGE FARM, lying on the steep chalk escarpment

immediately N of the church. The house is of the late C17, of flint
with red-brick dressings, and presents to the s two tall gabled
dormer cross windows. Sheahan tells us that the house was
'considered by the late Mr Pugin a very remarkable specimen
of brick work' (cf. his use of flint and brick in the Marlow
school, p. 199). Timber-framed barns.

In FERRY LANE, s of the Post Office and lying back from the
lane, PORTALS, 1958 by *John G. Fryman*. It is called Portals
because the structure is four welded portal frames. The house
stands on stilts, except for the garage and what might be called
a utility core. The house proper is a simple oblong, faced with
vertical red-cedar boarding.

At the end of the lane on the l. is the entrance to MEDMENHAM
ABBEY. The Abbey was a Cistercian house founded some time
early in the C13. Of the buildings no more is preserved than one
pier of quatrefoil section in the garden. The church lay to the
SE, s, and SW of the house. The present building is partly of
1595, partly C18 Gothic, and largely of 1898 etc. by *F. H.
Romaine Walker*. The Elizabethan contribution occupies part
of the E range of the cloister and part of the N transept. It can
most clearly be recognized in the E front with its three-storeyed
gabled porch, and the projecting wings as well, the SE of which
is continued by the principal C18 addition, a ruined tower. This
addition fills the inner bays of the N transept 'nave'. In the same
Gothick taste also the arcade or cloister of four bays along
the river front. This was, however, rationalized in the C19. In
the piers the original C13 pier was copied. The Gothick additions are connected with the time when the house was owned by
Francis Duffield and leased or rented by Sir Francis Dashwood
(*see* West Wycombe). It was here that his Hell-Fire Club met.
The name is apocryphal, the club is not. Yet of the indecent
ceiling painting in the chapel, the temple with an entrance in
the form of a female *vagina*, the statues with pornographic inscriptions, and what else more or less reliable C18 and recent
authors report, nothing understandably remains. The Late
Victorian house is Gothic and of stone. The area between it and
the house of 1595 marks the cloister garth. A timber-framed
wing with brick infilling was added in 1911 to the w of the Late
Victorian wing.

To the E of the Abbey lies DANESFIELD. The present house is
Romaine Walker's *magnum opus* without any doubt. It was built
for Mr Robert Hudson, mainly in 1899–1901, and tells of a
self-confidence which would have been unthinkable even twenty

years later. The same Robert Hudson had been responsible for the restoration of Medmenham Abbey in 1895 etc. Danesfield is vast and Tudor, of stone, with a tall gatehouse tower, two courtyards, and, towards the river, two symmetrical towers with enough space between them for five bay windows and a colonnade with Tuscan columns and four-centred arches. The Danesfield before Mr Hudson had been Charles Scott Murray's, who bought the Medmenham estate in 1831. He was a convert to Catholicism and Pugin's patron. *Pugin* built for him on the Danesfield estate a chapel (whose panelling, it is said, is that now in the Dining Room*), a presbytery, a school, and lodges. The LODGE on the main road may well be *Pugin*'s. It is of flint and red brick (*see* above). Mr Hudson, at the time he built his house, built for his agent KINGSWOOD, a very substantial gabled house, up the hill, to the N of the road.

WITTINGTON borders on the E on Danesfield. The house was built by *Sir Reginald Blomfield* in 1898 and is in the William-and-Mary style at which Blomfield's master, Norman Shaw, had arrived in the 80s. Brick with stone dressings and a hipped roof. Nine-bay entrance side with stone-faced, pedimented, pilastered, three-bay centre. Towards the river the steep three-bay pediment stands above a centre the ground floor of which is a loggia with Tuscan columns. It is a dignified, very acceptable design.

DANES DITCHES. At Danesfield, ¾ m. E of the church, an undated EARTHWORK. N and E of an area some 20 acres in extent a ditch with inner rampart and counterscarp bank. On the W side the defences have been destroyed. On the S the site was defended by the steep bank of the Thames.

WOOD END HOUSE, 2¼ m. N. Dated 1730. Nine-bay front with balustrade and pedimental gable. Porch on slender columns.

(VICARAGE. The W part is Early Georgian. Plaisted)

IRON AGE HILL-FORT. Lying SW of States House and much denuded by ploughing, this hill-fort encloses just under 17 acres and consists of a single rampart and ditch with an apparently original entrance to the NW, and to the SW a path protected by a bank leading to a stream.

MENTMORE   9010

ST MARY. Over-restored 1858 by *G. H. Stokes* (*see* below). He also rebuilt the chancel. Aisles must have been built *c.* 1200.

---

* But Plaisted says that this comes from a house in Gloucestershire.

Circular capitals with early stiff-leaf were re-used as the bases of the C14 piers. These are probably remodelled circular piers of *c.* 1200. Their new, Perp shape is quatrefoil with slender shafts in the diagonals. Capitals castellated; many-moulded arches. – STAINED GLASS. E window 1905 by *Kempe*. – SCULPTURE. Central-Italian Quattrocento relief of the Virgin and Child, demi-figure, style of *Desiderio da Settignano*. – PLATE. Cup and Cover Paten, 1570.

MANOR HOUSE. C18, of brick, five bays and two storeys, very handsome.

60 MENTMORE HOUSE. 1852–4 by *Sir Joseph Paxton* and his son-in-law *G. H. Stokes* for Baron Meyer Amschel de Rothschild. His daughter married Lord Rosebery. Very large and conspicuous. 'The style adopted by desire of the builder is that . . . of which Wollaton Hall is perhaps the finest example' (*The Builder*, 1857). The house is indeed actually inspired by Wollaton. It is also built like Wollaton of Ancaster stone, and has the same square angle towers or eminences and the same ornate Jacobean details – only more ornate than in the original. Also, where the central hall of Wollaton has solid walls and a solid ceiling, the central hall at Mentmore (48 by 40 by 40 ft) has a gallery with close and highly decorated arches on the upper floor and a glass roof (on Paxton's ridge-and-furrow principle) on an equally highly-decorated coving. The house was remarkable for its date for having hot-water heating and artificial ventilation throughout. All the window casements were of copper. Much plateglass in very large sheets was used. In the Great Hall a grand CHIMNEYPIECE in black and white marble from the house of *Rubens* at Antwerp. The Dining Room has *boiseries* throughout from the Hôtel de Villars in Paris (Hautecœur, vol. III, counts seven different Hôtels de Villars).* Other complete C18 *boiseries* from other houses, but also very skilful imitation *Dixhuitième*.

GRAFTON STUD FARM. Brick buildings of *c.* 1875 with barge-boarded gables.

7020

MIDDLE CLAYDON

CLAYDON HOUSE. Claydon House is a *locus classicus* of *bâtissomanie*, that universal complaint of the C18. What we call Claydon House is no more than half – perhaps one-third would be truer – of what Ralph, second Earl Verney, built from the

* Cf. Waddesdon, p. 276.

1750s to the 1780s. Hence the contrast between the relative simplicity of the exterior and the lavishness of the interior, unmatched, one can safely say, anywhere in England. The house as it stands today is a much remodelled Jacobean mansion – the remodelling dating from *c.* 1860 – and towards the S (really SW) and W (really NW) new mid-C18 fronts and three new major W rooms. This new work is ashlar-faced. To the S it has simply three windows on two-and-a-half storeys. To the W the same height appears as two storeys only. There are seven bays. The middle three project slightly and have a pediment. The entrance here is of the Venetian type and has a blank arch over all three parts. The other ground-floor windows are pedimented and have blank medallions above the pediments. The N section had to be remodelled about 1790, but it was clearly done with original materials. The reason for this remodelling is a sad one. The second Earl had succeeded to the title in 1752. He intended to make Claydon the political and cultural centre of the county in conscious, largely political, contrast to Stowe, i.e. the Temples and the Grenvilles. Apparently he first built the STABLES, to the E of the house, of brick and of moderate size (three sides of a quadrangle, pedimented centres, the one in the recessed part also with the usual lantern), and then modernized and enlarged the S front (later, as we have seen, re-Jacobeanized again). When he embarked on the bigger scheme is not certain. The most likely date is *c.* 1760. He must have built the existing wing first and completed it inside as well. He then continued to the N, adding a domed rotunda and, to the N of that, a companion-piece to the existing wing. The total length thus became 256 ft. The N wing contained one great ballroom – 90 by 50 by 40 ft – and no more. The architect for the extension was *Sir Thomas Robinson*. The centre had to the W giant columns, an attic with lunette windows, a balustrade, a recessed drum, and the dome. Verney ruined himself over this scheme and his interest in racing and the Ranelagh. He died bankrupt in 1791, and in 1792 the centre and the N wing were demolished. The ballroom had not even been completely decorated.

The interior of the SW wing was fortunately left intact. The house is now entered on the N by a door that leads into a subsidiary room, the Pink Room. It has a Venetian window to the E, a delightfully light and free (but symmetrical) Rococo overmantel of wood, and exceedingly pretty overdoors also of wood, the work no doubt of a *Mr Lightfoot* who was a carpenter and at the same time apparently in charge of the new work in a more

comprehensive way. Sir Thomas Robinson ascribes to him 'no
small trace of madness in his composition'. We gratefully agree.
The Pink Room is no more than an *hors d'œuvre*. The three main
rooms are from N to S the North Hall, the Saloon, and the
Library. The North Hall is a double cube, 50 by 25 by 25 ft –
the Palladio–Inigo-Jones ideal. The three N windows are
blocked. Here again the decoration is all wood-carved. The
ceiling has an oval centre with trophies and a surround of garlands and medallions, putti, genii, etc. Below the ceiling a triglyph frieze, the metopes filled with busts. Niches with Rococo
decoration of birds, heads, etc. Concave-sided open pediments
over the doors, with crowded decoration in the arch below the
pediments. The chimneypiece also is crowded and confused,
but full of ideas. Caryatids in profile l. and r. of the fireplace,
caryatids placed frontally in the overmantel. At the foot of the
overmantel a fantastical display of Rococo detail with swans,
as if taken from a pattern book. At the head brilliantly carved
garlands – a mixture of French and English ornamental materials. All motifs, in spite of their extreme arbitrariness, are
symmetrical. Robinson, who hated Lightfoot and the Rococo,
called the decoration absurd, Lightfoot called it work 'such as
the world never saw'. The saloon is more restrained and more
in the English Kentian tradition, as if Robinson had had a say
in it. Big, heavy, coffered coving, geometrical panels in the
ceiling with conventional antiquish foliage. Robinson's favourite plasterer was *Joseph Rose*, who also worked for Adam. No
doubt we have his work here. Straight-sided pediments on
fluted columns as door surrounds. Only the fireplace surround
is more exuberant, but that was a usual thing among English
Palladians. The same is true of the Library, another double-
cube room. Doorcases with fluted Ionic columns carrying
straight entablatures. Cherub brackets. Ceiling with decoration in the same style and probably by the same hand as in the
Saloon.

Behind these state-rooms lies the Staircase, sumptuously
appointed. The steps themselves are of mahogany, inlaid even
on their undersides. The balustrade is of the lightest, daintiest
wrought iron with ears of corn. Light stucco decoration on the
walls, Adamish not Rococo. Again broad coffered coving and
again of wood. Large oval glazed dome. On the first floor are
two more rooms decorated as luxuriantly as, or indeed more
luxuriantly than, any below: the Chinese and the Gothic rooms,
sacrificing to two fashions of the Rococo which culminated in

the 1750s and 1760s respectively. At Claydon they cannot be of an earlier date than *c.* 1765. The climax of the Chinese Room 55 is an alcove encrusted with Rococo *chinoiserie* carved with extreme boldness and gusto. Chinese of course also the over-doors and the fireplace surround. The Gothic Room has a ceil- 54 ing with three sunk octagonal centre panels, and Gothic shafts and panels around windows, doors, and fireplaces. A GOTHIC PAVILION of probably about the same time adjoins the SE of the house.

(In the Jacobeanized part C17 alabaster and marble fire-places and wooden panelling brought from Salden, Mursley. *Cole MSS.*)

ALL SAINTS. Small, on a hillock just S of the house. W tower, nave and chancel. The nave is of the late C13, but much renewed. Two-light lancets with Y-tracery. The chancel was rebuilt in 1519, the W tower is Perp too. In the chancel S wall a recess, now used for a door. This has against the underside of its arch three demi-figures of angels. – PULPIT. Simple, Elizabethan, with arched panels in perspective. – SCREEN. Simple, of one-light divisions. – PLATE. Cup and Standing Paten of 1663; Paten, 1667; Flagon, 1827. – MONUMENTS. Brasses to Isabella Giffard † 1523 (19 in.); Alexander Anne † 1526 (demi-figure of a priest; 11 in.); Roger Giffard † 1542 and wife (5 ft figures; he rebuilt the chancel). – Margaret Giffard † 1539. Alabaster. Recumbent effigy. Against the tomb-chest shields in elaborately cusped quatrefoils, etc., but somewhat coarse Renaissance balusters at the angles. – Tablet on the N wall, dated by the RCHM *c.* 1540, no inscription. With pilasters, strapwork, and the Giffard arms. – Sir Edmund Verney † 1642 in the battle of Edgehill. Also of his wife, his son, and his son's wife. By *Edward Marshall*, 1653. Many documents on the making of the tomb survive.* Large standing wall-monument of dark and white marble. In the centre inscription with draperies, to the l. and r. busts in two tiers in oval niches. Top with an open segmental pediment, a broad urn, and the word Resurgamus. – Lady Verney † 1694. Tablet with bust. – Sir Harry Verney, 1896 by *H. A. Pegram*. Bronze relief with portrait bust.

MILL END *see* HAMBLEDEN

* Originally the memorial was intended to be much more ambitious: two tombs facing each other like those in Michelangelo's Medici Chapel. In one Lady Verney was to be represented upright in her shroud. The original design was by *Burman*, revised and replaced by one done for Sir Ralph Verney in Rome by a Roman artist.

8030   MILTON KEYNES

ALL SAINTS. The oldest piece in the church is the chancel arch.
This is pointed, and has responds with broad simple upright
leaves and a stepped arch the corners of which are hollowed out.
The date probably *c.* 1200. The rest is externally and internally
Dec. Nave, chancel, N chapel, and to its W A N tower. Wide nave,
very light, thanks to large three-light windows. Of the window
tracery especially interesting that of the N chapel. The bell-
openings of the tower have intersected tracery. The N chapel
arcade has a circular pier with circular abacus and double-
chamfered arches, the chancel Sedilia, and Double Piscina with
ogee arches on shafts. The piscina in the N chapel with ballflower decoration. The same in the responds of the arch from
the tower into the nave. These responds have an odd shape,
rounded with a band projecting flat like a widened fillet. The
arches to W and E are blocked. – STAINED GLASS. In the chancel
by *A. Gibbs* (signed; bad) and by *Powell & Sons*, 1864 (Christ
and the Children and the Raising of Lazarus). – BRASS. To
Adam Babyngton † 1427, priest. A 16 in. figure (chancel, S wall).
RECTORY. A fine early C18 house of red brick. Five bays, two
storeys, hipped roof. Big three-bay pediment. Simple doorway.

8000   MONKS RISBOROUGH

ST DUNSTAN. Of flint, externally all Victorian (restoration
1863–4 by *Street*). W tower with knapped flintwork with
rectangular higher stair-turret. The details point to the early
C14. Most windows Perp, large in the chancel and the N transept. C14 arcades with octagonal piers and arches with two
double chamfers with a kind of cones at their springing. The
details of the N arcade a little earlier than those of the other. –
FONT. Norman, cup-shaped. Fluted below, and with a band
of almond shapes with palmettes above. – SCREEN. Perp. With
badly painted figures on the dado. The tracery in the upper
part all gone. – BENCHES. Two with poppy-heads, three with
small figures, a fourth with two heads of women. – STAINED
GLASS. A jumble of old fragments in the SE window of the S
aisle. – BRASSES. Robert Blundell † 1431, rector, the figure
2 ft 1 in. long. – Civilian and wife, demi-figures, 13 in. long
(S aisle E). – Two Sons and five Daughters, 6 in. long (by the
Lectern).
DOVECOTE, NW of the church. Square, of stone, with a small

lantern. Probably c16. The doorway, with odd posthumously
Gothic detail, supposed not to belong.

COTTAGES, s of the churchyard. An exceptionally picturesque
row.

WHITELEAF CROSS. Cut in the chalk on the hill E of the village.
It has a triangular base and measures some 80 ft across with
arms about 20 ft wide. It is generally similar to the Greek-cross
form of the Bledlow Cross some 4 m. SW, particularly in position and original date (see p. 67).

MOUND. On the crest of WHITELEAF HILL, N of the site of the
Neolithic barrow (see p. 15), an undatable mound.

MOULSOE 9040

ASSUMPTION. Mostly Dec of the earliest phase. The window
tracery is interesting. It favours spheric triangles and quadrangles with trefoils and quatrefoils and spurs connecting the
re-entrant angles with the corner of the triangles and quadrangles. Arcades of four bays with octagonal piers and double-
chamfered arches. The chancel arch is of the same design. The
W tower is Early Dec at the foot, a little later (flowing tracery)
higher up, and has a Perp top. – SCREEN. Perp, much c19.
One-light divisions and broad ogee-headed entrance. – MONU-
MENTS. Brasses to Richard Ruthall (?) † 1528 and wife, the
figures 2 ft 6 in. long. – Second Lord Carrington † 1868 by
Lerolle Frères of Paris. Bronze tablet with openwork; very
Baroque. – Second Lady Carrington † 1879. Alabaster tablet
in the English early c18 style. – In the churchyard Carrington
Enclosure, very Gothic with stone piers and iron grilles,
probably of c. 1870–80.

MOULSOE BUILDINGS. A Late Georgian three-bay house of red
brick. Two and a half storeys. With one-bay one-storey wings
with curved tops up to the house.

MURSLEY 8020

ST MARY. Short W tower of the c14 and c15. The rest looks all as
if of the restoration of 1867. The aisles are Dec, see the arcades
with octagonal piers and arches with one chamfer and one sunk
quadrant, and see the windows too. The tower arch has three
hollow chamfers and, to the N and S on the ground floor, deeply-
splayed lancets. The clerestory and the chancel interior are of
1867. – PULPIT. Jacobean, with two tiers of panels containing
broad arches filled with foliage. – MONUMENTS of the Fortes-
cues of Salden. Cecilia † 1570, tomb-chest with cusped panels,

probably earlier, and brass effigy on the lid. – Sir John † 1607 and wife with two of the usual kneelers. – Sir Francis and wife, also early C 17, also with kneelers.

MANOR HOUSE, E of the church. C 18 front with brick chequer-pattern, but groups of C 17 chimneys.

SALDEN, I m. NE. E wing of the Fortescue mansion. Built c. 1570–90. The house had an inner courtyard and fronts of 175 ft length. The wing has little of interest. Red brick with blue diapering. Formerly mullioned windows.

7030
NASH

ALL SAINTS. 1862 by *Street*. Of light brown stone. Nave with bellcote and chancel. Lancets and bar tracery. Not of special interest. – The STAINED GLASS in the E window is dated 1861.

NASHDOM see TAPLOW

7010
NETHER WINCHENDON

ST NICHOLAS. W tower with higher stair-turret.* No features of interest in the nave. Chancel rebuilt in 1891, except for the Dec chancel arch. – PULPIT. Jacobean, with small tester. – BOX PEWS and WEST GALLERY, probably early C 19. – STAINED GLASS. In a N window English C 15, in a S window Flemish C 16. – BRASSES. Knight and Lady, c. 1410–20, 23 in. figures. – John Barton *alias* Bayle † 1487 and wife, 12 in. figures.

Many picturesque timber-framed houses with brick infilling. MANOR FARM, bigger than the others, lies w of the church. A door has the date 1620.

NETHER WINCHENDON HOUSE. A very interesting house, too little known. In its structure it represents a medieval stone mansion with angle towers. Three of these remain, of the fourth the thickness of the wall near the SW corner tells. Only two ranges are preserved, but of a third some indications (but-tresses at its corner) survive. The house probably had its Hall in the same place as it is now, but the details all along this S range are Early Tudor. Excellent circular ornamented brick chimneys in various places in the two remaining ranges. In ad-
36a dition the Parlour, i.e. the SE room, has delightful Early Renais-sance decoration, foliage, little candelabra, heads in profile, grotesques, a mermaid, etc. Their date must be c. 1530. The linenfold panelling comes from another house, the fireplace is

* The Rev. G. H. Isaacson tells me that the base of the tower and part of the N wall are supposed to be of the C 11.

of the c 18. The Hall fireplace is of the early c 17. Then, c. 1780, according to the Bernard Papers, the house was enthusiastically re-gothicized. The picturesque N screen of three arches was built through which the Hall façade now appears. This is of brick, laid in English bond. The house was given battlements, the Hall two Gothick s windows. Next to them an exceedingly pretty little veranda on the upper floor.

NEW BRADWELL *see* WOLVERTON

NEWLANDS PARK *see* CHALFONT ST GILES

NEWPORT PAGNELL

ST PETER AND ST PAUL. The largest church in this part of Buckinghamshire. The N side close to and just behind the High Street, with the N porch opening to it, the s side above the river Lovatt and looking out into fields with Tickford beyond. Although the present church has a w tower, there was a cruciform predecessor of which the E or chancel arch with three continuous chamfers bears evidence and the stretch of wall w of the E bays of the arcades. This is where the w arch of the crossing tower was. The E bays then opened into transepts. The rest is mostly mid-c 14 but much restored. Especially the s aisle windows are all not original. The s aisle was rebuilt in 1827–8 by *Savage*. Latest Medieval the broad w tower with its pairs of two-light bell-openings. This was built between 1542 and 1548. The pinnacles (a rarity in Buckinghamshire) date from the c 19. The most rewarding Dec piece is the s porch and s doorway. The porch entrance and the doorway have cusped and subcusped arches, and the porch has along its w and E walls blank arcading to a high dado height. The N porch is two-storeyed and has on the ground floor a sexpartite vault (cf. Great Linford) with heavy hollow-chamfered ribs. The interior is spacious. Five-bay arcades. Quatrefoil piers with slender shafts in the diagonals. Finely-moulded arches. In the s aisle elaborate Sedilia with three arches under a straight top. The style is early c 14 and the piece was probably moved during the Savage restoration. Clerestory and nave roof Perp. – STAINED GLASS. E window 1860, designed by *Street* and executed by *A. Gibbs*, who also glazed the chancel s windows (1848 and 1864). – PLATE. Large Flagon 1634; Chalice and Paten 1638; Paten 1703. – MONUMENT. Brass to a Civilian, late c 14 (rood-stair door). The figure is 3 ft 9 in. long.

On the NE side of the churchyard modest one-storeyed ALMS-
HOUSES, built in 1763. E of the churchyard the old NATIONAL
SCHOOLS, dated 1816. Red brick and slate.

The PERAMBULATION starts from the Bridge a little to the NE of
the church. The bridge was built in 1810. Here at once the best
house in the town, now COUNTY LIBRARY. Late C17, of red
and vitreous brick, crowning parapet, giant pilasters. Seven
bays, oddly divided by pilasters into three and four. Later doorway. Early C19 room on the first floor. Now up and into HIGH
STREET. At the corner of the church, Messrs ODELL, a good
Early Victorian shop front, rounded, with unfluted Corinthian
columns. Then the SWAN REVIVED, front of c. 1830–40, but
a Jacobean staircase inside. Opposite, BARCLAYS BANK,
Gothic, dated 1870, and next to it the WHITE HOUSE, probably Early Victorian, with a handsome straight-sided oriel
window on the upper floor. The corner of St John Street and
the whole E side demolished at the time of writing to make way
for new development. Off St John Street is Silver Street and off
Silver Street PAGG'S COURT, where CHRISTIE'S SCHOOL
ought to be seen, a house dated 1702, one-storeyed, of brick
with diaper decoration. Hipped roof, segment-headed windows.
The house was built as a workhouse. On in the High Street the
URBAN DISTRICT OFFICES (No. 60), a five-bay house of c.
1700 with three storeys and quoins; doorway with Ionic pilasters and pediment. After that the former ANCHOR HOTEL
with a deep Tuscan porch across the pavement. Further on, on
the same side, the VICARAGE, lying back a little. Four bays,
two storeys. (Original C17 staircase, also other woodwork.
RCHM) Then the small BAPTIST CHAPEL, two windows and a
doorway, 1824. The simple predecessor of stone, dating from c.
1700, is at the back. Then on the other side No. 84, early C18,
of five bays and two storeys with quoins, a rusticated door surround, and a shell-hood. Finally, across the end of the street the
former TOWN HALL, 1845, of grey brick, with grand pilasters
and a pedimented gable. This was originally built as the British
School.

To TICKFORD one crosses the BRIDGE, cast iron of 1810, from
the end of St John Street. On the r. ST MARGARET'S, Victorian, on the l. the former WRESTLERS' INN, the front early
C18 but inside C16.* There is a TOLLHOUSE opposite the
steep-gabled lodge to TICKFORD ABBEY. Fragments of the
former PRIORY re-used in the walls of the house and its

* According to Mr Newman Cole.

outbuildings. Further s RENNY LODGE HOSPITAL, the former WORKHOUSE, built in 1836.

SOCIÉTÉ GENEVOISE (Sogenique), Green Farm Road. By *G. & U. Bowyer*, 1957–8. Simple, very finely-detailed two-storeyed office block with a short wing at the back containing staircase and cloakroom. Light brick and concrete. The panels below the sills of pale blue glass. Around the entrance also slate and teak strips.

NEWTON BLOSSOMVILLE

9050

ST NICHOLAS. Mostly of *c.* 1300 and soon after. Nave s wall, short with one tall lancet and one large three-light intersected window, i.e. *c.* 1300. N aisle windows minor early C14. Chancel all flowing tracery, N chapel E window reticulated tracery. Arcade of two bays with octagonal pier and double-chamfered arches. The W respond has a caryatid bust corbel. N chapel towards the chancel two bays, quatrefoil pier, double-chamfered arches. An arch also from the chapel to the aisle. Perp w tower with higher stair-turret. – FONT. Octagonal, Perp, with two-light blank panelling. – PULPIT. Simple, of *c.* 1700. – STAINED GLASS. N aisle E; C14 fragment in the tracery. – E window by *Kempe*, *c.* 1915, unsigned.

NEWTON LONGVILLE

8030

ST FAITH. Perp externally (except for the doorways and altered N aisle w window), but internally earlier. Late C12 arcades of two bays. Circular piers with square abaci, pointed arches. The capitals and other details differ. The N capital is flatter and has scrolly leaves and dragons, the s capital has plain flat upright leaves. The hood-mould of the s arches is plain, on the N side it has nailhead decoration. The chancel arch is of the same date. Semicircular responds with square abaci. Crocket leaves and monsters in the capitals. The arch rebuilt in the early C14 with many mouldings, including keeling and a hollow set out with dog-tooth and fleurons. Ambitious Perp N chapel. w respond with demi-figure of an angel. Inside no more than several corbel heads and a length of frieze. – SCULPTURE. Outside the N chapel on the E wall small statue of a female Saint; C14. – PLATE. Small Cover of an Elizabethan Cup; large Flagon, 1638; large Cup and Paten on foot. 1685. – MONUMENT. Head of a Knight of *c.* 1300 (E of the s arcade).

A village with many picturesque timber-framed cottages, with exposed timbers and thatched roofs.

MANOR HOUSE, s of the church. Brick with dark vitreous diapers. Recessed centre and symmetrically projecting gabled wings. The date probably Early Elizabethan.

9040   NORTH CRAWLEY

St FIRMIN. At the beginning stands the s arcade, of *c.* 1200. Five bays, octagonal piers. Low capitals with upright leaves, double-chamfered arches. The arcade must have been built in two operations, as after three bays from the E the thickness of the original, no doubt Norman, W wall remains, However, all the details tally; so the decision to lengthen the church must have been taken during building. The building of the W tower followed indeed shortly after. Low circular angle stair-turret. Lancet windows. Tower arch to the nave of three continuous chamfers. The upper parts of the tower are Dec. The chancel was rebuilt late in the C13, see the chancel arch and the bar tracery of the internally shafted windows. Foiled circles, and in the E window three foiled circles. The N arcade is of the early C14. Four bays for the length of the older five. Quatrefoil piers, double-chamfered arches. Finally Perp windows, Perp clerestory. – FONT COVER. 1640. Very pretty. Octagonal with panels with the usual blank arches. Castellated top with little ball finials at the corners. Recessed obelisk. – SCREEN. Late C15. Broad ogee-arched one-light divisions with tracery over. Ribbed W coving. Against the dado figures of prophets and saints, with inscription scrolls. The quality is creditable. – BENCH ENDS. Straight-headed with linenfold panelling. – BOX PEWS. – PLATE. Paten on foot of 1663; Cup of 1665.

CONGREGATIONAL CHURCH. 1821. Brick. Pedimented front with arched doorway and two arched windows.

CRAWLEY GRANGE. A sizeable Elizabethan brick mansion with a NE wing by *Tanner Jun.*, illustrated in 1907. The old front is on the E-plan with straight gables and mullioned and transomed windows. Plain porch. The addition is in the same style with canted bay windows. It contains chiefly a large ballroom. (Inside one elaborately carved chimneypiece, the fireplace surround dated 1686, the overmantel Jacobean.)

GRANGE FARM, $\frac{1}{2}$ m. NW. C16 and C17. Timber-framed with brick infillings. Picturesque and picturesquely placed inside a moat.

NORTH DEAN HOUSE *see* HUGHENDEN

NORTH MARSTON

ST MARY. Short, plain Perp w tower. Nave and aisles and sumptuous Perp chancel and s chapel, both restored at the expense of Queen Victoria in 1855. The work was done in memory of Mr J. C. Neild, who had left the queen property to the value of £250,000. The architect chosen was *Sir Matthew Digby Wyatt*.* The chancel and chapel are embattled and have pinnacles. The N aisle (W lancet!) and N arcade are of the C13. Quatrefoil piers and characteristic moulded capitals. Double-chamfered arches and a hood-mould with big nailhead. The s arcade has two bays of the Dec style. Arches with one sunk quadrant and one chamfer on pier and responds which are concave-sided octagonal. The latter the RCHM regards as a late C15 rebuilding. The E bay is later than the W bays. The RCHM suggests c. 1350. Oddly compound piers with circular capitals with big fleurons. Arches of many mouldings. Squint or window E of the arcade bay with fleurons. Flowing tracery in the E window, and in its jambs l. and r. niches. Fleurons in the arch. In the E wall at ground level a small recess with some bones was found in 1947–8, and this is supposed to be connected with the relics of John Schorne, the local vicar and wonder-worker who succeeded in imprisoning the devil in a boot. The wide Perp chancel is accompanied by a N transept chapel and a two-storeyed vestry with stair-turret, both of the same date as the chancel. The embattled clerestory is Late Perp. The roof rests on angels. Inside the chancel rich but defaced Sedilia with polygonally projecting canopies. Their undersides have pretty little rib-vaults. The decoration of the chancel is of c. 1855. – REREDOS by *Samuel Cundy*. – STAINED GLASS. By *Ward & Nixon*, designed by Miss *Harriet Clarke*. – STALLS. Perp, with poppy-heads, traceried fronts, and some MISERICORDS with foliage. – FONT. Perp, octagonal; the renewed bowl rests on defaced angels. – PLATE. Cup and Cover Paten of 1569. – MONUMENT. Stone tablet to John Virgin, 1694. Inscription in a circle: 'He lise dust dovne there'. A hand points downwards to the 'there'.

NOTLEY ABBEY

The abbey was founded for Augustinian canons early in the C12. The present house is the Abbot's Lodging built partly in the C15 and partly by the last abbot before the Dissolution, Richard

* Information given by Mr Nairn.

Rydge (1529–39).* The house contains the Abbot's Hall, the Parlour and Solar to its w and communication on the E side with the w range of the cloister. The Hall and the Upper Chamber above it have straight-headed two-light windows and panel tracery to the s. The Hall fireplace is a copy of an original one in the Solar, but the old door inside it, probably to a smoke chamber, is original. The w range has no features of special interest except a doorway. The church lay to the N of the cloister, and of it all that stands is the base of the circular E pier of the s arcade, the C12 sw pier of the crossing, the Perp SE pier of the crossing, and the SE corner of the whole church. Excavations have proved that the church was originally built c. 1160 with a crossing and transepts, that the nave had aisles dating from c. 1200 and was about 100 ft long, that a new E end of c. 120 ft length was built c. 1300, and that the crossing tower was remodelled in the Perp style. Along the E range of the cloister the site of the Chapter House has been found by excavation. It was rectangular and dated from the C13. Finally, the s range, which, as usual, contained the Refectory. Here, inside, against the E wall, is some beautiful C13 arcading: stiff-leaf capitals, the shafts of which are missing, pointed trefoil arches, and spandrels richly decorated with stiff-leaf foliage in relief. In the C18 the w wall still stood to the gable and had three tiers of lancet windows (see the Buck engraving). The doorway from the cloister to the refectory also has shafts with stiff-leaf capitals. To the E of the refectory, at the corner of the cloister, was the Warming House. The doorway of this survives, and a doorway from it to the undercroft of the refectory.

To the N of the church, higher up, is a square stone DOVECOTE, perhaps of the C14.

6010   OAKLEY

ST MARY. The arcade between nave and N aisle is puzzling. It is of five bays; the first must be a w extension, the next two piers are of the early C13, circular with octagonal abaci, the last is octagonal and represents a lengthening by two bays to which the two plain recesses in the N wall correspond. All arches are double-chamfered. w tower of c. 1300, see the cusped lancets and the tower arch of three continuous chamfers dying into the imposts. Perp top with higher stair-turret carrying a pediment. Of c. 1300 also the N aisle w window. The N windows are Dec.

* His name appears on panelling from Notley now at Winton Manor, Oxon.

Dec also the deep s transept with a three-light reticulated s window, below which a big cinque-cusped outer tomb recess. –
PLATE. Tasting Dish with pierced handle, 1686; Paten on foot,
c. 1700. – MONUMENTS. Coffin lids in the N recesses with
crosses, one quite elaborate.

OAKLEY HOUSE, at the s end of the village. Dated 1660. Brick
with stone dressings, including quoins. Two-light mullioned
windows, one canted bay window, and a doorway with an oval
window over, placed below a hood-mould, a typical late C17
motif. Big square-panelled central chimneystack.

OLNEY   8o5o

ST PETER AND ST PAUL. A Northamptonshire church in Bucks, 6b
unmistakable with its tall C14 spire. The tower is tall too. It has
diagonal buttresses. On its top the spire starts with very short
broaches, hardly noticeable as tall pinnacles stand on them. The
spire has four sets of lucarnes, all in the cardinal directions. The
early C14 is the period which prevails in the church. Very tall
three-light windows with flowing tracery. In the chancel the
five-light E window is over-restored. The chancel NW and SW
windows are of the low-side type and have transoms. Inside,
against the N wall, Easter Sepulchre. The tomb-chest has
quatrefoil panels in a very crisply and richly ornamented framework. Large and airy interior. Five-bay arcades with quatrefoil piers and arches with two sunk quadrants. Chancel arch
with three sunk quadrants dying into the imposts. Tower arch
triple-chamfered, also dying. It is a pity that the church has no
clerestory. The segmentally vaulted plaster ceiling lies somewhat low on the nave. – STAINED GLASS. E window by Holland
of Warwick, c. 1869. – MONUMENTS. In the churchyard many
tombstones by James Andrews, Cowper's friend (see F. Burgess,
Monumental Journal, June 1950).

Olney is one of the most attractive of the small towns in the county.
Cowper suits it to perfection. The walk starts by the church,
which lies at the very s end of a town stretching for a mile along
its High Street to the N. The church is placed in a triangle
between the roads from the bridge and from the mill. The
BRIDGE with its five fine segmental arches dates from 1832. To
the N of it, on the W side the first of the many stately Later
Georgian houses of the town. Stone (as most of them are), five
bays, three storeys, with a round-headed doorway and a broken
pediment (also a recurrent motif). The MILL is of four storeys,
partly stone and partly brick, and includes the Miller's house,

stone, of five bays and three storeys, with the same type of door-way.* The street bends round the churchyard, and N of this stands the VICARAGE, built in 1767, long and two-storeyed, with irregular fenestration. Then, on the other side, COURT-NEY HOUSE, early C19, with broad tripartite windows. After that the street joins up with that from the bridge. At the meeting point the former SCHOOL of 1847. Front of two big shaped gables with a big window under each of them. Opposite a graceful C18 shop-front. To its r. a house of 1717 with odd lunettes above the upper windows. After this WESTON ROAD joins from the W. In it ALMSHOUSES of 1819, two-storeyed, of chequered brick, with a central pediment, twelve tenements in all. Here the High Street starts, but almost at once the MARKET PLACE opens on the E. Overlooking it from the W the BULL HOTEL with an Early Victorian or slightly earlier front. White and black; deep, columned porch. In the Market Place the most important house is on the S side, COWPER'S HOUSE, now the Cowper Museum. This is probably mid-Georgian. Red brick, not stone, vertical bands and angle rustication in vitreous bricks. Six bays, three storeys, raised oblong panels below the windows. Two doorways with pulvinated friezes and pedi-ments. Behind the house Cowper's garden and his tiny unas-suming Summer House. Direct connexion existed in the past from here across one field to the Vicarage garden.

The HIGH STREET is nowhere interrupted by side streets, which gives it a most gratifying continuity. Of houses the following deserve notice. No. 6 is of three wide bays, three-storeyed, with the centre oddly emphasized by three tiers of pilasters. Doorway with slim Gothic triple shafts. The windows were no doubt originally tripartite. No. 14 is of the early C18, of three bays and two storeys, with quoins and with tripartite windows l. and r. of the pedimented doorway. Above the doorway a window with side volutes. Opposite, OLNEY HOUSE, a fine mid-Georgian house of three bays and two storeys. The whole ground floor is rusticated, the doorway is of the type already met. To the l. and r. Venetian windows, also a Venetian window in the l. hand annexe. After that several more nice doorcases. On the other side CLIFTON HOUSE, five bays, three storeys, with a doorcase as before.‡ Finally, again on the W side,

* (Inside, according to O. Ratcliff and H. Brown, very fine fireplaces from the former Great House.)

‡ Lying back, the monstrous CONGREGATIONAL CHURCH of 1879, with plate tracery and an indescribable turret.

ORCHARD HOUSE, C18 like its neighbour to the r., which has a pretty doorcase with some Gothic detail. Orchard House, however, has front excrescences in a kind of Arts-and-Crafts-Neo-Baroque. They are of 1904 and by *A. E. Anderson* of Northampton. After Orchard House less eventful houses.

ROMAN BUILDING. At ASHFURLONG, ¼ m. N of the bend of the Ouse and on the line of a possible Roman road (*see* p. 17), parts of a Roman building are still visible. From the neighbourhood came a hoard of silver coins of C3–4 date and a bronze figure of Mercury as well as contemporary 'terra sigillata' and coarse wares.

OVER WINCHENDON *see* UPPER WINCHENDON

OVING   7020

ALL SAINTS. Much restored (*Street*, 1867). The chancel is of the early C13. Lancet windows, group of three, stepped, at the E end. Later in the C13 the nave received aisles. The S arcade of two bays is complete. Octagonal piers, double-chamfered arches. Of the N arcade only one bay and the start of the second remain. The S doorway is simple with a continuous chamfer. Early in the C14 the S aisle received an E chapel. Reticulated tracery in the E window. Big ogee-headed recess in the S wall. W tower and clerestory Perp. Low-pitched Perp nave roof. Of the big arched braces one is dated 1657. – SCREEN. Simple, Perp, of one-light divisions. – BENCH ENDS. In the S aisle, simple, with knobs on the arms and the top. – PLATE. Cup and Cover Paten, small, 1569; Paten on foot 1708.

OVING HOUSE. Built in the early C17, completely remodelled in 1740–3, and enlarged in the late C18. Brick cemented and stone dressings. The entrance side has to the l. and r. of the centre projecting wings with gables. There are round windows in the gables. The wings are two bays wide. Centre doorway with Tuscan columns. On the garden front a three-bay centre with pediment, and to the l. and r. of it a Venetian window and a tripartite lunette over. Plain two-storeyed wings to the l. and r., l. four bays, r. three. Behind the centre on the garden side lies the principal room, with an elaborate, yet not too exuberant, plaster ceiling. The forms are small and busy. Neither in the classical Kent, nor in the Rococo vein. Staircase with three slim turned balusters to the tread and carved tread-ends. The other rooms have been georgianized with great skill and swagger by *Felix Harbord*, *c.* 1950. In the Hall the panel with a portrait in profile is original. So are the elaborate plasterwork of the Dining Room ceiling and the chimneypiece and overmantel in the same room. To the E STABLES with a pedimented doorway and a lantern turret.

The main street runs S–N from the gardens of the house to the church. Wide green edges and a number of pretty cottages.

7030
PADBURY

NATIVITY. C14 S doorway, but a re-used hood-mould of the C13 with nailhead decoration. The S aisle Piscina looks c. 1300. Dec the chancel. Lancet windows and windows with Y-tracery and reticulated tracery. The lancets are of the low-side variety. Dec also part of the tower – see the arch to the nave, on coarse head-corbels. The rest of the tower is C17 or C18. Dec arcades of standard details. Circular clerestory windows on the N side. – WALL PAINTINGS. N wall, from W, first the Wheel of the Deadly Sins, then two scenes from the life of St Catherine, both c. 1330. In the spandrels of the S arcade fragments of early C14 figures. All scarcely recognizable.*

NORBURY CAMP. A roughly circular, undated earthwork lying beside the N branch of the Claydon Brook and ¼ m. S of the station. It encloses about 15 acres and has a single rampart and ditch.

9000
PEDNOR

GREAT PEDNOR. Timber-framed C16 house with brick infilling. Added to it an irregular C18 façade. Inside very handsome original wall-paintings with interlocked quatrefoils on the ground floor, Elizabethan wall-painting in a room on the upper floor. Big BARN with fine, massive timbers.

LITTLE PEDNOR. By *Edwin Forbes*, 1911–12. A remarkably successful enlargement of some farm buildings to make a formal composition round a large oblong courtyard, through which runs the main road. In the courtyard a circular dovecote. The house on the W side, with lower cottages, all in one group, the cruciform garage, etc., on the E side. All dark red brick and Tudor details.

9090
PENN

HOLY TRINITY. An oddly mixed but not unattractive building. Short W tower, nave and chancel and several accretions. The tower is early C14, see the W lancet and the arch towards the

* Cf. *Rec. of Bucks.*, XVI, 2, 1955–6.

nave. Then the s aisle arcade, no more than a breaking through
a pre-existing s wall (of what date?) by means of arches dying
into the imposts. Perp the fine nave roof with tie-beams on
arched braces which rest on stone figures, heads, etc. Queen-
posts. Tracery spandrels above the braces, and tracery outside
the queenposts. Tall blank panelling up the roof between wall
plates and purlins. Wind-braces above the purlins. The chancel
N side a repair of 1736 (the pointed window and that at the SE
end perhaps of c. 1800). – PULPIT. C18 with marquetry, from
the Curzon Chapel in Mayfair. – PORCH DOOR. C15 with
traceried spandrels above the head. – PAINTING. Doom, late
C15, painted on boards (which is a rarity); Christ in Majesty
with angels, carrying the Instruments of the Passion; the Virgin
and the Apostles below. Not of high quality. – MONUMENTS.
A number of post-Reformation Brasses in the s aisle. – Mrs E.
Curzon; set up in 1765. Flat urn and above oval medallion with
profile portrait; fine quality, unsigned. – Assheton, Viscount
Curzon, † 1820. By *Chantrey*. Two mourning women. One
seated, the other standing behind. Pedestal with profile portrait in roundel and urn above. In the Grecian taste. – Two
simple tablets by *Chantrey*. – Many more tablets.

Several noteworthy buildings by the church: to the SE THE
KNOLL, of c. 1700, with a hipped roof, to the N the CROWN
HOTEL, gabled brick, much added to, then the SCHOOL, 1910
by *Harrison Townsend*. Further W along the village street, on
the s side, a cottage of brick with cross-windows and two shaped
gables, probably late C17, and further NW, behind the Red Lion
Inn, yet another with the same shaped gables.

¾ m. s of the church PARSONAGE FARMHOUSE, C17, timber-
framed with brick-nogging. Gabled projecting wings. Barn and
square granary.

RAYNERS SCHOOL. Begun for the London County Council in
1959. Designed by *Stillman & Eastwick Field*. This is a residential school, and it is added to a manor house. The old house
lies to the N, the new buildings are charmingly grouped round
a small courtyard to the s. There is a two-storeyed range with
classrooms and dormitory and, at r. angles to it, the Hall and
Dining Room. Red brick, like the old house, cedar facing and
glass.

PENN STREET

HOLY TRINITY. By *Ferrey*, 1849. Flint, in the Dec style. Very
competent and dignified. Placed against a background of woods.

With central tower carrying an octagonal bell-stage and a spire. Nave and chancel of the same height; transept. – Inside large PAINTING of the Transfiguration, a copy after *Raphael*'s famous picture. Brought by Earl Howe from the Curzon Chapel in Mayfair.

SCHOOL. Also 1849. With a recent and pretty addition.

PRIMARY SCHOOL. By the County Architect's Department, 1958–60.

7020   PITCHCOTT

ST GILES. Small and over-restored. The chancel lancet makes the C13 likely as the original date of the church. In one S window a stone book-rest in the E jamb. – PLATE. Cup and Cover Paten, 1569.

9010   PITSTONE

ST MARY. The oldest part of the church is the N arcade of the chancel. This has an octagonal pier and responds with big, mature stiff-leaf capitals and double-chamfered arches of c. 1230. Then follows the N wall of the N aisle, c. 1300, see the two lancet windows with rere-arches and the blocked doorway. The S doorway of about the same time, but more elaborate. The N arcade is a C15 rebuilding of the former arcade. Octagonal piers, moulded capitals, double-chamfered arches. The S arcade was pulled down at the same time, so that the chancel arch is now in a lopsided position. Perp W tower. – FONT. Late C12, circular, with fluting on stem and bowl as at Aylesbury. Re-cut top frieze. – PULPIT. Good, Jacobean, with tester. – PEWS. Box Pews; C17. – CHEST. Plain, iron-bound, C13 (Vestry). – TYMPANUM. Dated 1733 (5?). Filling the whole upper E wall of the nave. With Creed, Commandments, etc. – COMMUNION RAIL. C18 with thin twisted balusters. – PLATE. Large Paten on foot, 1662. – BRASS. Small early C14 brass of a lady; only 12 in. long (found in 1935), the earliest brass in Bucks.

PARSONAGE. 1856 by *G. E. Street*.* Yellow brick, with thin dark diapers. Heavily bargeboarded gables.

PITSTONE GREEN MILL, *see* Ivinghoe, p. 179.

TUMULUS. On MONEYBURY HILL, Pitstone Common, an undated tumulus.

DITCH. ½ m. E of the church an undated curved ditch running E–W for about 300 yds.

* According to Mr D. Cole.

POUNDON

6020

2 m. sw of Twyford

POUNDON HOUSE. Of *c.* 1910. Symmetrical. Neo-Georgian.

PRESTON BISSETT

6030

ST JOHN BAPTIST. Short w tower, doubly short-looking because of the C19 clerestory of the nave. Dec chancel with a transomed low-side window and an E window with flowing tracery. Sedilia with head-corbels carrying crocketed ogee arches. The chancel arch is on two crouching figures. Dec N aisle with intricate E window. Three-bay arcade with octagonal piers and double-chamfered arches.

RECTORY, N of the church. Cemented, gabled house in the Tudor style. Built in 1840.

PRESTWOOD

8000

1¾ m. sw of Great Missenden

HOLY TRINITY. By *E. B. Lamb*, 1849 (GR). Of flint. Nave and chancel with steep-pitched roofs. Bellcote at the w end. Odd roof-line at the E end of the s aisle, odd junction of the porch with the s aisle. The porch leads into a w extension of the nave, which serves as a baptistery. Wide, squat nave arcades, the E bays of miniature size. Tall, narrow chancel and baptistery arches. Very odd scissor-bracing of the roof in the nave (the struts actually hang from the trusses),* and even odder roof in the w baptistery.

VICARAGE. Also by *Lamb*, 1850. Roof with many gables, odd doors.

PRINCES RISBOROUGH

8000

ST MARY. Large, of flint. The distinguishing feature of the church is due to *John Oldrid Scott*: the tower of 1907–8, with its bell-openings, straight-headed and Dec, with reticulation motifs in the tracery and with its parapet of flint and stone chequer and recessed spire. Most of the rest of the interior is *Arthur Blomfield*'s, who restored the church in 1867–8, especially the N aisle and the clerestory. The arcades inside the church are very mixed, of seven bays of which the narrow last one is C19. The bulk of the others is assigned by the RCHM to the early C13, but seems too thin in its details for that date (octagonal

* So the Rev. S. F. Smith tells me.

8—B.

piers and double-chamfered arches). The w bays are late C13 to early C14, the details of the s one later than the N. The s doorway belongs to the same phase. In the s aisle a fine triplet of lancets, remarkably elaborately shafted inside with attached, and in front of them detached, shafts of Purbeck marble. In the s aisle also four ogee-headed tomb recesses. – PULPIT. Jacobean, with broad blank arches and arabesque panels above. – STAINED GLASS. E window by *Kempe & Tower*, 1909. – PLATE. Flagon of 1628; Chalice of 1752.

ST TERESA OF LISIEUX (R.C.). 1937–8 by *Giuseppe Rinvolucri*. Of brick with a prominent dome. The plan is interesting, a triangle with three apses in the middles of the sides. Under the hexagonal domical vault there are thus three apsidal chapels and two triangular ones – a Borrominesque idea (cf. St Ivo in Rome). The third triangle contains the porch. The statue outside and the STATUES inside are by *Richard Guino*. They are of ceramic ware. By Guino the altar relief too. The relief of Joseph and the COMMUNION RAILS by *Rosamund Fletcher*, 1957. Next to the church the PRESBYTERY, white and in the modern style of 1930, i.e. with flat roof and windows wrapped round corners, curiously dated now and out of place.

PERAMBULATION. To the E of the church the MANOR HOUSE, probably of *c.* 1670, and an early example of the type current about 1700, i.e. of red brick, five bays wide, two storeys high, and with a hipped roof. However, the front is distinguished from later ones by the wide distances between the windows and the use of broad, short brick pilasters in two orders to separate them. The windows originally had mullion and transom crosses (see one remaining one at the back) but were sashed later. To the same later date probably belongs the doorway with pediment on Doric pilasters. Small front garden with original gatepiers. Inside a spectacular Staircase, square with open well and a balustrade still within the strapwork tradition. The pattern is one of circles in two tiers, not quite closed but linked up into 'addossed' question-marks. Farm buildings to the l. and, next to them, on the N side of the churchyard, the OLD VICARAGE, a picturesque timber-framed C15 cottage.

To the SW of the church lay the CASTLE of the Black Prince. Some fragments of a rampart, a ditch, and walls have been found.

From the churchyard to the E runs CHURCH STREET, with some timber-framed houses, especially a long front on the N side with overhang. On the s side a C17 brick house with two gables. Then the MARKET SQUARE with the TOWN HALL. This was built in 1824. Brick with wooden posts around connected by lean-to roofs with the upper storey. Here one window on each side. Pyramid roof and bell-turret. No houses of special interest. One nice doorcase with Doric pilasters and a pediment due S from the Town Hall. The HIGH STREET then runs SE. Several more doorcases here, but nothing of real note.

QUAINTON   7020

ST MARY AND HOLY CROSS. Nave and aisles Dec. Octagonal piers and double-chamfered arches. The piers were heightened in the C15. At the same time the W tower was built, and the Dec W doorway and W window re-used. Aisle windows Perp, straight-headed, the SE window especially pretty. It has inside in the jambs an Angle Piscina; this placing of the piscina is very rare in Bucks, though usual in East Anglia. Perp also the castellated N chapel of two bays. To the chancel one wide arch with two hollow chamfers. – FONT. Octagonal, Perp, simple. – REREDOS and SEDILIA by *William White*, who restored the church and rebuilt the chancel in 1877. – SCREEN. Part of the dado of the rood screen with PAINTINGS of four Saints in the N aisle. This again is very unusual in Bucks but standard in East Anglia. – DESK or Lectern (S aisle). Dated 1682. Entirely undecorated. – STAINED GLASS. In the SE window, signed by *Warrington*, 1861. – PLATE. Cup and Cover Paten, 1569; Flagon, 1669; Paten, 1672. – MONUMENTS. Quainton church is exceptionally rich in large late C17 and C18 monuments. Brasses to Joan Plessi, *c.* 1350 (chancel S, demi-figure, 8 in.); to John Lewys, rector, † 1422 (chancel S, kneeling, 9 in.); to John Spence, rector, † 1485 (chancel N, 3 ft); to Margery Verney † 1509 (chancel N, 3 ft); to Richard Iwardby † 1510 (chancel S, 21 in.). – Fleetwood Dormer † 1638 (tower, S). This monument, a tablet with two columns and an oddly-shaped urn at the top, is the centre of a much larger standing wall-monument to John Dormer † 1679 and Fleetwood Dormer † 1696. The strange, tall obelisks l. and r. with their garlands and cherubs' heads belong to this, and the gross putti holding on to urns. – Sir John Dormer † 1675 and Lady Dormer † 1672. Erected before his death. Designed by *William Stanton*. Big inscription plate ending in Latin distychs. Busts at the top, a little awkwardly placed. Below hers it says: Praeivi, below his: Sequar. Many more inscriptions at the foot, including a Greek one and such passages as Cito cadit caduca vita. – Richard Winwood and his wife, 24b

erected in 1689, signed by *Thomas Stayner* (s aisle). White
figures on a black tomb-chest. He lies in armour, comfortably
recumbent with a hand on his heart. She is behind him, half
sitting up and contemplating him. Separate inscription cartouche behind. A HELM to the l. – Sir Richard Piggott (N aisle).
Signed by *Giacomo Leoni*, the architect, and made after 1735.
Big, heavy black sarcophagus on claw feet. Reredos background
of white and grey marbles with columns and pilasters and an
open pediment. Between the columns against the back wall a
kind of concave-sided truncated pyramid and putto-heads,
clouds and rays. No effigy. – Mr Justice Dormer, *c*. 1728–30.
Big with a big sarcophagus and a white reredos back wall with
pilasters and pediment. On the sarcophagus the recumbent
dead son, his head on pillows, a blanket over his legs. To the r.
kneeling, his mother in tears, to the r., upright, with wig and a
demonstrating gesture, his father. Mrs Esdaile attributed the
monument to *Roubiliac*, but he was not yet in England when it
was made. Who can its author be? It is of very high quality, and
compositionally as well as sculpturally exceptional. – Charlotte
Pigott † 1823. White tablet by *M. C. Wyatt*. Curtains pulled
away. Above the inscription some drooping branches of weeping willow.

To the r. and l. of the entrance to the churchyard are the WIN-
WOOD ALMSHOUSES and the Rectory. The Almshouses
date from 1687, but are still entirely pre-classical in style. One
storey and a row of dormers alternating between bigger and
smaller gables. Two porches with Dutch gables are the main
accent. Groups of diagonally-placed chimneystacks. To the l.
and r. at r. angles two outbuildings with semicircular gables.
The RECTORY has a Georgian front of vitreous and red brick
with a three-bay centre and two outer canted bays. Above the
entrance one dormer in the roof, curiously shaped, with a pedimental gable. (Inside C16 linenfold panelling, said to come from
Denham Lodge.) The front to CHURCH STREET is of four bays.
Along Church Street a number of worth-while houses, timber-
framed and otherwise, especially ALWYN with the big date
1722 in the brick infilling, and Nos 2–4, C16, also with brick
infilling. These stand at the corner of THE GREEN. The Green
is large, triangular, and nicely rough. It slopes down the hill. At
its head, more or less in a line, the base and shaft of the VILL-
AGE CROSS, C15; behind it, that is facing down S, CROSS
FARMHOUSE, with a cartouche dated 1723, chequered brick,
four bays plus a fifth for the doorway and a blank window over.

Behind Cross Farmhouse, higher up and partly hidden, the WINDMILL, a tower mill, *c.* 100 ft tall, dated 1830, and with only one sail left. More pretty cottages W of the Green and round its bottom.

¼ m. to the NE DENHAM LODGE. The house has a moat and a separate, simple, one-storeyed gatehouse of stone. The centre of the front of the house is also of stone and is no doubt older than its fenestration. This must be of the late C17. The centre is five bays wide and of two storeys. Projecting brick wings. The windows of the cross-type with transoms placed unusually high. Staircase with strong, vertically symmetrical balusters. (Brick walls extend from Denham Lodge a long distance, surrounding fields to the E and N, the former enclosure of a deer park. MHLG)

(DENHAM HILL FARMHOUSE. A picturesque C17–18 group with ilex trees to the E. MHLG)

GRANGE FARM, 1 m. NW. The mansion of the Dormer family was destroyed in the C18. There remains a pre-Reformation BARN with double-curved braces and queenposts in the roof.

¾ m. NNW from here DRY LEYS, early C18 front of five bays and two storeys. Vitreous and red brick.

DODDERSHALL HOUSE, *see* p. 108.

QUARRENDON 7010

1½ m. NW of Aylesbury

ST PETER. Ruins, in a field. The almost unrecognizable overgrown ruins represent the two W bays of the nave and N aisle. Late C13. Octagonal piers, double-chamfered arches. Square-headed aisle windows. Already in 1817 the ruin formed 'a melancholy object of contemplation' (*Gent. Mag.*).

Of the mansion of the Lee family, one of the most notable Bucks families (cf. Aylesbury church), nothing remains. Sir Henry Lee entertained Queen Elizabeth here for two days in 1592.

RADCLIVE 6030

ST JOHN EVANGELIST. S doorway and chancel arch *c.* 1200 or thereabouts. The doorway has two orders of shafts with shaft-rings and stiff-leaf capitals and a hood-mould of dog-tooth, but the arch with zigzag, meeting at a roll moulding a zigzag set at r. angles to the other. This is a Late Norman motif, the rest is Early English; so perhaps the doorway is later than 1200, and the zigzag is re-used from a former round arch. The chancel arch is much altered anyway. The jambs have Norman motifs,

especially a token beakhead reduced to triangles within triangles, and also simply-decorated abaci, but the arch is double-
chamfered and therefore C13 at the earliest. W tower of c. 1300.
Doorway with continuous roll mouldings, lancet windows, and
battlements. – BENCHES with poppy-heads, now in the porch. –
COMMUNION RAIL. Jacobean, with openwork balusters. –
Also Jacobean HAT-PEGS. – STAINED GLASS. Good C14 fragments in a nave N window.

8a   MANOR HOUSE. 1621. The fragment of a larger house. The best
feature is the Staircase with openwork panels of finial-spiked
ovals, and lozenges. Also the former Screen, bulgy Tudor
columns and segmental arches with pendants. A blocked doorway is in line with the screen. Several old fireplaces and chimneystacks (square set diagonally).

7090   # RADNAGE

ST MARY. With an imposing central tower of the C13. Of the same
time the chancel E window, three separate stepped lancets.
Other chancel and nave windows of the beginning of the C14.
Perp nave roof with tie-beams on arched braces decorated with
tracery. – WALL PAINTINGS. C13 figures in the E windows. A
St Christopher on the N wall (only head and child preserved).
Ashlaring in other places. – PLATE. Cup and Cover Paten of
1577. – BRASS. William Este † 1534 (nave E wall), 15 in. figure.

8050   # RAVENSTONE

ALL SAINTS. Some C11 herringbone masonry in the W wall. The
S arcade follows, of which the first two bays are of c. 1190. Circular pier with square abacus. Flat water-leaf capital. Unmoulded arches. The third bay is later. Unbuttressed C13 W
tower and chancel (one 'low-side' lancet). Sedilia of c. 1300 in
the S aisle. – Of the furnishings by far the most important is the
25   MONUMENT to the first Earl of Nottingham † 1682. The S
chapel was added for it, still with mullioned and transomed
windows. The monument is of great dignity, a large four-
poster of white and black marble. White curtains looped to the
black columns. Under its flat roof reclines the Earl in a half-
seated position, white on a black marble slab. An excellent portrait and competent in the draperies. The sculptor is unknown.
Mrs Esdaile has attributed it to *Cibber* and to *William Stanton*.
Mr Betjeman and Mr Piper support *Catterns*. – The chapel is
surrounded by a good SCREEN with sturdy twisted balusters.
The same pattern in the COMMUNION RAIL. – Of the same

date also the splendid PULPIT, quite unornamented, with an uncommonly large tester, and the PANELLING round the walls. – Other furnishings: FONT, early C14, tub-shaped with flat trefoiled arches and small quatrefoils in the spandrels. – ORGAN. Late Georgian; Gothic. – PLATE. Cup and Cover Paten of the late C17.

ALMSHOUSES. Immediately N of the churchyard and with gate-piers to it. Late C17. Two rows facing each other. One-storeyed, of chequered brick.

ROUGHWOOD FARM *see* CHALFONT ST GILES

RUSHYMEAD *see* AMERSHAM

ST LEONARDS   9000

ST LEONARD. An attractive little church, plastered walls and a short bell-turret with spire. Nave and chancel in one. The church was largely rebuilt after the Civil War, and much restored in 1845. – MONUMENTS. Seth Wood and wife, 1707, tablet with two mournful little girls l. and r. – General Cornelius Wood † 1712. Tablet with bust in front of a large fan of trophies. Putti seated on cannon-balls. Both monuments by *Nicholas Bigée* (Gunnis).

(HEN GROVE. By *Morley Horder*, 1910. Essentially symmetrical, in a nice simple neo-Tudor. Of brick.)

SALDEN *see* MURSLEY

SAUNDERTON   7000

ST MARY. Nave and chancel and shingled bell-turret with steep pyramid roof. Mostly rebuilt by *J. S. Alder*, 1888–91 (GR). Of old material the chancel windows and nave doorways, all early C14. – SCREEN. Late C14, with one-light divisions and simple, rather broad tracery at the top. – PLATE. Small Cup and Cover of 1691.

Close to the church a FARMHOUSE, very picturesque, placed behind a pond and reached by a white bridge.

FROGMORE FARMHOUSE, ½ m. W. C16. Timber-framed with brick infilling and a fine seven-bay BARN.

EARLY SETTLEMENT. On the S slopes of LODGE HILL, above the Upper Icknield Way and ½ m. W of Saunderton Lee, a number of shallow sub-circular depressions, presumably a native settlement site, from which have come surface finds of both early and Belgic Iron Age pottery as well as Roman 'terra sigillata'. To the w a bank and ditch forming the parish boundary, and to the s a bridle-path running beside a low hedgebank. To the E a shallow sickle-shaped ditch, lying NE–SW, with a slight bank on the E side, was examined in 1939 and revealed a causeway and occupation debris including Belgic pottery in a primary position.

BARROWS. Just NW of this site are two much ravaged barrows, dated by surface finds of late Neolithic 'grooved' and 'Beaker' sherds.

IRON AGE SITE. ⅓ m. NW of Lodge Hill an early Iron Age site is situated in SMITHS FIELD, on the scarp-and-dip slope above the Icknield Way. The settlement is indicated by shallow depressions marking the position of 'working hollows' and storage pits, partial excavation of which in 1939 confirmed the date of the site.

ROMAN VILLA. At SAUNDERTON MILL, near the church the site was excavated in 1926–8 of a Roman villa built in the mid C2 and rebuilt at the end of the C3 and again possibly later. It was of the corridor type and boasted some twelve rooms with a hypocaust or corn-drying kiln to the NE. Associated with the first period of occupation were three infant burials as, at Hambleden (see pp. 154–5).

SEER GREEN

9090

HOLY TRINITY. 1846. Nave, chancel, and bellcote. Lancet windows.

SEFTON PARK see STOKE POGES

SHABBINGTON

6000

ST MARY MAGDALENE. C11 nave and chancel, the date suggested by the herringbone laying of the rubble. Low Perp w tower with battlements. The chancel windows are characteristic of c. 1300, the nave windows are Victorian. – PULPIT Dated 1626. Plain panelling and two small friezes of foliage. – PLATE. Cup and Cover Paten of 1683.

SCHOOL HOUSE, somewhat N of the church. C17 with a nice C18 front of three bays, vitreous brick with red-brick dressings. At the back the schoolroom with a big pointed E window.

SHALSTONE   6030

ST EDWARD. Almost entirely by *Sir G. G. Scott*, 1862. Only the
N aisle was left in its previous state, that is the state of a rebuilding of 1828. The windows here have Y-tracery. The most impressive motifs of Scott's rebuilding are the W tower with a
higher stair-turret crowned by a spirelet, and the S arcade inside, where the capitals are carved with naturalistic palm-
fronds, roses, lilies, ivy, etc. Scott believed in the possibility of
improving over the C13 in this one way of close attention to
nature. The piers of the N arcade could be genuine Perp. –
STAINED GLASS. S aisle W by *Hughes* of London. – MONU-
MENTS. Brass to Susan Kyngeston † 1540 (2 ft figure). – Mrs
Purefoy, by *Richard Batchelor* of Buckingham. The contract
was made in 1759, in her lifetime, and the monument was to
cost £98. Inscription plate etc. and, at the top, in the middle of
an open pediment, portrait bust. A conservative piece. – Many
tablets, especially Mary Hawes † 1828 by *Sir R. Westmacott*
(seated Faith with book, cup, and chalice) and Geraldine Jer-
voise † 1852 by the younger *R. Westmacott* (two pretty, characteristically more sentimental, kneeling children).

SHALSTONE HOUSE. Georgian, of stone, very plain, five by six
bays, two storeys, with parapet and hipped roof. (A chimneypiece was supplied by *William Palmer* in 1739. Information
from Dr Girouard.)

SHARDELOES   9090
1 m. NW of Amersham

Built in 1758–66 for William Drake, M.P. for Amersham. The 57a
original architect was *Stiff Leadbetter*, but the house was altered
and completed by *Robert Adam*. It is brick, stuccoed, nine by
seven bays in size, and has one-and-a-half storeys only with a
top balustrade. To the N excellent giant pedimented portico of
stone, Corinthian columns, and Corinthian pilasters against the
wall of the house. The end bays have the ground-floor windows
pedimented and set in shallow niches. The same treatment of
the end bays to the E. Here the middle window has a pediment
too. Below the N front the river Misbourne forms a lake. Leadbetter's house was meant to have square angle towers like Holkham or Hagley. Adam cancelled these and added the portico.
Entrance Hall with large doorcases to N and S. They are early as
Adam forms go. Fluted Doric pilasters, metope frieze, and no
pediment. The Dining Room to the r. (NW) has large stucco

panels on the walls and a ceiling with oval panels. Vine and ivy trails play around their frames. The NE room also with good stucco work. The main E room is the Library, and here *James Wyatt* stepped in. However, Wyatt's style at this stage is not essentially different from Adam's. The painted panels above the bookcases are by *Rebecca*, the stucco of the ceiling by *Joseph Rose*, both favourite craftsmen of Adam. Surprisingly small Staircase behind the Entrance Hall, with subdued iron balustrade. To the W the STABLES, centre with clock-turret, projecting wings with hipped roofs. The centre has five archways. The grounds were laid out by *Repton*.

8030

SHENLEY CHURCH END

ST MARY. The unusual interest of the church centres in its chancel. This is of the ending C12. Shafted windows with shaft-rings, crocket capitals. Arches with several roll mouldings. The E window is Perp. Inside a roll moulding runs along the walls below the windows, and a frieze of nailhead above and encircling the window heads. The windows are again shafted. Between them a keeled shaft on a corbel, accompanied a little higher up by shorter shafts on their own corbels. This was clearly for vaulting purposes. The corbels have decoration closer to the Norman than anything else in this Transitional ensemble. A very interesting addition of the C13 is the Sedilia. Two seats separated by a stone arm with a short attached shaft. Both seats have one wide segmental arch in common. Keeled continuous moulding. This spectacular chancel was added to, or marked the completion of, a cruciform Norman church. Of this the E window in the s transept bears witness.* The crossing has later arches of three chamfers. They date from the C15 and cut on the W side into the aisle arcades. The s arcade is of *c.* 1200. Four bays, short circular piers, moulded capitals, square abaci, single-stepped unchamfered pointed arches. Hood-mould with small zigzag at r. angles to the walls. C14 N arcade with octagonal piers and double-chamfered arches. Of the C14 also the clerestory. The W window the same as the E window. – PULPIT. Incorporating early C17 panels with very elongated blank arches of the familiar kind. – MONUMENTS. Sir Edmund Ashfyld † 1577. Standing monument. Sarcophagus behind three columns (cf. Dr Caius, Cambridge), open pediment. – Thomas Stafford † 1607. Standing monument. Alabaster. The

---

* In the s transept NE corner a finely decorated Norman capital, re-set.

effigy stiffly reclining on its side. Smaller kneeling figures in relief below.

FARMHOUSE, s of the church. Big, L-shaped, timber-framed, C17.

ALMSHOUSES. 1654. Plain one-storey row of stone.

SHERINGTON   8040

ST LAUD. The chief interest of the church is the central tower. The arches to w and E inside characterize it as of the C13 (triple-shafted responds). The outside in its upper parts is Perp, and has most curious four-centred relieving arches high up. Pairs of two-light bell-openings. Also of the C13 the N arcade. Circular piers with circular abaci, double-chamfered arches. The piers stand (also in the s arcade) on such high bases that the floor of the church must be lowered. The bays are wide, and the nave is wide. Much Dec work. The s aisle has an arcade with octagonal piers and double-chamfered arches and an original window with flowing tracery and another which may be re-used, as it has bar tracery with three circles, i.e. ought to be of before 1300. The s porch is Dec too. Rib-vault and blank wall arcading with ogee motifs. In the N aisle also a Dec window. Perp several windows, especially that at the w end of the nave (five lights). Also the Sedilia, with a curious top as if the tracery of a Perp window had been re-used. – FONT. Perp, octagonal, with small Saints under flat ogee arches. – CHANDELIER (nave). Brass, given in 1783.

BANCROFT MANOR (Rectory), ¼ m. SE. Stone, dated 1607.

(BRIDGE, across the Ouse. Handsome; C18. NBR)

BARROW. Just E of the motte site a Bronze Age 'saucer' barrow.

SHIPTON see WINSLOW

SHRUB'S WOOD see CHALFONT ST GILES

SIMPSON   8030

ST THOMAS. Cruciform, with a tall, rather slender crossing tower. Mostly of the early C14. Of the late C13 only the arches of the crossing tower, with semicircular responds and double-chamfered arches. Of early C14 indications there are more than need be mentioned, mouldings of the s and N doorways, window tracery, the E recess in the N transept with its ogee arch, etc. Good, unusual nave roof with tie-beams, two collars, both on braces, and two tiers of wind-braces. – MONUMENT. Sir Waldon Hanmer, 1789 by *John Bacon*. White base, black obelisk with a medallion in which Justice with her scales, mourning. Inscription:

> Absent or Dead, still let a Friend be dear
> A sigh the Absent claims, the Dead a tear.

A canal village with hump bridges.

SLAPTON

9020

HOLY CROSS. All Perp exterior, except that the chancel was rebuilt in the C19 and its exterior re-faced in brick, and the N and S doorways have details clearly of the Dec style. Not large, but with W tower, aisles, and clerestory. The aisles are narrow, the arcades of the early C14 (octagonal piers, double-chamfered arches). The chancel arch is a little earlier, see its capitals. – TILES. C14, in the chancel. – PLATE. Cup of 1662; Flagon of 1689. – BRASSES. Reynold Manser † 1462, demi-figure of priest, 13 in. long; Thomas Knyghton † 1529, priest, 13 in. long; James Tornay † 1519 and wives, 18 in. figures.

SLOUGH

9080

Slough, with 66,000 inhabitants, is the biggest town in the county. It is a town without tradition, did not become a Civil Parish until 1894, and has not made efforts yet to build up any visual centre of dignity. It could have done, but has not.

ST MARY. By *J. Oldrid Scott*, begun in 1876 in replacement of a neo-Norman church of 1835. The dominating NW tower was built only in 1912. It has a fine tall spire with big flying buttresses against the four pinnacles. The church is in red brick with details in stone, flint, and dark brick. The style is E.E. Interior all circular piers carrying stiff-leaf capitals. Circular clerestory windows. Wide aisles connected with transepts by double arches. – STAINED GLASS. By *Kempe* S aisle E 1885; chancel E 1889; chancel N and S 1891–2; S aisle 1893. – In the W windows a most remarkable display. Four tall lancets filled with irregular geometrical shapes in glowing colours, and in entirely abstract and, moreover, non-symmetrical, completely free patterns. They were designed by *Alfred A. Wolmark* in 1915 and are thus pioneer work of high significance, a parallel to Wyndham Lewis's designs for 'Blast', and, as far as stained glass in England goes, not emulated again until the new windows for Coventry Cathedral were designed.

ST LAURENCE, Upton. Of brown stone. If it were not for the S
aisle of 1851 (by *Ferrey*) the church would be a perfect example
of the Norman parish church. Nave, central tower, and 9b
straight-headed chancel are all Norman. In the nave two
phases can be observed, the early one remembered by one
blocked N window, and the later one by the rest of the church.
Windows in chancel, tower, and nave. N doorway with one
order of shafts and nook-shafts. Capitals with upright leaves;
zigzag. Very fine rib-vaulted chancel of two bays. They are
divided by semicircular responds and an unmoulded transverse
arch. The ribs are rolls on a flat unmoulded band and rest on
corbels. All capitals are scalloped. The PAINTINGS of the ribs
may well represent what was originally there. The pattern is
simple, the colours are black, red, and yellow. A very curious
arch is in the new part, unrecorded apparently as to its provenance. It is oaken, of the C13, with shafts, crocket capitals, and
profuse dog-tooth. Does it come from a house ? (cf. e.g. Great
Bricett, Suffolk). – FONT. Cylindrical, Norman, with tall blank
arches on thin colonnettes. – SCULPTURE. An alabaster Trinity
of the C15, somewhat damaged, in the nave S wall. – STAINED
GLASS. In the S aisle a S window of 1857, signed with the monogram of *Thomas Willement*. – Several early and interesting
Kempe windows: S aisle E and nave W of 1877, N side third from
W of 1882, first from W 1893. – MONUMENTS. Brass of a Knight
with his two wives, early C16, 2 ft 1 in. figures. – Brass to E. Bulstrode † 1599 and wife. – Monument to Sir William Herschel,
the astronomer, † 1822. By *J. Theakston*. Simple, heavy Grecian
tablet.

ST PAUL, Stoke Road. 1905 by *J. E. K. & J. P. Cutts*.

ST PETER, Chalvey. By *Street*, 1860–1. Nave, lower chancel,
low N aisle, and bellcote. Knapped flint and brick bands. The
arcade with big, rather clumsy foliage capitals. In the E wall a
circular window with odd foiling. Much spiky nailhead decoration. Stone PULPIT.

TOWN HALL, Bath Road. By *C. H. James & Bywaters* and *Rowland Pierce*, 1934–6. Neo-classical in the Swedish way, see the
graceful bell-turret and the prettily framed centre windows.
This centre is three bays wide and pedimented. The plan for
the rest is only half executed, a nine-bay lower wing with a band
of windows on the ground floor, separate windows on the upper
floor, and a projecting end wing. It was to be balanced by a
broad, short wing with the assembly hall.

LAW COURTS AND POLICE STATION, Windsor Road. By the

County Architect, *F. B. Pooley*, 1956–7. A remarkably friendly group of buildings at r. angles to each other. The Police Station faces Windsor Road. The Law Courts consist of two self-contained parts side by side, without internal communication. Each has court rooms with subsidiary rooms. The E part is two-storeyed.

FIRE STATION, Tuns Lane, off Bath Road. By *F. B. Pooley*, 1956. A good group with the flat-roofed garage, the drill-tower, and the low-pitched roof of the two-storeyed dormitory behind the low, square ambulance station.

COLLEGE OF FURTHER EDUCATION, Bath Road, W of William Street. By the County Architect, *F. B. Pooley*, 1957–61. Three tall blocks of six storeys and one- to two-storeyed ranges between. The tall blocks have a steel frame and timber curtain walling to the E and W. The N and S ends are bare and sensitively proportioned, partly of sheer brick, partly of cast stone. One vertical glazed band only between these parts. A slightly-recessed canopy on the roof.

LICENSED VICTUALLERS' SCHOOL, Mackenzie Street. By *Leathart & Granger*, 1936. Big, neo-Georgian, of light brick, with four projecting wings and a copper-sheathed bell-turret.

ORCHARD COUNTY SECONDARY MODERN SCHOOL. By the County Architect's Department. For 600 children. Completed in 1952. Steel-frame and brick panels.

ST JOSEPH'S SECONDARY MODERN SCHOOL (R.C.), Shaggy Calf Lane. 1957–8 by *Sterrett & Blouet*.

WESTERN HOUSE INFANT SCHOOL, Cippenham. By *F. A. C. Maunder*, 1949–50. Built in an old orchard. Spreading plan with two classroom blocks facing S and connected by a con-course and cloakrooms running N–S. Hall and Kitchen at the N end of this concourse projecting to the N. One-storeyed through-out.

UPTON HOSPITAL, Albert Street. The former Workhouse. De-signed by *Kempthorne*. Yellow brick, Late Classical, plain and utilitarian, with the usual octagonal centre. Built in 1835–6.

SLOUGH GENERAL HOSPITAL, Wexham Park, *see* p. 291.

STATION. Built in 1882. One-storeyed, of red brick, with five oddly metropolitan-looking French pavilion roofs. The com-position has a big middle pavilion and two end pavilions.

PERAMBULATION

Of the centre of Slough very little need be said. The main shop-ping street might be the main shopping street in any other town of the same size. There is no shopping district. The scenery changes at once behind this one line, as one can study in MACKENZIE STREET to the N, where Early Victorian semi-detached villas and a Late Victorian large house, such as the one by *Cave* of 1893 at the S end of the street, stand at a stone's throw from the centre. It is the same in WINDSOR ROAD to the S.

What is special and deserves a glance is the industrial development to the W along the BATH ROAD. Coming from the Town Hall one passes first one or two Georgian houses, the THREE TUNS on the r. (five bays, two storeys, parapet) and the SALTHILL HOTEL on the l. (big bow window), and then comes to the Trading Estate on the r.

The SLOUGH TRADING ESTATE was created in 1920, making use of a 600-acre site and buildings erected during the first World War by the War Office in an effort to centralize all military workshops and stores. The principle of letting factories to companies gradually established itself, and in 1927 the company began to build factories in advance of requirements, and the growth justified the erection in 1936 of a Community Centre as a headquarters for recreation, welfare, etc. This and the factories along the Bath Road, as far as they were built before 1939, were designed by *Wallis Gilbert & Partners*. They are in a streamlined modernistic idiom which has by now acquired a period flavour. The factories are individually symmetrical throughout. The ENTRANCE GATES are especially characteristic. After the Second World War the style changed, as is illustrated by, e.g., the FLEXELLO factory (by *J. C. Richardson*). Outside the Trading Estate some more noteworthy examples of factory architecture, especially Berlei of before and Aspro of after the war. BERLEI is by *O. R. Salvisberg* and *Sir John Brown & Henson*, and dates from 1937. The offices, with the prominent semicircular glazed staircase tower on the l., are along the road, the workshops behind. The proportions of the whole relatively small building are very good. Next to it, to the W, ASPRO NICHOLAS, by *E. D. Jefferiss Mathews*, 1956–8. One large oblong and intended to be enlarged further to the W. The E part contains laboratories, offices, canteen, etc., the W part, which is much bigger, factory and warehouse. Steel framing and brick facing. The W part has very small, widely spaced windows. The factory space is entirely artificially lit and air-conditioned. On the bare brick wall towards the Bath Road the name of the firm in large lettering. The E part is more open, with much glazing. The entrance to the offices is comparatively insignificant. It leads to a curved 'flying' staircase. The general office has a wavy ceiling between 90 ft-long structural beams.

As an appendix to this C20 factory style, HORLICK'S ought to be mentioned, to the N of the railway, off STOKE POGES LANE, with its long, even, three-storeyed brick front and the odd castellated tower at one end which even has tourelles. This is still entirely Victorian in style. It dates from 1908 and was built on the pattern of Horlick's American factory.

In WEXHAM ROAD a big new office building for I.C.I. PAINTS DIVISION. By *T. P. Bennett & Son*, 1956–7, a tri-radial star with raised centre. Four-storeyed, of light brick with much glass. Towards the road the ground floor is recessed, and the upper floors are carried on blue mosaic columns. Curtain walling above; the sills of the windows of blue glass. The end wall has windows only in its r. half, the l. half has plain brick with a big emblem.

BAYLIS HOUSE, Stoke Poges Lane. Built *c*. 1695 for Dean Hascard of Windsor. A simple, pleasantly proportioned brick house of seven bays and two storeys, with a slight three-bay projection and a three-bay pediment. The entrance and the garden sides are identical except for the doorways. That towards the forecourt is a C19 alteration, the other, which has a pediment on brackets, seems to belong to alterations of 1725–6 or 1733–5. The former were done for Dr Godolphin of Eton by *Thomas Rowland (see* Eton), the latter for his son by *John James*. To James's time belong the STABLES with their pretty lantern (the clock is dated 1735) and probably also the quadrant wall connecting them with the house. This has a Tuscan colonnade at its back. Further Georgian additions are the pavilions at the ends of the forecourt with their pyramid roofs, a subsidiary wing of the house, and a second, quite stately range of stables. Good wrought-iron GATES with the dolphin of the Godolphins.

(UPTON COURT, SW of St Lawrence, Upton. Basically late C15, with a porch to the E and a spiral staircase in the NE corner. Three original oak doorways on the staircase. Richly-moulded jambs, four-centred arches. RCHM)

(CIPPENHAM PLACE, Lower Cippenham Lane. Timber-framing and brick. Mid-C16. Originally L-shaped. Oversailing upper floor on moulded beams. On the ground floor two original windows with wooden mullions. On the upper floor two rooms with carved ceilings. C19 additions.)

MOUND. On SALT HILL, s of Upton, is the mound once used in
the Eton College 'Montem' ceremony abolished in 1864. It
is probably a prehistoric burial mound, though built up in
recent times.

SOULBURY   *8020*

ALL SAINTS. Over-restored. Dec chancel and Dec N aisle win-
dows. s aisle Perp, both arcades inside Perp. – FONT. Octagonal,
Perp, with the usual panels. – PLATE. Large Cup and Paten on
foot of 1630; large Flagon of 1672; large Dish on foot of 1678. –
MONUMENTS. Low ogee-headed recess in the N chancel wall. –
Brass of John Turnay † 1502 and wife (18 in.); Brass of John
Mallet's wife (he died in 1516; 20 in.). – Large number of
monuments to Lovetts of Liscombe Park: Sir Robert † 1609
and wife, with the usual kneelers. – Robert † 1690, by *Grinling
Gibbons* (unsigned but documentarily certain).* Surprisingly
c18-looking. All white marble. No effigy. Big urn on a big
sarcophagus. To the l. and r. standing putti in front of tall
obelisks. Putto-heads and clouds above the urn. One of the putti
has a crown and a palm-frond. Exceedingly elaborate flower
frieze at the foot of the sarcophagus and band of flowers round
the urn. – Eleanor Lovett † 1786. Of Coade stone and signed by
Coade & Sealy. Reclining figure on a base on which the inscriptions are set in cusped Gothic panels.
LOVETT'S SCHOOL. Dated 1724. A nine-bay front of two storeys.
Two doorways with segmental hoods on carved brackets. The
windows with wooden crosses. A very attractive front.
THREE LOCKS, 1 m. NE. A good piece of canalscape.
CHELMSCOTE MANOR, *see* p. 84.

STANTONBURY   *8040*

ST PETER. 1 m. WNW of Great Linford. In ruins. The intersected
E window and the Norman chancel arch have been removed.
ROMANO-BRITISH SETTLEMENT. s of Stanton Low and in a
bend of the Ouse is the site of a Romano-British settlement. A
group of possibly four buildings was indicated in rescue excavations in 1957. Signs of a hypocaust were also found, as
well as a scatter of early Iron Age sherds.
The MOUND sw of the old parish church has produced Roman
pottery. To the SE is a bank, with, to the E, a berm.

* According to Mr Gunnis.

6020
STEEPLE CLAYDON

St Michael. Not an architecturally satisfactory building. Restored and enlarged various times, the last by *Sir G. G. Scott* and his son *J. Oldrid Scott*, to whom the tower with its broach-spire is due. The brick transepts with re-used Perp windows look more like 1842, the date of an early restoration. The chancel is largely original, of the c14. Wide and bare interior. The Scott touch in the naturalistic foliage of the chancel arch and tower arch. – PULPIT. Jacobean. – PLATE. Cup and Cover Paten, 1569. – MONUMENT. Sir Harry Verney † 1894 and Lady Verney † 1857, two good profile medallions in a wooden frame.

PUBLIC LIBRARY, built in 1656 as a school by Sir Thomas Chaloner, enlarged and added to in 1841 and later. Brick, with a c17 bell-turret and later gables.

Quite a number of picturesque timber-framed cottages with white walls and thatched roofs. New housing in connexion with the Calvert brickworks.

8020
STEWKLEY

St Michael. The most splendid piece of Norman parochial architecture in Buckinghamshire, and in addition exceptionally complete and unaltered. The most likely date is 1140–50. All parts are sumptuously decorated, but there is little of special inventiveness in the motifs. Nave, central space with tower, and straight chancel. The w front has a doorway flanked by slightly lower blank arches. Capitals with scallops as well as foliage trails and beasts. Strangely-shaped tympanum, its bottom cut out in two lunettes. The surface of the tympanum is covered with dragons with twisted tails; also some foliage trails. Arches with double zigzag. Above this zone a zigzag course which runs right round the church. The window above the doorway also has zigzag. In the gable circular window with zigzag. The front is reminiscent of that of Iffley, which had the same plan too, before it was enlarged. The N and S windows have zigzag also. S doorway with one order of shafts, a lintel concave at the foot, zigzag in the arch, and a hood-mould with pellets. This stands on dragons' heads. The central space and the chancel have the same zigzag windows. Up at the top of the tower intersected zigzag arches. Perp pinnacles. The chancel E wall has (renewed) flat, shafted angle buttresses. The interior has a double frieze of nutmeg and all windows surrounded by zigzag. Towards the central space an arch on two orders of shafts (both to the w) carrying scalloped capitals. The arch has one order of beakhead, one of zigzag, and a hood-mould of zigzag. The chancel arch, i.e. the arch at the E end of the central space, is identical. The chancel finally is vaulted. The vault is quadripartite and has broad rectangular ribs, the top surface of which carries a band of lozenges each with a head inside. – STAINED GLASS. E window, 1864, could well be by *Saunders*.

A long village with occasional worthwhile houses and cottages, e.g., near the S end, MANOR FARMHOUSE, with one star-topped group of chimneys, and an octagonal dovecote, dated 1704. (It has about 800 nesting places. MHLG)

EMBANKMENT. About ½ m. E of North End an embankment some 100 yds long; undatable. Human skeletal remains found in the area seem to point to the site of a battle.

STOKE GOLDINGTON 8040

ST PETER. Norman chancel arch, unmoulded. C13 arcades with circular piers, circular abaci, and double-chamfered arches. Simple C13 N doorway. S chapel (windows with Y-tracery) of *c.* 1300. Perp W tower. – STAINED GLASS. E window by *Kempe*, 1902. – PLATE. Paten on foot, given in 1673.

SCHOOL. One-storeyed front of three groups of three arched windows. Built in 1837.

STOKE HAMMOND 8020

ST LUKE. Of ironstone with a Dec central tower. Dec chancel with flowing tracery. Perp transepts and most windows, also the E window. The crossing has responds only to E and W. To N and S the arches die into the former walls of the central space. – FONT. C14. On four shafts with moulded capitals. Quatrefoil bowl with the capitals penetrating into the re-entrant angles. – ALMSBOX. Dated 1618. On pillar. – PLATE. Cup, late C16, parcel-gilt; small Paten of 1685. – MONUMENT. Members of the Disney family, *c.* 1690. Tall tablet with thin columns and an open pediment, very unclassical in the details.

To the E nice canalscape, with the THREE LOCKS and several hump bridges.

STOKE MANDEVILLE 8010

ST MARY, 1886. In a prominent position but alas singularly un-attractive. Flint with copious red brick and stone dressings. S W porch tower. The fenestration by cusped single pointed windows and windows with plate tracery. – FONT. Perp, octagonal, with pleasant leaf motifs, also a shield with the symbol of the Trinity and a shrine. – BENCH. One plain old one. – PLATE. Cup and Cover Paten of *c.* 1570. – MONUMENT. Brudenell children, *c.* 1600. Not in its original state. The eldest daughter semi-reclining on her side. Inscription:

> Cruell death by mortall blades
> Hath slaine foure of my tender babes
> But God which never man deceaved
> Hath ther soules to Him received
> This death to them is greatest gayne
> Increasinge their Joy freeing them from payne
> O Dorothye my blesséd Childe
> Thou wert my tenth even God's own choyce
> In the exceedingly I did rejoyce
> On Good Friday at night my Doll departed
> Adieu my sweete and mòst true harted
>   etc.

OLD ST MARY. ½ m. s. In full decay. Of the late C17 brick tower only the stair-turret remains with the tower arch to the nave, of the DEC S arcade only the E respond, no chancel arch, but the PERP E window, also the N and S walls with their doorways.

42a STOKE HOUSE. A perfect example of the English house of *c.* 1700, as good as any in the country. It has, needless to say, five bays by five bays and two storeys with a hipped roof. But the eaves are carved with a large egg-and-dart motif and the two doorways have exquisite and very rich carving, one just brackets for a straight head, the other brackets carrying a generous shellhood and a frieze with a flower garland worthy of the best carver.

7090   STOKENCHURCH

ST PETER AND ST PAUL. What meets the eye first is the funny, shapeless, slate-hung W tower with its tiny open bellcote on the top.* This tower is actually Norman – see the small W window. Norman also, or rather Transitional, the chancel arch, although clearly muddled up later. One order of keeled nook-shafts and zigzag in the arch at r. angles to the wall. Late C13 S doorway with one order of shafts and dog-tooth in the hood-mould. The S windows of *c.* 1300–10, see the characteristic tracery. Of the C14 the E arch of the N arcade which opened originally into a transept. Head corbels on the imposts. The N aisle otherwise

* It is under reconstruction at the time of going to press.

dates from 1893, as does the bell-tower. – PLATE. Cup and
Cover Paten of 1574; Paten of 1684. – MONUMENTS. Brasses
to two Knights, both called Robert Morle, one † 1410, the
other † 1415. Almost identical. Both figures 2 ft high. – Bartholomew Tipping † 1680. Cartouche with fat bad fruit and fat bad
putti.

Large Green SE of the church. Bordering on it the KING'S ARMS
HOTEL, the front apparently C18, but in fact C20. Also the
PRIMITIVE METHODIST CHAPEL of 1893, a hideous-looking
building, in a belated and debased Italianate. The central window and its plate tracery is particularly hard to appreciate. A
little further E the BOARD SCHOOL of 1877, flint and red brick,
with a tower next to a half-hipped gable.

STOKE POGES

ST GILES. A picturesque sight from the E with the three gables of
the Hastings chapel, the chancel, and the nave. The church is
essentially Norman, as witnessed by one Norman N window in
the chancel and the Norman masonry of the W wall. Much was
done in the C13 to enlarge the church. The E end of the chancel
is E.E., see the lancet windows and the piscina. E.E. also the N
transeptal tower, again with lancets. The tower has a C19 pyramid roof. E.E. aisles, see the arcades, that on the N side, with
circular pier and octagonal abaci, and double-chamfered arches
with thin hood-moulds, is older by a little than that on the s
side, which has circular abaci and no hood-moulds. Excellent
Dec s porch of timber. The sides are opened in twice five ogee-
headed lights with quatrefoils in the spandrels. Heavy timbers
in the front with a Jacobean finial. The nave roof is also ascribed
to the C14. It is single-framed but has big tie-beams and king-
posts with four-way struts. The Hastings Chapel is of brick
with straight-headed windows whose lights have depressed
arches. It was built about 1560. – ALTAR CROSS. Bronze base
of an altar cross (chancel s) dating from c. 1480 and no doubt
English. Six-lobed foot, an inscription engraved above, and a
pretty cresting to hold the candle. A great rarity. – STAINED
GLASS. C17 heraldic glass in the Hastings Chapel. – In the s
aisle a two-light window signed by *Mayer* of Munich. It is still
entirely pictorial, and in addition very engagingly sentimental.
One can hardly assume a date later than 1845. – MONUMENTS.
Tomb-chest in the chancel, Dec, with crocketed ogee arch. –
Brasses to Sir William Molyns † 1425 and wife (chancel N), the
figures 2 ft 6 in. long. – Nathaniel Marchant, 1816 by *Flaxman*.

Inscription, and in the Grecian gable a female figure seated on the ground and holding a medallion with George III on horseback. Marchant was an engraver of gems.

GRAY MONUMENT, E of the church. Erected in 1799 by John Penn to *James Wyatt*'s design. A huge sarcophagus with straight tapering sides on a pedestal 20 ft high. The pedestal is square, of yellow stone with white stone inscription panels. The panels of the sarcophagus are strigillated. The placing of the monument is said to be due to *Repton*.

MANOR HOUSE, N of the church. Of red brick, built *c.* 1550–60, but only fragmentarily in its original state. The original part contains the Hall. It has a big chimneybreast and shafts with star tops. To the l. a bay window with two transoms, to the r. a window of three lights also with two transoms. The house was built for Sir Henry Hastings, Earl of Huntingdon, and later inhabited by Sir Edward Coke, the great lawyer. (The Hall chimneypiece is very elaborate but is not *in situ*. Caryatids, carved panels, twisted pilasters, and the Hastings arms. On the upper floor one other fireplace with caryatids. RCHM).

58b STOKE PARK. A large and uncommonly interesting Late Georgian mansion. It was built for John Penn, grandson of Penn of Pennsylvania. Three-storeyed core of seven bays width, plastered white. This must have been quite a simple building; its architect was *Robert Nasmyth*. Very soon after, however, Penn called in *James Wyatt*, and he gradually added one-storeyed extensions which changed the character of the building and, furthermore, a commanding dome, a feature of which few private houses can boast. The extensions consist of a one-storeyed Greek Doric portico of twelve columns on the S side with two-bay solid ends, a conservatory of six Greek Doric columns on the E side, again with solid ends, which here, however, have five bays. Of these, three are big bows. To the entrance, i.e. the N, there are ten Greek Doric pilasters between one-bay solid ends. On the S portico originally there was a four-column Ionic portico as well, behind which the original arched windows remained. This upper portico has disappeared. Wyatt's use of Greek Doric columns deserves mention, as this was still an innovation in English architecture at the time when Stoke Park was rebuilt. Soane had used them as early as 1778 in Rome and in the 1790s in England, for instance inside Tyringham, and Bonomi's Greek Doric columns at Packington church in Warwickshire date from 1789–90. What is the date of Wyatt's use here? Mr Colvin says 1793–9, an anonymous *Historical Account of Stoke Park* published in 1813 gives the (more convincing) date 1808, but the colonnades are mentioned in Repton's *Observations* of 1803 and illustrated in *The Beauties of England and Wales* in 1801. In this the dome however is missing, and it is still missing in the plate in Neale (vol. 1, 1822–3). If Neale is correct, then the dome was built after Wyatt's death. It is as interesting as the colonnades and more unusual. It has a drum, provided with oddly fragile and widely-spaced Composite columns. It is leaded and merges with the lantern in almost a double curve. The lantern has closely-set pilasters. Inside Wyatt arranged an oval Entrance Hall, followed by the spectacular Staircase Hall which is covered with a groined vault extended to the N and S by strips of segmental vault. The flying Staircase itself must be later. On the upper floor aedicules with fluted Ionic columns and pediments. The centre of the S side is taken by the former Library, 125 ft long and divided by four screens of grey marble columns with arches (the 'Venetian' motif) into five parts. Fine details also in the NE and SE corner rooms. The grounds were first landscaped by *Capability Brown* in 1771 and again by *Repton* about 1790. In the grounds a large lake crossed SE of the house by a handsome three-arch BRIDGE (of 1798), and a memorial COLUMN to Sir Edward Coke set up by Penn in 1800 to the N of the house. It was also designed by *Wyatt*. It is of the Roman Doric order, 60 ft high, with a statue by *Rossi* on top. The S LODGES have Greek Doric porches with pediments, and there are fine iron GATES between them.

MOUND. On the golf course, in the SW corner of Stoke Park, the mound by the thirteenth hole is probably a Bronze Age barrow, as suggested by the discovery in 1911 of a 'cinerary urn' in making the bunker.

HOSPITAL, to the N of the road N of the church. Built by Thomas Penn in 1765. An unusually composite group in red brick, to the r. the dwellings of the three poor men and three poor women, wings at the back, a clock-tower on the S front. Then to the l., attached to the dwellings, the Master's House, i.e. the vicarage, as the vicar was master. It is of five bays and two storeys. To its l., finally, the small Chapel with a S window with Y-tracery.

VICARAGE. The vicarage which replaced the house in the middle of the hospital front was built by *Wyatt* in 1802 a little to the w. It is of brick, cemented, three bays wide, two-storeyed, and castellated. On the ground floor four-centred arches, on the first floor hood-moulds.

TYTHE FARM HOUSE, ¼ m. W of the Vicarage. Pretty. C16. Of brick, with a gable and an original chimneystack.

(STOKE PLACE, Stoke Green, ½ m. SW. The centre completed in 1698. The wings added c. 1750–60. At the same time interior alterations. Brick. The centre has five bays and two storeys. Hipped roof. Entrance Hall with a screen of Roman Doric columns. Staircase with Rococo decoration. The grounds were laid out by *Capability Brown c.* 1771.)

STOKE HOUSE, N of the above (corner of Stoke Green and Gray's Park Road). Early Victorian, of yellow brick. With a veranda along the S front and behind an asymmetrically-placed Italianate tower.

STOKE COURT, I m. N of the church. This was West End Cottage, in which Gray used to stay. The house was rebuilt by Mr Penn about 1845 and added to in 1873. It is all very Gothic now, irregular and castellated. The N end seems the addition. The house is threatened with demolition. To its S a lake, and by it Gray's ALCOVE, a Gothic arch of conglomerate with a semicircular niche behind.

SEFTON PARK, I m. SE. Late Georgian. Two storeys, plastered. Six-bay centre and two three-bay bow windows close to the angles. Low hipped roof.

FRAMEWOOD MANOR. By *G. C. Horsley, c.* 1903–4. Red brick and partly tile-hung. Picturesquely asymmetrical. Neo-Tudor, somewhat conservative for its date.

7010

STONE

ST JOHN BAPTIST. Early C14 W tower with C19 saddleback roof. C13 chancel and transepts, the chancel with lancet windows, the S transept with a group of three stepped lancets to the S, the N transept with a N window of two lights with a foiled circle, i.e. a motif of 1260 at the earliest. But earlier than all this is, as one enters, the S doorway: Norman, with one order of shafts and a zigzag arch. Capitals with palmette and leaf motifs. The N arcade is only a little later, or at least its three E bays. Circular piers with scallop and leaf-crocket capitals, square abaci, three-stepped, unchamfered, round arches. The W bay was added in the C13 with a round pier and round abacus and pointed double-chamfered arches. The W respond, however, was re-used. Round arches from S transept to nave and from N transept to N aisle. The tower arch is clearly of the early C14. – FONT. Cylindrical, Norman. Decorated with beaded symmetrical patterns

16

of close interlace, of interlaced stars, rosettes, etc., and one complicated scene the most prominent part of which is a man fighting a beast. To the l. a fish (the sign of Christ), to the r. a smaller man fighting another beast. The dove also pecks into this beast. In the mouth of the beast a human head. – BENCHES. Some, in the nave, primitive, with poppy-heads. – BRASSES. William Gurney † 1472 and wife, 12 in. figures; Thomas Gurney † 1520 and wife, 18 in. figures (nave).

ST JOHN'S HOSPITAL. The s part, running E–W with two wings at each end projecting N and s, is by *T. H. Wyatt and D. Brandon*, 1850–3. Red brick, Italianate, and remarkably reticent. The entrance of stone, with the Italianate ('debased') tower centrally placed, is later. Separate E.E. chapel with wooden bellturret, by *Brandon*. The buildings were constructed with iron floor joists and iron roofs.

New Admission Unit by *Gollins, Melvin, Ward & Partners*. Not yet completed. The design is cruciform. In the two long arms wards and rooms, in the two short arms Treatment Rooms, Dining Room, Kitchen, etc. The two-storeyed ward block is still to be built. The rest single-storeyed. Brick and glass.

STONY STRATFORD

7040

ST GILES. A fire in 1742 destroyed much of the E half of the town together with one parish church of Stony Stratford of which only the tower survives (*see* below, Perambulation). The other parish church was rebuilt in 1776–7 by *Francis Hiorne* of Warwick, who again allowed the tower of the former church to remain.* This has a clearly recognizable Perp arch to the nave. The upper parts have clasping buttresses. The nave starts with a pediment which is cut into by the tower. The windows received new unfortunate tracery by *Street* in 1876. Chancel, tall and weakly Gothic towards the High Street, 1928 by *C. G. Hare*. The pleasure of the church is inside. It is a hall-church with tall wooden piers of eight very thin clustered shafts carrying plaster rib-vaults. Two galleries of timber not very convincingly placed. – STAINED GLASS. w window by *Kempe*, 1903.

ST MARY, London Road, Wolverton End. 1864 by *Sir G. G. Scott*. In the E.E. style. Nave with bellcote and N aisle with a

---

* Actually both churches were chapels of ease, St Giles of Calverton, St Mary Magdalene (*see* below) of Wolverton. They became parochial under one incumbent in 1661 (information received from the Rev. C. L. G. Hutchings).

separate gable. Apsidal chancel. Lancet windows. Arcade of narrow arches on octagonal piers. Arches dying into them.

ST MARY MAGDALENE (R.C.). By *Deakin & Laing*, 1957–8. Light brick and much glass. Low-pitched roof. Wide nave and no aisles. Façade glass centre, with uninterrupted uprights to the roof, and narrow recessed angle bays with grid of elongated hexagons of tile. w gallery above a low lobby. To the l. and r. of the altar five-light windows with two transoms. Simple interior with well designed benches and altar rail.

MR FEGAN'S HOMES, High Street. Founded as a school in 1863. Since repeatedly enlarged. Chapel by *Goldie & Child*. Rock-faced stone with red brick dressings. Pointed windows. The main accent the front of the chapel with a big rose window filled by four still big circles. To its r. archway and then an asymmetrically placed turret. The interior of the chapel has, surprisingly, a plaster tunnel-vault on Corinthian columns placed against the walls on brackets. Transepts.

PERAMBULATION

Stony Stratford to the passing traveller is one long High Street, roaring with the traffic of the A5. On a Sunday the town is quiet and pleasant with much that is enjoyable in the High Street and in the backwater to its s. Not much in the High Street E of the church. At the E end of the High Street to the N the CONGREGATIONAL CHURCH of 1823, two-storeyed, of three bays, with arched doorway and window and a pediment right across. s from the same place to HORSEFAIR GREEN, where, facing many friendly minor Georgian houses, the BAPTIST CHURCH, also of 1823, and of similar design. Then from the church down CHURCH STREET between more minor Georgian houses to the Market Place. The MARKET PLACE might be miles away from the arterial road. It has to the N the church appearing behind houses, to the s among others the nice Nos 12–13 with a date 1790 and leaf carving over the door that looks more like 1700, to the E especially No. 4 which is of vitreous and red brick with quoins, three-storeyed, and must date from c. 1700. Aprons to the top windows. The w side is alas occupied by the fiery red Police Station, Gothic, of 1865.

So finally those parts of the HIGH STREET which matter. There are more plain, satisfactory Georgian houses of red brick than can be mentioned. Much had to be rebuilt after the fire of 1742. The first to be singled out is the COCK HOTEL, of brick, seven bays and two and a half storeys. Above the entrance a lunette window. This and the surrounding windows have Gibbs surrounds. The door surround is of wood and looks as though imported from the interior of a mid-c18 house of the first order (the destroyed parts of Claydon?). Fluted Corinthian columns, frieze with garlands, no pediment. No. 75 opposite has an early c19 shop-front with pilasters with Grecian details. Nos 92–96, again on the N side, are a nine-bay brick house with a central carriageway in. No. 97 opposite has a shop-front with interlaced Gothic glazing. By No. 98 a passage leads to the Perp W tower of the former church ST MARY MAGDALENE and so to the end of the perambulation.

STOWE

INTRODUCTION

There are two phases of the picturesque laying-out of grounds in the c18 in England, the first more evocative, the second more natural. The chief exponent of the first is *Vanbrugh*, already in his memorandum of 1709 about Blenheim; of the second *Capability Brown*, who was only ten when Vanbrugh died. *Kent*, who returned from Italy in 1719 – still a painter and neither an architect nor a designer of gardens – and who died in 1748, stood mid-way between them. Stowe contains the work of all three, although what share Vanbrugh had in the landscape planning, which was in the hands of *Charles Bridgeman*, we cannot say, and although Brown is only known with certainty to have started as an under-gardener at Stowe in 1740. The importance of Vanbrugh and Bridgeman is attested as early as 1745, in a description to be found in Virtue's *Notebooks* which says: 'Vanbrugh was the most concerned in the direction of Lord Cobham's Gardens, or rather buildings, because Mr Bridgeman had the direction and disposition of the gardens.'* Bridgeman's principles of gardening are still transitional between the formal and the informal. He combines straight avenues with wiggly wildernesses, and wanted at Stowe a straight avenue from the house to an octagonal pond which was later merged with the picturesque serpentine lake, at the same time that his avenue was thinned out sufficiently not to appear an avenue any longer. Speaking of the ruin of the old manor house at Woodstock in his memorandum on Blenheim, Vanbrugh pleads for its preservation because buildings of distant times 'move more lively and pleasing Reactions on the Persons who have Inhabited them; or the Remarkable things which have been transacted in

---

* *Walpole Society*, vol. 22, p. 133.

them; or the extraordinary Occasions of Erecting them'. Here is
the case for the evocative building in a garden formulated to perfection. The evocative phase indeed went in with great zest for
temples, columns, rotundas, umbrellos, alcoves, and the like, and
no other gardens in England have preserved more of these than
Stowe. 'Such a profusion', wrote Horace Walpole in 1753, 'gives
inexpressible richness.' The house itself is the largest and the only
spectacular Georgian mansion in Buckinghamshire and would
hold its own in any county, but it is the number of furnishings
scattered through the grounds that is unique. Nor have all that
were built survived. Many, and among them some of the most interesting, such as Vanbrugh's Egyptian Pyramid, 60 ft high, and
the Chinese House of the 1740s, have disappeared. Even as it is,
however, those who were in favour of the gentler, less dramatic,
and more natural mid-Georgian style of Capability Brown found
that there was too much of occasional building at Stowe. The
same Horace Walpole, writing of the 'Albano glut of buildings',
added: 'let them be ever so much condemned'. And Piper, the
Swedish painter-gardener (in 1799), suggested that they were
mainly built for 'a duke to gain renown and to exceed all others in
point of expense and size'. Stowe during the crucial decades belonged to Sir Richard Temple, who had inherited it in 1697 and
was made Viscount Cobham in 1718. He began work on the
gardens in 1713. In 1719 Vanbrugh wrote in a letter that Cobham
'spends all he has to spare . . . on the improvement of his house and
gardens', and in 1724 Lord Percival wrote that Stowe 'within
these five years has gained the reputation of being the finest seat
in England'. In 1731 Pope in his Epistle to Lord Burlington uses
it as the climax of what he has to say on natural gardening, and in
1736 Thomson in his *Liberty* brackets it with Richmond (Marble
Hill) and Chiswick in a similar context. A nephew of Cobham,
Gilbert West, wrote a descriptive poem on Stowe in 1732, and
from 1744 onwards guide-books began to appear. Gilpin's
very first publication dealing with his future domain, the Picturesque, was his anonymous *Dialogue upon the Gardens at Stowe* of
1748. Cobham died in 1749. His nephew, George Grenville of
Wotton Underwood, later Earl Temple, succeeded. The son of
this George Grenville was made Marquis of Buckingham, the
grandson Duke of Buckingham and Chandos.

THE MANSION

When Cobham, in temporary disgrace between 1710 and 1714,
began improvements at Stowe, there was a late C17 house there,

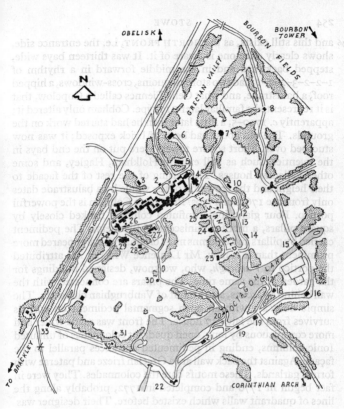

PLAN OF STOWE

46 and this still exists, as the NORTH FRONT, i.e. the entrance side,
shows clearly once one is aware of it. It was thirteen bays wide,
stepped backward and in the middle forward in a rhythm of
1–2–2–3–2–2–1, had two storeys, quoins, cross-windows, a hipped
roof, a balustrade, and what Celia Fiennes called a Cupelow, that
is it represented a familiar later C17 type. Cobham only altered it;
apparently *c.* 1720–5, a little later than he had started work on the
grounds. The old house had been of brick exposed; it was now
stuccoed over. Short square towers were put on the end bays in
the twenties, such as still exist at Holkham, Hagley, and some
other Palladian houses. The raising of the rest of the façade to
their height and the crowning of the whole by a balustrade dates
only from the 1760s or 1770s. But due to Cobham is the powerful
portico. Four giant Ionic unfluted columns flanked closely by
square pillars, a motif reminiscent of Blenheim. The pediment
carried by pillars and columns must originally have appeared more
prominent than it is now. Mr Laurence Whistler has attributed
the portico to *Vanbrugh*, who, we know, designed buildings for
the garden at the same time. The pillars are connected with the
wall behind by arches, also a motif of Vanbrughian character. The
simple doorcase with an open segmental pediment on corbels
survives from the late C17 house. The front was made wider and
more conspicuous by long, open quadrant colonnades of unfluted
Ionic columns, ending in pedimented entrances parallel to the
façade. Against the back wall are a Grecian frieze and paterae with
formal garlands. These motifs date the colonnades. They were in
fact begun in 1770 and completed in 1772, probably along the
lines of quadrant walls which existed before. Their designer was
in all probability *Giovanni Battista Borra*, who had been at
Palmyra and Baalbek with Wood in 1750 and at Turin before and
after. He became a kind of resident architect – not necessarily of
his own designs only – and died after 1783. Beyond the colonnades there follows a piece of blank wall on either side with a big
Wrenian Tuscan doorway, then a projecting wing of five bays set
at r. angles to the façade and decorated with Ionic pilasters and
niches between them and with very broad even rustication at the
angles. On the face of the wing close to the angle is an inscription,
on the W side 'Templa quam dilecta',* on the E side 'Deo Patriae
Amicis'. In the middle of the wall which continues the face of the
wing a big doorway rather like that of an Italian C16 fortress or
town-gate. In the base and the shanks of the pediment blocks of
raw, unworked-looking stone (i.e. with vermiculated rustication)

* A pun on the name Temple, of course.

are inserted, a strange Mannerist idea taken over direct from Serlio's *Libro Extraordinario* which was available to any curious architect and patron. Finally, again at r. angles, yet another length of wall and yet another doorway. These latter, in the Italian Baroque mode, are the work of *Giacomo Leoni* and date from *c.* 1735, i.e. were connected with a layout still very different from the present. Part of this early layout was service wings flanking the North Lawn. In their place is now the SPORTS PAVILION of the school (by *Dodd*, 1935), with its coupled Tuscan columns. Between the forecourt and the lawn the equestrian STATUE of George I, made of lead in 1727, and now in a very unhealthy state.

The SOUTH FRONT is the show-piece of the house, but it became that only when *Robert Adam* had re-designed and enlarged it and *Borra* had altered and executed Adam's design in 1774. The front is as wide as the whole N forecourt with all its appendages. It consists of three parts, a centre, then straight, recessed, lower seven-bay wings, and finally higher end pavilions of three wide bays. Beyond these run another five low bays of outbuildings. The front is of yellow and buff stone. Centre and pavilions have a rusticated basement at ground level, the connecting wings a plain arcading instead. There is only one upper floor, but this is extremely high in centre and pavilions, of normal height in the connecting wings. The centre of the centre is a pedimented giant portico of six unfluted Corinthian columns reached by a wide open staircase. To the l. and r. no more than one bay, but treated broadly and monumentally. The window is large and tripartite and has a blank arch over with a medallion. To the l. and r. of the window pilasters, coupled at the ends, single towards the portico. Garlands between the capitals of the pilasters. In the lower links the upper floor has a fenestration of normal proportions and Ionic columns in addition. The pavilions take up the Adam motif of the tripartite window with its blank arch and medallion and repeat it three times. Single pilasters and garlands as before. Top balustrading on all parts of this splendidly spacious and beautifully detailed façade. It is seen to greatest advantage from the other side of the lake (*see* p. 260).

The INTERIOR of the house is on the whole a little disappointing. The large ENTRANCE HALL has a coved painted ceiling and on the w wall high up a relief of Caractacus by *Banks* (1774–7). Opposite, lower down, relief of the family of Darius before Alexander by *Christophe Veyrier*, *c.* 1680. Behind it the fine oval HALL 49 with pink scagliola columns, trophies on the walls, and a frieze by *Valdré* with hundreds of small figures. Coffered dome with

glazed centre. There are two main STAIRCASES, but neither is
large nor specially elegantly appointed. They have thin wrought-
iron balustrades. From the entrance hall they can be reached only
by a narrow passage. On the w side this is followed by a piece of
corridor with a coffered tunnel-vault. To the w and to the E of the
oval Hall a room with an apse and giant Corinthian columns. The
eastern one of the two has Pompeian decoration. In the eastern
connecting link is the LIBRARY, the full seven bays long with a
good white plaster ceiling. The corresponding w room is the
school DINING HALL. It has Kentian wooden fireplaces and over-
doors. At the rear of the E wing was the CHAPEL. The room was
divided horizontally in the 1920s and deprived of its principal
furnishings (see p. 264). In the upper part the patterned coffered
ceiling with stars, etc., remains. The E pavilion has three large
rooms with original ceilings, the w pavilion two, i.e. one of two
bays. No rooms of importance in the basement or ground floor
57b except the following three. The GOTHIC LIBRARY, now Headmaster's Study, was gothicized in 1803–6 by an unlikely architect
for such a job, *Sir John Soane*. Even the chimneypiece (by *Thomas
Catherwood*) and the surround and tools of the fireplace are Gothic.
Elaborate bookcases, gently coved ceiling. Above the entrance a
strange RELIEF, representing the Battle of Bosworth. It is ascribed to the late C16 and comes from Gosfield Hall, Essex, or
originally from Castle Hedingham. The room is in the centre, w
of the open staircase. There is also a GOTHIC ANTE-ROOM to it,
and, odder still, on the N side behind the outer staircase there is an
EGYPTIAN LOBBY. Neither its date nor its designer seems to be
recorded. A date before 1800 is not likely.

THE GROUNDS

Work on the grounds, as has already been said, started in 1713.
It was in the hands of *Bridgeman* to about 1725. He laid out the
part w of the avenue and the octagonal pond. *Kent* turned his
attention to the E part and made the Elysian Fields and the Grecian
Valley. If Bridgeman had left this part untouched, the reason was,
according to Mr Whistler's convincing suggestion, that the village
of Stowe had not been removed yet. Kent could include its site in
his plans. The village church was left standing. Bridgeman, to
re-emphasize a point already made, still kept his main avenues
straight. Kent was the first – to quote Sir Thomas Robinson – to
work 'without either level or line'. But the scale of his improvement was still limited. *Brown* about the middle of the century
abolished Bridgeman's formalities and gave the whole a superior

scale and unity. For the buildings in the garden Lord Cobham secured the best architects: *Vanbrugh, Gibbs, Kent.* Among buildings by *Vanbrugh* which are no longer in existence there were, apart from the Egyptian pyramid, an obelisk or *guglio* in Bridgeman's octagonal pond, a Temple of Bacchus, a Sleeping Parlour, Dido's Cave, Nelson's Seat, and a Bagno. Of *Gibbs*'s contribution the Saxon Temple and the Temple of Diana have disappeared. Later on *Borra* altered some of the buildings and shifted some. In perambulating the grounds and examining the buildings, no fixed route can be prescribed. The route followed here is that of Mr Whistler's *A Guide to the Gardens* (first edition 1956), as it can be assumed that every visitor will have it. It is more detailed than the following account and also has a more detailed map. Only on architectural description and comment a little more is here attempted than in Mr Whistler's *Guide*.

The best approach is by the STOWE AVENUE from Buckingham, which runs absolutely straight for about a mile and a half and ends by the Corinthian Arch. Avenue and arch are the work of the sixties, but the avenue, which, if continued, would end straight in the centre of the S front, is no doubt part of *Bridgeman*'s original conception. The avenue starts with the BUCKINGHAM LODGES, two balustraded cubes of one storey. Pleasant panels with reliefs above doorway and windows. The CORINTHIAN ARCH was designed in 1767 by Walpole's friend *Thomas Pitt*, Lord Camelford. It has coupled Corinthian pilasters and a balustrade and is one window deep. From here the visitor today must turn W and join up with the OXFORD AVENUE from Brackley. Late C18 LODGES S of the lake called Oxford Water. The piers, pierced by arches and pedimented above an attic, are attributed by Mr Whistler to *Kent* and regarded as *ex situ*. The lodges with their low Chinese roofs he gives to *Valdré*. Across the handsome three-arched BRIDGE and to the two BOYCOTT PAVILIONS (called after a former hamlet). They are by *Gibbs* and were originally far more dramatic (and Vanbrughian) than they are now. There were gatepiers connected by an arch, and the pavilions had octagonal pyramids instead of domes (alteration by *Borra, c.* 1760). The domes are octagonal with four main sides and four short diagonal sides and have a lantern. The walls are rusticated. There are four pedimented entrances. From here to the house and from its SE angle southwards into the ELYSIAN FIELDS, a beautiful gentle slope down towards the Lake, laid out by *Kent* about 1735. At once on the l. the GRENVILLE COLUMN, originally set up in 1748 and moved to its present site in 1754, a rostral column with the lead statue of

Heroic Beauty on the top holding out a scroll towards the British Worthies (*see* below). On the r. the church.

CHURCH OF THE ASSUMPTION. Hidden by trees from the house. Nave and aisles, chancel and N chapel, W tower. E window with steep reticulation, *c.* 1330. Double-curved E gable, probably of the C18. The E window of the S aisle also with reticulation. Dec also the W tower, see its doorway and two-light bell-openings. Big niche with miniature vault and miniature buttresses above the doorway. Arcades of three bays with octagonal piers and double-chamfered arches, that on the N side probably late C13, that on the S mid C14. N chapel Early Tudor, two bays without any caesura between jambs and arches. Jambs as well as arches are panelled. – Former REREDOS. Jacobean, originally an overmantel (RCHM). – MONUMENTS. C14 effigy of a praying Civilian, his head on a pillow. Much defaced. – Brass to Alice Saunders † 1462, the figure 12 in. long. – Martha Penyston † 1619. White marble effigy in shroud. Black marble sarcophagus.

SE of the church the TEMPLE OF ANCIENT VIRTUE, by *Kent*, *c.* 1735. Originally there was a sham ruin corresponding to it which was satirically called the Temple of Modern Virtue. The Temple of Ancient Virtue is a rotunda with unfluted Ionic columns and a stone dome. View across the Elysian Fields and the Lake to the Temple of British Worthies. But first to the S and the DORIC ARCH, a late-comer, set up in 1768 to commemorate the visit of Princess Amelia. Roman Doric pilasters to the W, columns to the E. Coffered vault inside the arch. The view to be enjoyed from here was to the Palladian Bridge and distant Stowe Castle.*

48b   The TEMPLE OF BRITISH WORTHIES, on to the NE, is one of the most original conceptions and designs of the Stowe *ensemble*. It is by *Kent* and of 1733. It consists of a circle with as its centre a stepped pyramid with a very odd horseshoe-shaped empty recess. In the recess was originally a Mercury, as the god who leads souls to Elysium – apparently British as well as Grecian. Along the semicircle and at its end, i.e. facing us as we approach, are eight low niches on either side. They contain busts. Each bust is in a bay slightly projected on its own and with its own pediment. In the niches are eight busts made by *Rysbrack* in 1732 for Gibbs's former Saxon Temple and eight made for Kent's new building in 1733, either by *Rysbrack* (Mrs Webb's view) or by *Scheemakers* (Mr Gunnis's view). The first eight are Queen Elizabeth, Shakespeare, Bacon, Milton, Hampden, Newton, Locke, and William III (in Roman dress). The others are King Alfred, the Black

* This view was drawn by Piper in 1779.

Prince, Gresham, Sir John Barnard, Drake, Raleigh, Inigo Jones, and Pope. The whole is an eminently significant demonstration of national pride versus the worship of antiquity, and also interesting for the 'historicism' demonstrated in the care for accurate costume.

N of the Temple of British Worthies is the small SHELL BRIDGE, also by *Kent*, a lively composition with a pedimented centre and pedimented end piers and smaller gabled piers between, the whole originally encrusted with shells. The bridge really dams the river between the upper and the lower part of the lake. Next the COOK MONUMENT, erected to the memory of Captain Cook in 1778, with a medallion on the pedestal and originally a globe on the top, and the small FOUNTAIN OF THE SEASONS, to the NE of the Grenville Column, a pedimented back panel and a small basin into which water flowed from a lion's head.

Now out of the Elysian Fields and across the lawn to the E. The GOTHIC TEMPLE cannot be missed. It is one of the most promi- 47b nent of the furnishings of the grounds – and also one of the most interesting. For one thing it dates from after 1739 and before 1745, and the Gothic fashion was at that time only in its beginnings. Horace Walpole did not choose it at Strawberry Hill until 1749. Kent had practised it, it is true, as early as the 1730s (Hampton Court 1732, Esher Place c. 1730), but – and this is the other re- markable fact – it is not by Kent but by *Gibbs*. The Gothic Temple is surprisingly big, it is built of ironstone, and it is also lively in its composition and details and remarkably ignorant. The plan is a triangle with pentagonal towers at two angles and a higher square one at the third, which is at the back. The pentagonal towers have recessed little turrets and cupolas, the square tower has a flat em- battled top with pinnacles. The front between the pentagonal towers is divided into three bays by what can only be called Gothic pilasters, with palm-leaf capitals. They appear in two orders, below set between arched openings, above between arched two-light windows with a quatrefoil in the spandrel. A similar arrangement on the other sides. The front ends in a castellated gable. Circular interior with a balcony all round. Stuccoed Gothic dome.

Down S from here to the PALLADIAN BRIDGE. This also was built before 1745. The design is by *Palladio* (drawing in the Burlington–Devonshire Collection at the R.I.B.A., published in Bertotti-Scamozzi's edition of Palladio) and had been carried out in England about 1737 at Wilton House by Lord Pembroke and Roger Morris. Another replica (of 1750) is at Prior Park, Bath. The effect at Stowe is superb, if approached from the S rather than the

N. The bridge is roofed. It has unfluted Ionic columns, carrying pediments over the entrances and the first and last bays to E and W. Between these are even colonnades of four columns. Originally the E side was solid, but it was opened less than twenty years after.

S of the Palladian Bridge and separated from it by the unsightly but unavoidable Tennis Courts of the School is the TEMPLE OF FRIENDSHIP, by *Gibbs*, dated 1739. This has been in ruins for a century, but ought to be made safe, as it is a key building in the scheme of Stowe. The front has four bulgy Tuscan columns and a pediment, inspired perhaps by Inigo Jones's St Paul, Covent Garden. A considerably raised brick structure behind with blank panels. One-storeyed arched side bays.

Next, W of the Temple, the PEBBLE ALCOVE by *Kent*, self-explanatory, and the MONUMENT TO CONGREVE, on the island, a little NW. This is of 1736, by *Kent*, and consists of an obelisk of big blocks of stone with an urn with bacchic and silenic heads awkwardly stuck on to it, and a monkey seated at the top. Further SW, and exactly in line with the S façade of the house, Bridgeman's avenue, and the Grand Avenue from Buckingham, the LAKE PAVILIONS, designed by *Vanbrugh c.* 1719 and remodelled by *Borra c.* 1770. In Vanbrugh's time they had unfluted columns and stood more closely together. The view from here of the house is the best of all. The lake in front of the Pavilions is called the Octagon Lake, because it replaces Bridgeman's formal octagonal pond. It is separated from the Eleven Acre Lake by the CASCADE, a picturesque rocky little dam with a rough pointed arch.

Mr Whistler from here conducts us direct to the centre of the 48a big lawn S of the school buildings and to *Vanbrugh*'s ROTONDO, a noble design, entirely transparent, with Tuscan columns. The dome was alas altered by *Borra*. Vanbrugh's work is of *c.* 1719, Borra's of *c.* 1763 (Whistler). The view from it and towards it has been disastrously impaired by recent school buildings. On these see p. 263.

Straight N of the Rotondo lies the SCHOOL SHOP, an extremely pretty building of 1781, originally built as a menagerie. One-storeyed. Concave recessed centre and one-bay end pavilions. The concave part consists of a domed centre with Ionic pilasters and wings of five bays with glazed walls divided by Ionic columns.

Instead of thus returning one can continue from the Cascade to the SW. Here the HERMITAGE (or Shepherd's Cove) by *Kent*, a shelter with a heavily rusticated and pedimented arch and a turret at one corner, and then to the extreme S end. Here Bridge-man had originally made a bastion as a companion to another at

the SE end, where the Temple of Friendship stands. On the
former S bastion the TEMPLE OF VENUS, identified by Mr 47a
Whistler with 'a spacious building' with 'spreading wings' which
West mentions in 1732 as by *Kent*. But did Kent work so early
at Stowe? Whoever the author and whatever the date, the Temple
of Venus is one of the best designs at Stowe. The centre is a pedimented alcove with two niches in the side piers and a screen of two
Ionic columns and an entablature across the entrance. Heavily
arcaded short quadrant wings to rusticated end pavilions, with an
arched opening and a broken pediment. The room behind the
screen has a coffered apse and contained originally what Mr
Whistler calls 'indelicate murals'. A good deal NW of the Temple
of Venus QUEEN CAROLINE'S MONUMENT, erected *c.* 1730, but
in a different position. It is a cluster of four fluted Ionic columns
with thin joint entablature, and on it stands a statue of the Queen
by *Rysbrack*. S of the Monument another shelter named (probably
apocryphally) SHEPHERD'S COTE, small, square, with a somewhat military arched frieze below the top of the walls and a pyramid roof.

Mr Whistler proposes a separate walk to the NE of the house,
starting (past the school GYMNASIUM by *Clough Williams-Ellis*, a
pretty building with an attenuated Adam portico, erected to be
temporary) at the TEMPLE OF CONCORD, one of the most ambitious of the Stowe temples. It is by *Kent*, built towards the end of
his life and completed by *Borra* about 1764. It has been treated
ignominiously by Lorimer and the school, who took part of its
fine peristyle and used the columns inside the chapel. The
columns are fluted Ionic, the pediment has a relief by *Scheemakers*.
Coffering on the ceiling of the peristyle. Interior with niches and
blue and white plaques. The inscription referring to Concordia
not only Civium but also Foederatorum refers to the victorious
end of the Seven Years' War.* The view N along *Kent*'s Grecian
Valley is exquisite. There is also a diagonal view to the Cobham
Monument.

But before this can be visited, there is still the QUEEN'S
TEMPLE to come, designed between 1744 and 1749 probably by
Gibbs and altered to great advantage by *Borra* in the seventies. It
is used as a music school now. Noble portico of four fluted Corinthian columns at the head of a wide open staircase. Rusticated

---

* N of the Temple, outside the boundaries, and NNE, inside the boundaries, two SHELTERS. The former is polygonal and Gothick, with windows
with Y-tracery. The latter was called the FANE OF PASTORAL POETRY and is
square with chamfered corners and carries a dome. It is partly fallen.

pediment. Frieze with delicate honeysuckle carving. Fine view towards the Temple of Friendship. Interior of the 1920s. The back opens on to a very effective semicircular terrace with Ionic columns. In the Queen's Temple is the 8 ft square tessellated pavement with a geometric design in red, white, and blue-grey cubes from the C4 Roman villa at Foscott (*see* p. 137). NE from here the COBHAM MONUMENT, erected in 1747 by Lord Cobham as a belvedere. Designed by *Gibbs*. Altered by *Valdré*. The octagonal pillar is 115 ft high. Each side has one gigantic flute. On the belvedere cage was the statue of Lord Cobham.

From here one can leave the grounds by a gate and a bridge and have a look at Stowe monuments outside the Stowe grounds, and first and foremost at *Vanbrugh*'s BOURBON TOWER, originally no more than a Keeper's Lodge. The earthwork around it was added only in 1845. The name refers to the visit from Hartwell of the exiled future Louis XVIII. This is the earliest piece of medievalism at Stowe; for Vanbrugh died in 1726. Built of ironstone on a strongly buttressed base of grey conglomerate. In the base circular windows, above arched windows in two storeys. Blank arched top frieze of Romanesque character and originally a conical roof. The recessed little octagon above with a frieze of small blank quatrefoils in ovals dates from 1845.

More than a mile E Lord Cobham provided towards the end of his life an eye-catcher of surprising size, STOWE CASTLE. It is really (to the E) a group of two-storeyed cottages. They have a lean-to roof, i.e. roofs which lean against a tall stone wall which forms an elongated half decagon and has at its angles five square towers. It is this very fortified, castellated side which is seen from the grounds of the house.

Finally, also outside the grounds, SW of Stowe Castle and N of the house, the OBELISK, erected in 1759 to commemorate the death of General Wolfe in the battle for Quebec. The obelisk is over 100 ft high.

Stowe is an object lesson in visual planning. The buildings are placed with a view to multiple vistas forward and backward. There are long axes and the surprises of unexpected *dénouements*. The architecture is enhanced in its effect by nature, and *vice versa*. No one can say that the buildings and monuments today are quite in the state in which they ought to be, nor that the vegetation is kept wholly under control. It is easy to blame the school, but it ought not to be forgotten that if it were not for the school there would be no Stowe. The demolition merchants were waiting when the school stepped in. To that extent the school deserves all gratitude. Even so, the job of maintenance is clearly beyond the means of a public school, and the authorities of the school ought to agree to an arrangement by which the Ministry of Works would take over the responsibility for the preservation of those buildings in the grounds which are of no practical use to the school.

THE SCHOOL

If the suggestion is made that the architecture of the gardens of Stowe ought to be taken from the school, one additional reason is that its recent architectural record is not good. This is the story. The school was founded in 1923. Additional buildings were soon required. They were at first treated as adjuncts or placed in conveniently concealed positions. When more was needed, all attempts at a consistent plan were given up, and the result is a visual mess. The one thing that should have been done in the interests of Stowe and of the school was not even contemplated: to purchase a few acres to the NW of the North Lawn, outside the boundaries, and to build there, according to a plan, axial or otherwise. There would have been space here for the erection of a dignified campus of which the house could have formed the splendid southern range. Instead, buildings crowd together w of the house and have begun, with their vanguard, especially the recent Headmaster's House, seriously to interfere with the principal C18 vistas.

The buildings are as follows, in the order in which they appeared. First, in 1923, Mr *Clough Williams-Ellis*, to whom so much is owed for the salvation of Stowe, began to build a range continuing the ORANGERY. This was of the mid C18, thirteen bays long with a two-storeyed pedimented three-bay centre. Clough Williams-Ellis added a wisely and tactfully designed piece with an open lantern and repeated the orangery to the l. of his piece which now became the centre of a successful composition.* In 1924–5 Clough Williams-Ellis also built the pretty neo-Adam GYMNASIUM which has been mentioned on p. 261.

Then, however, he broke with this sensible programme. His next building, CHATHAM HOUSE of 1924–5, started the confusion. It is three-storeyed, of seventeen bays with a four-column portico of extremely attenuated columns and wings now appearing too heavy for this centre, because they were planned to have two storeys. It stands boldly inviting comparison with Vanbrugh's

---

* It is said at Stowe that the idea was *Sir Reginald Blomfield*'s, who was consulted in the matter and at the same time suggested the position of the future chapel.

Rotondo and the Temple of Venus, and thereby assumed new responsibilities. It cannot be said that the building discharged them well, partly because of its proportions, and partly because it does not stand in line with any of the previous buildings. So the school had come out into the open, and not promisingly.

What followed next was the CHAPEL. This was designed by *Sir Robert Lorimer*, begun in 1927, and completed in 1928. It is large and ambitious and achieves grandeur by the re-use of the splendid giant columns taken utterly unjustifiably from the Temple of Concord. The roof is awkward, with its tie-beams and canted wooden vault, and doubly awkward above the columns. The odd boxes for the masters with their baluster screens are doubtful too. On the other hand, the chapel enjoys the presence of the very fine wooden FURNISHINGS of the old chapel, i.e. the Panelling (Corinthian pilasters and a garland frieze), the Pulpit (with marquetry and garlands), the Royal Arms, and part of the West Gallery. The carver was *Michael Clarke*. The Panelling and the Pulpit were originally at Stowe House in Cornwall, built in 1680 by John Grenville, Earl of Bath, where Lord Cobham bought them when that house was pulled down in 1739 (Gunnis, p. 101). The chapel forms the W boundary of what was intended as a court or quad in the university sense. Mr Williams-Ellis's lantern may not have been a strong enough accent, but the idea of progressing in the development of school buildings in this way was right. Chatham House had, however, been an ominous sign that things would not proceed in such an orderly way throughout.

R. Fielding Dodd's WALPOLE HOUSE of 1934 was worse as architecture, and, by nibbling at the grounds towards the Elysian Fields and the Grecian Valley, worse for the future. For the back especially, that is the E elevation, there is nothing to be said. The style of the front is again neo-Georgian. For the same architect's much happier SPORTS PAVILION of 1935 *see* p. 255.

Near the chapel there then came gradually more disjointed structures, a modern ART SCHOOL, also by *R. Fielding Dodd* (1935), some smaller pieces without any ambitions, and finally the HALL, by *G. Forsyth Lawson* of Banbury, in an odd, timid 1950 style with Georgian hankerings. It is hard to describe it. The front has a low-pitched roof along, not across, and a thin balcony on the upper floor.

The HEADMASTER'S HOUSE of 1955–6 (by *Ronald Fielding*) has no ambitions either. But it should have them in so extremely prominent and exacting a position. Like Chatham House, it is out in the open and faces Vanbrugh's Rotondo and one of the finest landscape settings in England. Has its architect taken that into consideration? Was he justified in providing a seven-bay brick house like hundreds of others in the well-to-do streets of cities and towns?

SWANBOURNE

ST SWITHIN. Fine early C13 chancel, externally much renewed. The E wall has three lancets, internally part of a shafted five-arch arcade. The chancel arch has three hollow chamfers, the inner on corbels. One of the corbels starts with a saucy little twist and then turns into many small trumpet scallops. The tower arch is similar; only the corbels differ. Perp tower top. The S doorway also is of the C13. The arch has seven bold cusps and many fine mouldings. Thin shafts l. and r. In the N wall from the W first an unexpectedly sumptuous Perp window, then a short N aisle with arcade of very raw details. The nave S wall was rebuilt in 1630 with battlements and still quite acceptable Perp windows of three and four lights. Inside they are framed by an odd frill. – LECTERN. Plain, C17. – WALL PAINTINGS, N wall, c. 1500, hardly recognizable.

Near the church a group of good houses, especially the MANOR HOUSE, Elizabethan, sizeable, of stone, with several gables and mullioned and transomed windows. Also of stone, DEVERELL'S FARM, SE of the church, with the date 1632, an asymmetrically placed porch, and mullioned windows. Opposite, a picturesque timber cottage with brick infilling. Several more and also attractive brick houses in the road N of the Manor House. SE of Deverell's Farm the OLD HOUSE, externally rambling C18, but with a C16 core of timber and brick.

TAIDSWOOD see IVER HEATH

TAPLOW

ST NICOLAS. 1912, by *Fellowes Prynne*, Gothic, with tall spire. Nave and aisles and chancel. Tall stone SCREEN. – FONT. The bowl is of the table-top type, Norman, of Purbeck marble, with four shallow blank arches on each side. – BRASSES. Nichole de Aumberdene, c. 1350. Small bearded figure, 12 in. long, in the head of a very pretty foliated cross. This is the earliest surviving brass of a civilian in England. – Richard Manfeld † 1455 with brother and sister. The figures are 3 ft long and uncommonly good. – Thomas Manfeld † 1540 and two wives. 1 ft 9 in. figures; not good.

ELIBANK HOUSE, Rectory Road, w of the church. c18, brick, of five bays and two storeys, with a three-bay pediment. This middle part has quoins too. On the first floor the first and fifth windows are of the Venetian type.

TAPLOW COURT. Ascribed to *Sir Charles Barry* – an improbable attribution. 1855. Big, Early Tudor with gables and finials and an angle tower. The windows with arched lights. Lofty square tower in the centre. Under it the Hall with two tiers of galleries, 38 ft by 16 ft in size, and in a bleak Norman style. The piers of polished marble. On the lawn in front of the entrance STATUE of a Roman Emperor; c18. The provenance seems unknown.

BURIAL MOUND. The c7 Saxon burial mound at Taplow Court, within the old churchyard on the high ground above the Thames, was opened in 1883. Within a timber-lined area were the fragmentary skeletal remains of a man, buried fully extended, clothed in a gold embroidered garment, with his arms about him. The rich assortment of grave goods included a bronze Cufic bowl, four drinking horns with bronze and silver-gilt mounts, four lobed glass beakers, about thirty bone gaming counters, and a great gold buckle with filigree ornamentation and cloisonné work similar in style to the jewellery of the Sutton Hoo ship burial (*see The Buildings of England, Suffolk*) and indicative of an origin in Jutish Kent. There is a reference in Domesday to one Taeppa and his mound, which suggests the derivation of the name 'Taplow'. The finds are now in the British Museum.

IRON AGE SETTLEMENT. On the cricket field s of the mound two slight lines of entrenchment mark the site of an Iron Age settlement.

TAPLOW HOUSE. Originally a three-bay Georgian house,* but much added to in the early c19 (architect *Basevi*). Castellated. Entrance Hall with columns.

NASHDOM, 1¼ m. NW. By *Lutyens*, 1910, for Princess Dolgor-ouki. The house was to be large and 'not so expensive'. Uncommonly pure and bare neo-Georgian, brick, simply white-washed. The site slopes steeply. This is overcome by a part basement and a great levelling of the garden with a retaining wall at the w end. The doorways are interesting, in a loggia with to the l. the main, to the r. the staff entrance. A recessed apsidal court between. The main rooms face the garden and are *en suite*, 106 ft long. Also facing the garden two bow windows, one continued in a circular room. At the NE entrance to the grounds

* Built in 1751. MHLG.

a complex gateway with lodges. The gateway has Tuscan columns and a straight entablature breaking into the eaves of the roofs of the lodges, which run through above the gateway.

MAIDENHEAD BRIDGE. Built in 1772–7 to the design of *Sir Robert Taylor*. Beautiful stone arches and stone balustrade. Georgian masonry at its best.

RAILWAY BRIDGE. By *Brunel*, 1839. Two segmental brick arches 123 ft long, called in Murray's Handbook of 1902 (by John Meade Falkner) 'perhaps the largest brickwork span in the world'. Sheahan writes in 1862: 'To the eye familiar with geometrical beauty, the perfect execution of an elliptical arch, on so large a scale, and so high a degree of eccentricity, is an uncommon gratification; but when the practical mechanician considers the difficulties and risks which must have attended its construction. . . , then indeed, and only then, will he sufficiently appreciate the courage and the capacity which have approached so near the verge of possibility without transgressing its bounds.' The bridge is painted in Turner's 'Rain, Steam and Speed'.

TATHALL END FARMHOUSE see HANSLOPE

TATTENHOE *8030*

ST GILES. Entirely on its own, by the deserted moat of the former mansion. Nave and chancel in one; wooden bellcote. – PLATE. Cup and Paten on foot of 1662.

TERRICK HOUSE see ELLESBOROUGH

THORNBOROUGH *7030*

ST MARY. (Herringbone masonry in the S wall.) C13 N arcade with standard details and late C13 chancel with intersected tracery in the E window. Perp windows with panel tracery and Perp W tower. – MONUMENTS. William Barton † 1389, brass, a 2 ft figure. – Pretty tablet to Charles Wodnoth † 1778.

THORNBOROUGH BRIDGE. An impressive medieval bridge with three pointed ribbed arches. Hood-moulds, with a head-stop at the NW end. Three breakwaters on the S side. Two more arches (to the E) unribbed.

BURIAL MOUNDS. W of the village on the N side of the road, 500 ft before reaching the bridge, two Roman burial mounds. One was opened in 1839 by the Duke of Buckingham. Amongst the finds – now in the Cambridge Museum of Archaeology and Ethnology – were two bronze jugs, amphorae, a bronze lamp, and 'terra sigillata' ware with a potter's stamp possibly that of 'Tittius' of Lezoux, all in all indicative of a late C2 date.

THORNTON

7030

St Michael. Opposite Thornton House. All but rebuilt *c.* 1850, i.e. at the time the house was rebuilt, and so probably by the same architect, *John Tarring*. The effect however, thanks to the use of plenty of old materials, is not Victorian. – The survival of box pews, two-decker pulpit, squire's pew, etc., at so late a date is surprising. – Plate. Cup and Cover Paten, possibly c17. – Monuments. Knight and Lady, mid-c15, alabaster effigies. – Robert Ingylton † 1472 and three wives. Tomb-chest with shield-bearers in ogee-headed recesses. Outstandingly good brasses under quadruple canopy. The figures are 2 ft long. Sixteen kneeling children below.

Thornton House. By *John Tarring*, 1850. The vch says that it incorporates parts of a medieval house modernized in the c18. Neo-Tudor, cemented. Symmetrical front towards the church and extensive asymmetrical parts to the l. of this with a tower with higher stair-turret. Gothic interiors, including a vaulted screen to the staircase and a vaulted passage. Also contemporary stained glass.

Thornton Hall, ½ m. se. Red brick, Georgian, with two canted bay windows and a wooden doorcase with open pediment. Wide view to the n.

TICKFORD *see* NEWPORT PAGNELL

TINGEWICK

6030

St Mary Magdalene. Tall Perp w tower. n aisle with n arcade of *c.* 1200. Three bays, circular piers, square, chamfered abaci, round arches with small zigzag at r. angles to the wall. The w bay later. It is narrower and has a pointed arch. The pier is square and chamfered, i.e. probably a fragment of the former w wall. Perp chancel. s aisle of 1851. – Brass. Erasmus Williams, rector, † 1608. Small brass plate with kneeling figure and elaborate allegorical conceits. They deserve close study. The plate is signed by *Richard Haydock* (cf. Queen's College, Oxford, and Carlisle).

ROMAN VILLA. E of Tingewick Mill, and about 200 yds from the Ouse, in a field called STOLLIDGE, is the site of a Roman villa partially excavated in 1860–2. It seems to have been of the corridor type with, on the s, a separate small building, possibly a dye-works. Coins indicated an early C4 date.

TURVILLE 7090

Round Turville and Turville Heath is the most secluded and perhaps the most beautiful part of the Chilterns.

ST MARY. Of knapped flint, externally all Victorian, with a short broad w tower. The N aisle of brick was built in 1733. Simple Norman N doorway, simple early E.E. s doorway. Tower arch and chancel arch perhaps also C13. – SCULPTURE. Openwork panel with acanthus foliage and putti, late C17 or early C18 and perhaps Flemish. – STAINED GLASS. Armorial glass of the C16 and C18. – PLATE. Cup of 1565; Cover Paten of 1637. – MONUMENT. In the N aisle to members of the Perry family, 1740, signed by *Thomas Cooper* of Henley. White, black, and grey marble. Standing, without figures. At the top two urns and a shield in a cartouche.

It is very pretty by the church, all timber-framed and brick houses. Only the row of council houses to the N jars badly, far more than the harmless modern one-storey house by *Ernö Goldfinger*, 1954, could ever jar. Yet this caused a fight with the County Council. To the w of the church the jolly VICARAGE. The centre is of knapped flint and brick and has a steep gable with a tall Gothic window flanked by little low blank gables. The brick verticals have intermittent flint rustication – a rustic later version of the Bradenham Vicarage.

On the hill above the village a former WINDMILL, twelve-sided, a smock-mill, of brick below, weatherboarded above. It is converted into a house.

At Turville Heath, 1½ m. w, TURVILLE PARK, a big, rambling, cemented house, supposed to date from the C17 and C18 but externally now, it seems, mostly Early Victorian.

TURVILLE GRANGE, facing the Heath, is an early C18 house of vitreous and red brick, five bays, two storeys, with picturesque barns by its side, including a weatherboarded tower.

TURWESTON 6030

ASSUMPTION. Externally all Victorian (1863) by *Street* (D. Cole). Big w tower with saddleback roof. The building history

starts with nave and N aisle. One small Norman aisle W window,
and an arcade of two bays which, with the odd shape of the
pier, really some wall left standing, and the responds to E and
W, seems to indicate that the aisle was an addition to the nave.
The responds have semicircular projections and nook-shafts.
The capitals with waterleaf crockets and stiff-leaf. The arches
are still round and unchamfered of one step. All this looks *c.*
1190. The S arcade is of the C13, but the E arch on tripartite
responds with moulded capitals is still round. The W arch was
re-done in the C14. The chancel arch goes with the older part
of the S arcade. The arch has two big hollow chamfers. Pointed
single windows in chancel and S aisle (W). In the chancel a C14
ogee-headed recess. – STAINED GLASS. S aisle E by *Willement*,
1851, not bad. – Chancel E by *O'Connor*, 1870, bad. – PLATE.
Cup of 1684. – MONUMENTS. Brass to a Priest, 2 ft figure (chancel N). – Brass to Thomas Grene and two wives, *c.* 1490, 9 in.
figures. – Tablet to Symon Haynes † 1628. With small kneelers.

TURWESTON HOUSE, W of the church. Georgian, of stone, seven
bays, with pedimented three-bay centre.

MANOR HOUSE. In the main street. C17 and much enlarged.
(Staircase of the late C17 with carved balusters. Three C17 overmantels. RCHM)

6020

TWYFORD

ASSUMPTION. Ornate Norman S doorway. Inner order with
thick continuous zigzag. Three orders with shafts, their capitals
decorated with beasts, and beakhead along the arch. Up the
jambs seven stars on top of each other. Norman too, but altered
in the C13, the chancel arch. Of the C12 the zigzag on the r. and
the beakhead, stylized and simplified out of recognition, on the l.
Of the C13 the Sedilia in the chancel, the S aisle arcade with low
quatrefoil piers and double-chamfered arches, and the S aisle E
bay which was originally a transept, wider than the aisle, and
with, in its E wall, a triplet of lancets. The W tower in its lower
part (see the single-chamfered arch towards the nave) is of
the C13 too. Above it is Perp. Perp also the nave roof with
tiebeams on arched braces, kingposts, and two diagonal queen-
posts. The posts and the principals are all cusped. Perp probably too the considerable widening of the S aisle, though two of
the windows (Y-tracery) are of *c.* 1300. – PULPIT. Jacobean,
with one tier of blank arches and gadrooned panels over. –
SCREEN. The dado only, with quatrefoils cut out of the panels.
White flowers painted on the panels. – BENCHES. Plain, C15,

with simple trefoiled poppy-heads. – SCULPTURE. One Norman capital, among other stones, in a recess in the S aisle. It may have belonged to the chancel arch. – PLATE. Cup of 1569, with band of ornament on the bowl and band of egg and tongue on the base. – MONUMENTS. Cross-legged Knight, of Purbeck marble, later C13, defaced (S aisle). – Brass to John Everden † 1413, priest. A 15 in. figure (chancel N wall). – Front of a Perp tomb-chest with quatrefoils (S aisle). – Tomb-chest with, against the short sides, ogee recesses with shield-bearers. On the lid brass to Thomas Gyffard † 1550.* – Richard Wenman † 1572. Painted wooden panel, surrounded by columns and pediment. – Viscount Wenman † 1640. Big oval inscription plate in a gristly cartouche. Black columns and a steep pointed pediment. Putti on it. Not good. – CHURCHYARD CROSS. The base looks C13, a very early date. Trefoiled arches also broken round the corners (cf. e.g. the W front of Salisbury Cathedral). Figures below them, very defaced.

(VICARAGE, to the NE. Incorporates the remains of a late C15 Hall of three bays with adjoining Solar. The Hall roof has braced collar beams. The Solar roof also remains. In place of the C15 kitchen, etc., a wing was built c. 1560. The roof of this is also still intact. RCHM)

POUNDON HOUSE, see p. 225.

TYLERS GREEN

9090

ST MARGARET. 1854 by *Brandon*. Flint. Nave with lancets. An addition of 1891 the curious SE turret, whose bell-stage is tall and entirely of wood, with tracery. Steep pyramid roof. The chancel was lengthened and altered in 1934.

RAYNERS. Red brick, gabled, Elizabethan. Built in 1847. The architect is unrecorded.

DISRAELI MONUMENT, see Hughenden, p. 173.

TYRINGHAM

8040

ST PETER. Except for the W tower by *E. J. Tarver*, 1871 (GR). The tower appears Perp from outside, but its arch to the nave is of the late C12: low, round, single-stepped, and on the simplest imposts. Rock-faced nave and chancel with apse. Two-light windows with plate tracery. The carved decoration outside and inside, especially in the apse and chancel arch, rather on the way to the Arts and Crafts than conventionally Gothic. – PLATE.

* The brass is palimpsest. One part belongs to a priest of c. 1350.

Cup of 1570. – MONUMENTS. Brass to a Knight, late C15, a 2 ft figure. – Brass to a Lady, early C16, 14 in. figure. – William Praed † 1833 (*see* below) by *William Behnes*. Inscription and lunette above with a relief of a lock and a barge.

TYRINGHAM HOUSE. Built by *Soane* in 1793–7 for William Praed, banker and entrepreneur. Tyringham was Soane's first mature work, and so one would give much for having it in its original shape and with its original interiors, including the noble entrance hall with its Greek Doric columns in the corners supporting a shallow groined vault. However, only the GATE-WAY remains unaltered. This is, in spite of its small scale, a monument of European importance. It is a screen of the same kind as Adam's at Syon House or the Hyde Park Corner screen. What is so remarkable about it is that it is entirely independent of period precedent, a sign of a daring only matched at that moment by what Ledoux was designing in France and Gilly in Germany. The Tyringham gateway, which is built of elephant-grey stone, is in addition an extremely exacting piece of design, with emphatically nothing of the elegance of Holland and Wyatt. It consists of a segmental arch on heavy, square, completely unmoulded pillars. The arch is carved out of a big, massive slab, again unmoulded. On top of this is a thin slab, slightly thicker in the centre. The segmental arch is coffered inside, and a band of incised lines marks its edge. Another such band of lines runs along the place on the pillars where one would expect a capital or an abacus, and then runs on across a connecting link to the l. and r. which has a blank niche and ends at the two end pavilions of the screen composition. These have Tuscan columns *in antis* (with hardly any entasis), the only detail for which a precedent existed. Soane had been in Rome in 1778–9, but such Tuscan columns were more a recent French than an ancient Roman motif.

From the gateway one reaches the house by way of a hump BRIDGE in one elegant arch, again with the incised lines of which Soane was so fond.

The house should then form the climax. If it does not, this is due to the early C20 owner, F. A. Konig of New York and London, and his wife, a Frenchwoman. They ruthlessly swept away Soane's interior and altered his exterior drastically. The work was done in 1909, the architect being *G. F. Rees* of Stanmore. The entrance received a French-looking door but was otherwise left alone. Its central bow with attached giant columns, its characteristic incised Grecian decoration, and its balustrade are Soane's. On the garden side the door surround and the enrichments of the attic are of 1909. Soane's STABLES, however, dignified and utilitarian, with the deep eaves of the pediment above the entrance arch, survive. The GARDENS were also made more ornate about 1910, but it is not easy to judge of this now because of what *Lutyens* did after the first World War. Of *c.* 1910 the forecourt with its gatepiers and gates and railings,* also on the garden side the Pergola and the pool in front of it, and in addition the Service Wing to the l. of the garden front and the nice neo-Georgian cottages facing Soane's stables. *Lutyens* in 1926 made two long pools, one behind the other, in axis with the garden front and stretching away for 150 yards. Between the two is a round pool with two columns carrying leopards of lead. To the l. and r. of the first pool are two grand stone-domed pavilions, identical in front but different at the back. One is a Bathing Pavilion, the other a Music-Room-cum-Chapel. In the bathing pavilion dressing rooms are ingeniously tucked away behind black scagliola columns so as to present the grand and unused space under the dome. The Temple of Music is larger and comprises a central space like that of the bathing pavilion, then a second narrower central space where organ music rises through a grating from an instrument placed below ground, an altar space, and a retrochoir. Massive black and green scagliola columns. The main altar panels are by *McMillan*, the panelling on the end wall is by *Sir Frank Dicksee*, P.R.A.

TYTHROP HOUSE *see* KINGSEY

UPPER WINCHENDON

7010

ST MARY MAGDALENE. Norman nave and slightly later Norman N aisle. This has an arcade consisting simply of three unmoulded round arches cut through the wall. Rich later Norman S doorway. One order of shafts, one shaft twisted, the other with a lozenge pattern. Scalloped capitals, arch with roll moulding. Early C13 chancel arch, pointed with one slight chamfer. Lancet fenestration. In the E wall two lancets. N aisle windows Dec. Perp W tower with higher stair-turret crowned by a spirelet. – PULPIT. Of wood and probably as early as the C14. Two-light panel with a reticulation motif at the top. Crenellated rim. – SCREEN. Perp, with one-light divisions. – Plain C16 BENCHES.

* The SCULPTURE on the terrace is by *McMillan*, 1928.

Straight moulded tops to the ends, and elementary panels with cusped heads. – BRASS. Sir John Studeley † 1502, vicar (2 ft 7 in. figure).

THE WILDERNESS. A small fragment of a large mansion. What survives is the kitchen and offices. The brickwork seems of *c.* 1700, the time when the great first Marquess of Wharton enlarged and remodelled the house and gave it its famous, extensive gardens, of which the terraces and avenue can still be traced. Of the Marquess's buildings the only one that has fully preserved its original character is a SUMMER HOUSE to the NE of the house, of brick, two-storeyed with lower two-storeyed wings. The main windows of the centre to both sides are triplets with two lower and one higher and wider arch. This and the completely unmoulded blocks between jambs and arches are reminiscent of *Vanbrugh*. The house itself, i.e. the surviving kitchen wing, though brick-faced, is of stone. It may thus well be, as is so often the case, the surviving medieval core of the later and bigger house.

EYTHROPE. In the extensive grounds by a lake the PAVILION, a house built by *Devey* for Alice de Rothschild in 1883 and recently much enlarged. Brick with stone frieze. The original work was in a free neo-Tudor style. Of the many garden furnishings of the former mansion of the Dormers and Stanhopes, 'sham ruins and turreted buildings', as Lipscomb says, nothing remains, except a very small GROTTO by the lake and a nice C18 BRIDGE. There are however pretty LODGES on the estate, of rubble, brick, and timber, and picturesquely gabled. Plaques in the walls with the Rothschild arms and the mottos Concordia, Industria, Integritas, on a background of naturalistic plant sprays.

UPTON *see* SLOUGH pp. 237, 240, 241

VALE FARM *see* CHESHAM

WADDESDON

ST MICHAEL. A complicated history. It starts at the entrance to the church. The s doorway is Latest Norman, *c.* 1185, pointed but Norman in detail, with the characteristic late motif of zigzag at r. angles to the wall. Especially characteristic the trumpet scallops of one of the capitals of the one order of colonnettes. Of the same date the s arcade. Four bays, sturdy circular piers, square abaci with low many-scalloped capitals, the lunettes of the scallops decorated. Three of the piers have strange brackets

attached to their tops towards the nave, and two of these carry
colonnettes. Were they meant to support transverse arches?
The w end and the arches are clearly disturbed. The first pier
from the w is slenderer and has a circular abacus. The first two
bays have double-chamfered arches. This is probably a lengthening of the nave, in which case the w respond of the 1190
building was re-used. The arches of the other bays are, however, not of c. 1190 either but of c. 1310. Complex mouldings,
hood-moulds, from E to w, first with nailhead then with ballflower, petering out to the w. Chancel of c. 1300, see the window
tracery to E and W, and the S doorway. The N arcade is of the
early C14. Windows with Y-tracery. Arcade of six bays with
short octagonal piers and moulded arches. At the same time the
S arcade was lengthened to link up with the new chancel. The
chancel arch corresponds. C14 tower arch, but the rest of the
tower rebuilt in 1891–2. Perp clerestory. – FONT. Perp, octagonal, with quatrefoil panels. – PULPIT. Of alabaster, given
by the Duke of Marlborough. It was in Blenheim Palace before,
and is said to have been purchased at the 1851 Exhibition. –
SEAT. S aisle w end. Probably French, early C16. With canopy
on four pendant arches. – MONUMENTS. Knight, mid-C14,
badly preserved. – Brass to Roger Dynham † 1490 (from
Eythrope, Upper Winchendon). In armour, figure 4 ft 9 in.
long under a triple canopy. – Brass to Richard Huntyndon
† 1543. Priest, 15 in. figure. – Brass to Hugh Brystowe † 1548.
A 22 in. figure in a shroud.

WADDESDON MANOR. The land was bought by Baron Ferdin-
and de Rothschild in 1874. There was no house on the hill nor
much in the way of trees. The planting had to be done and the
top of the hill to be levelled off to make the mansion and its
formal gardens possible. The mansion is an utter surprise in its
Chiltern setting. 'Its lofty tourelles and skyward elaborations
might well be lifted above the swelling foliage of thick woods in
Touraine'; so *Country Life* wrote in its innocent young days.
Touraine is correct; the more prominent motifs are indeed derived from Chambord and Blois, even if there is more than a
dash of Louis XIII in the mixture. The architect who could
provide all this with so much zest and at the same time combine
it with great skill and experience in internal planning was *Hip-
polyte Alexandre Gabriel Walter Destailleur* (1822–93), architect also of the town houses of Prince Pless at Berlin and of
Albert de Rothschild in Vienna. Work was completed in 1880
(date on the service wing).

61b   A front view from the entrance or garden side tends to stun
you, and it is hard to get down to a description – partly because
motifs jostle each other too much to isolate them mentally.
Baron Ferdinand certainly got as much as anyone could have
demanded. The house is of Bath stone, two storeys high, with
dormers and a later three-storeyed part on the W side. The entrance side has a symmetrical centre with a one-storey porte-
cochère. Here and above, columns crowd together. A pavilion
roof is almost hidden by an erection reminiscent of the so-called
sarcophagi on the terrace at Anet. To the l. and r. of this centre a
calmer mood reigns, though even there the dormer windows in
the roof are lively enough and the tall chimney-shafts have odd
pedimented tops. Wings project, l. and r., and in the re-entrant
angles are domed spiral staircases à la Chambord. To the l.
plainer parts, more like Azay-le-Rideau, with very steep roofs
and a very fat angle tower. To the W the late addition by *Destailleur Jun.* (W. A., born in 1867.) This is of 1889.

       The garden façade is similar. Eleven bays, the main accents
marked by columns, the angle pavilions by coupled columns
with curved open pediments. The crowning motif, which again
almost hides the pavilion roof, is wilder even than on the other
side. In the later addition the architect here has cunningly gone
back to Louis XII details, as if there were older parts incorporated. To the r. a curved conservatory, and then with a *trompe* to
emulate the best of Delorme's the connexion is made to the big
Bachelors' Wing. The Billiard Room here has a coved ceiling
and panelling from Montmorency.

       Altogether the *boiseries* are the most spectacular of the
fixtures inside. The paintings, furniture, objets d'art, do not
concern us here. There are *boiseries* from the Hôtel de Richelieu
(Breakfast Room), the Hôtel de Lauzun (Grey Drawing Room),
Villa Beaujon (Tower Room), and other unrecorded French
sources. The superb mirrors in the Marble Dining Room come
from the Hôtel de Villars (cf. Mentmore, p. 206). From the
point of view of this book it is perhaps more important to add
that Destailleur's own work is of a high order, as designs in
period styles go. The Dining Room especially is all his, and its
marble panelling and the chimneypiece with the two putti
sitting on the mantelshelf and holding candles are both original
and successful.

       The GARDENS were laid out by *Lainé*. Long view to the N.
FOUNTAIN, S of the house. Said to be Italian of the C17, but
more probably of the C19.

At the foot of the hill extensive GREENHOUSES with a dome and Frenchy STABLING.

THE VILLAGE. Here also all is under Rothschild patronage. By the main drive to the house, LODGE on the r., SCHOOL on the l. Much estate housing, not at all French but English half-timbered; perhaps by *W. Taylor & Son* of Bierton, near Aylesbury, who designed the FIVE ARROWS HOTEL (1887). The VILLAGE HALL by the same architects is two years younger and hence more in the Arts and Crafts taste. To the l. of this ALMSHOUSES of 1893, very plain. CLUB and Reading Room of 1883. French in style alone the NE LODGE of brick with stone dressings (at the crossroads on A41, 1 m. E of the village).

WALTON
8030

ST MICHAEL, s of the Hall, not in the village. Limestone and ironstone. Perp w tower, and Dec nave and chancel. – MONU-MENTS. Bartholomew Beale † 1660 and wife (chancel N). Com- 23b missioned from *Thomas Burman* in 1672 by *Mary Beale*, the painter. She and her brother paid £45 for it. Two busts in oval medallions, excellent portraits. A black pilaster between. Black columns l. and r. carrying an open segmental pediment. – Sir Thomas Pinfold (nave s). He died in 1701, but the monument is signed by *Nollekens* and must have been made about 1780. Oval medallion with bust against an obelisk. Books at the foot of the obelisk.

WALTON HALL. Built in 1830. Cemented brick. Three by three bays; parapet. Porch of two pairs of Tuscan columns. Tripartite window over. The entrance hall is connected with the staircase by a screen of two Tuscan columns.

MANOR HOUSE, ½ m. SE. C16 to C17 with gables and many diagonally set chimneys.

WATER STRATFORD
6030

ST GILES. A small church in a small hamlet, but distinguished by some uncommonly good Norman sculpture. The church has a w tower with pyramid roof, not higher than the nave, and a low chancel. Dec and Perp windows, all material re-used when the church was rebuilt in 1828 – a case of piety unusual at that date. The s doorway has in the tympanum Christ in Majesty sup- 5 ported by two angels. The head of Christ unfortunately is not original. The style of the draperies is extremely lively, the composition is close to that of the Prior's Door at Ely. Below the tympanum, lintel with a long row of tiny intersected arches One order of shafts, capitals with interlace, arch with zigzag. The N chancel doorway is interesting for its combination of the usual motif of the lamb and cross, in the tympanum, set against a background of ornamented diaper, with a Viking dragon on the lintel. – (MONUMENT. Incised slab to Mary Franckyshe † 1630. She lies in bed; her husband and children kneel round it.)

WAVENDON

9030

ST MARY. Dec and Perp w tower. The rest of the exterior mostly from the restoration by *Butterfield* in 1848–9. His e.g. the clerestory, the chancel E window, and the other similar windows. The W doorway of the tower is in its mouldings correct and shows early C14 design. Early C14 also the arcades of four bays. Quatrefoil piers. Arches with one chamfer and a pair of small hollows. – PULPIT. From St Dunstan-in-the-West in London, late C17. With marquetry panels and garlands and cherubs' heads at the angles. – STAINED GLASS. All the glass of the Butterfield restoration is by *O'Connor*. Mr Betjeman praises its 'rich purples, reds and golds' and the 'dark mystery of the chancel'. – MONUMENT. George Wells † 1713. Good tablet.

PARSONAGE, W of the church. Built in 1848, and hence probably also by *Butterfield*. Very Gothic and gabled.

WAVENDON HOUSE. A big composite house of which the featureless lower E part is said to be the latest. The centre clearly represents an Early Georgian house of seven bays with a three-bay pediment. Various internal features such as doorcases and panelling correspond. Then a Late Georgian w front and s front were added, the latter with two canted bays and a Tuscan porch of two pairs of columns. The building history needs clearing up. Picturesque N lodge.

DANESBOROUGH. In Wavendon Wood, above Apsley Heath, an IRON AGE HILL-FORT with single ditch and rampart enclosing about 9 acres. To the SW the ditch has both a slight rampart and counterscarp bank. The defences are much denuded. A hollow way leads up to the SW corner of the camp and passes through and out to the N.

WEEDON

8010

MANOR FARMHOUSE. C17, partly early, partly late. A datestone 1649 on the front, 1687 on an archway, 1674 on the barn.

Timber-framed with brick infilling. (In a room a classical scene painted over the fireplace. MHLG)

WHEATSHEAF INN. Timber-framed with brick infilling. Inserted the pedimental brick gable of a window, cf. Whitchurch.

HOUSE at East End, at the SE corner of the village. This also has a window-head like the Wheatsheaf Inn.

WELDERS see CHALFONT ST PETER

WENDOVER 8000

ST MARY. Early C14 tower arch, SW arcade responds, and chancel arch. Later C14 arcades of five bays. The arches still have sunk quadrant mouldings, but the square piers with semicircular shafts carry capitals mostly with foliage of a type more familiar in Perp work. Early C14 N doorway with ballflower in one continuous moulding. Chancel E window with reticulated tracery, i.e. also early C14. W tower with battlements and spire. The exterior looks all Victorian (restoration by *Street*, 1869). – PLATE. Cup of 1569; Cup and Cover Paten of 1571. – MONUMENTS. Brass plate to William Bradschawe † 1537 and wife. Small kneeling figures, below them their nine yet smaller kneeling children, and below them, pedigree-wise, the names of twenty-three grandchildren.

MANOR HOUSE (Wendover House School). Victorian, in the Elizabethan style, gabled. Architect and date seem to be unknown.

PERAMBULATION. As the church is outside the village, the perambulation starts from the CLOCK TOWER, erected in 1842, a red brick square with a truncated pyramid roof, a clock stage, and a spire. From here to the N the piece of Wendover which one does not forget, a short stretch of the AYLESBURY ROAD flanked by nothing but attractive houses, two rows without breaks, and in the wide space between a row of trees closer to the E than the W side. The houses are mostly brick-fronted, but some timber-framing with plastered white infillings and occasional flint help variety. The sequence starts with the CORNER HOUSE HOTEL on the W, early C18, of nine bays, with the former central archway blocked. Then on the other side the RED HOUSE, so called although it has a front entirely of pale greyish-purple vitreous bricks, five bays, plus three more on the l., two storeys, doorway with Doric pilasters and pediment. After that CHILTERN HOUSE, dated 1725, red brick,

straight-headed windows, and a doorway with a straight hood
on simple brackets. OLD HOUSE, of about the same date and
with segment-headed windows, also has such a doorway. (THE
GRANGE is of the late C17, of brick with two gabled dormers.
RCHM)

From the Clock Tower to the E in TRING ROAD, at once BANK
FARMHOUSE, facing us. Vitreous and red brick, of four bays,
with weatherboarded barns. To the W from the Clock Tower
HIGH STREET. Here also there are good and nice minor
houses, but they are not so concentrated as in the Aylesbury
Road. The start is neither good nor minor, the LITERARY
INSTITUTE, founded in 1862, red brick and Gothic. Then
WOOLLERTON HOUSE opposite, of seven bays with a broad
doorcase with Doric pilasters, a metope frieze, and a pediment.
The curious thing is the top frieze of brick as if meant to imitate
Early Tudor Gothic brick friezes of little foiled pendant arches.
Then on the N side, lying back and actually in Back Street,
VINE TREE FARMHOUSE, early C18 with parapet. Opposite,
the POST OFFICE and its neighbour, once a private house, a
fine building of the C16 with a tall gabled carriageway on the l.
with an oversailing gable. Timber-framing with brick infilling.
At the r. end circular brick chimneyshafts. The continuation of
High Street is POUND STREET. Here on the l. timber-framed
cottages, on the r. the very handsome LIME TREE HOUSE,
mid-Georgian, of three bays, with simple Venetian windows l.
and r. of the door and a segment-headed window above it. The
door has a straight hood on modestly carved brackets.

OUTER WENDOVER. To be examined in three directions. First,
in continuation of Pound Street to the w, WELLWICK MANOR,
dated 1616. The front is now Early Georgian, but the four-
centred door-arch and the three-light transomed window
remain of the original building. Octagonal chimneyshafts.
Handsome contemporary weatherboarded BARNS. Then,
further out, on the S side, below the BOER WAR MEMORIAL
on Coombe Hill (erected in 1901), COOMBE HILL HOUSE, by
Leonard Stokes, 1901. This is white and has a front picturesquely gabled in various sizes and with well-placed tapering
chimneys. Garden side with recessed centre, a terrace stretched
out between the wings. Two porches with the typical short
columns of that date tucked into the angles. The wings differ
in bulk and detail. Altogether a lively and attractive design.

To the E of the church in HALE LANE the HOUSE IN THE
FIELDS, by Richardson & Gill, 1935, an example from many

around Wendover, Chesham, etc., of the quiet neo-Georgian then in vogue among the well-to-do and not-too-enterprising. At the end, THE HALE, dated 1743. This has a cemented six-bay front with quoins and a parapet and an indifferent doorway. Finally to the S along LONDON ROAD. Here, out at WENDOVER DEAN, lying back a good deal, MANOR FARM, Early Georgian, of seven bays with a parapet. The windows next to the centre are narrower than the others. Doorway with straight hood on carved brackets. Weatherboarded Barns. Then the FARM SCHOOL, also Early Georgian, with segment-headed windows and vitreous and red brick. Doorway with straight hood on carved brackets.

TUMULUS. A small tumulus, presumably a Bronze Age barrow, on BACOMBE HILL, 1000 yds W of the church.

GRIM'S DITCH. See p. 149.

WESTBURY

6030

ST AUGUSTINE. Early C13 W tower, unbuttressed with C19 saddleback roof. The arch towards the nave pointed and single-chamfered. Hood-mould with small zigzag at r. angles to the wall. Late C13 chancel (one N lancet). S aisle of 1863. The arcades inside are C14, three bays, octagonal piers, double-chamfered arches. The S capitals look earlier than those on the N. – Chancel decoration in red lines, ornament, and figure-work of 1884. – STAINED GLASS. In the chancel N and S windows, by *Kempe*. – PLATE. Cup and Cover Paten of 1592.

WESTBURY MANOR, C18 (a print dated 1769), but much added to in 1903, in a neo-Tudor style.

WESTCOTT

7010

ST MARY. 1867 by *G. E. Street*, and easily his best work in the county, very austere and without any compromise with what prettiness or sumptuousness the Gothic Revival was capable of. Stone exterior, nave with narrow aisles and lower chancel. A bellcote mid-way down the nave and a dormer with a timber-framed gable further E in the S side of the roof. The windows with bleak, large plate tracery. The aisles are shorter than the nave and extremely narrow. The nave has a plain single-framed roof, the aisles single-framed lean-to roofs. The S aisle starts only E of the porch, the N arcade a little further W. Bare, short circular piers with the barest capitals. Tall single-chamfered arches. The interior is faced with pale pink brick left untreated.

– Completely undecorated circular stone PULPIT on the l. side of the low stone SCREEN. To vary a fashionable term, the whole interior might well be called the New Brutalism of the mid C19.

SCHOOL, to the E. By *Street*.

8010   WESTON TURVILLE

ST MARY. Of flint. The exterior is of little interest. The building history begins with the two E bays of the S arcade, which date from the C13. Circular piers with octagonal abaci and double-chamfered arches. The nave was lengthened in the C14 and the N arcade built. Here there are taller square piers with demi-columns attached. The chancel may be a little older, see the chancel arch and the piscina. The E window dates from 1860 (restoration by *D. Brandon*). Perp W tower with higher stair-turret and Perp clerestory and nave roof. This has tie-beams on arched braces with tracery in the spandrels. – FONT. Norman, of cup shape. Fluted below, a band of symmetrically arranged leaf scrolls at the top. The foot is like a reversed block capital with decoration in the lunettes. – PULPIT. Mid-C17. – SCREEN. At the E end of the S aisle. Only the top, but the simple ogee arches with encircled quatrefoils in the spandrels suggest a C14 date. – SCULPTURE (chancel S). Part of a Norman shaft with lozenge decoration; two small figures of the late C13 in relief; a length of dog-tooth; a bust. – STAINED GLASS. Virgin, C15, E window. – CURIOSUM. A wooden panel formerly attached to a post and with the inscription: Faith not exercised, so one waxeth sicke. Ano Domini 1578 (S wall). – PLATE. Flagon, 1694; Cup, 1697.

RECTORY. By *G. G. Scott*, 1838, but not Gothic. In a Late Classical style, of flint with red brick trim, especially vertical bands. Three bays, the middle one projecting and pedimented. Doorway arched and door surround all of red brick. Rusticated red-brick quoins.

MANOR HOUSE. Mid-Georgian. Brick. Of five bays and three storeys with segment-headed windows. Porch with elongated columns. The window above the porch is arched. The other windows tripartite with three arches, narrow–wide–narrow, under one relieving arch.

CASTLE. In the grounds of the Manor House, to its NE, remains of a Norman motte-and-bailey castle. There were two baileys.

(MANOR FARM. In the house is the Hall of an early C16 house. Of the roof the handsome carved wall plate survives and three pairs of carved, heavily-moulded struts on corbels. G. Eland in *Rec. of Bucks.*, XI.)

WESTON UNDERWOOD   *8050*

ST LAURENCE. The arcades come first. Of their four bays three are of *c.* 1200, with round piers, octagonal abaci, and double-chamfered pointed arches. The fourth pier (round abacus) is a little later. Early C14 doorways and chancel arch (tripartite responds). Perp W tower and most windows. The E window is quite large and has a transom. – COMMUNION RAIL. With twisted balusters; *c.* 1700. – STAINED GLASS. In the E window nearly a dozen little whole C14 figures. At the top Christ and two angels. The others are Saints. – PLATE. Cup and Cover Paten of 1700. – MONUMENTS. Brass to John Olney † 1405. Only the large surround remains with inscription, and at the corners barbed quatrefoils with the Signs of the Evangelists. – Throckmorton family, probably shortly after 1688. Tablet with scrolly open pediment.

WESTON MANOR was pulled down early in the C19. The Roman Catholic chapel of 1838 also does not survive, except for one window with intersected tracery. What is preserved is only the STABLES with their clock-turret and some GATEPIERS. Of the gardens described by Cowper the WILDERNESS remains with some urns and busts. In Cowper's time there were also a rustic bridge, a Gothic alcove, and a Gothic temple.

THE VILLAGE has a goodly number of pleasant Georgian houses, especially one of seven bays with segment-headed windows and a pedimented doorway. The house itself is older, see a mullioned window on the l. side. Next to this house a mid-C17 (?) one with regularly arranged mullioned windows under hood-moulds.

WEST WYCOMBE   *8090*

ST LAURENCE, *see* p. 287.
ST PAUL, *see* p. 290.

West Wycombe is the creation of Sir Francis Dashwood, Lord Le Despencer. Churches and village must take their place in this description. The house is the unquestionable centre.

WEST WYCOMBE PARK. The house was built in the early C18, as the segment-headed windows prove and the general plainness behind the later enrichments confirms. The gardens were still formal by 1740. Sir Francis Dashwood began his bold re-modelling about 1750, and it was completed round about 1780.

The exact dates may be in the family papers, but these are not yet fully known. One can guess the dates however from the illustration of the completed work in volume IV of *Vitruvius Britannicus* in 1771 and from the fact that, according to Mr Gunnis, fireplaces were still being bought in 1779–80. The house is long and curiously irregular in that the N and S façades are not of identical length and the E and W porticoes not even axially in line.

Sir Francis Dashwood was born in 1708 and died in 1781. He was a traveller who knew Russia and Turkey, a dilettante, an M.P., for a time a bad Chancellor of the Exchequer, and for a subsequent time a good Postmaster-General. In 1763 he became Lord Le Despencer. He is best known and most notorious as the creator of the so-called Hell-Fire Club, a name current for clubs of rakes about 1720, but not used for his club originally. It was known as the Brotherhood of St Francis, or Dashwood's Apostles, or under similar names. The club met apparently once or twice a year for a whole week or more to devote their time exclusively to wining and whoring. The members of the inner circle included a First Lord of the Admiralty, a Regius Professor at Oxford, John Wilkes, and a number of pamphlet-eers and poets. Much more is stated about it than is known. Benjamin Franklin, e.g., spent sixteen days one July at West Wycombe. Was this to attend one of the Chapters? He certainly was a friend of Dashwood, and the two men published a simplified version of the Book of Common Prayer in 1773 (called *Liturgics*) 'to attract the young and lively and retrieve the well-disposed from the infliction of interminable prayers'. The reports on Dashwood's character are controversial. Of his interest in architecture there can be no doubt. He was one of the founders of the Society of Dilettanti.

West Wycombe Park is approached from the W, and there greets the visitor with a deep Ionic portico of six unfluted columns by two. Under the portico there is a coffered ceiling with three frescoes by *Giuseppe Borgnis* † 1761 or his son *Giovanni*, in a style à la Carracci and Veronese. This portico is an addition of *Nicholas Revett* and is supposed to date from 1771. In the back wall are two aedicule-framed doorways. In front of the portico on the r. against a hedge an ALCOVE with Tuscan pilasters and a pediment, the first of more than a dozen garden ornaments which were Sir Francis Dashwood's answer to the challenge of Stowe and which will be described in due course. The N front of the house faces the lake, a lake formed by damming the river Wye. It gives the first impression of the exquisite landscaping of the grounds which in its present form is the work of *Humphry Repton,* done before 1803. Here as well as anywhere in England the genius and the sensitivity of the garden makers can be admired, the way the clumps of trees are arranged and the way in which even planting on distant hills is controlled. The lake is framed by two little BRIDGES, and on the island appears a fragmentary view of a temple which is in full view from the E. The N front of the house is of eleven bays, yellow stucco and stone dressings, with its accents in the middle (three bays) and at the ends (one bay). These accents are a rusticated ground floor and arched upper windows. In the centre there are in addition Ionic columns between them and a pediment above them. The E side of the house has a painfully asymmetrically set deep Tuscan portico, also by *Revett.* Back wall and ceiling are again frescoed. Against the ceiling the fresco is a copy of *Reni*'s celebrated 'Aurora'. Finally the s front, set against the rising hill and thus the back of the house, yet remodelled about 1760 more sumptuously than the rest. The architect of this side seems to be *John Donovell.* The eleven bays of the façade were grouped in the old house with projecting three-bay wings. These the architect left more or less in their early C18 state. But he connected them by a two-storeyed colonnade all along the front, a bold and unusual motif looking more like painting than like real architecture. Moreover, the first, the last, and the middle three bays of this colonnade project so that the columns at their angles stand in pairs in depth. The columns are Tuscan below and Corinthian above. Pediment over the three centre bays. Small doorway with two attached unfluted Ionic columns and a broken pediment. Carving of two cornucopia below the pediment.

If the house is entered from the W, the visitor has to leave it again and pass through part of the s colonnade to reach the main entrance. This leads into the Hall, which has a screen of Tuscan columns separating its E end and another on the W side dividing it from the beautiful mahogany staircase with its dumb-bell balusters and sparse and dainty marquetry patterns. To the E of the Hall is the Blue Drawing Room, with a boldly coved ceiling and paintings inspired by the Carracci's Galleria Farnese. To the E again the State Drawing Room with a very rich fireplace in pink and white, carved by *Sir Henry Cheere,* and another coved ceiling. In this, motifs from the Farnese Gallery are mixed with others from Raphael's Villa Farnesina. In front of

this room is the E portico. The centre of the N side is the Saloon
(now Dining Room). The doorway to the Hall has Corinthian
columns, the fireplace a fine mythological relief by *Thomas
Carter*. The ceiling is flat and painted again with a fresco after
Raphael's Farnesina. On pedestals three of the four seasons by
Delvaux, made of *Coade* stone. To the W of the Saloon the
Tapestry Room with a Pompeian ceiling and doorcases of the
early C18, to the E of the Saloon the Small Drawing Room with
a ceiling painting by *William Hannen* after Cortona's in the
Palazzo Barberini. The Staircase runs up in a spacious open
well to a large room on the first floor above the Hall which has
the same arrangement of columns; but they are here Ionic
and fluted. The staircase then continues into the second floor.
The staircase walls have paintings derived from Raphael's
Loggie in the Vatican.

The perambulation of the ornamental GROUNDS is easy. They
are not as extensive as those of Stowe, and the garden ornaments
must once have been very close together; for Repton is known
to have removed many. Starting from the S front one turns r.
first and sees at once the so-called COCKPIT, a large flint
structure 'Libertati amicitiaeque sacrum'. Coupled attached
Tuscan columns carry a pediment. A tall arch opens between
and reveals the Apollo Belvedere in a rustic niche. This niche
and the sham façade to which it belongs screen the STABLES
and OFFICES, which incidentally were designed by *Robert
Adam* in 1767–8. Turn S and W for a glance towards the small
ROUND TEMPLE, with its fan-shaped Tuscan portico and
pointed roof.* Then in a straight line along the S boundary of
the gardens proper to their SE corner, where lies the TEMPLE
OF THE FOUR WINDS, an octagonal tower, copied from the
Temple of the Winds at Athens, as *Revett* had done at Shug-
borough. In front of the ground floor a flint screen of arches and
obelisks. On the first floor a surprisingly large doorway, chiefly
surprising because, with its broad broken segmental pediment
and its big keystone head, it looks definitely earlier than the
rest. It might be the original doorway of the early C18 house.

Now the boundary walk, the pathway inside the shrubbery
which in C18 gardens had to 'conceal the bounds', takes us N.
A tiny cascade leaves the lake, and here is the vantage point for
the ISLAND TEMPLE, built by *Revett* in 1778–80. It has an odd
shape with a rounded E end but a straight W one, the latter prob-

* Further S and up the hill in the plantation the DRUID'S HUT, a plain
cottage in its today's state.

ably not meant to be seen. The rounded end has six tall Ionic columns unfluted, flanked by square pillars, the S and N sides three, flanked by pillars. It is an exquisite sight on a fine day, with the Mausoleum and church on the hill behind. At the N end of the walk two Lodges, set at an angle, KITTY'S LODGE, square, one bay each side and with pyramid roof, and the TEMPLE OF DAPHNE, which appears a lodge as one approaches it from the road but is an open temple, as one recognizes from the inside. Unfluted Ionic columns.

One should leave the grounds here and examine the buildings outside their ornamental parts further E (never shown to the public). They are the following. Visible from CHAPEL LANE first the TEMPLE OF ST CRISPIN, a sham chapel of flint with red-brick dressings, as all the others in this area also are. At the W end tower with obelisk finials. In the middle of the E front steep-arched screen. Three-bay lower wings l. and r. One of the chimneys nightmarishly with an outline of one zig and one zag. S of this, l. and r. of the river Wye, the PEPPER BOXES, two turrets with pyramid roofs. Then, by the side of the road to the E entrance of the estate, the ROUND HOUSE, with circular windows to the E. Further back, in line from here with the Temple of the Winds, the house, and the lake, PARK FARM, with a three-bay centre and three-storeyed polygonal angle towers – a façade as of a house, not a farm. The SAWMILLS lie yet further W. Also three-storeyed and with a two-bay centre and low connecting links to one-bay pavilions; centre and pavilions hip-roofed. The arches are all pointed. N of this the TEMPLE OF FLORA, a lodge with a pediment on pilasters. To the grounds three-storeyed with flint surrounds.*

Across the main Oxford road and the village (see p. 290) the ornamental work of Lord Le Despencer continues, and indeed culminates. On the steep isolated hill lie his church and the Mausoleum. To reach them one has to pass the fork of the Oxford and the Aylesbury roads where a COLUMN with a ball finial serves as a signpost and also commemorates the completion of the building of the road in 1752. The main directions are indicated as 'To the City', 'To the University', 'To the County Town'.

ST LAURENCE. The church, although it will be hardly noticed, is medieval, and it seems strange at first that it was built on the hill and not where the village is. However, it was the church of

* At the NW end of the grounds also a LODGE, the one which one usually passes in entering.

a village called Haveringdon, which has disappeared. C 14 W tower. Low long C 13 chancel – see the outline of the arch of the E window and the blocked S doorway. But the church was made Georgian with great flourish. Charles Churchill calls it

> A temple built aloft in air
> That serves for show and not for prayer.

The tower was heightened and finished in the famous golden ball, inside which there are seats. Wilkes, a member of the Hell-Fire Club, and later an author of scandalous remarks about it, called the Ball 'the best Globe Tavern I was ever in'. The nave was rebuilt with five arched side windows and a blank circle above the middle one, and the interior of the whole building was given an entirely new look. In the nave are giant attached columns with richly carved Corinthian capitals. Richly carved frieze. Stucco garlands between the columns. Painted coffering on the ceiling. The effect was rightly called by a visitor in 1775 that of 'a very superb Egyptian Hall' – the term of course used in the sense of Vitruvius. Low, panelled and stuccoed chancel arch. Low chancel with a delightfully decorated ceiling. Nave and chancel beautifully marble-paved. In the centre of the chancel ceiling barbed quatrefoil painted with the Last Supper by *Borgnis*, probably *Giovanni* (who was paid for it in 1765) and not the father, Giuseppe, who had died in 1761 and is buried in the churchyard. Gothick ogee quatrefoils E and W and plenty of Rococo scrolls. The REREDOS and carved COMMUNIONRAIL, the STALLS and the PANELLING form a noble group. – FONT.
20a The oddest perhaps in the country. A claw tripod, a shaft up which winds a serpent, and four doves around what must have been a tiny bowl. A fifth dove reaches up from the shaft. –
20b LECTERN and two STALLS. These also must be among the oddest in the country, and in looking at them and perhaps at the seats in the golden ball high up, one is for the first time reminded of Lord Le Despencer's and Bub Dodington's Hell-Fire Club. Lectern and stalls are comfortable and very beautiful rosewood armchairs on platforms, with desks in front of them, one shaft for the lectern and an eagle above, two shafts for the stalls. – STAINED GLASS. Flemish medallions in the E window. – MONUMENTS. Hugh Darrell † 1667, wife, and grandson, clearly of his, not his grandfather's time. Hanging monument with Corinthian pilasters and a broken segmental pediment with garlands. Volutes at the sides ending at the top in harpies. – Sir Francis Dashwood † 1724. Opposite, and almost identical,

only without the harpies. – George Dashwood † 1801, by *Nollekens*. Plain sarcophagus with obelisk and a putto by an urn. Opposite a yet plainer tablet by *Nollekens*. – Walter Rankin Johnson † 1844. By *R. Brown* of London. Standing woman bending over a sarcophagus.

MAUSOLEUM. A spectacular and passing strange structure of flint, placed to the E of the church on the brink of the hill, and exactly in axis with the London road into High Wycombe. Hexagonal and entirely open to the sky. The three front sides are moreover open as screens with triumphal arch motifs of Tuscan columns carrying metope friezes. Parapet with urns. Large centre arch. The bays l. and r. of this with small arched openings and oblong openings over. The three W sides were originally used as a columbarium. The money for building the mausoleum was left to Lord Le Despencer in 1762 by George Dudington of Melcombe Regis, Dashwood's friend and a principal member of his club. Its designer was *John Bastard* the younger of Blandford. It was built in 1763–4. Three inscriptions on the friezes of three sides to Dudington, Dashwood, and the Earl of Westmorland, Baron Le Despencer and Burgersh, brother of Dashwood's mother. In the centre Urn on pedestal to Lady Le Despencer, 1769. The only big monument was taken out of the former church. It is to the two wives of Sir Francis Dashwood who died in 1710 and 1719. Two kneeling figures placed nearly frontally. Columns l. and r. and putti outside. No pediment. The r. figure looks as if it could be by *Bird*, the l. is not good in quality.

Half-way down the hill towards the village are the CAVES, made by Dashwood in 1750–2 with local labour. They go ¼ m. into the chalk and are a surprising experience. The excavations were undertaken in connexion with the building of the straight road from High Wycombe to West Wycombe, but general opinion is that they also served as a meeting-place for Dashwood's Club. There is little evidence to confirm this, and the 'indescribable scenes' referred to with glee by the notices must be left to the fantasies of visitors, inflamed by the names given* to the halls, chambers, and cells of the caves. They are (in this order) the Robing Room, the Catacombs, the Banqueting Hall, with access to four Monks' Cells, the Buttery, the river Styx, the Cursing Well, and the Inner Temple. The front of the cave is 50b exceedingly pretty. Side walls of flint with short obelisks and a

* Apparently recently; *see* D. McCormick: *The Hell-Fire Club*, 1958, p. 168 etc.

triptych façade with pointed-arched sides and a ruinous high
centre. In the area between the side walls a gay Café with a concave Chinese roof has recently been installed (architect *Guy
Shepherd;* date 1955).

Finally the VILLAGE, a village in which (except for the Methodist
Church of 1894) nothing is visually wrong. Yet there are not
many houses that need singling out. They are from E to W as
follows. The VICARAGE, placed raised and away from the
street. Flint, of two storeys, with a handsome four-bay one-
storeyed Ionic portico ending in a pediment. One-bay wings.
The N side a pretty flint composition (cf. Bassetsbury Manor,
High Wycombe, and the Vicarage, Bradenham). The CHURCH
OF ST PAUL in the garden of the Vicarage is of 1845 (architect
unknown), red brick with an apse and lancet windows. Now
along the village street, and first on the r. (N) CHURCH LOFT, a
timber-framed house with an overhanging upper floor and a
gable on the r., a carriageway on the l. More timber-framing
and also a five-bay Early Georgian brick house with segment-
headed windows and a hipped roof. Queer coving above the
ground-floor windows. Then, opposite, the GEORGE AND
DRAGON, Early Georgian, with irregular fenestration on
three-and-a-half storeys. Originally no doubt of nine bays.
Giant, even, rusticated angle strips with tiny Ionic capitals,
also to the three-bay centre. The strips continue in the attic.
The inn sign has a date 1726. After that a low, late C17, nine-
bay house with a central carriageway and, again on the N side,
APPLE ORCHARD, another pretty timber-framed house with
overhanging upper floor. Square brick chimneystack with
dentilled arched panelling.

CHIPPS'S FARM, 1½ m. SW. A fine early C18 brick house of five
bays and two storeys. Parapet with urns. Doorway with
straight hood on brackets; nothing special. A little carved
decoration below the middle window.

DESBOROUGH CASTLE. A well-preserved small HILL-FORT
enclosing about 1 acre with an entrance to the SE; to the N and
W traces of an outer work. It is probably of Iron Age date.

On CHURCH HILL, at the S end of the ridge and enclosing the
church itself, is a second small single-ditched HILL-FORT of
some 3 acres. To the SE a large part has been destroyed subsequent to the erection of the Dashwood Mausoleum, but elsewhere the ditch has both inner rampart and counterscarp
bank. The original entrance may have coincided with the NW
churchyard gate.

WEXHAM

ST MARY. Norman nave and chancel. The circular W window and one N window survive. Weatherboarded bell-turret with pretty spire. A strange fact is the slight (quoined) projections of the W third of the nave to the N and formerly the S. The E window of *c.* 1300 has cusped intersected tracery. An ogee-headed crocketed recess in the chancel S wall.

PRIMARY SCHOOL. By the County Architect, *F. B. Pooley*. Completed in 1956. For 480 children. A timber-framed structure.

SLOUGH GENERAL HOSPITAL, Wexham Park. By *R. Llewelyn Davies* and *J. Weeks*. Begun in 1959, and promises to be of outstanding architectural quality. The ward units are pavilions with small gardens along an L-shaped spine. The administrative offices and residential staff are to have one tower block with split floor levels inside. The first part to be built consists of operating theatres, X-ray department, out-patients' and casualty departments, and space for 300 beds.

WEXHAM SPRINGS, 1½ m. N. Research Station of the Cement and Concrete Association. For this a laboratory was designed by *Christopher Nicholson* and executed by *Sir Hugh Casson & N. Conder*.

MIDDLE GREEN MANOR HOUSE, ¾ m. SE. Georgian, red brick, five bays, three storeys. Doorway with broken pediment on Tuscan columns.

WHADDON

ST MARY. Externally mostly early to mid C14, internally earlier. The arcades seem to have been built at the end of the C12, but the order and the details of the operations are obscure. On the S side there are three bays, on the N side four, of which the fourth is much narrower than the others. The N piers are circular with square abaci,* the S piers have octagonal abaci. So probably the three N bays came first, and the S bays and the fourth N bay were a slightly later lengthening. But one S capital still has a Late Norman trumpet-shaped scalloped capital, the others have flat capitals, with leaves. The arches are pointed and single-chamfered. Big C14 N chapel with the arch on two small corbel heads. In the chancel Sedilia, below the S window, simply two seats, separated by a stone arm. – FONT. Of tub

---

* On the capital of the NW respond two peacocks pecking at the same morsel.

shape, on four shafts, separated by vertical bands of dog-tooth. – COMMUNION RAIL. Jacobean. – STAINED GLASS. E window 1889 by *Kempe*. – PLATE. Paten of 1683. – MONUMENTS. Thomas Pygott † 1519 and two wives. Tomb-chest with complexly cusped fields containing shields. Brasses with kneeling figures, 13 in. long. Twisted shafts support a horizontal top with a quatrefoil frieze and cresting. Underside with much blank tracery. – Lord Grey de Wilton † 1593 and wife. High, completely bare tomb-chest in the wall, and on it two short fluted columns carrying an entablature. The underside of this is decorated with a pattern of squares and circles connected by bars.

WHADDON HALL. Plain brick mansion of *c.* 1820, rendered. The N side with a centre with giant attached Ionic piers and columns. The Entrance Hall has at its back a screen of two pairs of purple scagliola columns. Behind this the Staircase, unexpectedly grand for the size of the house. Square with a circular coffered dome leaving Pantheon-fashion a glazed eye in the middle. The stair has a simple iron balustrade and rises in three flights round a large open square well. On the first floor a gallery all round with four wide tripartite openings towards the stairs. These openings again have scagliola columns. Above their straight entablatures segmental arches.

TUMULUS. On CHURCH HILL an undatable tumulus with encircling ditch and signs of a central robber pit.

WHELPLEY HILL *see* ASHLEY GREEN

8020 ## WHITCHURCH

ST JOHN EVANGELIST. Happily unscraped. The W doorway is E.E., with three orders of colonnettes with stiff-leaf capitals (re-set ?). Of the late C13 the chancel, which has windows with simple bar tracery (sexfoiled circles) and two doorways with continuous sunk-quadrant mouldings. Sedilia and Piscina in four steps, but the Sedilia covered by one broad segmental arch. Probably also late C13 or a little later the S aisle: W lancet, arcade of four bays with circular piers, circular capitals, octagonal abaci, and double-chamfered arches. The N aisle is different and again a little later: octagonal piers, double-chamfered arches, E window with flowing tracery, the N and W windows and the N doorway of the same style. The S doorway also is early C14, not late C13. The W tower was built into the church so that its buttresses cut into the N as well as the S arcade. It has triple-chamfered arches to E, N, and S. W window with two niches in the outer jambs and a niche over. All this is still no later than the mid C14. Perp clerestory and nave roof. – BENCHES. Plain, with straight tops, except for the poppy-heads. – POOR BOX. Simple, early C17. – CHANDELIER. Brass, given in 1755. – MONUMENT. John Westcar, by *John Gibson*, † 1833. Gentle- 31 man standing like an Athenian of the Parthenon, or like a faith-ful follower of Bakewell, in front of a bull. Some sheep to the r.

OLD HOUSE, NW of the church. Broad stone front with two shaped brick gables. The picturesque N front is a recent re-modelling.

PRIORY, SW of the church. Charming timber-framed house with brick infilling. Stone base. Oversailing upper floor. Diagonally placed chimneys.

Many more attractive houses, both S of the Priory (e.g. No. 28 High Street, timber-framed with brick infilling and a pedi-mentally gabled window head of brick – cf. Weedon) and along the streets NW of the church, e.g. in Castle Lane (a house with a pedimentally gabled door-head of brick), in Market Hill (terrace of cottages) and in Buckingham Road. Here, at the E end, SCHOOL HOUSE, timber-framed with oversailing upper floor, and further W WHITCHURCH HOUSE, with an C18 front. Set in it (not *in situ*) a cartouche with two cherubs, rustic work, probably of the late C17.

CRESLOW MANOR HOUSE, *see* p. 101.

WIDMERE *see* MARLOW

WILLEN   8040

ST MARY MAGDALENE. Built at the expense of Dr Busby of 8a Westminster School by *Robert Hooke* in 1679–80. Hooke had been a boy in Dr Busby's house. On an eminence and reached from the W by a straight avenue of lime trees. Tall short nave and W tower. The apse was added remarkably successfully by *T. H. Lewis* (?) in 1861. Red brick with stone dressings. W tower with the doorway in a stone-faced apsidal recess, just as in Wren's doorway of St Mary-le-Bow, 1670–83. Tall upper storey with Corinthian angle pilasters. Originally the tower had a lead cupola. One-storeyed side-chambers l. and r. to make up the width of the nave. They are tied to the tower by rising curves. Nave quoined with tall arched windows. E gable. The C19 apse is lower and also has arched windows. The interior has a tunnel-vault with penetrations and stucco panelling. The frames of the panels with flower scrolls. Also the date 1680. The plaster pattern is continued in the apse. – The FURNISHINGS are very complete. Original PEWS with curious tops to the ends and candle-holders. – STALL FRONTS with twisted balusters. – WEST DOOR with some openwork scrolls. – WALL PANELLING. – ORGAN CASE with cherubs' heads and scrolls. – Finally the FONT. This has a black polygonal baluster, and a white marble bowl with cherubs' heads. – FONT COVER, ogee-shaped with an urn on top. By *Bates*, who also carved the font cover in Wren's St Anne and St Agnes in London. – PLATE. Set given by Dr Busby and inscribed 1682.

9090

WILTON PARK
1 m. NE of Beaconsfield

An early C18 house of seven bays and two and a half storeys to which some time about 1800 one-storey wings with big arched windows were added. Mr Colvin reports activity of *Richard Jupp c.* 1790 and of *C. H. Tatham* in 1803–5. The house is entirely plastered white. Flat W side, E side with a large shallow bow in the middle. Good plasterwork inside of the Adam–Wyatt type. Also in the Entrance Hall, as well as the room to the l. of the central room with the bow, screens of paired columns to divide off the back part. Again two columns to mark the entrance to the stair. This has an open square well with a circular glazed dome. Restrained ironwork balustrade. The room to the r. of the bow room has instead of columns the back part of the room lower and covered by a segmental vault, in its details very Soanian and therefore no doubt by Tatham. The one-storey wing on the s has one big room, the biggest in the house; the N wing is subdivided into offices, etc.

BRONZE AGE BARROW. *See* Beaconsfield.

8020

WING

4a ALL SAINTS. Wing is one of the most interesting Anglo-Saxon churches in England, for its polygonal apse (cf. Deerhurst), for its crypt beneath (cf. Hexham and Ripon), for its aisles (cf. Brixworth), and also for its size. It is, without its Perp W tower, about 90 ft long, and the aisle externally and several of the internal details prove that it also had a respectable height. The apse is of seven sides of an elongated polygon of sixteen sides. It is externally articulated by tall lesenes carrying thin arches, and above these there were lesenes again, carrying triangular heads or straight-sided arches, motifs familiar from Earls Barton, Barton-on-Humber, and other churches. In this upper storey there are two original windows. The E arch was higher than the others and the details above show that the apse walls were originally higher. The ground-storey windows are of the C15. Below this apse there is a low crypt which consists of a small centre in the form of an elongated hexagon and a narrow ambulatory around which follows approximately the outlines of the centre and the apse. The ambulatory has three windows. The crypt is roughly vaulted. The nave is tall and has its original chancel arch – wide and unmoulded – and above it a twin-window with Roman tiles and a turned shaft. The arcades are no more than unmoulded arches on stepped imposts cut into the wall. Four bays, but the fourth remodelled in the late C13. The masonry of the N aisle is Anglo-Saxon too. In its E wall an original doorway, probably connected with the crypt. Above the W ends of the N and S walls of the nave, high up, two door-ways were found in 1954. They must have led to a W gallery, no doubt the lord's gallery, or rather the lady's, as the manor belonged to the Lady Aelfgifu in the late C10, to which date the work is assigned. It is thus contemporary with Deerhurst, Earls Barton, and Barton-on-Humber. She was the widow of the brother and predecessor of King Eadgar. Later work is no more than the rebuilding of the S aisle in the early C14 with a delightful Dec E window and the building of the W tower with a very tall arch to the nave, and of the clerestory in the C15.

FURNISHINGS. FONTS. Base of a Norman font in the porch, very similar to that of the late C12 font at Aylesbury. The form is that of a reversed two-scallop capital, with the lunettes of the scallops decorated with foliage. – Perp Font, octagonal, with demi-figures of angels carrying the bowl. On small shields the Instruments of the Passion. – PULPIT. Jacobean with the typical blank arches. – SCREENS. Tall Rood Screen of three-light divisions (cf. Edlesborough near by), but the tracery destroyed. Ribbed W coving. – Simple Screens to the SE chapel. – STAINED GLASS. In the S chapel E window, by *Kempe*, 1901. In the tracery head genuine C14 glass. Small figures of the Corona-tion of the Virgin. – PLATE. Small Cup and Cover Paten, 1569; large silver-gilt Cup and Cover Paten, 1644; two silver-gilt Plates, 1644; silver-gilt Flagon with lions, 1676; Paten on foot, 1700. – MONUMENTS. Brasses to a Civilian and wife, *c.* 1470, 17 in. figures (N aisle), and to Harry Blackwell † 1460 and wife,

22a   18 in. figures (s chapel). – Sir Robert Dormer, dated 1552, the
finest monument of its date in England and of an unparalleled
purity of Renaissance elements. Sarcophagus with bucranion
and two garlands. The architectural surround surprisingly wide.
Coupled fluted Corinthian columns l. and r. on tall bases with
strapwork. Against the wall coupled pilasters on bases correspond to these. The columns and pilasters carry a straight
entablature elaborately detailed. The soffit has simple repeating
strapwork motifs. The monument at first sight resembles
North Italian work, such as Sammicheli's Bembo Monument
at Padua. Another comparison is with the most classical interior
details of Ecouen, which are, however, not earlier, but in all
probability a little later. Moreover, the stone is local, and the
strapwork is local too. So one should perhaps rather think of the
admittedly less pure Sherington Monument at Lacock Abbey
in Wiltshire (1553) and thus of the circle round the Lord
Protector and the Duke of Northumberland.* – Sir William
Dormer and wife, inscribed 'Finished Anno 1590 the 20
October'. Two recumbent effigies, his behind and a little above
hers. His head rests on the rolled-up end of a mat. Columns l.
and r., pair of arches against the back, top with shields and
strapwork. – First Lord Dormer † 1617 and wife. Big kneeling
figures between columns. The smaller figures of the children
kneel along the base. – Lady Anne Sophia Dormer † 1695.
Above the inscription plate portrait bust between two putti. –
Henry Fynes † 1758. With a big putto lifting drapery from an
urn. Ascribed by Mrs Esdaile to *Roubiliac*.

SCHOOL, s of the church. Picturesque and gabled. Built in 1850.

DORMER'S HOSPITAL. Founded 1569, but much remodelled in
the C19. Four doors and four dormers. The doors and windows
have brick frames.

CASTLE HILL. Norman castle mount, *c.* 300 yds N of the church,
c. 20 ft high.

8010

WINGRAVE

ST PETER AND ST PAUL. Much renewed in 1887. C13 W tower
with higher stair-turret (rebuilt 1898). Nave and aisles and lower
chancel. The chancel is of *c.* 1190, lengthened a little later. It has
inside on the N wall blank pointed arcading on short shafts with
leaf capitals of the pre-stiff-leaf stage. Three tall arches, then a

* Dr Girouard has recently drawn my attention to the fact that the Duke
in 1552 married the sister of Sir Robert Dormer's son's wife, Mary Sidney,
and that this son, Sir William, no doubt commissioned the monument.

depressed one and a simple doorway into a strange narrow gangway-like chamber with a pointed tunnel-vault. On the s side remains of the same arcading. Two more capitals of shafts belonging to it now re-used in the E wall of the chancel. Among the chancel windows one lancet and one cusped 'low-side' lancet. A little later the tower arch, a fine piece with mature stiff-leaf capitals and a triple-chamfered arch. The N and s arcades were built in the C14. They have octagonal piers and double-chamfered arches. – FONT. Circular, Norman, with one band of rope. – SCREEN. Perp, simple, under the w tower. – PLATE. Cup of 1568; Paten on foot of 1671.

(DENE LEYS, Nup End. In an upstairs room later C16 arabesque wall-painting; cf. Loughton Manor House. E. C. Rouse)

WINSLOW 7020

ST LAURENCE. Mostly Dec, i.e. the arcades with their octagonal piers and double-chamfered arches, the foiled circular windows of the clerestory, the chancel, and the lower parts of the w tower. The latter is embraced by the aisles. Perp the E window, most of the aisle windows (but not that at the w end of the s aisle), the straight-headed clerestory windows, and the top of the tower. N chapel of 1889, and probably also of that time the curious half-timbered E gable of the chancel. – PULPIT. Jacobean, elaborately carved, with book-rest. – WALL PAINTINGS. Traces of a Murder of St Thomas, C15; also St Christopher, C15; both N aisle w wall. Doom, oil painting of c. 1500, also N aisle wall, not easily recognizable. – STAINED GLASS. In one s aisle window by *A. J. Mingaye*, 1868 (TK). – In the chancel E window by *Kempe*, 1897. – PLATE. Cup of unusual shape (cf. several in Worcestershire), c. 1550; Cover Paten, 1569; large Cup and Cover Paten, 1639; Salver, 1686; Paten on foot, 1693; two silver-gilt Spoons, 1699; Cup and Cover Paten, 1716; Paten on foot, 1723.

CONGREGATIONAL CHURCH, Horn Street, 1884 by *Sulman*. Red brick with asymmetrical tower. Perp detail.

BAPTIST CHURCH, off Market Walk, adjoining the Market. With a date-plate 1695. Simple cottage. The furnishings inside complete, very humble, probably Late Georgian.

WINSLOW HALL. Dated 1700. Built for William Lowndes, 43 Secretary to the Treasury. The design in all probability by *Sir Christopher Wren*, who certainly checked the accounts (*Rec. of Bucks.* XI) and occasionally pruned the bills. The bricks were locally made, the names of bricklayer and mason are known, and also the fact that the woodwork was done by *C. Hopson*, the King's Joiner, and *M. Bankes*, the King's Carpenter. The iron GATE to the E by *Stephen Big*. The trees for the garden were bought by *Wise* and *London*, the King's Gardeners. The house is very stately, very restrained, and very urban. Vitreous and red brick and stone dressings. Seven bays, two main floors, a basement for kitchen and offices, and a half-storey. Hipped roof with four big narrowly-oblong panelled chimneyshafts in a row on the ridge. Quoins of stone and quoins to the slightly-projecting three-bay centre, which carries a big pediment. Doorway with segmental pediment on elongated brackets. The garden front is exactly identical with the street front. The plan of the house is very simple. Two staircases in the shallow E and W projections, the E stair characterized as principal by being a little wider. Turned balusters, not over-thick. Two main front-rooms and two main back-rooms on each of the three floors, small subsidiary rooms N and S of the staircases. Typical 'Queen Anne' panelling and chimney-pieces. On the first floor in a back room wall-paintings of ideal landscape in heavy and elaborate ornamental surrounds including caryatids. Surprisingly rustic in so metropolitan-looking a house.

PERAMBULATION. The centre of the little town is the MARKET SQUARE. On its S side the BELL HOTEL, early C19, with three nice bay windows on the ground floor, a naive, broad, columned doorway, and giant and other pilasters with incised ornament. Across in the SW corner the GEORGE HOTEL with a mid-C18 wrought-iron balcony of fabulously ornate workmanship. This stranger comes from Claydon House. On the N side of the Square a Georgian brick house of three storeys whose upper windows are all Venetian. To its r. nice Georgian shop-front. From the NW corner a passage leads to the church. From the NE corner HIGH STREET runs N. On its E side, facing the churchyard, nice minor houses and cottages. Nothing worth singling out. From the SW corner HORN STREET goes W. It has several attractive houses, especially No. 3 with two late C18 doorcases and, at its bend, the two called Parson's Close. Their r. end is a barn. The roof runs through. From the SE corner of the Market Square to the E goes SHEEP STREET, past BROOK HALL (early C18, six bays, vitreous and red brick), past Wins-low Hall, past a number of cottages to the two isolated ones at its end, in the hamlet of SHIPTON. One is of the C16 and has timber-framing with brick infilling.

HOSPITAL, former Workhouse. 1835 by *G. G. Scott*, but still entirely Georgian. The principal house is of two and a half storeys and five bays, the three middle ones forming a canted bay. The usual utilitarian premises are behind.

WOLVERTON   8040

Wolverton consists of Old Wolverton and New Wolverton. Old Wolverton the traveller does not notice, New Wolverton he cannot overlook.

OLD WOLVERTON

HOLY TRINITY. 1815 by *Henry Hakewill*, neo-Norman and a bafflingly early example of that particular revival. With w tower and transepts. Big w portal and big, preposterously low-placed E rose window. Thin vault over the chancel, the rest with a panelled ceiling, probably belonging to the remodelling of *c.* 1870 by *E. Swinfen Harris*. The WALL PAINTINGS of that time are by Bell of *Bell & Almand*. – Neo-Norman PULPIT. – MONUMENT. Sir Thomas Longueville † 1685. Semi-reclining figure in Roman armour, hand on heart. He lies on a big sarcophagus. Reredos background.

To the N of the church across fields in the distance the AQUEDUCT crossing the valley of the Ouse. This was built in 1811 for the Grand Union Canal. The water runs in a big square iron trough. Stone piers.

RECTORY, by the church. Built in 1729. Five bays, two storeys, of stone. But the portal comes from the earlier Manor House. It has Corinthian columns and a steep wide-open pediment and appears to be of *c.* 1600. (For more fragments, *see* RCHM.)

To the NE, off the road, MANOR FARM (early C19; stone. MHLG). SW of this MANOR COTTAGES, early C18, stone, of five bays and two storeys. One of the cottages has a pretty door dated 1629.

WOLVERTON HOUSE, ½ m. SW of the church. Three-bay stone range of *c.* 1800 added to a rambling C16 to C17 house. The front of the house of *c.* 1800 has giant pilasters. Tripartite windows, segment-headed. Doorway with pilasters and pediment.

NEW WOLVERTON

Some medieval towns grew out of markets; Wolverton and Swindon are the outcome of the establishment of railway works. The Midland Railway started its carriage works in 1838, the year in

which the London–Birmingham railway was inaugurated. They
stretch along, N of the main road and s of the canal, and the town
was planned and built to their s, a grid of streets with the same
or very similar long avenues of two-storeyed red brick cottages
with bay windows. No climax in either a parish church or a
market place with town hall. The carriage-works themselves
have nothing monumental or conspicuous about them either.

St GEORGE. The main parish church, indifferently placed. By
Wyatt & Brandon, 1843–4, transepts by *Oldrid Scott*, 1894
(GR). E.E. and quite big. Lancet windows mostly with red
sandstone dressings. NE tower with insignificant spire.

NEW BRADWELL

New Bradwell is a smaller edition of New Wolverton, a little to its
w. The same grid of brick cottages, the same lack of accents. The
Illustrated London News in 1858 speaks of 150 cottages and the
church and school.

St JAMES. 1858 by *Street*. Nave and s aisle and chancel. The NW
tower was never built. A rather shameful little wooden bell-
turret instead. N aisle of 1898. Street's church has lancets and
windows with plate tracery. The arcade piers with big stiff-leaf
and flowers. Quatrefoil clerestory windows with shafts inside
and foliage capitals. – STAINED GLASS. In the N window, signed
M. B. Cantab. Who may he be ? The glass is very surprising for
its date. The faces still somewhat Pre-Raphaelite, but the
strong, warm colours and their areas point forward from the
Arts and Crafts to Expressionism.

SCHOOL, s of the church. By *Street*.

WINDMILL, just w of the railway. Tower-mill without sails.

WOOBURN
9080

St PAUL. Almost entirely Victorian, although never really re-
built. Restoration by *Butterfield* 1856–7, and again 1868–9.
Knapped flint. w tower and higher stair-turret crowned by a
spirelet. Whitewashed interior. The arcade piers of the ending
C12, but completely re-done. Circular with flat capitals and
square abaci. Unmoulded arches. – ROOD SCREEN. Very
ornate with rood and two seraphim. 1899 by *Comper*. –
STAINED GLASS. w window by *Heaton & Butler*. – BRASSES.
John Godwyn † 1488. – Christopher Askowe and wife, c. 1510.
– Thomas Swayne † 1519, priest. – Man in shroud, c. 1520.
Nice cottages and houses behind the church.

WOOBURN HOUSE. Built in 1769 in the place of a palace of the bishops of Lincoln, which had been remodelled by the Duke of Wharton. Red brick, five bays with two pedimented slightly projecting wings. Two storeys, hipped roof. Stables on the l. and one odd gabled piece of flint and red brick with a stepped gable and a Gothick window. In the gardens to the S a BRIDGE, the former posts of the handrail of which stand on C15 head-corbels from the medieval palace.

CLAPTON REVEL, 1¼ m. N, off a lane between the A40 and A4094 roads. Brick. Five by three bays with hipped roof.

WOOD END HOUSE see MEDMENHAM

WOODROW HIGH HOUSE see AMERSHAM

WORMINGHALL   6000

ST PETER AND ST PAUL. Norman s doorway with one order of shafts. Capitals with broad upright leaves ending in corbels. The N doorway also is, or was, Norman, but the whole N wall was rebuilt in 1847. C14 chancel, C15 W tower. – STAINED GLASS. E window of 1847; characteristic and not discreditable. – PLATE. Large Cup and small Cover Paten of 1629. – MONUMENT. Brass tablet to Philip Kinge † 1592. Kneeling figures and a chrysom child at their feet. Philip Kinge's uncle was the last abbot of Oseney and first bishop of Oxford. The inscription on the tablet runs as follows:

> The aged roote that twelve times frvite did beare
> (Though first and last were blasted in their prime)
> Is withered now, and warnes his children deare
> Thovgh yet they springe, to know their wint^{rs} time.
> So labovr'd he and so is gone to rest.
> So liv'd, so died, as all (bvt cvrsed) blest.
> Blesse Lord his fellow roote that lives as yet.
> Bvt as a vine withovt hir proppe decaies:
> And blesse their branches wch these two did get,
> And send them sap to novrish them alwaies.
> Blesse roote and branch, y^{t} all may grow in Thee
> And meet at length to eat of Thy life tree.

ALMSHOUSES. Founded in 1675 by John King in memory of his father Henry King, bishop of Chichester, H-shaped, of brick with stone quoins, etc., and a hipped roof. Mullioned windows. Quite a stately building.

WOTTON UNDERWOOD

ALL SAINTS. Nave and chancel, and early C19 w tower with lead
spire. The s aisle rebuilt in 1867 by the Duke of Buckingham,
and the whole then over-restored. Of that time especially the
nave roof carried by angels. But the Duke's most conspicuous
14b   contribution is the STONE SCREEN to the family chapel, heavily
detailed Early Dec. The IRON SCREEN of the same part of the
church to the E, on the other hand, is a splendid piece of Georgian wrought-iron work with wrought-iron Corinthian pilasters
and comes probably from the house. – SCULPTURE. A part of a
Norman frieze with saltire crosses over the doorway from the
tower to the nave. – STAINED GLASS. In the family chapel many
coats of arms by *Francis Eginton*, 1800, re-set by *Powell*'s, 1868.
– PLATE. Cup and Cover Paten, 1589. – MONUMENTS. The
extensive columbarium arrangement is of 1800. – Duchess of
Buckingham † 1836. Tablet with kneeling woman by an urn. –
So-called Agnes de Grenville. Elizabethan. Recumbent effigy.
In a Gothic recess of 1867. Above, not *in situ*, two small kneeling
Elizabethan figures. – Also Victorian Gothic tablets.

44b   WOTTON HOUSE. Wotton House was built for Richard Grenville (cf. Stowe, p. 252) between 1704 and 1714. *John Keene* is
given as the architect, but recently *Thornhill* has been suggested,
by whom a drawing of the house with one of the pavilions
exists. The house has two independent pavilions or service
buildings, and these are one-storeyed, of five by five bays, and
have hipped roofs and a lantern. This ensemble and the dormers
with alternating triangular and segmental pediments are conservative for their date. As for the house itself, its evidence is
confused by the fact that it was damaged by fire in 1820 and rebuilt by *Soane*. However, the fire cannot have been too disastrous for the exterior; for this is close to the Thornhill drawing. Brick, with stone dressings. Eleven bays, two storeys, with
giant pilasters at the angles and at the angles of the three-bay
centre, and an attic storey above the cornice, all motifs familiar
from such early C18 houses as Chicheley (*see* p. 93), Buckingham House, London, of 1705, or Cound of 1704. Lysons indeed
says that Wotton was built after the model of Buckingham
House. However, the dates make such a dependence improbable. The garden side is the same as the entrance side, except
that here Soane, rather than the architect of 1704, gave the
whole three-bay centre a portico of giant pilasters. The attic
also seems to be altered. w as well as E doorway have segmental

pediments. That on the W (garden) front has splendid carved decoration and carries the date 1704. The entrance front is preceded by a forecourt closed by splendid railings and iron gates. The Vanbrughian decoration of the Hall is not of direct Vanbrughian but rather of Lutyensian derivation. It belongs to the remodelling of the interior after another fire in 1929 and was designed by *A. S. G. Butler*. Below this remodelling arches and mouldings and remains of the dome have been discovered, as *Soane* had done them in remodelling the early C18 house. Of the early C18 however the wrought-iron stair balustrade.*

The gardens of Wotton were probably laid out originally by *Bridgeman*. They are large and have quite a number of ornamental buildings, mostly at present derelict. The spectacular CHINESE HOUSE has found a new home in Ireland. What remains is a large twin LAKE with a five-arch BRIDGE. W of the house, nearer the house, at the E end of the S lake, two Tuscan TEMPLES (soon to be moved?), on the W side of the N lake a ROTUNDA and an OCTAGON, on the NE side of the N lake a Turkish TEMPLE, and parts of the GROTTO on Grotto Island.‡

WOUGHTON-ON-THE-GREEN 8030

ASSUMPTION. Perp W tower, but mostly Dec, namely the chancel, S aisle, S porch, and the renewed N windows. S arcade of quatrefoil piers and double-chamfered arches. Nice Dec decoration above the doorway to the rood-stair. In the chancel N wall an ogee-headed recess. In the chancel S wall a window with reticulated tracery. The S porch has pretty two-light openings to W and E. – PLATE. C15 Paten, silver-gilt, a great rarity. Circular with an inscription round the rim. Sexfoiled centre with leaf ornament in the lobes and the monogram of Christ in the middle. – MONUMENTS. Defaced effigy of a Priest, C14, chancel N. – Martha James † 1735. Tablet with pilasters, pediment, and urn. Good.

WRAYSBURY 0070

ST ANDREW. By *Brandon*, 1862, the W tower with broach-spire and the S aisle. The rest medieval, but externally over-restored. Internally the arcades of three bays and the chancel arch have the same curious and unusual details. Square, heavy piers, i.e. probably chunks of former wall left standing, but at the corners

* This information was kindly given me by Mrs Brunner.
‡ This also I was told by Mrs Brunner.

provided with thin keeled nook-shafts. These continue and form thin keeled roll mouldings at the angles of the otherwise unmoulded arches. In the chancel one blocked N lancet. All this work is probably of the beginning of the C13. – PLATE. Cup and Cover Paten of 1634. – MONUMENTS. Brasses to a Knight and Lady, c. 1500, under a double canopy, 2 ft 6 in. figures. – Brass to John Stonor † 1512, in student or legal dress, 9 in. figure. – Harriett Paxton † 1794. Standing monument of unusual design. Urn on a sarcophagus under a plain arch; the inscription above. – William Gyll † 1806 (N aisle). Seated female figure with anchor and heraldic shield in front of an obelisk.

KING JOHN'S HUNTING LODGE, Old Ferry Drive, ½ m. NW. Timber-framed pre-Reformation house, carefully restored. Projecting two-storeyed central porch. (Inside, Hall with one truss with cambered tie-beams on braces and a tall octagonal kingpost. MHLG)

Along the road to Staines first OAST HOUSE, Georgian with the addition of an Italianate brick tower, then after a while ANKER-WYCKE PRIORY, long white two-storeyed house of the early C19 (after 1805). In the grounds three lengths of stone walling of ANKERWYKE NUNNERY. In the walls one C13 window and two later ones. Yet further on at the end of a drive WRAYSBURY HALL, by *T. E. Collcutt*, 1892, originally called Rivernook. Brick, in a free Early Tudor, with half-timbered gables. Pretty porch with a short column and two arches.

WYRARDISBURY see WRAYSBURY

GLOSSARY

ABACUS: flat slab on the top of a capital (q.v.).

ABUTMENT: solid masonry placed to resist the lateral pressure of a vault.

ACANTHUS: plant with thick fleshy and scalloped leaves used as part of the decoration of a Corinthian capital (q.v.) and in some types of leaf carving.

ACHIEVEMENT OF ARMS: in heraldry, a complete display of armorial bearings.

ACROTERION: foliage-carved block on the end or top of a classical pediment.

ADDORSED: two human figures, animals, or birds, etc., placed symmetrically so that they turn their backs to each other.

AEDICULE, AEDICULA: framing of a window or door by columns and a pediment (q.v.).

AFFRONTED: two human figures, animals, or birds, etc., placed symmetrically so that they face each other.

AMBULATORY: semicircular or polygonal aisle enclosing an apse (q.v.).

ANNULET: see Shaft-ring.

ANTEPENDIUM: covering of the front of an altar, usually by textiles or metalwork.

ANTIS, IN: see Portico.

APSE: vaulted semicircular or polygonal end of a chancel or a chapel.

ARABESQUE: light and fanciful surface decoration using combinations of flowing lines, ten-

drils, etc., interspersed with vases, animals, etc.

ARCADE: range of arches supported on piers or columns, free-standing; or, BLIND ARCADE, the same attached to a wall.

ARCH: round-headed; i.e. semi-circular pointed, i.e. consisting of two curves, each drawn from one centre, and meeting in a point at the top; segmental, i.e. in the form of a segment; pointed; four-centred, see Fig. 1(a); Tudor, see Fig. 1(b); Ogee, see Fig. 1(c); Stilted, see Fig. 1(d).

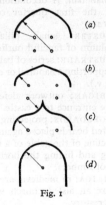

Fig. 1

ARCHITRAVE: lowest of the three main parts of the entablature (q.v.) of an order (q.v.) (see Fig. 12).

ARCHIVOLT: under-surface of an arch (also called Soffit).

ARRIS: sharp edge at the meeting of two surfaces.

ASHLAR: masonry of large blocks wrought to even faces and square edges.

ATRIUM: inner court of a Roman house, also open court in front of a church.

ATTACHED: *see* Engaged.

ATTIC: topmost storey of a house, if distance from floor to ceiling is less than in the others.

AUMBRY: recess or cupboard to hold sacred vessels for Mass and Communion.

BAILEY: open space or court of a castle.

BALDACCHINO: canopy supported on columns.

BALLFLOWER: globular flower of three petals enclosing a small ball. A decoration used in the first quarter of the C14.

BALUSTER: small pillar or column of fanciful outline.

BALUSTRADE: series of balusters supporting a handrail or coping (q.v.).

BARBICAN: outwork defending the entrance to a castle.

BARGEBOARDS: projecting decorated boards placed against the incline of the gable of a building and hiding the horizontal roof timbers.

BASILICA: in medieval architecture an aisled church with a clerestory.

BASTION: projection at the angle of a fortification.

BATTER: inclined face of a wall.

BATTLEMENT: parapet with a series of indentations or embrasures with raised portions or merlons between (also called Crenellation).

BAYS: internal compartments of a building; each divided from the other not by solid walls but by divisions only marked in the side walls (columns, pilasters, etc.) or the ceiling (beams, etc.). Also external divisions of a building by fenestration.

BAY-WINDOW: angular or curved projection of a house front with ample fenestration. If curved, also called bow-window; if on an upper floor only, also called oriel or oriel window.

BEAKER FOLK: small bands of metal-using artisan-warriors from the Continent, heralding the onset of the Bronze Age.

BEAKHEAD: Norman ornamental motif consisting of a row of bird or beast heads with beaks biting usually into a roll moulding.

BELFRY: turret on a roof to hang bells in.

BELGAE: powerful warrior bands from the Continent who established themselves in SE Britain shortly before the Roman Occupation. They came in two waves, *c.* 75 and 50 B.C., and gave rise to what is known as the Iron Age C culture.

BELL BARROW: type of Bronze Age barrow with a wide level shelf between edge of mound and ditch.

BELLCOTE: framework on a roof to hang bells from.

BILLET FRIEZE: Norman ornamental motif made up of short raised rectangles placed at regular intervals.

BLOCK CAPITAL: Romanesque capital cut from a cube by having the lower angles rounded off to the circular

shaft below (also called
Cushion Capital) (Fig. 2).

Fig. 2

BOND, ENGLISH or FLEMISH:
see Brickwork.
BOSS: knob or projection usually
placed to cover the intersection of ribs in a vault.
BOW-WINDOW: see Bay-Win-
dow.
BOX PEW: pew with a high
wooden enclosure.
BRACES: see Roof.
BRACKET: small supporting
piece of stone, etc., to carry a
projecting horizontal.
BRESSUMER: beam in a timber-
framed building to support the,
usually projecting, superstructure.
BRICKWORK: *Header:* brick laid
so that the end only appears on
the face of the wall. *Stretcher:*
brick laid so that the side only
appears on the face of the wall.
English Bond: method of laying

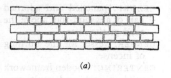

(a)

(b)

Fig. 3

bricks so that alternate courses
or layers on the face of the wall
are composed of headers or
stretchers only (Fig. 3a).
Flemish Bond: method of laying
bricks so that alternate headers
and stretchers appear in each
course on the face of the wall
(Fig. 3b).
BROACH: see Spire.
BROKEN PEDIMENT: see Pediment.
BUTTRESS: mass of brickwork or
masonry projecting from or
built against a wall to give additional strength. *Angle Buttresses:* two meeting at an angle
of 90° at the angle of a building
(Fig. 4a). *Clasping Buttress:*
one which encases the angle
(Fig. 4d). *Diagonal Buttress:*
one placed against the right
angle formed by two walls, and
more or less equiangular with
both (Fig. 4b). *Flying Buttress:*
arch or half arch transmitting
the thrust of a vault or roof
from the upper part of a wall
to an outer support or buttress.
Setback Buttress: angle buttress set slightly back from the
angle (Fig. 4c).

CABLE MOULDING: moulding
imitating a twisted cord.
CAIRN: any prehistoric mound
of stones. Sometimes the stone
core of a Chambered Tomb
from which the earth has been
eroded.
CAMBER: slight rise or upward
curve of an otherwise horizontal structure.
CAMP: Camps are generally
either the simple rural en-
campments of the New Stone

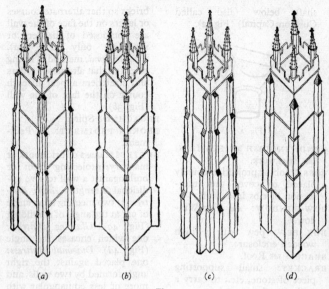

(a)   (b)   (c)   (d)

Fig. 4

Age or the heavily fortified
structures of the Early Iron
Age. In Northern Britain they
were being constructed during
the whole of the Roman Occupation and beyond.

CAMPANILE: isolated bell
tower.

CANOPY: projection or hood
over an altar, pulpit, niche,
statue, etc.

CAP: in a windmill the crowning
feature.

CAPITAL: head or top part of a
column (q.v.).

CARTOUCHE: tablet with an
ornate frame, usually enclosing
an inscription.

CARYATID: human figure used
instead of a column.

CASTELLATED: decorated with
battlements.

CELTS: The Celtic incursions
into England occurred from
c. 250 B.C. onward. The most
important settlements were in
Yorkshire and the SW. (N.B.
Celt, pronounced with a soft
c, is also a technical word for
an axe of Old or New Stone
Age origin.)

CELURE: panelled and adorned
part of a wagon-roof above the
rood or the altar.

CENSER: vessel for the burning
of incense.

CENTERING: wooden framework
used in arch and vault construction and removed when
the mortar has set.

CHALICE: cup used in the
Communion service or at
Mass.

CHAMBERED TOMB: a burial

mound of New Stone Age date, with a stone structure at the centre of an earthen mound. Wooden chambers were sometimes built in the Long Barrows of the New Stone Age.

CHAMFER: surface made by cutting across the square angle of a stone block, piece of wood, etc., at an angle of 45° to the other two surfaces.

CHANCEL: that part of the E end of a church in which the altar is placed, usually applied to the whole continuation of the nave E of the crossing.

CHANCEL ARCH: arch at the W end of the chancel.

CHANTRY CHAPEL: chapel attached to, or inside, a church, endowed for the saying of Masses for the soul of the founder or some other individual.

CHEVET: French term for the E end of a church (chancel, ambulatory, and radiating chapels).

CHEVRON: sculptured moulding forming a zigzag.

CHOIR: that part of the church where divine service is sung.

CIBORIUM: a baldacchino.

CINQUEFOIL: see Foil.

CIST: a small slab-lined receptacle to hold the bones or ashes of the dead in an inhumation burial.

CLAPPER BRIDGE: bridge made of large slabs of stone, some built up to make rough piers and other longer ones laid on top to make the roadway.

CLASSIC: here used to mean the moment of highest achievement of a style.

CLASSICAL: here used as the term for Greek and Roman architecture and any subsequent styles inspired by it.

CLERESTORY: upper storey of the nave walls of a church, pierced by windows.

COADE STONE: artificial (cast) stone made in the late C18 and the early C19 by Coade and Seely in London.

COB: walling material made of mixed clay and straw.

COFFERING: decorating a ceiling with sunk square or polygonal ornamental panels.

COLLAR-BEAM: see Roof.

COLONNADE: range of columns.

COLONNETTE: small column.

COLUMNA ROSTRATA: column decorated with carved prows of ships to celebrate a naval victory.

COMPOSITE: see Order.

CONSOLE: bracket (q.v.) with a compound curved outline.

COPING: capping or covering to a wall.

CORBEL: block of stone projecting from a wall, supporting some horizontal feature.

CORBEL TABLE: series of corbels, occurring just below the roof eaves externally or internally, often seen in Norman buildings.

CORINTHIAN: see Orders.

CORNICE: in classical architecture the top section of the entablature (q.v.). Also for a projecting decorative feature along the top of a wall, arch, etc.

COVE, COVING: concave undersurface in the nature of a hollow moulding but on a larger scale.

COVER PATEN: cover to a Communion cup, suitable for use

as a paten or plate for the consecrated bread.

CRADLE ROOF: see Wagon-roof.

CRANNOG: prehistoric lake-dwelling on piles.

CRENELLATION: see Battlement.

CRESSWELLIAN CULTURE: term relating to the hunters who inhabited Cresswell Crags in Derbyshire during the Upper Palaeolithic. By extension, to similar cultures elsewhere in Britain.

CREST, CRESTING: ornamental finish along the top of a screen, etc.

CROCKET, CROCKETING: decorative features placed on the sloping sides of spires, pinnacles, gables, etc., in Gothic architecture, carved in various leaf shapes and placed at regular intervals.

CROCKET CAPITAL: see Fig. 5.

Fig. 5

CROMLECH: obsolete word, often used of a free-standing stone, but more properly applied to a Bronze Age stone circle.

CROSSING: space at the intersection of nave, chancel, and transepts.

CRUCK: big curved beam supporting both walls and roof of a cottage.

CRYPT: underground room usually below the E end of a church.

CUPOLA: small polygonal or circular domed turret crowning a roof.

CURSUS: long strips enclosed between narrow banks at Stonehenge, in the Thames valley, and in Wessex. The best known is the one at Stonehenge. Their use is unknown, and they are of New Stone and Bronze Age date.

CURTAIN WALL: connecting wall between the towers of a castle.

CURVILINEAR: see Tracery.

CUSHION CAPITAL: see Block Capital.

CUSP: projecting point between the foils in a foiled Gothic arch.

DADO: decorative covering of the lower part of a wall.

DAGGER: tracery motif of the Dec style. It is a lancet shape rounded or pointed at the head, pointed at the foot, and cusped inside (see Fig. 6).

Fig. 6

DAIS: raised platform at one end of a room.

DEC ('DECORATED'): historical division of English Gothic architecture covering the period from c. 1290 to c. 1350.

DEMI-COLUMNS: columns half sunk into a wall.

DIAPER WORK: surface decoration composed of square or lozenge shapes.

DISC BARROW: Bronze Age

barrow in which the outer ditch and bank are more prominent than the inconspicuous mound.

DOG-TOOTH: typical E.E. ornament consisting of a series of four-cornered stars placed diagonally and raised pyramidally (Fig. 7).

Fig. 7

DOLMEN: obsolete word, signifying the stone chamber of a megalithic tomb after the outer structure of earth has been eroded away.

DOMICAL VAULT: see Vault.

DONJON: see Keep.

DORIC: see Order.

DORMER (WINDOW): window placed vertically in the sloping plane of a roof.

DRIPSTONE: see Hood-mould.

DRUM: circular or polygonal vertical wall of a dome or cupola.

E.E. ('EARLY ENGLISH'): historical division of English Gothic architecture roughly covering the C13.

EASTER SEPULCHRE: recess with tomb-chest usually in the wall of a chancel, the tomb-chest to receive an effigy of Christ for Easter celebrations.

EAVES: underpart of a sloping roof overhanging a wall.

EAVES CORNICE: cornice below the eaves of a roof.

ECHINUS: Convex or projecting moulding supporting the abacus of a Greek Doric capital,

sometimes bearing an egg and dart pattern.

EMBATTLED: see Battlement.

EMBRASURE: small opening in the wall or parapet of a fortified building, usually splayed on the inside. See Loop.

ENCAUSTIC TILES: earthenware glazed and decorated tiles used for paving.

ENGAGED COLUMNS: columns attached to, or partly sunk into, a wall.

ENGLISH BOND: see Brickwork.

ENTABLATURE: in classical architecture the whole of the horizontal members above a column (that is architrave, frieze, and cornice) (see Fig. 12).

ENTASIS: very slight convex deviation from a straight line; used on Greek columns and sometimes on spires to prevent an optical illusion of concavity.

ENTRESOL: see Mezzanine.

EPITAPH: hanging wall monument.

ESCUTCHEON: shield for armorial bearings.

EXEDRA: the apsidal end of a room. See Apse.

FAIENCE: decorated glazed earthenware.

FAN TRACERY: see Tracery.

FAN VAULT: see Vault.

FERETORY: place behind the High Altar where the chief shrine of a church is kept.

FESTOON: carved garland of flowers and fruit suspended at both ends.

FILLET: narrow flat band running down a shaft or along a roll moulding.

FINIAL: top of a canopy, gable, pinnacle.

FLAGON: vessel for the wine used in the Communion service.

FLAMBOYANT: properly the latest phase of French Gothic architecture where the window tracery takes on wavy undulating lines.

FLÈCHE: slender wooden spire on the centre of a roof (also called Spirelet).

FLEMISH BOND: see Brickwork.

FLEURON: decorative carved flower or leaf.

FLUSH WORK: decorative use of flint in conjunction with dressed stone so as to form patterns: tracery, initials, etc.

FLUTING: vertical channelling in the shaft of a column.

FLYING BUTTRESS: see Buttress.

FOIL: lobe formed by the cusping (q.v.) of a circle or an arch. Trefoil, quatrefoil, cinquefoil, multifoil, express the number of leaf shapes to be seen.

FOLIATED: carved with leaf shapes.

FOSSE: ditch.

FOUR-CENTRED ARCH: see Arch.

FRATER: refectory or dining hall of a monastery.

FRESCO: wall painting on wet plaster.

FRIEZE: middle division of a classical entablature (q.v.) (see Fig. 12).

FRONTAL: covering for the front of an altar.

GABLE: *Dutch gable*: A gable with curved sides crowned by a pediment (Fig. 8a).

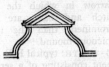

Fig. 8a

Shaped gable: A gable with multi-curved sides (Fig. 8b).

Fig. 8b

GADROONED: enriched with a series of convex ridges, the opposite of fluting.

GALILEE: chapel or vestibule usually at the W end of a church enclosing the porch. Also called Narthex (q.v.).

GALLERY: in church architecture upper storey above an aisle, opened in arches to the nave. Also called Tribune (q.v.) and often erroneously Triforium (q.v.).

GARGOYLE: water spout projecting from the parapet of a wall or tower; carved into a human or animal shape.

GAZEBO: lookout tower or raised summer house in a picturesque garden.

'GEOMETRICAL': see Tracery.

'GIBBS SURROUND': of a doorway or window. A surround with alternating larger and smaller blocks of stone, quoinwise, or intermittent large blocks, sometimes with a narrow raised band connecting them up the verticals and along the face of the arch (Fig. 9).

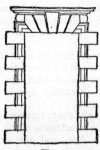

Fig. 9

GROIN: sharp edge at the meeting of two cells of a cross-vault.

GROINED VAULT: see Vault.

GROTESQUE: fanciful ornamental decoration: see also Arabesque.

HAGIOSCOPE: see Squint.

HALF-TIMBERING: see Timber Framing.

HALL CHURCH: church in which nave and aisles are of equal height or approximately so.

HALLSTATT CULTURE: the culture known as Iron Age A, brought from the Continent *c.* 500 B.C.

HAMMERBEAM: see Roof.

HANAP: large metal cup, generally made for domestic use, standing on an elaborate base and stem; with a very ornate cover frequently crowned with a little steeple.

HEADERS: see Brickwork.

HERRINGBONE WORK: brick, stone, or tile construction where the component blocks are laid diagonally instead of flat. Alternate courses lie in opposing directions to make a zigzag pattern up the face of the wall.

II—B

HEXASTYLE: having six detached columns.

HILL FORT: see also Camp, supra. The great hill forts of the Iron Age were, for obvious reasons, usually sited on promontories, generally where the terrain afforded a natural barrier on one or more sides.

HIPPED ROOF: see Roof.

HOOD-MOULD: projecting moulding above an arch or a lintel to throw off water (also called Dripstone or Label).

ICONOGRAPHY: the science of the subject matter of works of the visual arts.

IMPOST: brackets in walls, usually formed of mouldings, on which the ends of an arch rest.

INDENT: shape chiselled out in a stone slab to receive a brass.

INGLENOOK: bench or seat built in beside a fireplace, sometimes covered by the chimney breast, occasionally lit by small windows on each side of the fire.

INTERCOLUMNIATION: the space between columns.

IONIC: see Orders (Fig. 12).

JAMB: straight side of an archway, doorway, or window.

KEEL MOULDING: moulding whose outline is in section like that of the keel of a ship.

KEEP: massive tower of a Norman castle.

KEYSTONE: middle stone in an arch or a rib-vault.

KING-POST: see Roof (Fig. 14).

LABEL: see Hood-mould.

LABEL STOP: ornamental boss at the end of a hood-mould (q.v.).

LAKE DWELLINGS: villages of Late Iron Age date found in Yorkshire, East Anglia, Breconshire, and Somerset. Those of Glastonbury and Meare are by far the most extensive.

LANCET WINDOW: slender pointed-arched window.

LANTERN: in architecture, a small circular or polygonal turret with windows all round crowning a roof (see Cupola) or a dome.

LANTERN CROSS: churchyard cross with lantern-shaped top usually with sculptured representations on the sides of the top.

LA TÈNE CULTURE: the culture known as Iron Age B, brought from the Continent by Marnian overlords between 300 and 250 B.C.

LEAN-TO ROOF: roof with one slope only, built against a higher wall.

LESENE or PILASTER STRIP: pilaster without base or capital.

LIERNE: see Vault (Fig. 21).

LINENFOLD: Tudor panelling ornamented with a conventional representation of a piece of linen laid in vertical folds. The piece is repeated in each panel.

LINTEL: horizontal beam or stone bridging an opening.

LOGGIA: recessed colonnade (q.v.).

LONG AND SHORT WORK: Saxon quoins (q.v.) consisting of stones placed with the long sides alternately upright and horizontal.

LONG BARROWS: earthen structures characteristic of the New Stone Age, and not known subsequently.

LOUVRE: opening, often with lantern (q.v.) over, in the roof of a room to let the smoke from a central hearth escape.

LOZENGE: diamond shape.

LUNETTE: tympanum (q.v.) or semicircular opening.

LYCH GATE: wooden gate structure with a roof and open sides placed at the entrance to a churchyard to provide space for the reception of a coffin. The word lych is Saxon and means a corpse.

LYNCHETS: the eroded terracing of primitive field systems, usually in carefully devised strips: hence 'strip lynchets'.

MACHICOLATION: projecting gallery on brackets constructed on the outside of castle towers or walls. The gallery has holes in the floor to drop missiles through.

MAGLEMOSIAN CULTURE: term denoting the hunter-fishing culture of Baltic origin established along the eastern margin of Britain in Middle Stone Age times. By extension to similar cultures.

MAJOLICA: ornamented glazed earthenware.

MANSARD: *see* Roof.

MEGALITHIC TOMBS: the chambered cairns of the New Stone Age, found with variations over SW England, Wales, Scotland, and particularly Ireland, with a small outlier in Kent. The inner tomb is constructed of large stone slabs, often disposed in accordance with an elaborate ground plan.

MENHIR: obsolete word, synonymous with Dolmen or Cromlech, which are similarly vague and antique.

MERLON: *see* Battlement.

METOPE: in classical architecture of the Doric order (q.v.) the space in the frieze between the triglyphs (Fig. 12).

MEZZANINE: low storey placed between two higher ones.

MISERERE: *see* Misericord.

MISERICORD: bracket placed on the underside of a hinged choir stall seat which, when turned up, provided the occupant of the seat with a support during long periods of standing (also called Miserere).

MODILLION: small bracket of which large numbers (modillion frieze) are often placed below a cornice (q.v.) in classical architecture.

MOTTE: steep mound forming the main feature of C11 and C12 castles.

MOUCHETTE: tracery motif in curvilinear tracery, a curved dagger (q.v.) (Fig. 10).

Fig. 10

MULLION: vertical post or upright dividing a window into two or more 'lights'.

MUNTIN: vertical part in the framing of a door, screen, etc., stopped by the horizontal rails.

NAIL-HEAD: E.E. ornamental motif, consisting of small pyramids regularly repeated (Fig. 11).

Fig. 11

NARTHEX: enclosed vestibule or covered porch at the main entrance to a church (*see* Galilee).

NEWEL: central post in a circular or winding staircase; also the principal post when a flight of stairs meets a landing.

OBELISK: lofty pillar of square section tapering at the top and ending pyramidally.

OGEE: *see* Arch (Fig. 1c).

ORATORY: small private chapel in a house.

ORDER: (1) *of a doorway or window:* series of concentric steps receding towards the opening; (2) *in classical architecture:* column with base, shaft, capital, and entablature (q.v.) according to one of the following styles: Greek Doric, Roman Doric, Tuscan Doric, Ionic, Corinthian, Composite. The established details are very elaborate, and some

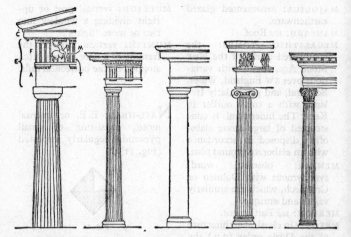

Fig. 12 – Orders of Columns (Greek Doric, Roman Doric, Tuscan Doric, Ionic, Corinthian) E, Entablature; C, Cornice; F, Frieze; A, Architrave; M, Metope; T, Triglyph.

specialist architectural work should be consulted for further guidance (*see* Fig. 12).

ORIEL: *see* Bay-Window.

OVERHANG: projection of the upper storey of a house.

OVERSAILING COURSES: series of stone or brick courses, each one projecting beyond the one below it.

PALIMPSEST: (1) *of a brass:* where a metal plate has been re-used by turning over and engraving on the back; (2) *of a wall painting:* where one overlaps and partly obscures an earlier one.

PALLADIAN: architecture following the ideas and principles of Andrea Palladio, 1518–80.

PALSTAVE: technical term for a Bronze Age celt with a pronounced stop-ridge to facilitate hafting.

PANTILE: tile of curved S-shaped section.

PARAPET: low wall placed to protect any spot where there is a sudden drop, for example on a bridge, quay, hillside, housetop, etc.

PARGETTING: plaster work with patterns and ornaments either in relief or engraved on it.

PARVIS: term wrongly applied to a room over a church porch. These rooms were often used as a schoolroom or as a store room.

PATEN: plate to hold the bread at Communion or Mass.

PATERA: small flat circular or oval ornament in classical architecture.

PEDIMENT: low-pitched gable used in classical, Renaissance, and neo-classical architecture above a portico and above doors, windows, etc. It may be straight-sided or curved segmentally. *Broken Pediment:* one where the centre portion of the base is left open. *Open Pediment:* one where the centre portion of the sloping sides is left out.

PENDANT: boss (q.v.) elongated so that it seems to hang down.

PENDENTIF: concave triangular spandrel used to lead from the angle of two walls to the base of a circular dome. It is constructed as part of the hemisphere over a diameter the size of the diagonal of the basic square (Fig. 13).

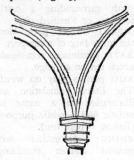

Fig. 13

PERP (PERPENDICULAR): historical division of English Gothic architecture covering the period from *c.* 1335–50 to *c.* 1530.

PETERBOROUGH CULTURE: term denoting culture of Baltic origin that flourished during the New Stone Age.

PIANO NOBILE: principal storey of a house with the reception rooms; usually the first floor.

PIAZZA: open space surrounded by buildings, in C17 and C18 England sometimes used to mean a long colonnade or loggia.

PIER: strong, solid support, frequently square in section or of composite section (compound pier).

PIETRA DURA: ornamental or scenic inlay by means of thin slabs of stone.

PILASTER: shallow pier attached to a wall.

PILLAR PISCINA: free-standing piscina on a pillar.

PINNACLE: ornamental form crowning a spire, tower, buttress, etc., usually of steep pyramidal, conical, or some similar shape.

PISCINA: basin for washing the Communion or Mass vessels, provided with a drain. Generally set in or against the wall to the S of an altar.

PLAISANCE: summer-house, pleasure house near a mansion.

PLATE TRACERY: see Tracery.

PLINTH: projecting base of a wall or column, generally chamfered (q.v.) or moulded at the top.

POPPYHEAD: ornament of leaf and flower type used to decorate the tops of bench- or stall-ends.

PORTCULLIS: gate constructed to rise and fall in vertical grooves; used in gateways of castles.

PORTE COCHÈRE: porch large enough to admit wheeled vehicles.

PORTICO: centre-piece of a house or a church with classical detached or attached columns and a pediment. A portico is called *prostyle* or *in antis* according to whether it projects from or recedes into a building. In a portico *in antis* the columns range with the side walls.

POSTERN: small gateway at the back of a building.

PREDELLA: in an altar-piece the horizontal strip below the main representation, often used for a number of subsidiary representations in a row.

PRESBYTERY: the part of the church lying E of the choir. It is the part where the altar is placed.

PRINCIPAL: *see* Roof (Fig. 14).

PRIORY: monastic house whose head is a prior or prioress, not an abbot or abbess.

PROSTYLE: with free-standing columns in a row.

PULPITUM: stone screen in a major church provided to shut off the choir from the nave and also as a backing for the return choir stalls.

PURLIN: *see* Roof (Figs. 14, 15).

PUTTO: small naked boy.

QUADRANGLE: inner courtyard in a large building.

QUARRY: in stained-glass work, a small diamond or square-shaped piece of glass set diagonally.

QUATREFOIL: *see* Foil.

QUEEN-POSTS: *see* Roof (Fig. 15).

QUOINS: dressed stones at the angles of a building. Sometimes all the stones are of the same size; more often they are alternately large and small.

RADIATING CHAPELS: chapels projecting radially from an ambulatory or an apse.

RAFTER: *see* Roof.

RAMPART: stone wall or wall of earth surrounding a castle, fortress, or fortified city.

RAMPART-WALK: path along the inner face of a rampart.

REBATE: continuous rectangular notch cut on an edge.

REBUS: pun, a play on words. The literal translation and illustration of a name for artistic and heraldic purposes (Belton = bell, tun).

REEDING: decoration with parallel convex mouldings touching one another.

REFECTORY: dining hall; *see* Frater.

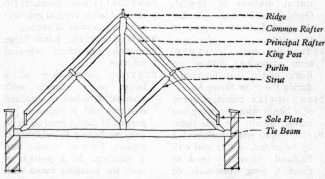

Ridge
Common Rafter
Principal Rafter
King Post
Purlin
Strut

Sole Plate
Tie Beam

Fig. 14

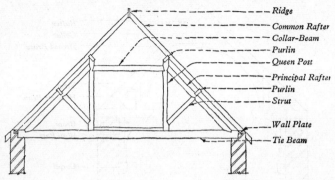

Fig. 15

RENDERING: plastering of an outer wall.

REPOUSSÉ: decoration of metal work by relief designs, formed by beating the metal from the back.

REREDOS: structure behind and above an altar.

RESPOND: half-pier bonded into a wall and carrying one end of an arch.

RETABLE: altar-piece, a picture or piece of carving, standing behind and attached to an altar.

RETICULATION: *see* Tracery (Fig. 20).

REVEAL: that part of a jamb (q.v.) which lies between the glass or door and the outer surface of the wall.

RIB VAULT: *see* Vault.

ROCOCO: latest phase of the Baroque style, current in most Continental countries between *c.* 1720 and *c.* 1760.

ROLL MOULDING: moulding of semicircular or more than semicircular section.

ROMANESQUE: that style in architecture which was current in the C11 and C12 and pre-ceded the Gothic style (in England often called Norman). (Some scholars extend the use of the term Romanesque back to the C10 or C9.)

ROOD: cross or crucifix.

ROOD LOFT: singing gallery on the top of the rood screen, often supported by a coving.

ROOD SCREEN: *see* Screen.

ROOD STAIRS: stairs to give access to the rood loft.

ROOF: *Single-framed:* if consisting entirely of transverse members (such as rafters with or without braces, collars, tie-beams, king-posts or queen-posts, etc.) not tied together longitudinally. *Double-framed:* if longitudinal members (such as a ridge beam and purlins) are employed. As a rule in such cases the rafters are divided into stronger principals and weaker subsidiary rafters. *Hipped:* roof with sloped instead of vertical ends. *Mansard:* roof with a double slope, the lower slope being larger and steeper than the upper. *Saddleback:* tower roof

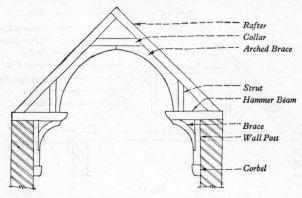

Fig. 16

shaped like an ordinary gabled timber roof. The following members have special names: *Rafter:* roof-timber sloping up from the wall plate to the ridge. *Principal:* principal rafter, usually corresponding to the main bay divisions of the nave or chancel below. *Wall Plate:* timber laid longitudinally on the top of a wall. *Purlin:* longitudinal member laid parallel with wall plate and ridge beam some way up the slope of the roof. *Tie-beam:* beam connecting the two slopes of a roof across at its foot, usually at the height of the wall plate, to prevent the roof from spreading. *Collar-beam:* tie-beam applied higher up the slope of the roof. *Strut:* upright timber connecting the tie-beam with the rafter above it. *King-post:* upright timber connecting a tie-beam and collar-beam with the ridge beam. *Queen-posts:* two struts placed symmetrically on a tie-beam or collar-beam. *Braces:* inclined

timbers inserted to strengthen others. Usually braces connect a collar-beam with the rafters below or a tie-beam with the wall below. Braces can be straight or curved (also called arched). *Hammerbeam:* beam projecting at right angles, usually from the top of a wall, to carry arched braces or struts and arched braces (*see* Figs. 14, 15, 16).

ROSE WINDOW (or WHEEL WINDOW): circular window with patterned tracery arranged to radiate from the centre.

ROTUNDA: building circular in plan.

RUBBLE: building stones, not square or hewn, nor laid in regular courses.

RUSTICATION: *rock-faced* if the surfaces of large blocks of ashlar stone are left rough like rock; *smooth* if the ashlar blocks are smooth and separated by V-joints; *banded* if the separation by V-joints applies only to the horizontals.

Saddleback: *see* Roof.

Saltire cross: equal-limbed cross placed diagonally.

Sanctuary: (1) area around the main altar of a church (*see* Presbytery); (2) sacred site consisting of wooden or stone uprights enclosed by a circular bank and ditch. Beginning in the New Stone Age, they were elaborated in the succeeding Bronze Age. The best known examples are Stonehenge and Avebury.

Sarcophagus: elaborately carved coffin.

Scagliola: material composed of cement and colouring matter to imitate marble.

Scalloped capital: development of the block capital (q.v.) in which the single semi-circular surface is elaborated into a series of truncated cones (Fig. 17).

Fig. 17

Scarp: artificial cutting away of the ground to form a steep slope.

Screen: *Parclose screen:* screen separating a chapel from the rest of a church. *Rood screen:* screen below the rood (q.v.), usually at the W end of a chancel.

Screens passage: passage between the entrances to kitchen, buttery, etc., and the screen behind which lies the hall of a medieval house.

Sedilia: seats for the priests (usually three) on the S side of the chancel of a church.

Segmental arch: *see* Arch.

Set-off: *see* Weathering.

Sexpartite: *see* Vaulting.

Sgraffito: pattern incised into plaster so as to expose a dark surface underneath.

Shaft-ring: ring round a circular pier or a shaft attached to a pier.

Sheila-na-gig: fertility figure, usually with legs wide open.

Sill: lower horizontal part of the frame of a window.

Slatehanging: the covering of walls by overlapping rows of slates, on a timber substructure.

Soffit: underside of an arch, lintel, etc.

Solar: upper living-room of a medieval house.

Sopraporte: painting above the door of a room, usual in the C17 and C18.

Sounding board: horizontal board or canopy over a pulpit. Also called Tester.

Spandrel: triangular surface between one side of an arch, the horizontal drawn from its apex, and the vertical drawn from its springer, also the surface between two arches.

Spire: tall pyramidal or conical pointed erection often built on top of a tower, turret, etc. *Broach Spire:* spire which is generally octagonal in plan rising from the top or parapet of a square tower. A small inclined piece of masonry covers the vacant triangular space at each of the four angles of the square and is carried up to a point along the diagonal sides of the octagon. *Needle Spire:* thin spire rising from the centre of a tower roof, well inside the parapet.

SPIRELET: *see* Flèche.

SPLAY: chamfer, usually of the jamb of a window.

SPRINGING: level at which an arch rises from its supports.

SQUINCH: arch or system of concentric arches thrown across the angle between two walls to support a superstructure, for example a dome (Fig. 18).

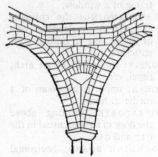

Fig. 18

SQUINT: hole cut in a wall or through a pier to allow a view of the main altar of a church from places whence it could not otherwise be seen (also called Hagioscope).

STALL: carved seat, one of a row, made of wood or stone.

STAUNCHION: upright iron or steel member.

STEEPLE: the tower of a church together with a spire, cupola, etc.

STIFF-LEAF: E.E. type of foliage of many-lobed shapes (Fig. 19).

Fig. 19

STILTED: *see* Arch.

STONE CIRCLES: rings of standing stones without external earthworks. Probably of Middle and Late Bronze Age date.

STONE ROWS: single or double rows of standing stones, often associated with Stone Circles and of similar date.

STOUP: vessel for the reception of holy water, usually placed near a door.

STRAINER ARCH: arch inserted across a room to prevent the walls from leaning.

STRAPWORK: C16 decoration consisting of interlaced bands, and forms similar to fretwork or cut and bent leather.

STRETCHERS: *see* Brickwork.

STRING COURSE: projecting horizontal band or moulding set in the surface of a wall.

STRIP LYNCHETS: *see* Lynchets.

STRUT: *see* Roof.

STUCCO: plaster work.

STUDS: Upright timbers in timber-framed houses.

SWAG: festoon formed by a carved piece of cloth suspended from both ends.

TABERNACLE: richly ornamented niche (q.v.) or free-standing canopy. Usually contains the Holy Sacrament.

TARDENOISEAN CULTURE: Middle Stone Age culture named after a French type-site and extended to similar British cultures.

TAZZA: shallow bowl on a foot.

TERMINAL FIGURES (TERMS, TERMINI): upper part of a human figure growing out of a pier, pilaster, etc., which tapers towards the base.

TERRACOTTA: burnt clay, un-glazed.

TESSELATED PAVEMENT: deco-rative floor or wall covering made up of tesserae or small coloured cubes of stone, fitted into a bed of cement.

TESTER: see Sounding Board.

TETRASTYLE: having four de-tached columns.

THREE-DECKER PULPIT: pulpit with Clerk's Stall below and Reading Desk below the Clerk's Stall.

TIE-BEAM: see Roof (Figs. 14, 15).

TIERCERON: see Vault (Fig. 21).

TILEHANGING: see Slatehang-ing.

TIMBER-FRAMING: method of construction where walls are built of timber framework with the spaces filled in by plaster or brickwork. Sometimes the timber is covered over with plaster or boarding laid hori-zontally.

TOMB-CHEST: chest-shaped stone coffin, the most usual medieval form of funeral monument.

TOUCH: soft black marble quar-ried near Tournai.

TOURELLE: turret corbelled out from the wall.

TRACERY: intersecting ribwork in the upper part of a window, or used decoratively in blank arches, on vaults, etc. *Plate tracery:* early form of tracery where decoratively shaped openings are cut through the solid stone infilling in a window head (Fig. 20a). *Bar tracery:* intersecting ribwork made up of slender shafts, continuing the lines of the mullions of windows up to a decorative mesh in the head of the win-dow. *Geometrical tracery:* tracery consisting chiefly of circles or foiled circles (Fig. 20b). *Y-tracery:* tracery consisting of a mullion which branches into two forming a Y shape (Fig. 20c). *Inter-sected tracery:* tracery in which each mullion of a window branches out into two curved bars in such a way that every one of them is drawn with the same radius from a different

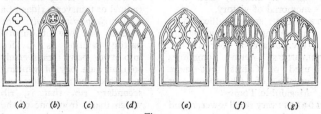

(a)   (b)   (c)   (d)   (e)   (f)   (g)

Fig. 20

centre. The result is that every light of the window is a lancet and every two, three, four, etc., lights together form a pointed arch (Fig. 20*d*). *Reticulated tracery:* tracery consisting entirely of circles drawn at top and bottom into ogee shapes so that a net-like appearance results (Fig. 20*e*). *Panel tracery:* tracery forming upright straight-sided panels above lights of a window (Fig. 20, *f & g*).

TRANSEPT: transverse portion of a cross-shaped church.

TRANSOM: horizontal bar across the openings of a window.

TRANSVERSE ARCH: see Vaulting.

TRIBUNE: see Gallery.

TRICIPUT, SIGNUM TRICIPUT: sign of the Trinity expressed by three faces belonging to one head.

TRIFORIUM: arcaded wall passage or blank arcading facing the nave at the height of the aisle roof and below the clerestory (q.v.) windows. (*See* Gallery.)

TRIGLYPHS: blocks with vertical grooves separating the metopes (q.v.) in the Doric frieze (Fig. 12).

TROPHY: sculptured group of arms or armour, used as a memorial of victory.

TRUMEAU: stone mullion (q.v.) supporting the tympanum (q.v.) of a wide doorway.

TUMULUS: term sometimes used of Cairns, but more usually of Chambered or Megalithic Tombs.

TURRET: very small tower, round or polygonal in plan.

TUSCAN: see Order.

TYMPANUM: space between the lintel of a doorway and the arch above it.

UNDERCROFT: vaulted room, sometimes underground, below a church or chapel.

VAULT: *Barrel vault: see* Tunnel vault. *Cross-vault: see* Groined vault. *Domical vault:* square or polygonal dome rising direct on a square or polygonal bay, the curved surfaces separated by groins (q.v.). *Fan vault:* vault where all ribs springing from one springer are of the same length, the same distance from the next, and the same curvature. *Groined vault* or *Cross-vault:* vault of two tunnel vaults of identical shape intersecting each other at right angles. *Lierne:* tertiary rib, that is, rib which does not spring either from one of the main springers or the central boss. *Quadripartite vault:* one wherein one bay of vaulting is divided into four parts. *Rib vault:* vault with diagonal ribs projecting along the groins. *Ridge-rib:* rib along the longitudinal or transverse ridge of a vault. *Sexpartite vault:* one wherein one bay of quadripartite vaulting is divided into two parts transversely so that each bay of vaulting has six parts. *Tierceron:* secondary rib, that is, rib which issues from one of the main springers or the central

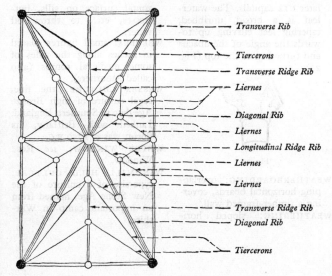

Transverse Rib

Tiercerons

Transverse Ridge Rib

Liernes

Diagonal Rib

Liernes

Longitudinal Ridge Rib

Liernes

Liernes

Transverse Ridge Rib

Diagonal Rib

Tiercerons

Fig. 21

boss and leads to a place on a ridge-rib. *Transverse arch:* arch separating one bay of a vault from the next. *Tunnel vault* or *Barrel vault:* vault of semi-circular or pointed section (Fig. 21).

VAULTING SHAFT: vertical member leading to the springer of a vault.

VENETIAN WINDOW: window with three openings, the central one arched and wider than the outside ones.

VERANDA: open gallery or balcony with a roof on light, usually metal, supports.

VESICA: oval with pointed head and foot.

VESTIBULE: ante-room or entrance hall.

VILLA: according to Gwilt (1842) 'a country house for the residence of opulent persons'.

VITRIFIED: made similar to glass.

VOLUTE: spiral scroll, one of the component parts of an Ionic column (*see* Order).

VOUSSOIR: wedge-shaped stone used in arch construction.

WAGON-ROOF: roof in which by closely set rafters with arched braces the appearance of the inside of a canvas tilt over a wagon is achieved. Wagon-roofs can be panelled or plastered (ceiled) or left uncovered.

WAINSCOT: timber lining to walls.

WALL PLATE: *see* Roof.

WATERLEAF: leaf shape used in

later C12 capitals. The water-leaf is a broad, unribbed, tapering leaf curving up towards the angle of the abacus and turned in at the top (Fig. 22).

Fig. 22

WEATHERBOARDING: overlapping horizontal boards, covering a timber-framed wall.

WEATHERING: sloped horizontal surface on sills, buttresses, etc., to throw off water.

WEEPERS: small figures placed in niches along the sides of some medieval tombs (also called Mourners).

WESSEX CULTURE: the fine, regal culture of high Bronze Age date in Southern England. Linked with Brittany, its floruit was *c.* 1750 B.C.

WHEEL WINDOW: *see* Rose Window.

WINDMILL HILL CULTURE: type-site of a culture of the New Stone Age, named from an important camp in Wiltshire.

INDEX OF PLATES

INDEX OF ARTISTS

INDEX OF PLACES

ADDENDA

(MARCH 1960)

p. 167 [High Wycombe.] A little further down the river BOWDEN MILL, brick and weather-boarding, whitewashed, with only the small wheel remaining; a little up the river, in Easton Street, PANN MILL, whitewashed, brick, with a restored wheel happily still in use.

p. 177 [Iver.] $\frac{3}{4}$ m. WSW of Iver Grove, close to Shreding Green, MOAT HOUSE (formerly Parsonage Farm), brick, the S half of c. 1600, the N half of the late C17. Two large BARNS of c. 1600. House and barns lie in a moat.

p. 182 [Langley Marish.] ROYAL ARMS. Dated 1625. Carved and painted. On the wall above the gallery in the N aisle.